VOL. 20
Action Edition

Story and Art by
RUMIKO TAKAHASHI

English Adaptation by Gerard Jones

Translation/Mari Morimoto
Touch-Up Art & Lettering/Bill Schuch
Cover and Interior Graphics & Design/Yuki Ameda
Editor/Avery Gotoh
Supervising Editor/Michelle Pangilinan

Managing Editor/Annette Roman
Director of Production/Noboru Watanabe
VP of Publishing/Alvin Lu
Sr. Director of Acquisitions/Rika Inouye
VP of Sales & Marketing/Liza Coppola
Publisher/Hyoe Narita

© 1997 Rumiko Takahashi/Shogakukan, Inc. First published
by Shogakukan, Inc. in Japan as "Inuyasha."

New and adapted artwork and text
© 2004 VIZ, LLC
All rights reserved.

Printed in Canada.

Published by VIZ, LLC
P.O. Box 77010
San Francisco, CA 94107

Action Edition
10 9 8 7 6 5 4 3 2
Second printing, May 2005

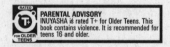

store.viz.com

INUYASHA ™

VOL. 20   Action Edition

STORY AND ART BY
RUMIKO TAKAHASHI

CONTENTS

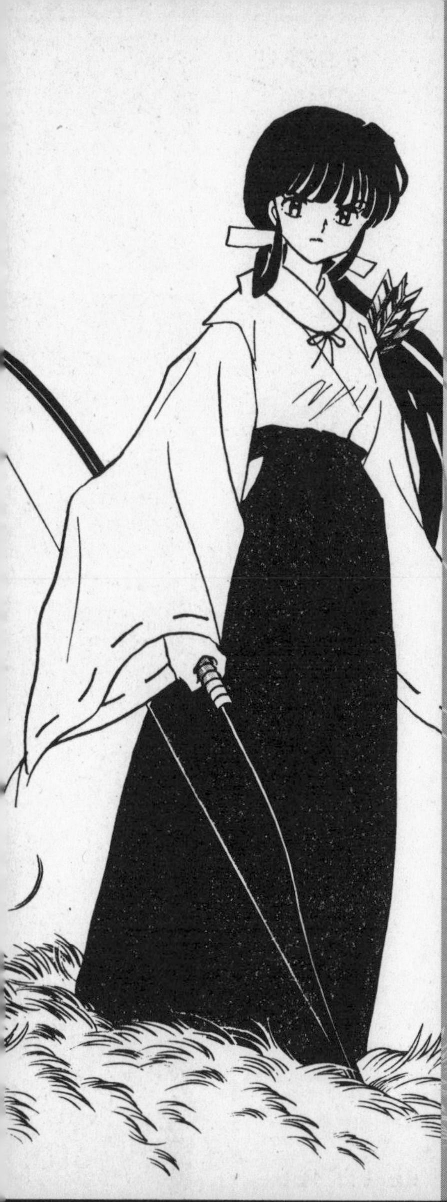

Long ago, in the "Warring States" era of Japan's Muromachi period (Sengoku-jidai, approximately 1467-1568 CE), a legendary dog-like half-demon called "Inu-Yasha" attempted to steal the Shikon Jewel, or "Jewel of Four Souls," from a village, but was stopped by the enchanted arrow of the village priestess, Kikyo. Inu-Yasha fell into a deep sleep, pinned to a tree by Kikyo's arrow, while the mortally wounded Kikyo took the Shikon Jewel with her into the fires of her funeral pyre. Years passed.

Fast-forward to the present day. Kagome, a Japanese high-school girl, is pulled into a well one day by a mysterious centipede monster, and finds herself transported into the past, only to come face to face with the trapped Inu-Yasha. She frees him, and Inu-Yasha easily defeats the centipede monster.

The residents of the village, now 50 years older, readily accept Kagome as the reincarnation of their deceased priestess Kikyo, a claim supported by the fact that the Shikon Jewel emerges from a cut on Kagome's body. Unfortunately, the jewel's rediscovery means that the village is soon under attack by a variety of demons in search of this treasure. Then, the jewel is accidentally shattered into many shards, each of which may have the fearsome power of the entire jewel.

Although Inu-Yasha says he hates Kagome because of her resemblance to Kikyo, the woman who "killed" him, he is forced to team up with her when Kaede, the village leader, binds him to Kagome with a powerful spell. Now the two grudging companions must fight to reclaim and reassemble the shattered shards of the Shikon Jewel before they fall into the wrong hands...

THIS VOLUME Locked in battle with Ryôkotsusei—the same demon responsible for his father's death—nu-Yasha may have a chance at victory...but not if he can't master the "Backlash Wave" (Bakuryû-ha). Meanwhile, when Kagome is bitten by Tsubaki's familiar, the Shikon Jewel shards themselves are affected.

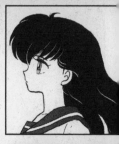

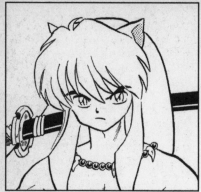

INU-YASHA
Half-demon hybrid, son of a human mother and demon father. His necklace is enchanted, allowing Kagome to control him with a word.

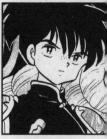

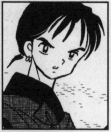

MIROKU
Lecherous Buddhist priest cursed with a mystical "hellhole" in his hand that's slowly killing him.

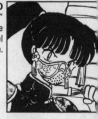

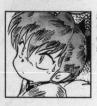

SHIPPO
Orphaned young fox-demon who likes to play shape-changing tricks.

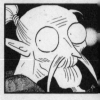

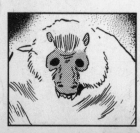

NARAKU
Enigmatic demon-mastermind behind the miseries of nearly everyone in the story.

KAGOME
Modern-day Japanese schoolgirl who can travel back and forth between the past and present through an enchanted well.

KOHAKU
Killed by Naraku—but not before first slaying both his own and Sango's father—now he's back again in a newer...if somewhat *slower*...form.

SANGO
"Demon Exterminator" or slayer from the village where the Shikon Jewel was first born.

TÔTÔSAI
Quirky (some might say "crazy") maker of swords—the genius-smith behind both Tetsusaiga and Tenseiga.

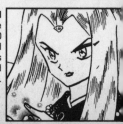

TSUBAKI
Mistress of the Black Arts who, 50 years ago, battled Kikyo for the shards of the Sacred Jewel.

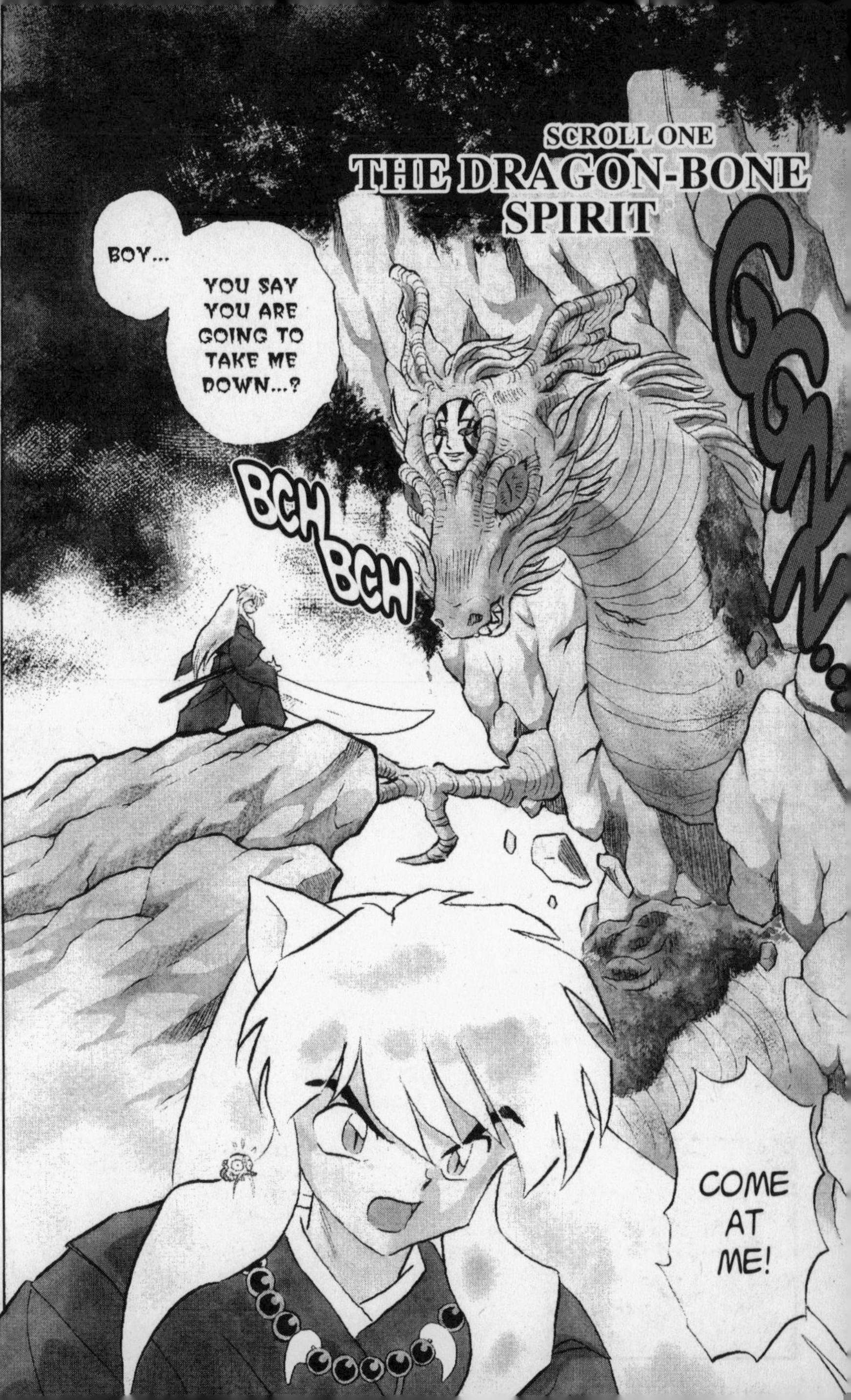
SCROLL ONE
THE DRAGON-BONE SPIRIT
BOY...
YOU SAY YOU ARE GOING TO TAKE ME DOWN...?
BCH BCH
COME AT ME!

SCROLL ONE
THE DRAGON-BONE SPIRIT

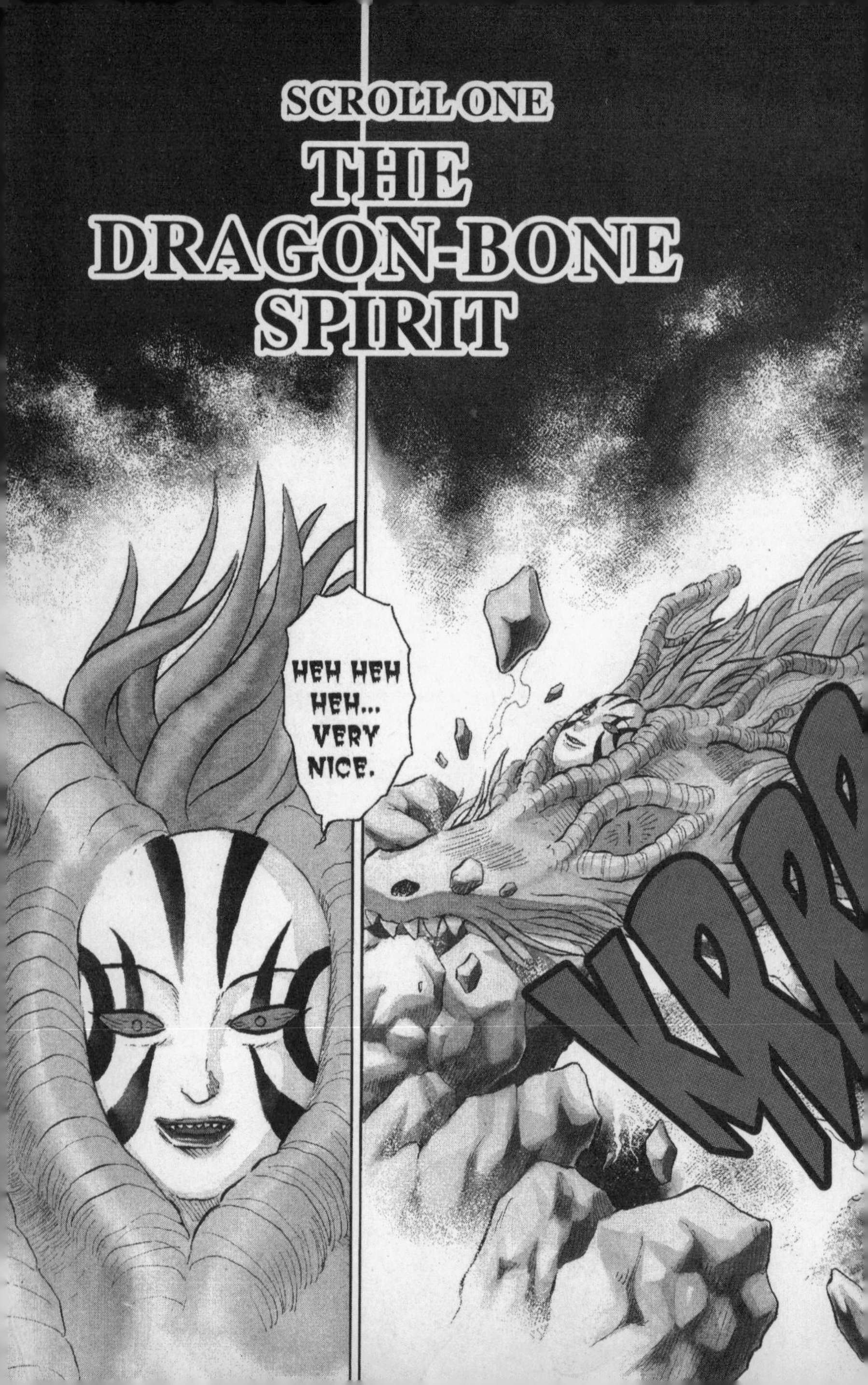
HEH HEH HEH... VERY NICE.

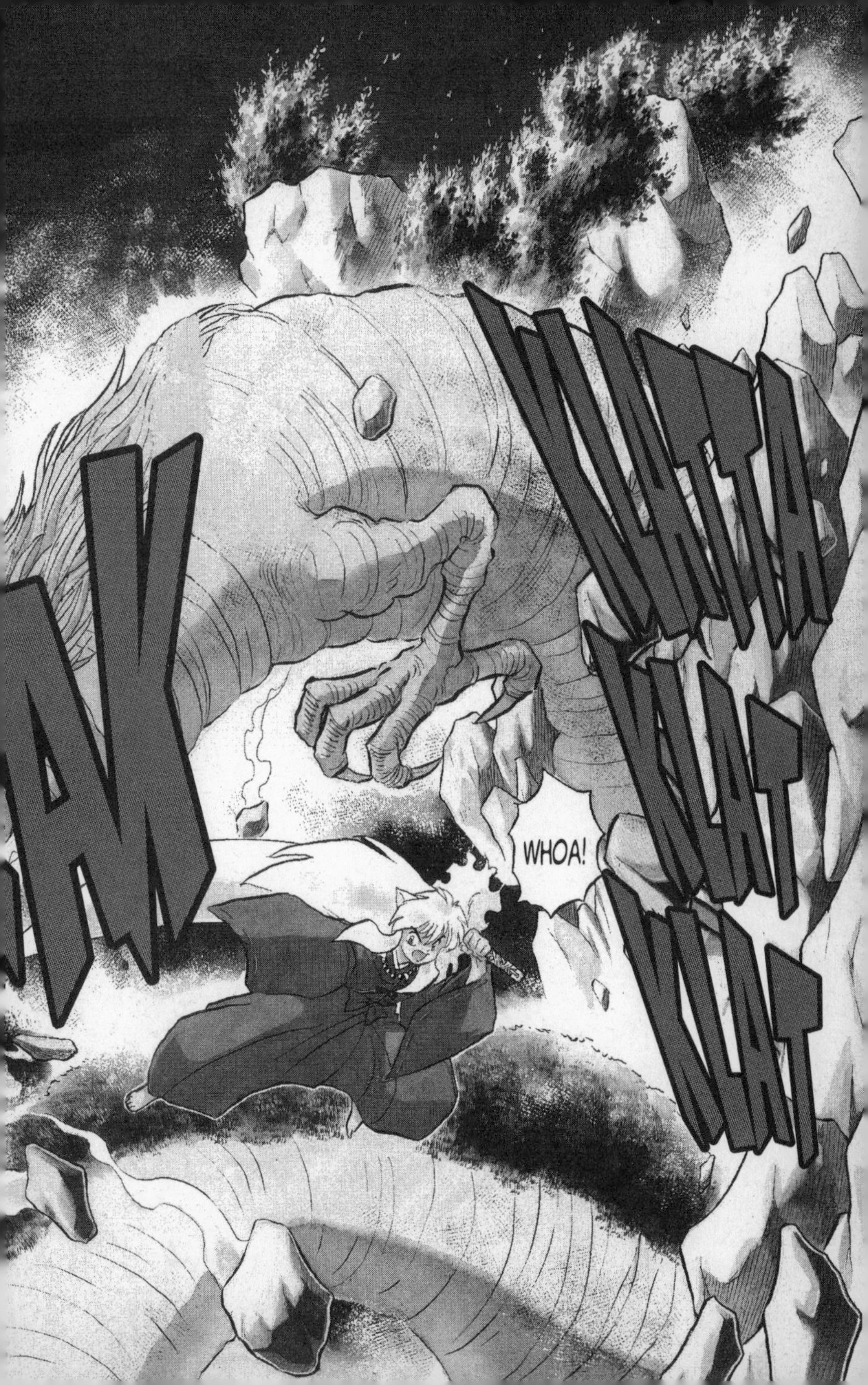

AK
WHOA!
WHATTA
WHAT
WHAT

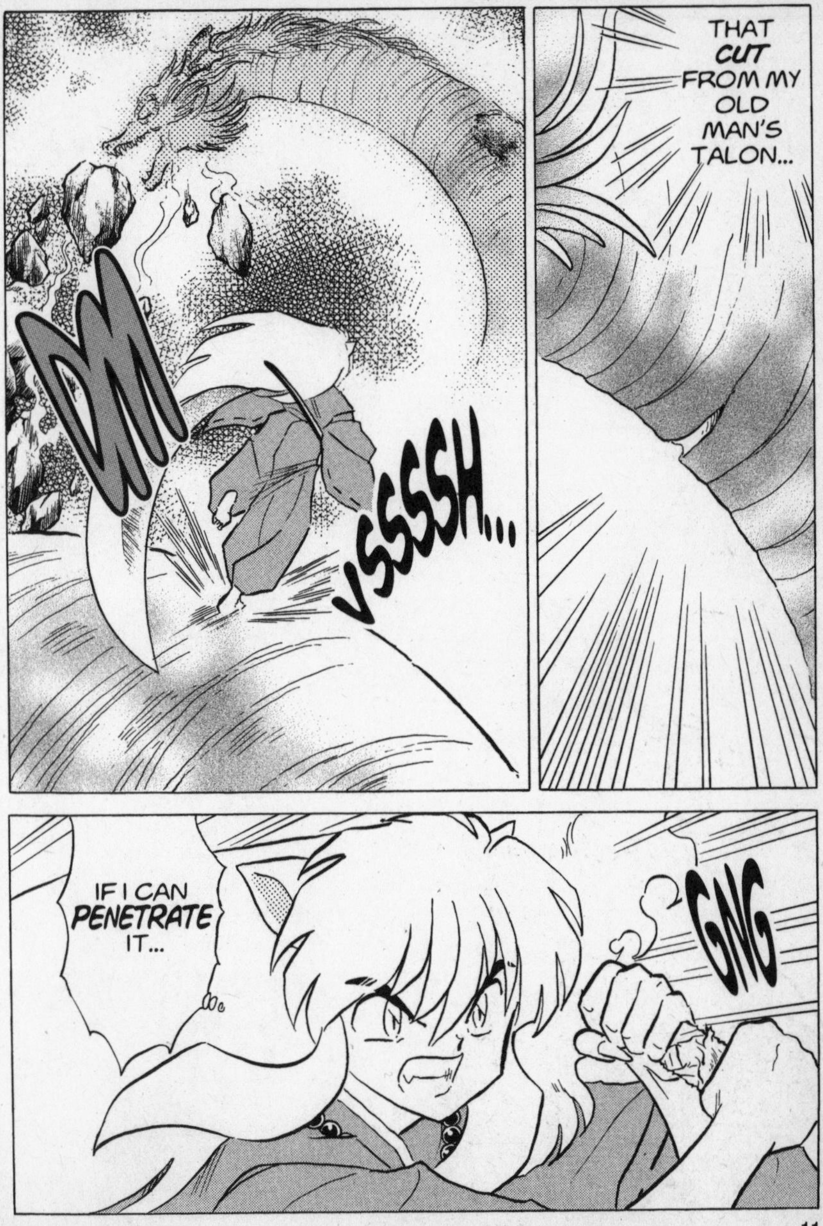
DM
VSSSSH...
THAT
CUT
FROM MY
OLD
MAN'S
TALON...
IF I CAN
PENETRATE
IT...
GNG

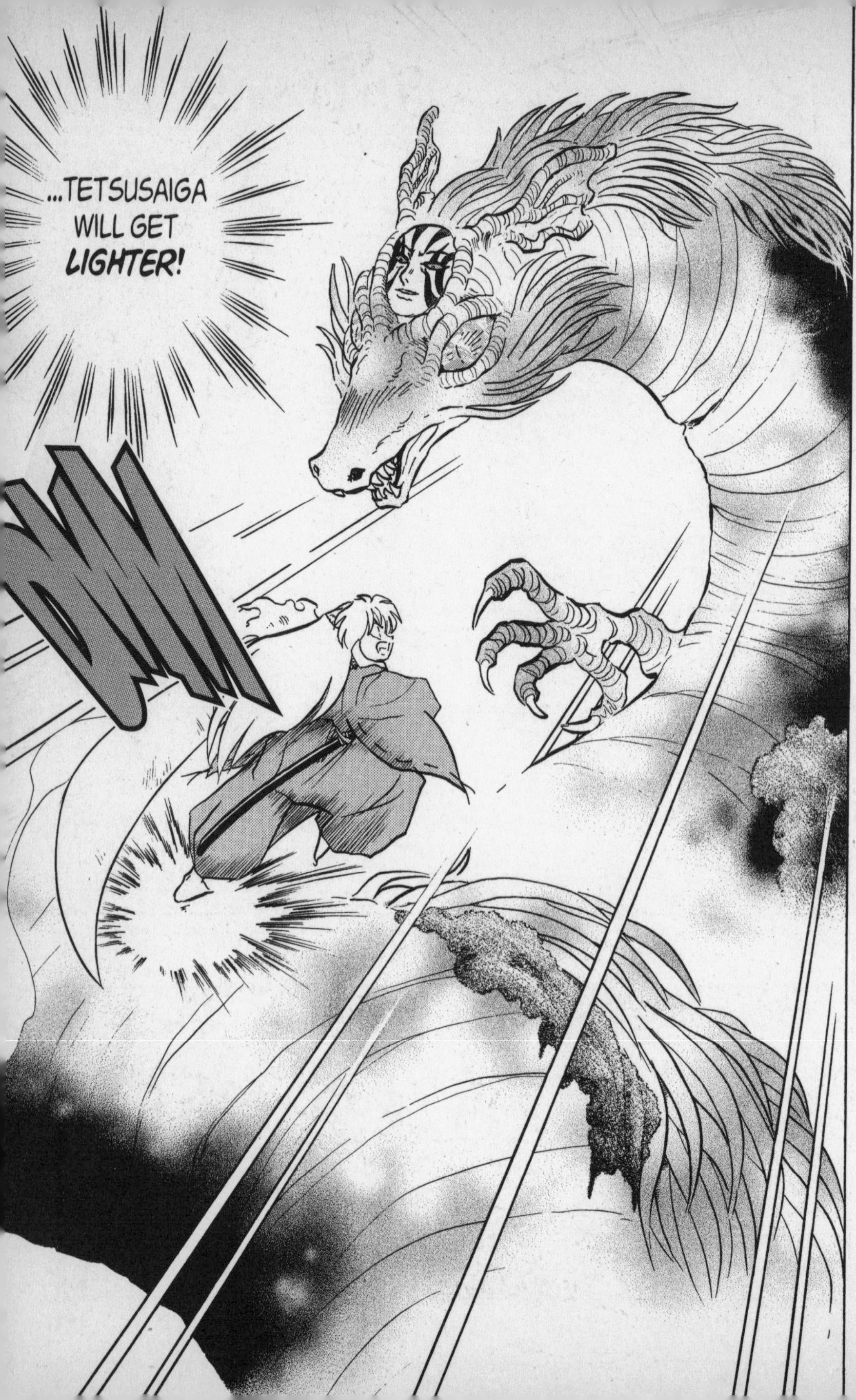
...TETSUSAIGA WILL GET LIGHTER!

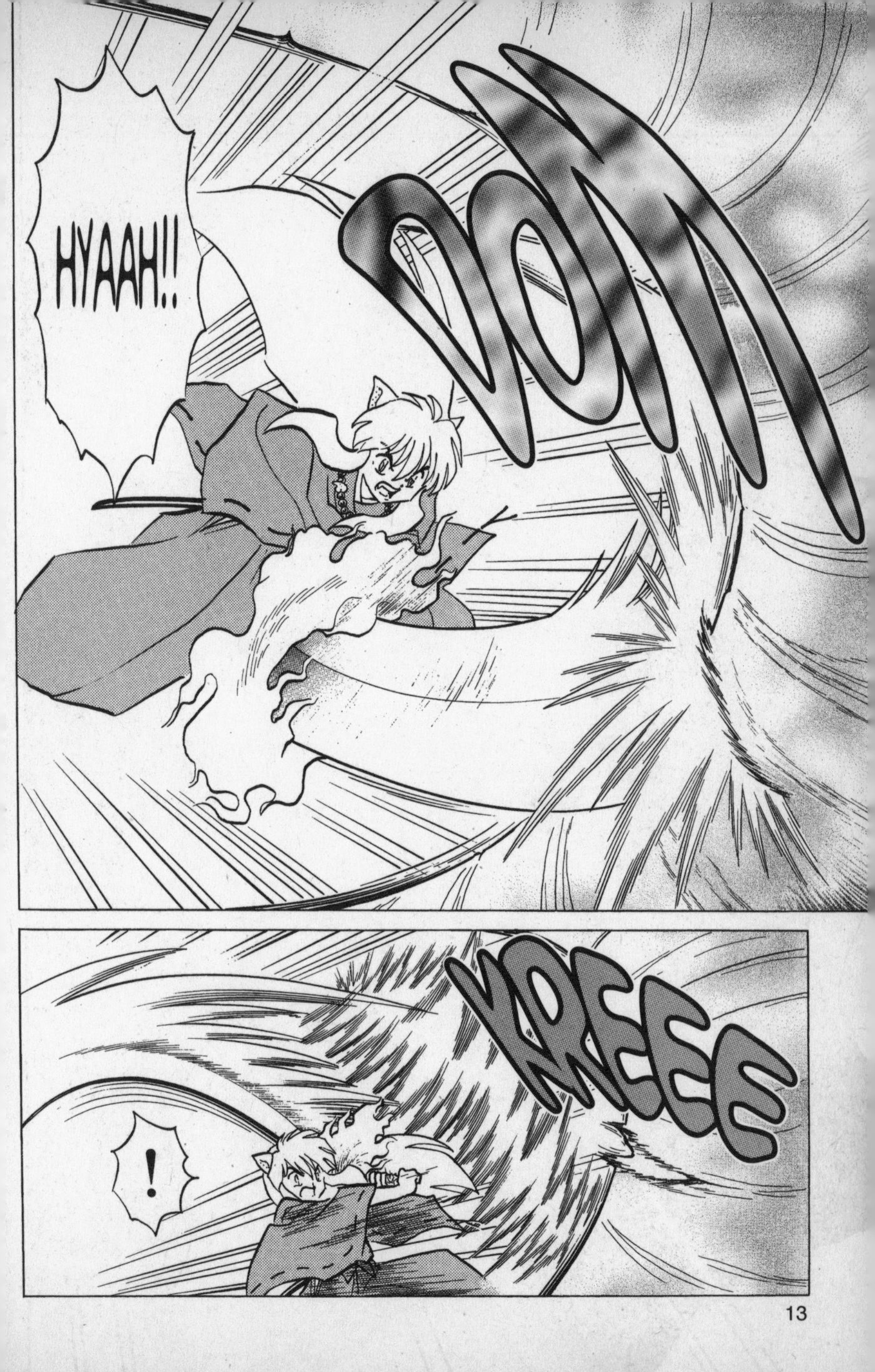
HYAAH!!
KREEE
!

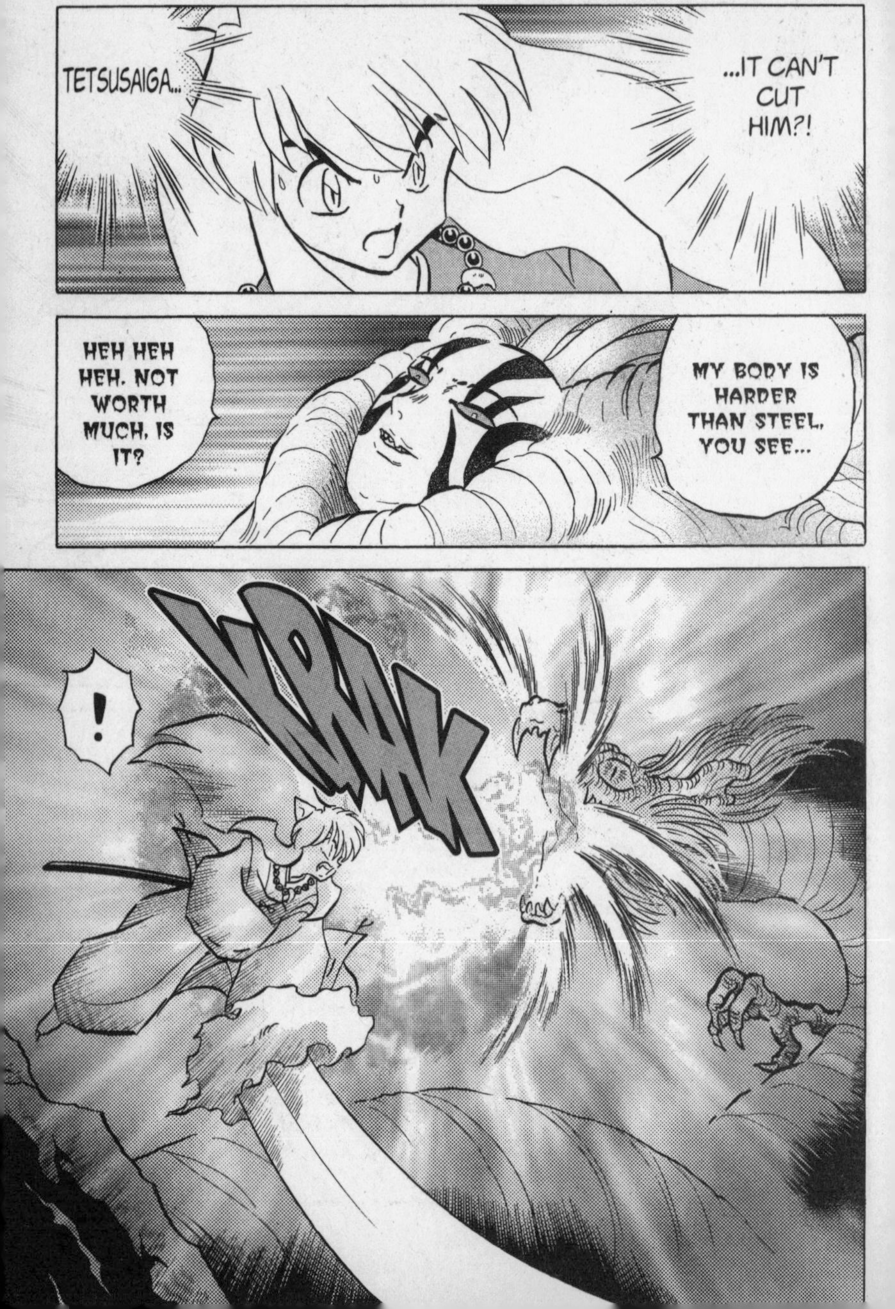
TETSUSAIGA...
...IT CAN'T CUT HIM?!
HEH HEH HEH. NOT WORTH MUCH, IS IT?
MY BODY IS HARDER THAN STEEL, YOU SEE...
!
VRAK

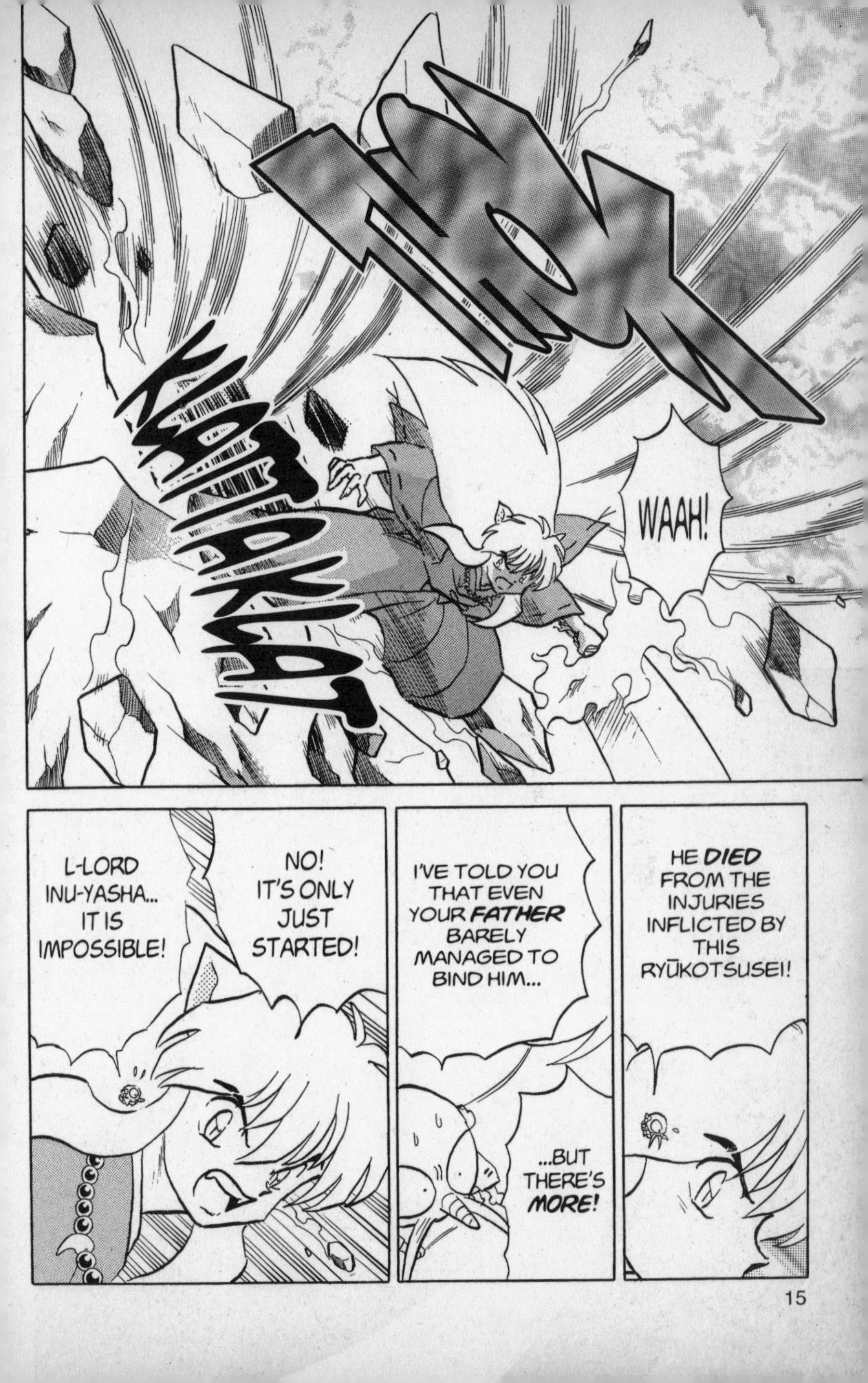
WAAH!
L-LORD INU-YASHA... IT IS IMPOSSIBLE!
NO! IT'S ONLY JUST STARTED!
I'VE TOLD YOU THAT EVEN YOUR **FATHER** BARELY MANAGED TO BIND HIM...
...BUT THERE'S ***MORE!***
HE **DIED** FROM THE INJURIES INFLICTED BY THIS RYŪKOTSUSEI!

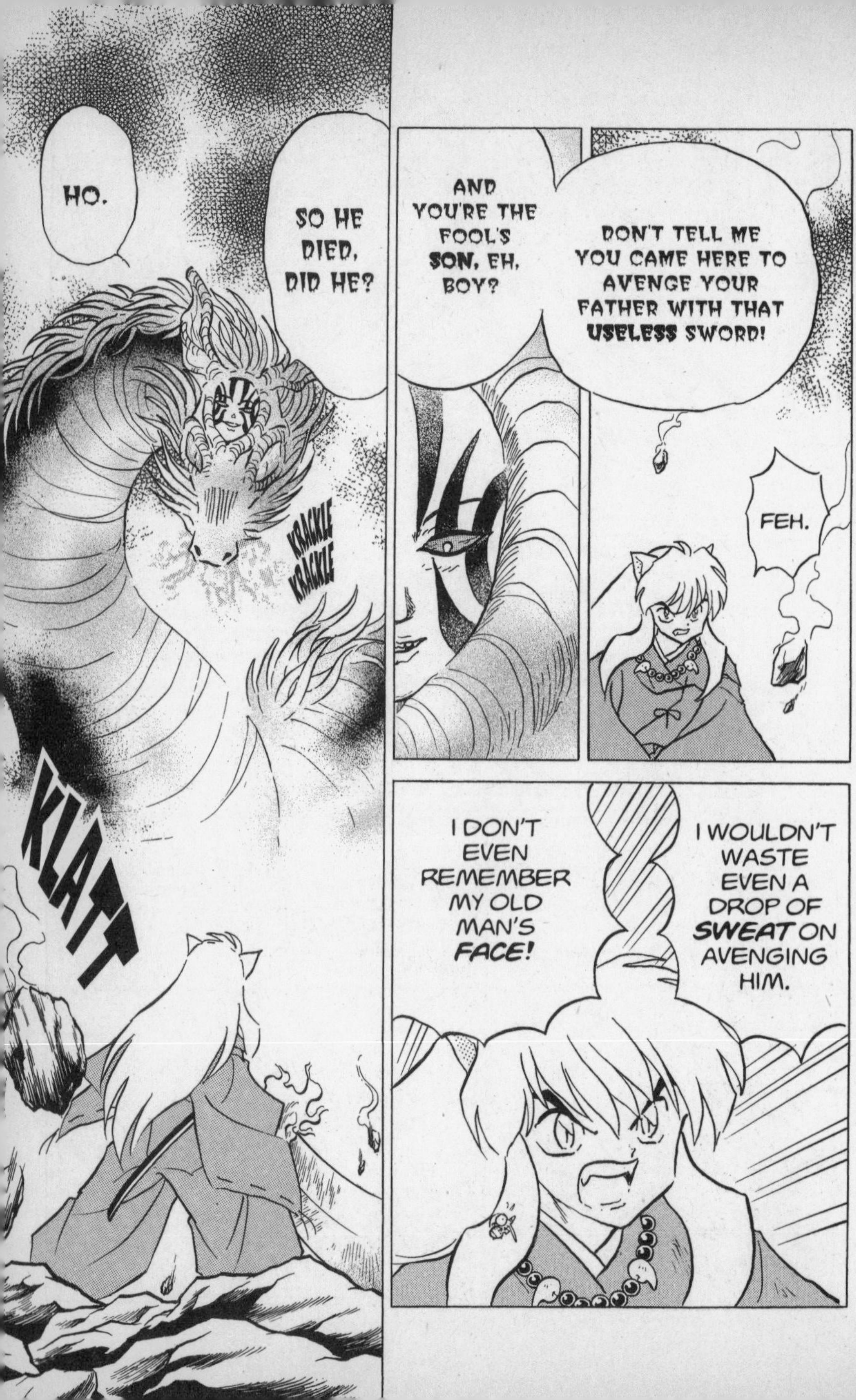
HO.
SO HE DIED, DID HE?
KRACKLE KRACKLE
KLATT
AND YOU'RE THE FOOL'S SON, EH, BOY?
DON'T TELL ME YOU CAME HERE TO AVENGE YOUR FATHER WITH THAT USELESS SWORD!
FEH.
I DON'T EVEN REMEMBER MY OLD MAN'S FACE!
I WOULDN'T WASTE EVEN A DROP OF SWEAT ON AVENGING HIM.

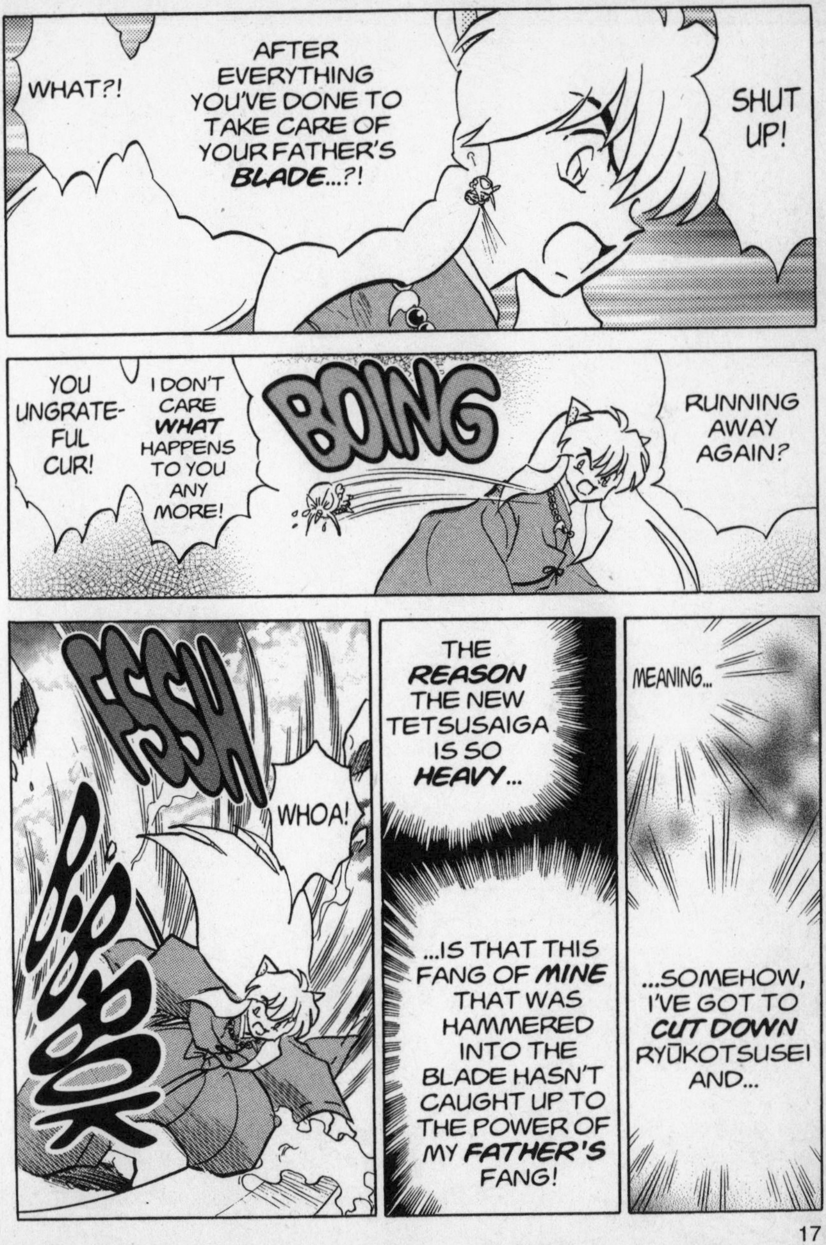
WHAT?!
AFTER EVERYTHING YOU'VE DONE TO TAKE CARE OF YOUR FATHER'S BLADE...?!
SHUT UP!
YOU UNGRATE-FUL CUR!
I DON'T CARE WHAT HAPPENS TO YOU ANY MORE!
BOING
RUNNING AWAY AGAIN?
FSSH
WHOA!
THE REASON THE NEW TETSUSAIGA IS SO HEAVY...
...IS THAT THIS FANG OF MINE THAT WAS HAMMERED INTO THE BLADE HASN'T CAUGHT UP TO THE POWER OF MY FATHER'S FANG!
MEANING...
...SOMEHOW, I'VE GOT TO CUT DOWN RYŪKOTSUSEI AND...

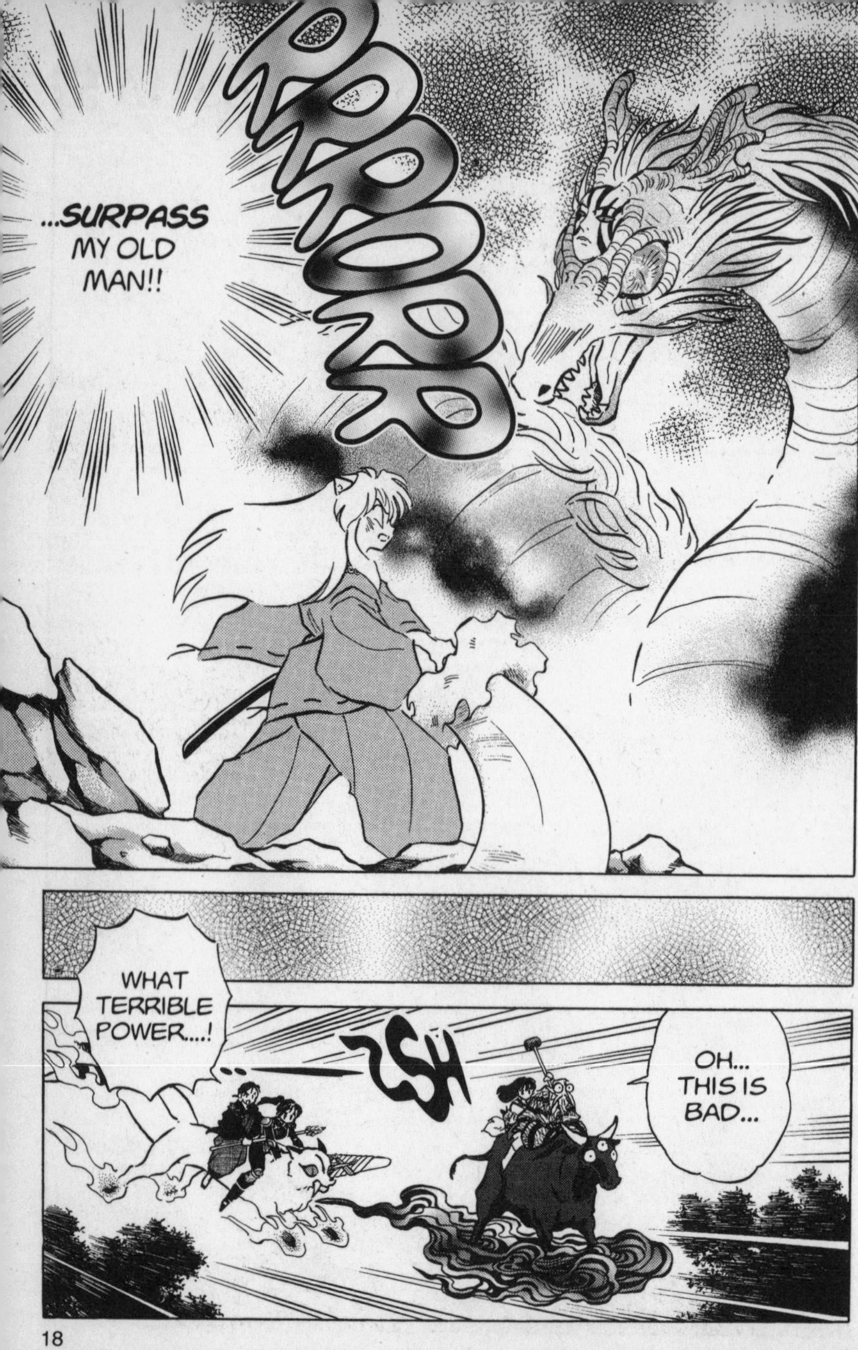

...SURPASS MY OLD MAN!!
RRROOORR
WHAT TERRIBLE POWER....!
ZSH
OH... THIS IS BAD...

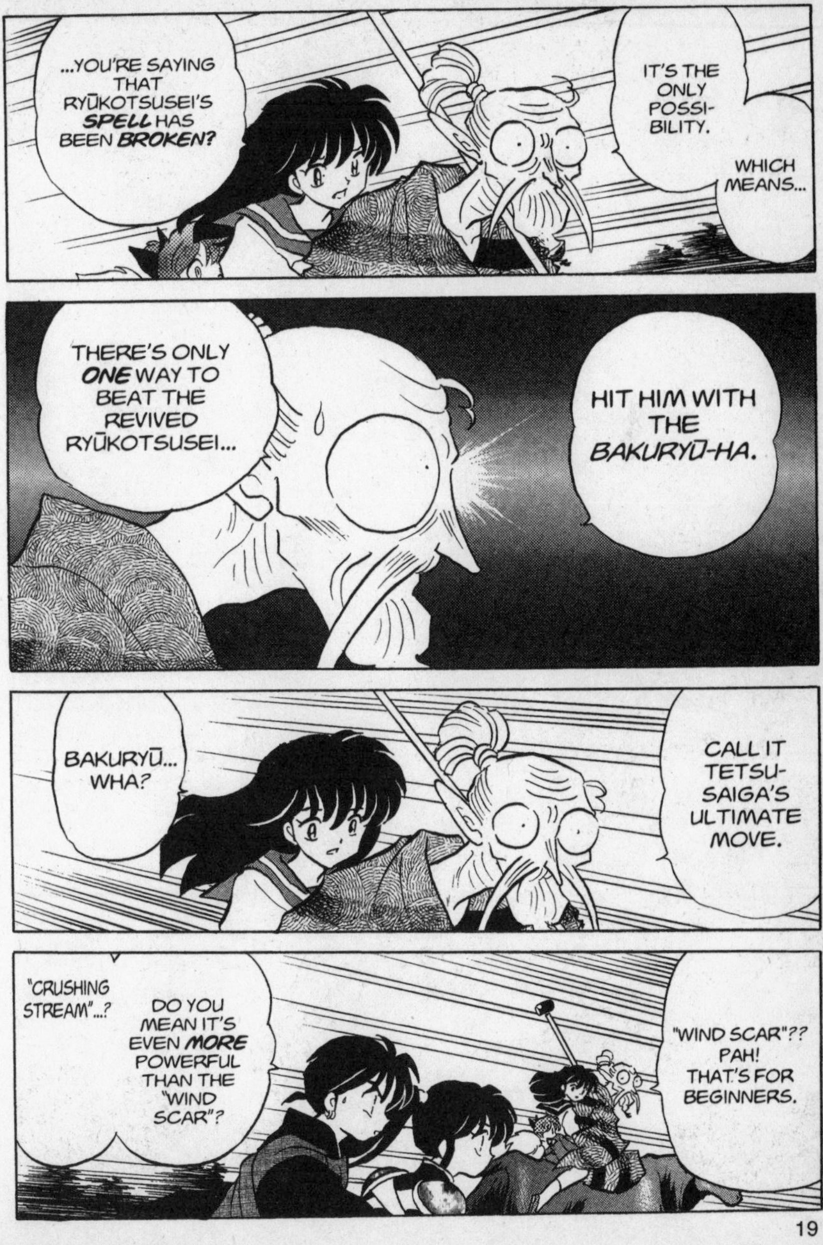
...YOU'RE SAYING THAT RYŪKOTSUSEI'S SPELL HAS BEEN BROKEN?
IT'S THE ONLY POSSI-BILITY.
WHICH MEANS...
THERE'S ONLY ONE WAY TO BEAT THE REVIVED RYŪKOTSUSEI...
HIT HIM WITH THE BAKURYŪ-HA.
BAKURYŪ... WHA?
CALL IT TETSU-SAIGA'S ULTIMATE MOVE.
"CRUSHING STREAM"...?
DO YOU MEAN IT'S EVEN MORE POWERFUL THAN THE "WIND SCAR"?
"WIND SCAR"?? PAH! THAT'S FOR BEGINNERS.

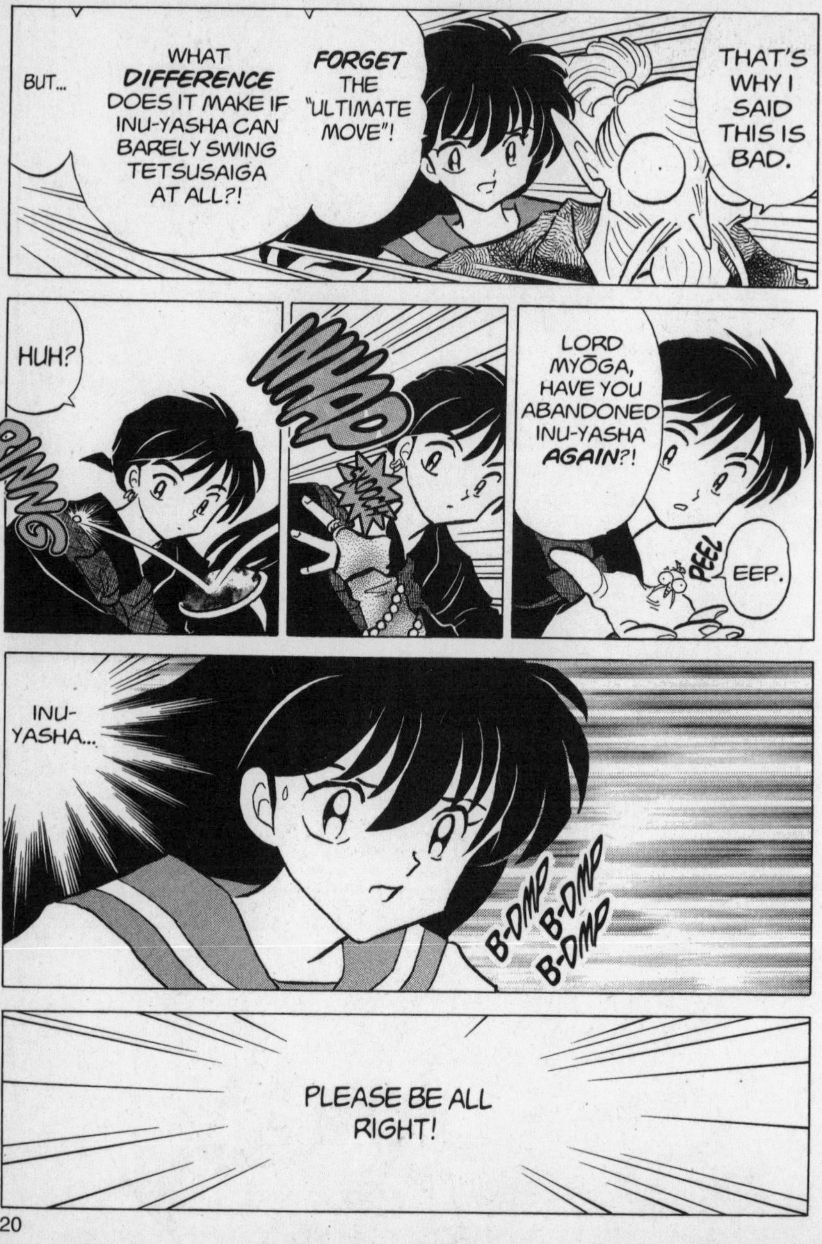
BUT...
WHAT *DIFFERENCE* DOES IT MAKE IF INU-YASHA CAN BARELY SWING TETSUSAIGA AT ALL?!
FORGET THE "ULTIMATE MOVE"!
THAT'S WHY I SAID THIS IS BAD.
HUH?
BINNG
WHAP
LORD MYŌGA, HAVE YOU ABANDONED INU-YASHA *AGAIN*?!
PEEL
EEP.
INU-YASHA...
B-DMP B-DMP B-DMP
PLEASE BE ALL RIGHT!

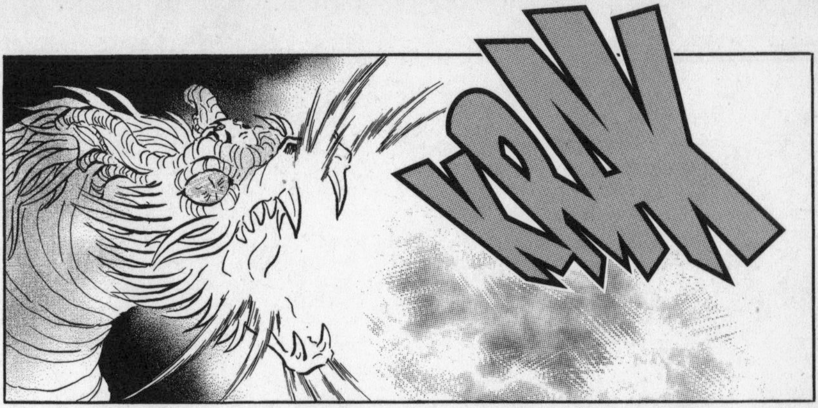
KRAK
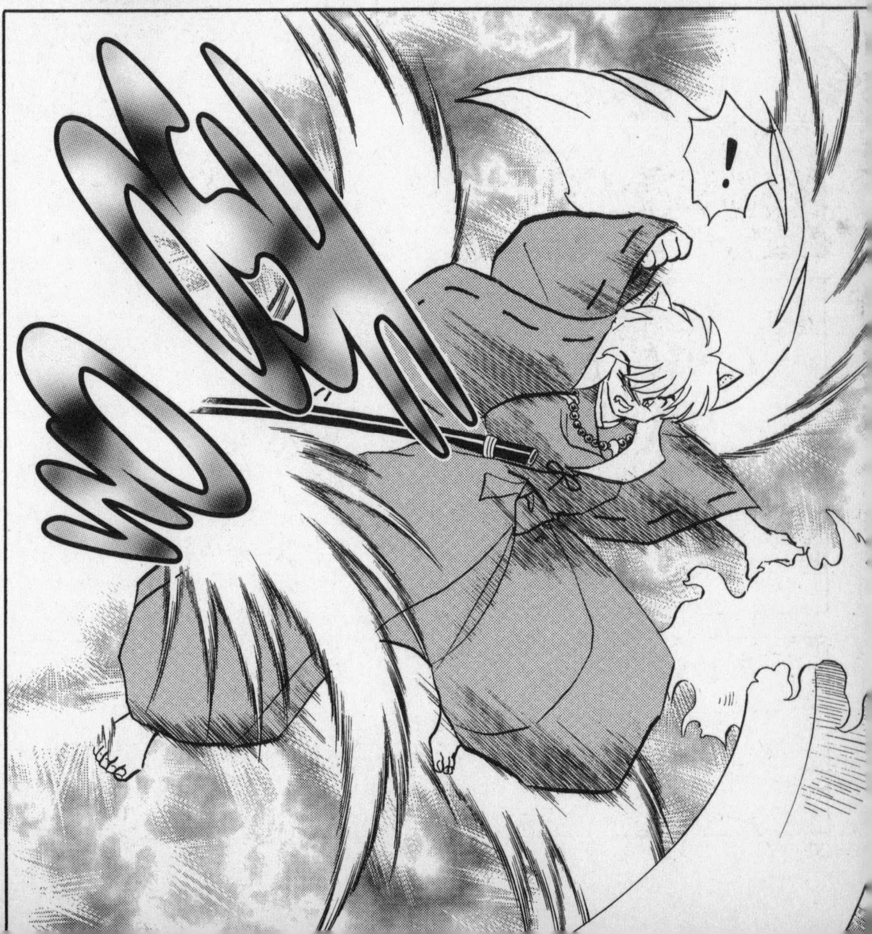
!

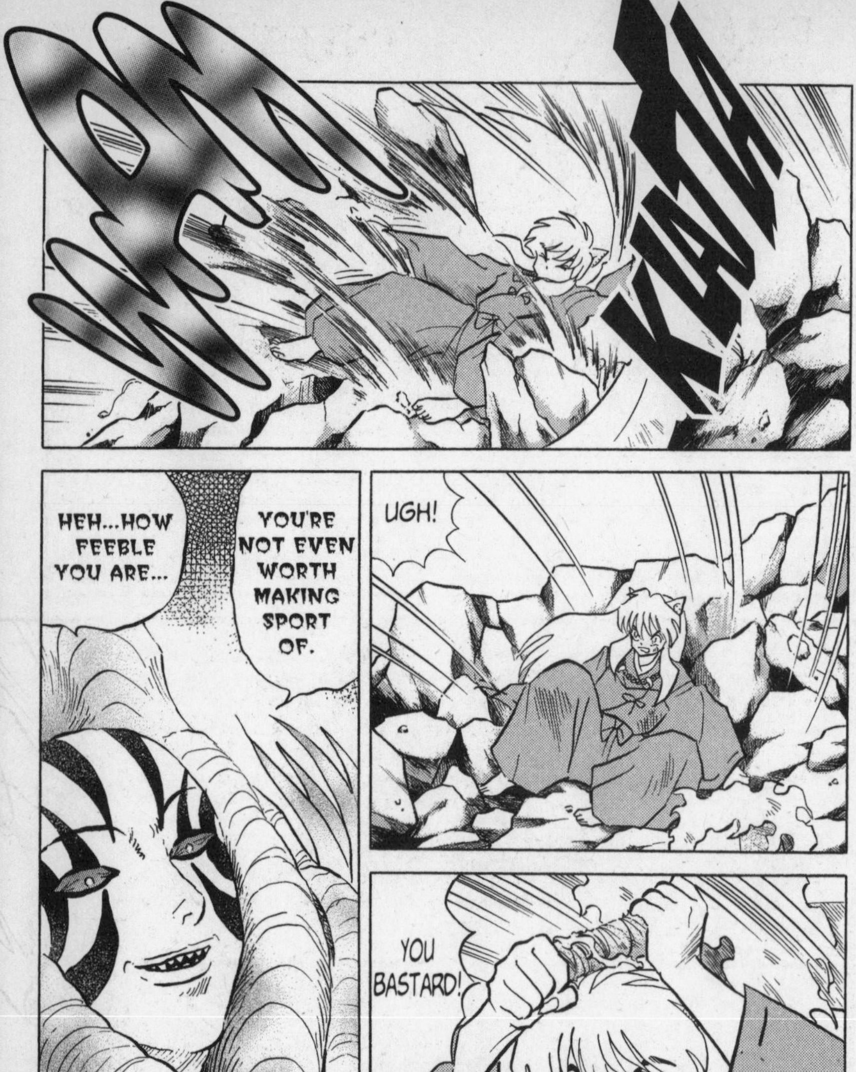
HEH...HOW FEEBLE YOU ARE...
YOU'RE NOT EVEN WORTH MAKING SPORT OF.
UGH!
YOU BASTARD!

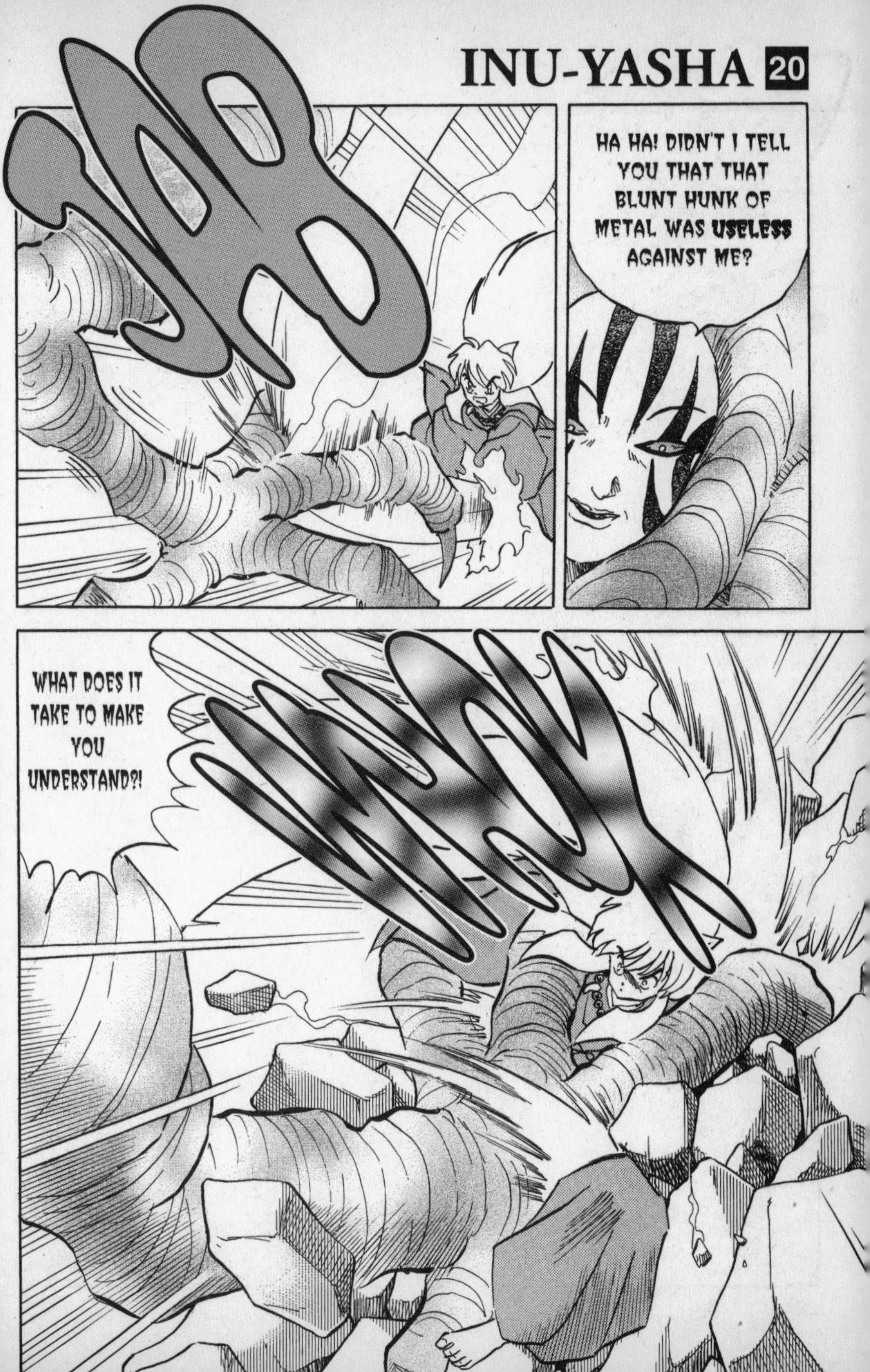
HA HA! DIDN'T I TELL YOU THAT THAT BLUNT HUNK OF METAL WAS **USELESS** AGAINST ME?
WHAT DOES IT TAKE TO MAKE YOU UNDERSTAND?!

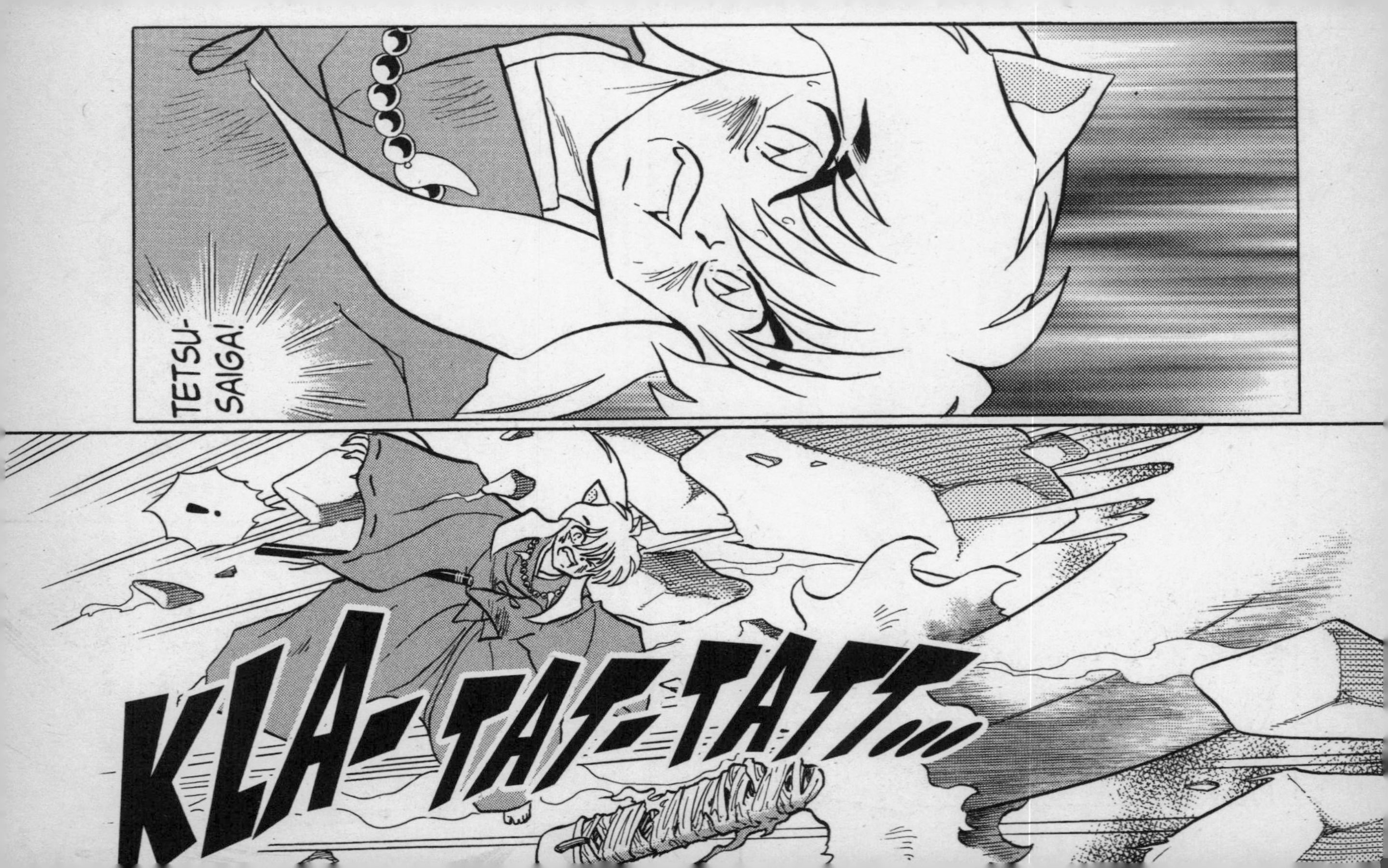
TETSU-SAIGA!
!
KLA-TAT-TATT...

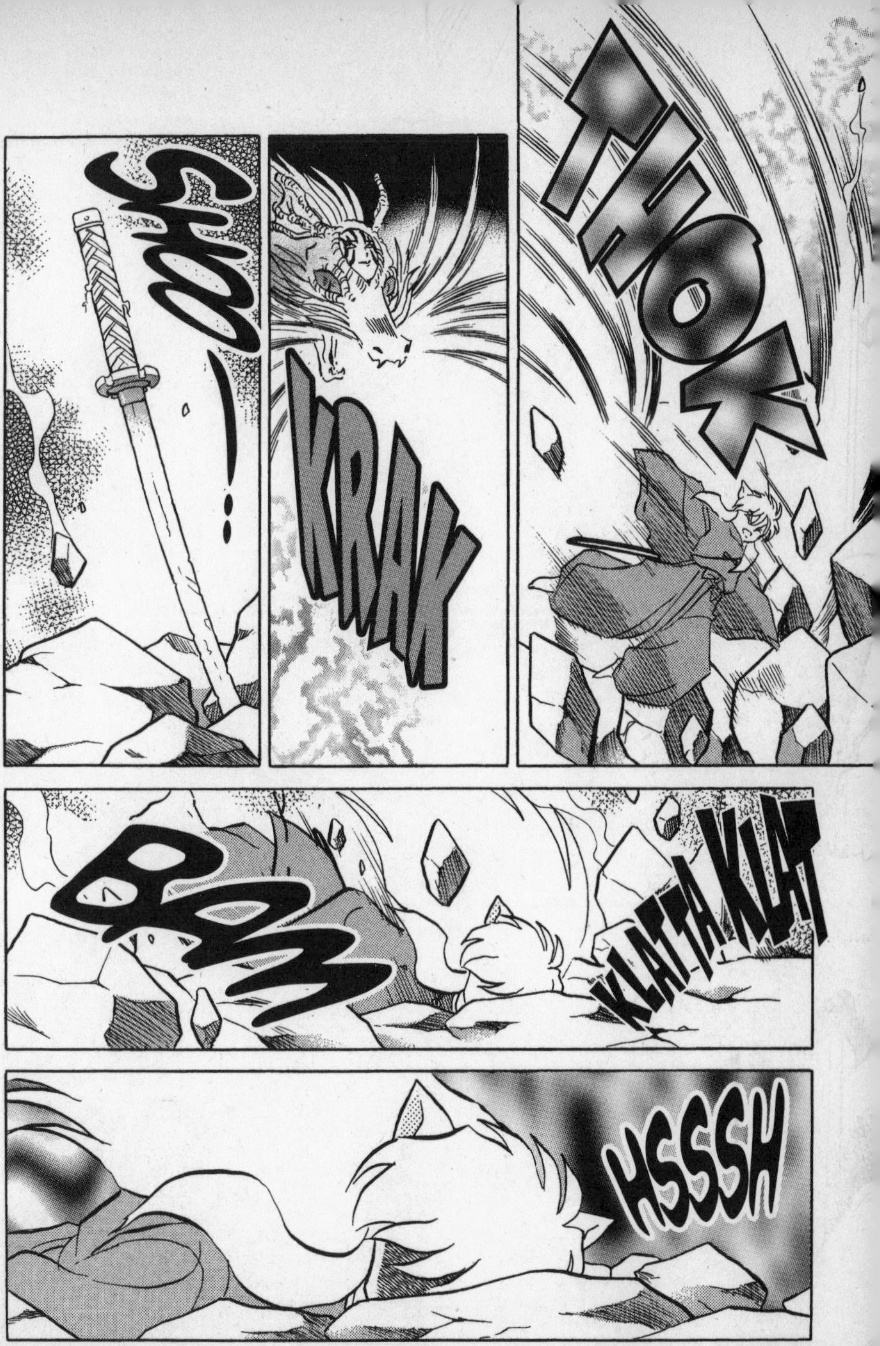
SHOO--!!
KRAK
THOK
BOOM
KLATTA KLAT
HSSSH

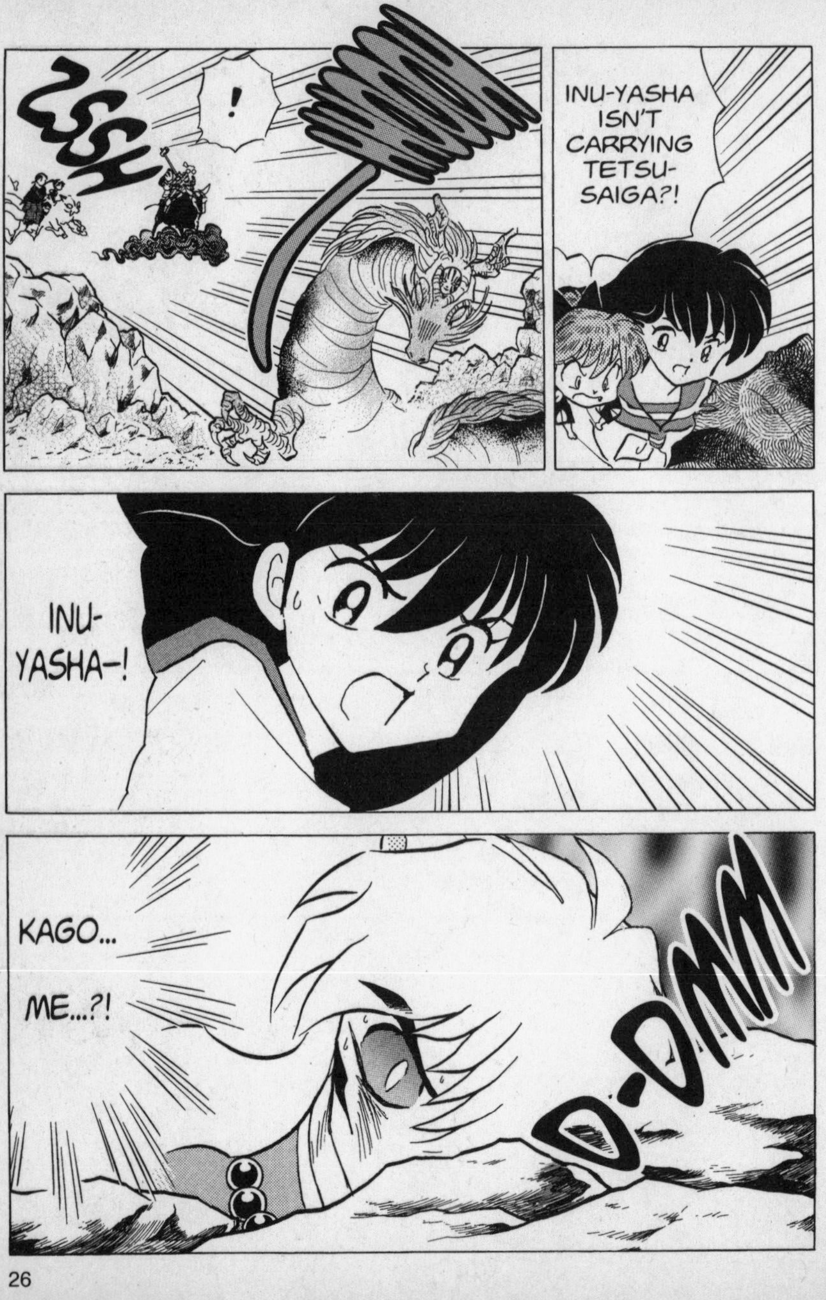
ZSSH
!
INU-YASHA ISN'T CARRYING TETSU-SAIGA?!
INU-YASHA-!
KAGO...
ME...?!
D-DMM

SCROLL TWO

TALONS AND BLADE

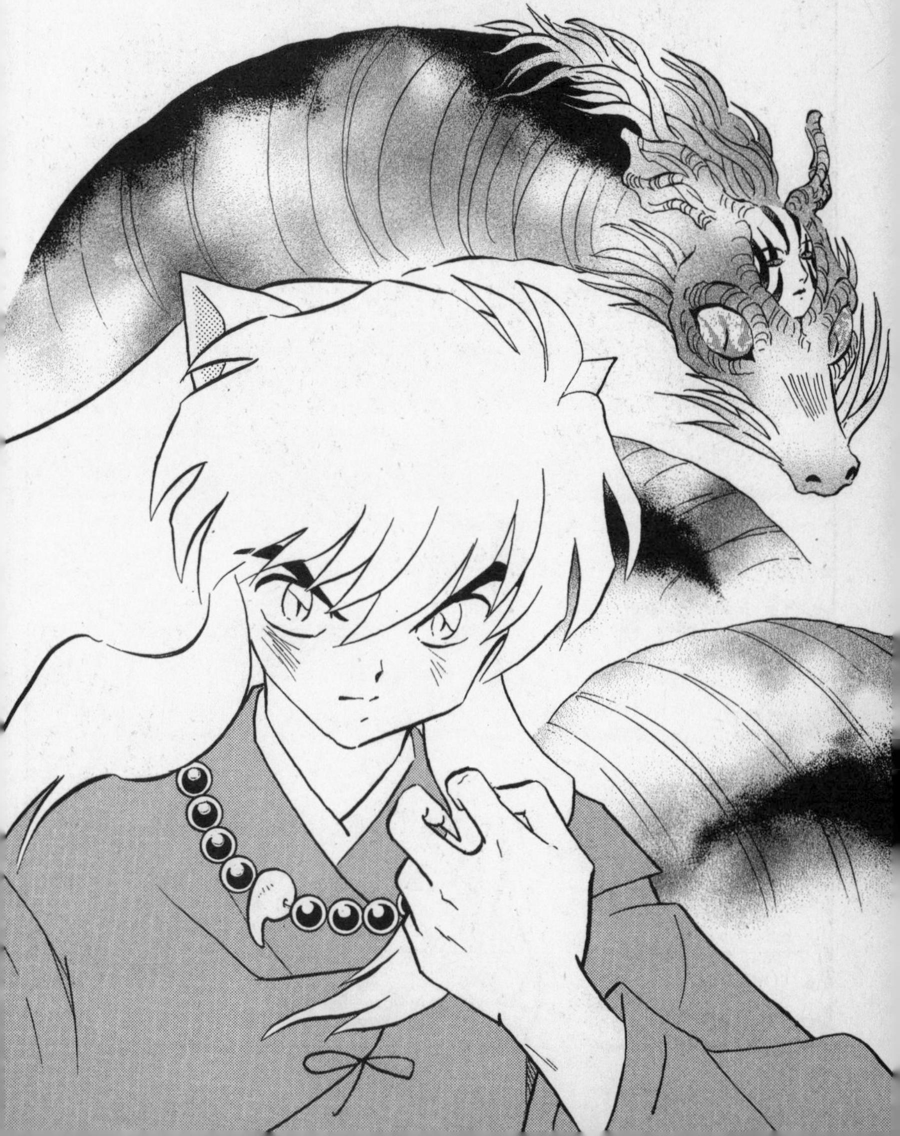

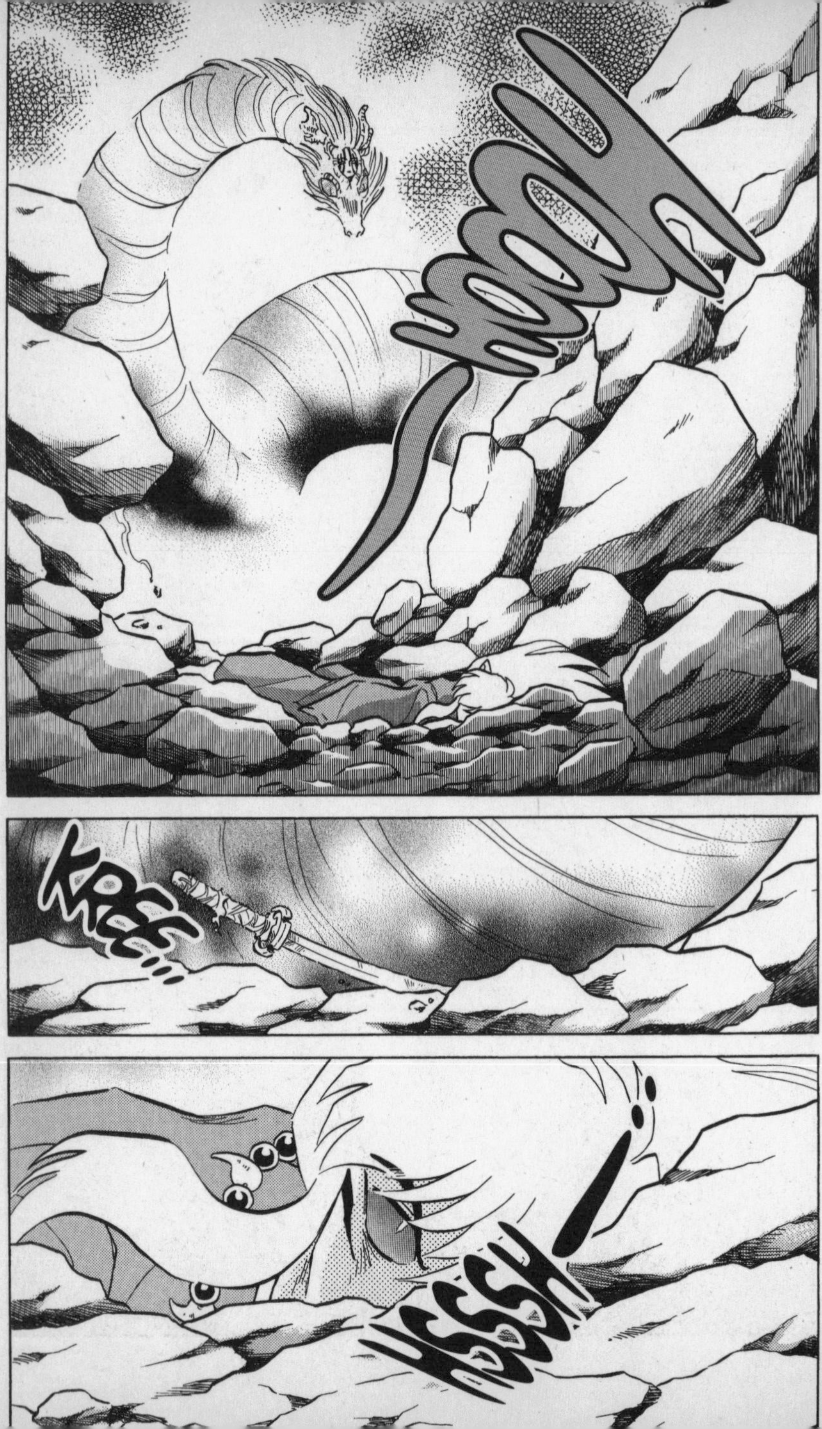
WHOOSH
KREE...
HSSH!

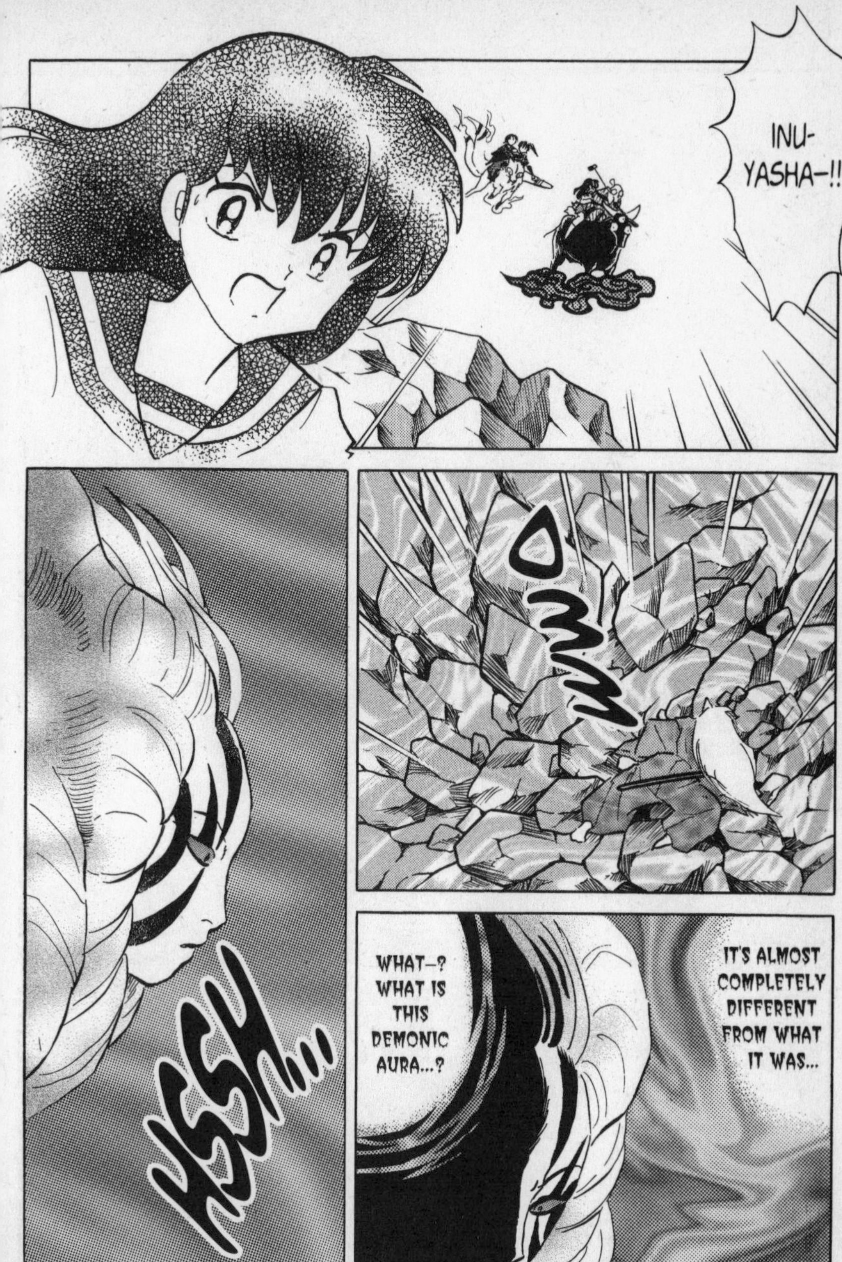
INU-
YASHA--!!
HSSH...
DMM
WHAT--? WHAT IS THIS DEMONIC AURA...?
IT'S ALMOST COMPLETELY DIFFERENT FROM WHAT IT WAS...

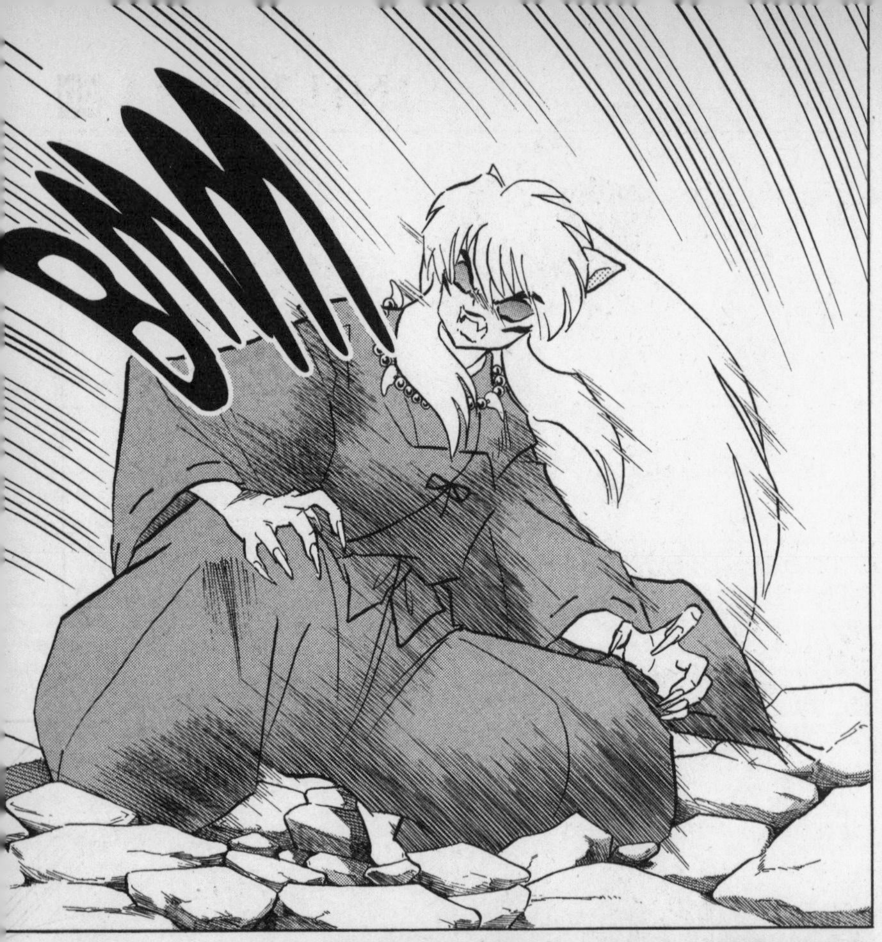
BAM
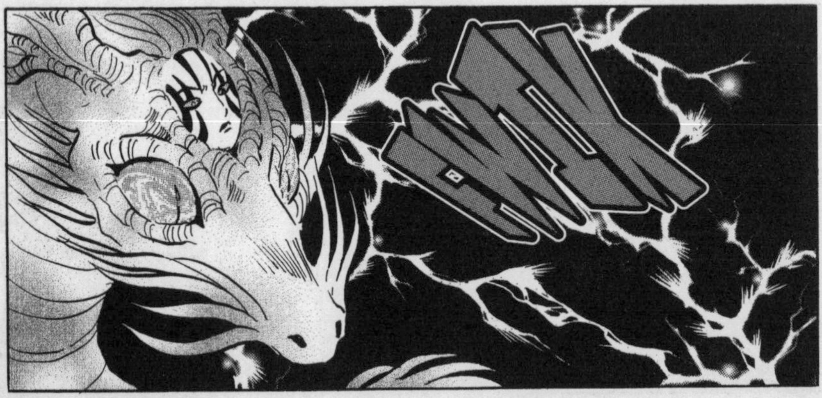

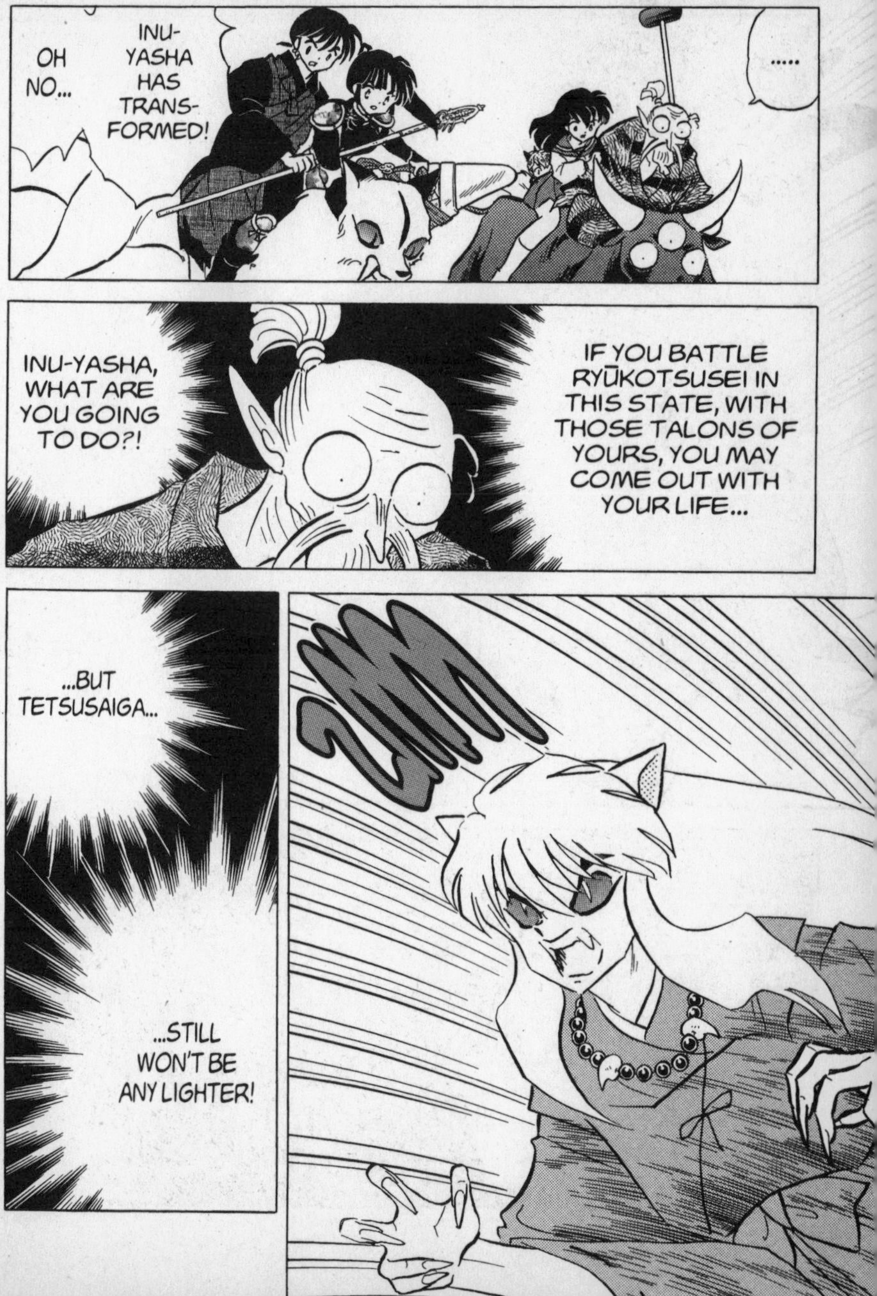
OH NO...
INU-YASHA HAS TRANSFORMED!
.....
INU-YASHA, WHAT ARE YOU GOING TO DO?!
IF YOU BATTLE RYŪKOTSUSEI IN THIS STATE, WITH THOSE TALONS OF YOURS, YOU MAY COME OUT WITH YOUR LIFE...
...BUT TETSUSAIGA...
...STILL WON'T BE ANY LIGHTER!

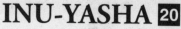

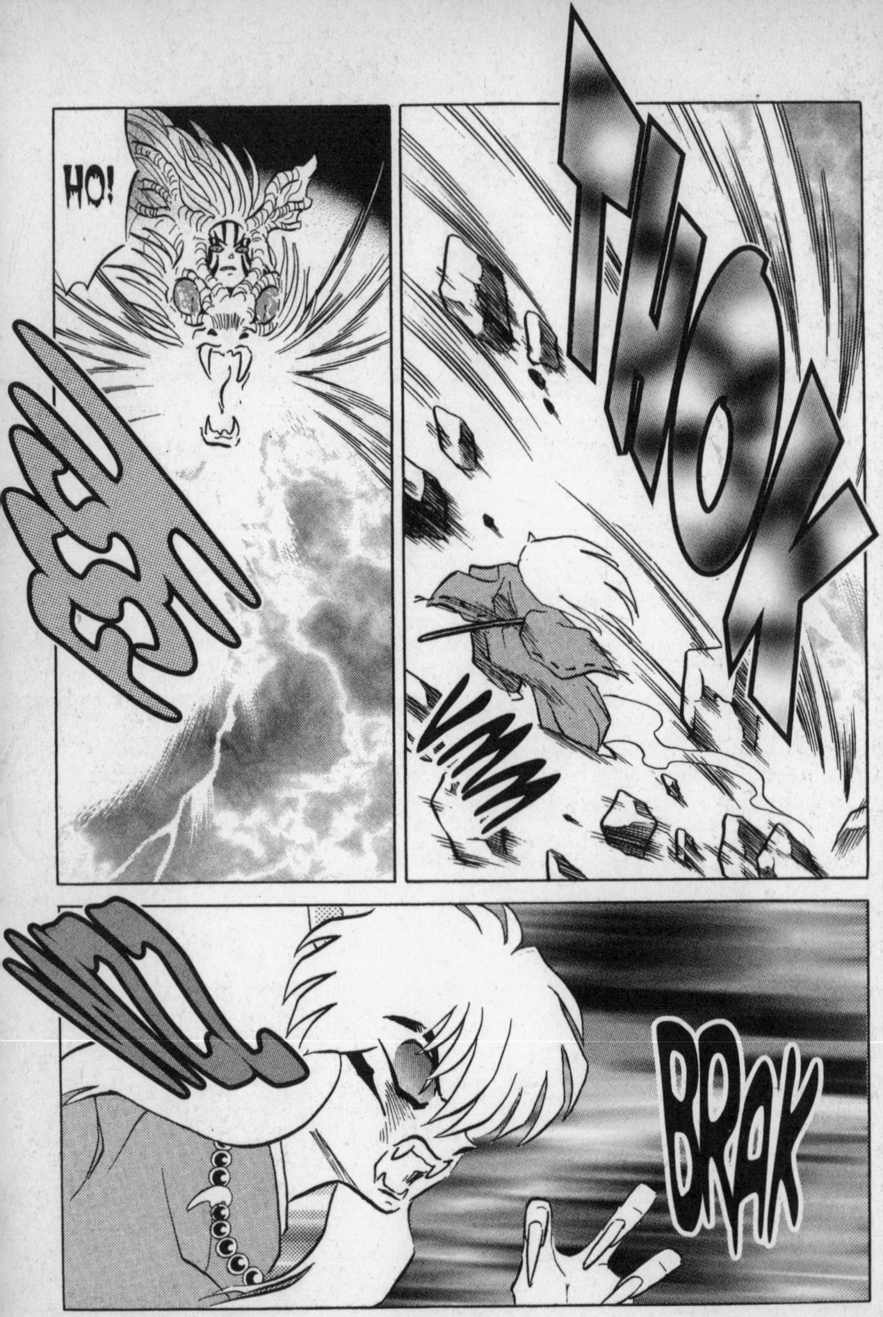
HO!
THOK
VMM
BRAK

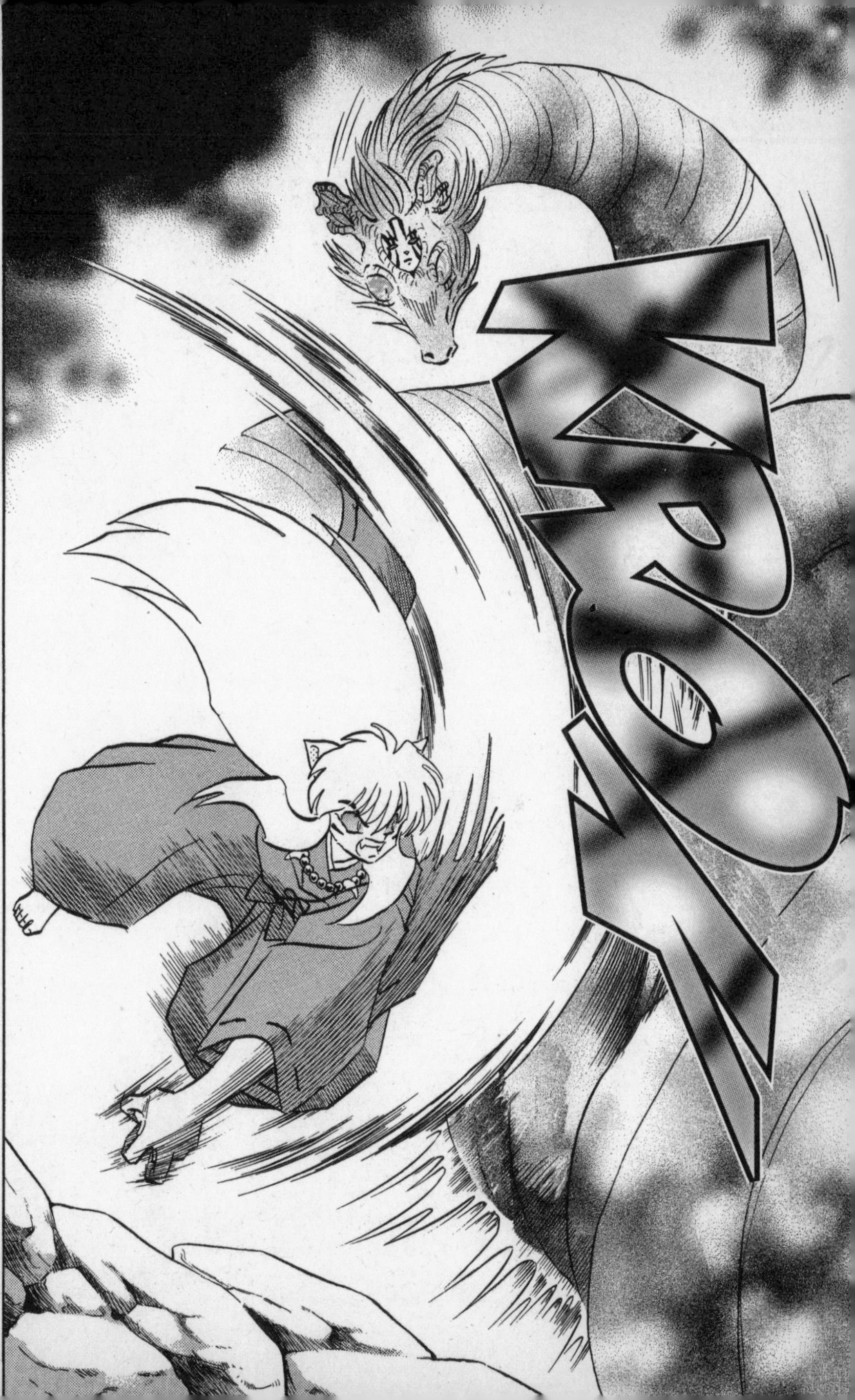

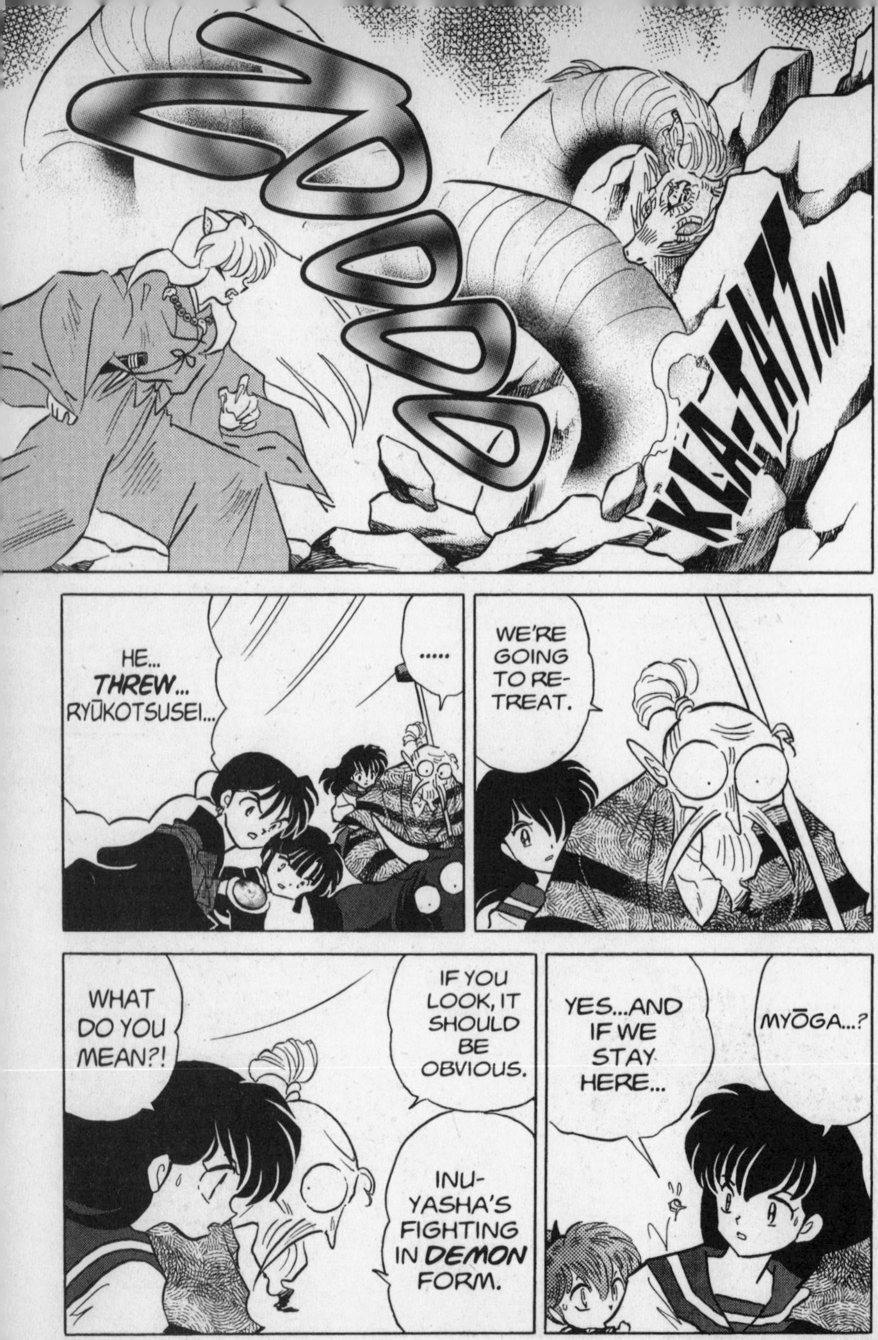
KA-TAT...
HE... THREW... RYŪKOTSUSEI...
.....
WE'RE GOING TO RE-TREAT.
WHAT DO YOU MEAN?!
IF YOU LOOK, IT SHOULD BE OBVIOUS.
INU-YASHA'S FIGHTING IN DEMON FORM.
YES...AND IF WE STAY HERE...
MYŌGA...?

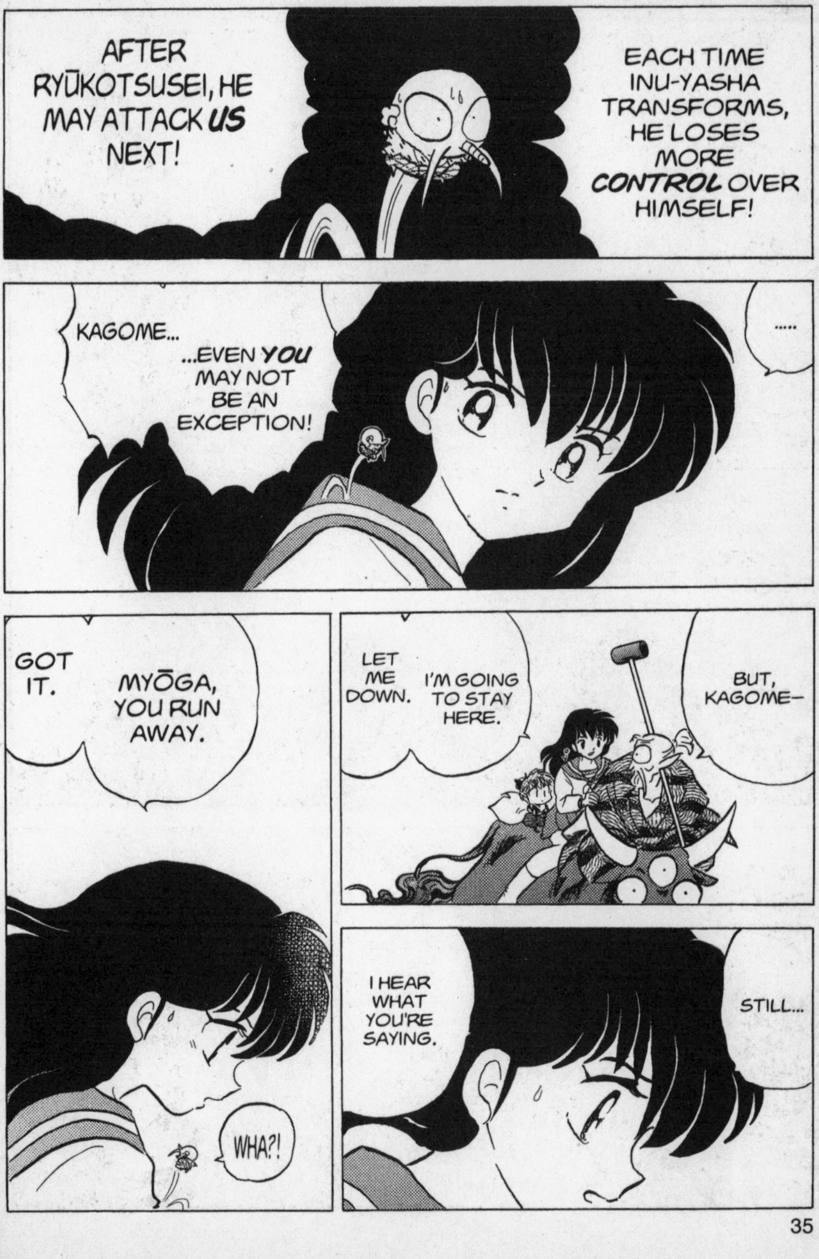
AFTER RYŪKOTSUSEI, HE MAY ATTACK **US** NEXT!
EACH TIME INU-YASHA TRANSFORMS, HE LOSES MORE **CONTROL** OVER HIMSELF!
KAGOME...
...EVEN **YOU** MAY NOT BE AN EXCEPTION!
.....
GOT IT.
MYŌGA, YOU RUN AWAY.
WHA?!
LET ME DOWN.
I'M GOING TO STAY HERE.
BUT, KAGOME–
I HEAR WHAT YOU'RE SAYING.
STILL...

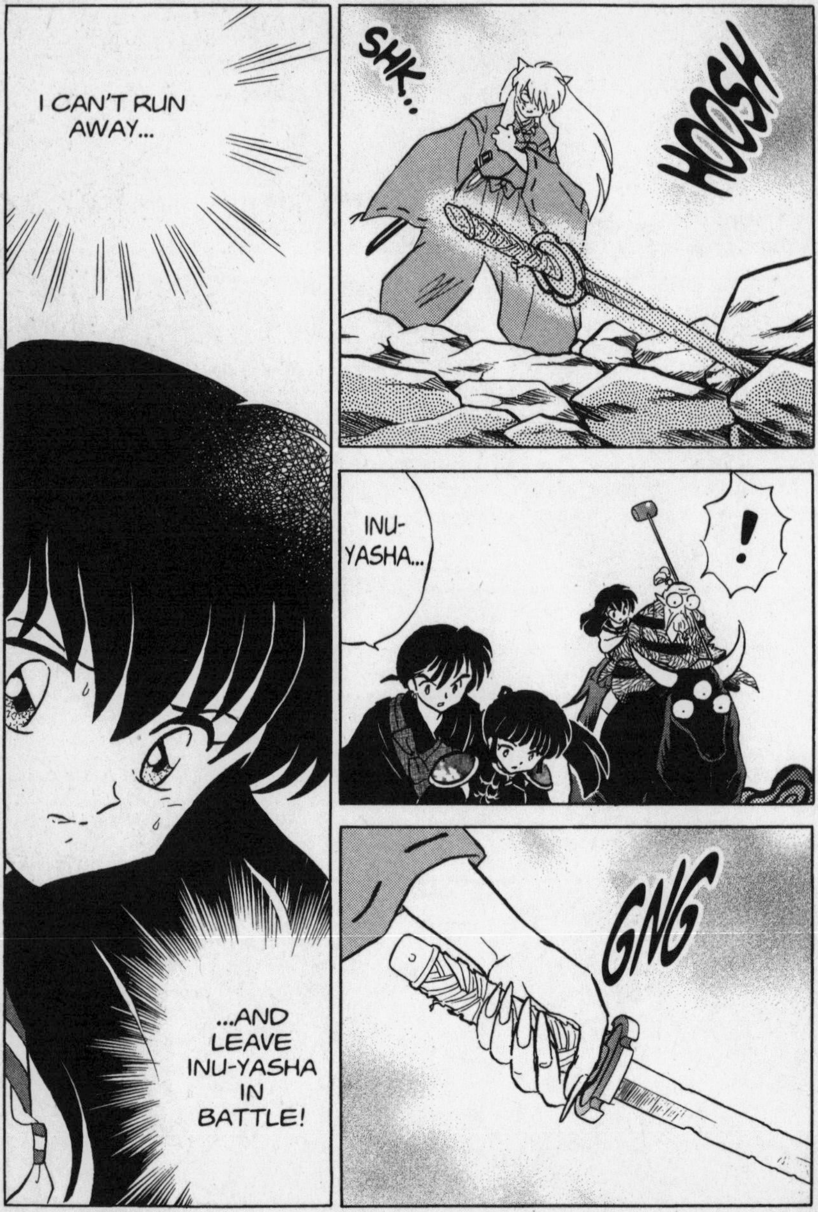
I CAN'T RUN AWAY...
...AND LEAVE INU-YASHA IN BATTLE!
SHK...
HOOSH
INU-YASHA...
!
GNG

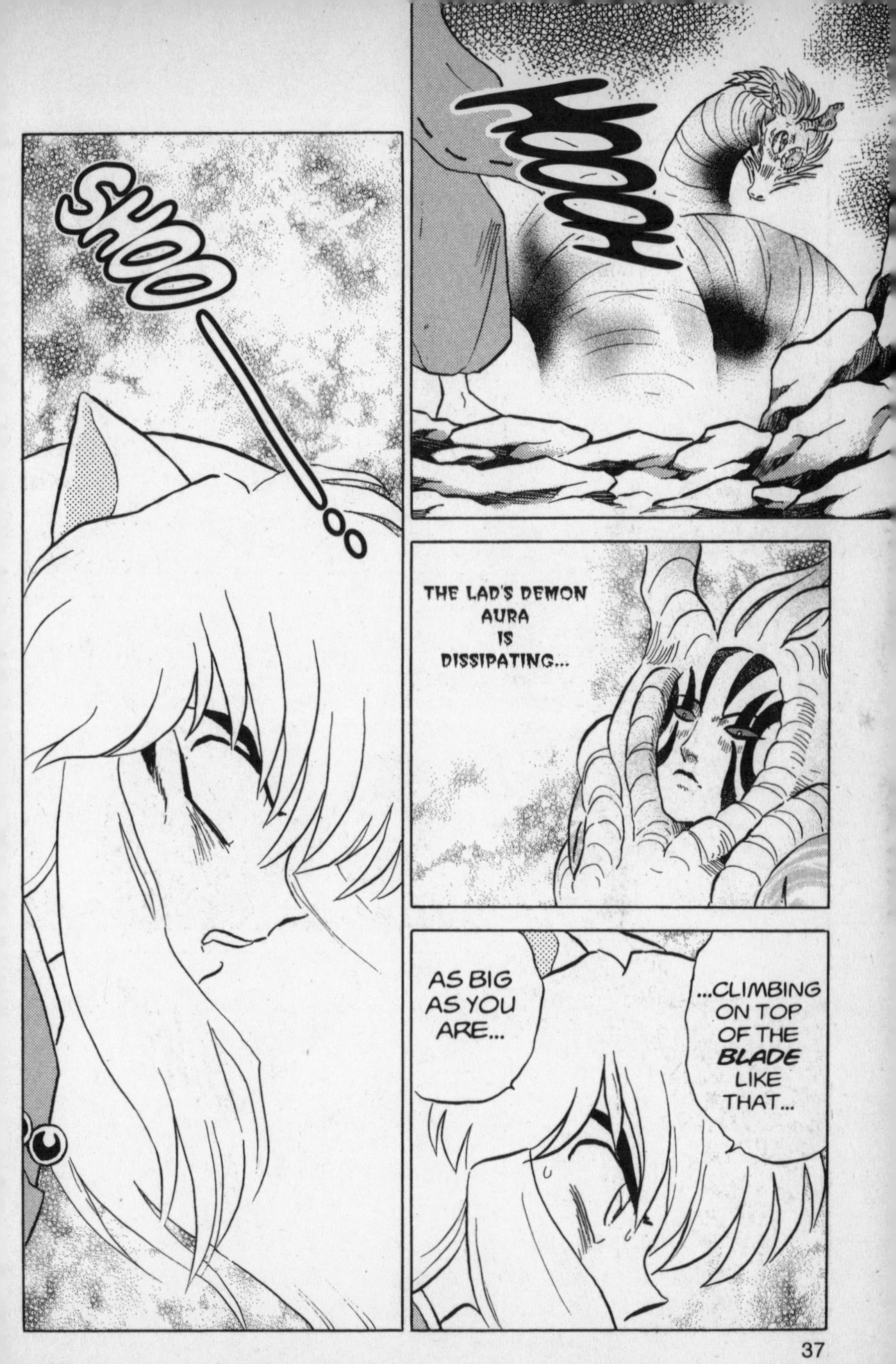
SHOO...
HOOOH
THE LAD'S DEMON AURA IS DISSIPATING...
AS BIG AS YOU ARE...
...CLIMBING ON TOP OF THE *BLADE* LIKE THAT...

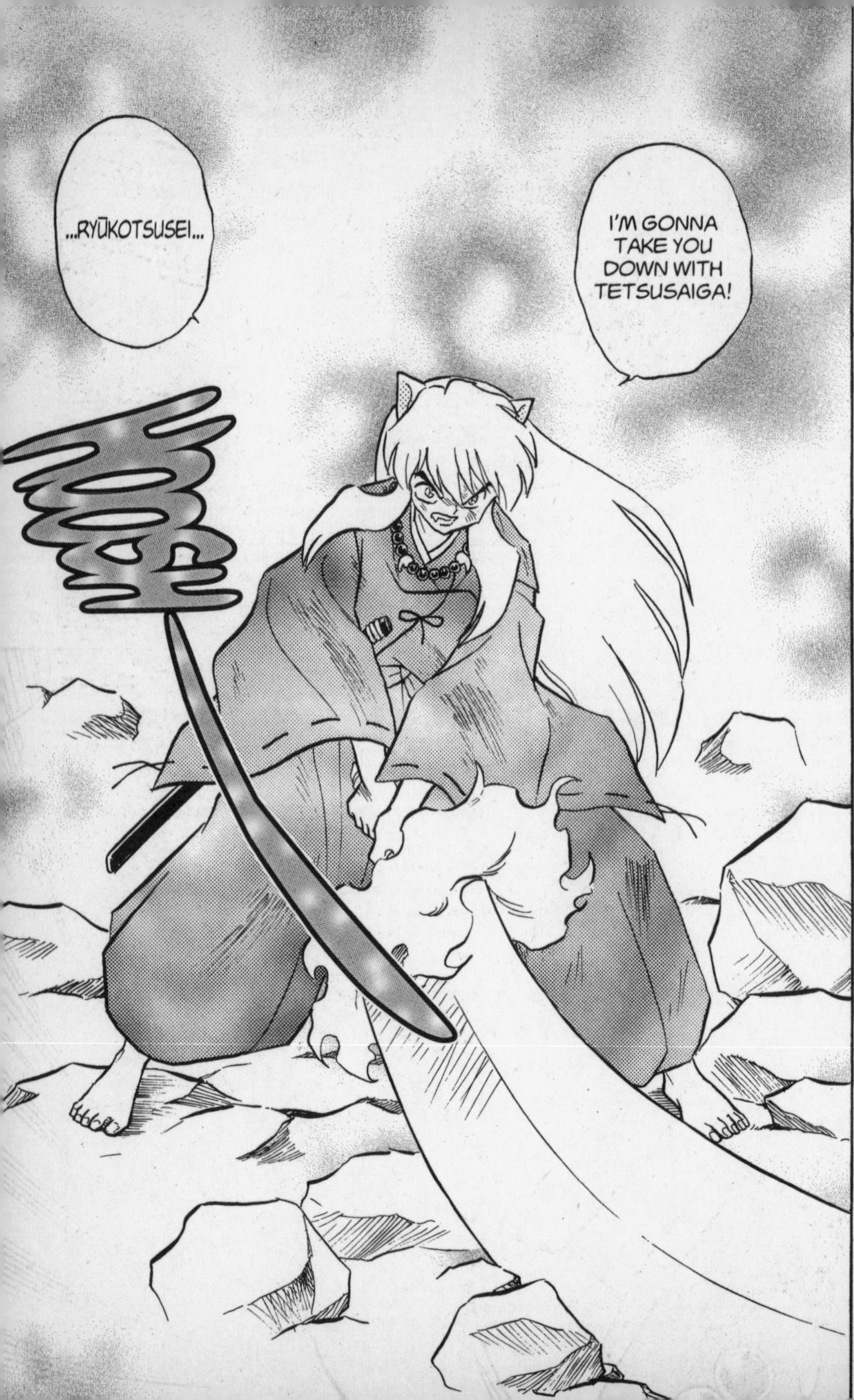
...RYŪKOTSUSEI...
I'M GONNA TAKE YOU DOWN WITH TETSUSAIGA!
WOOSH

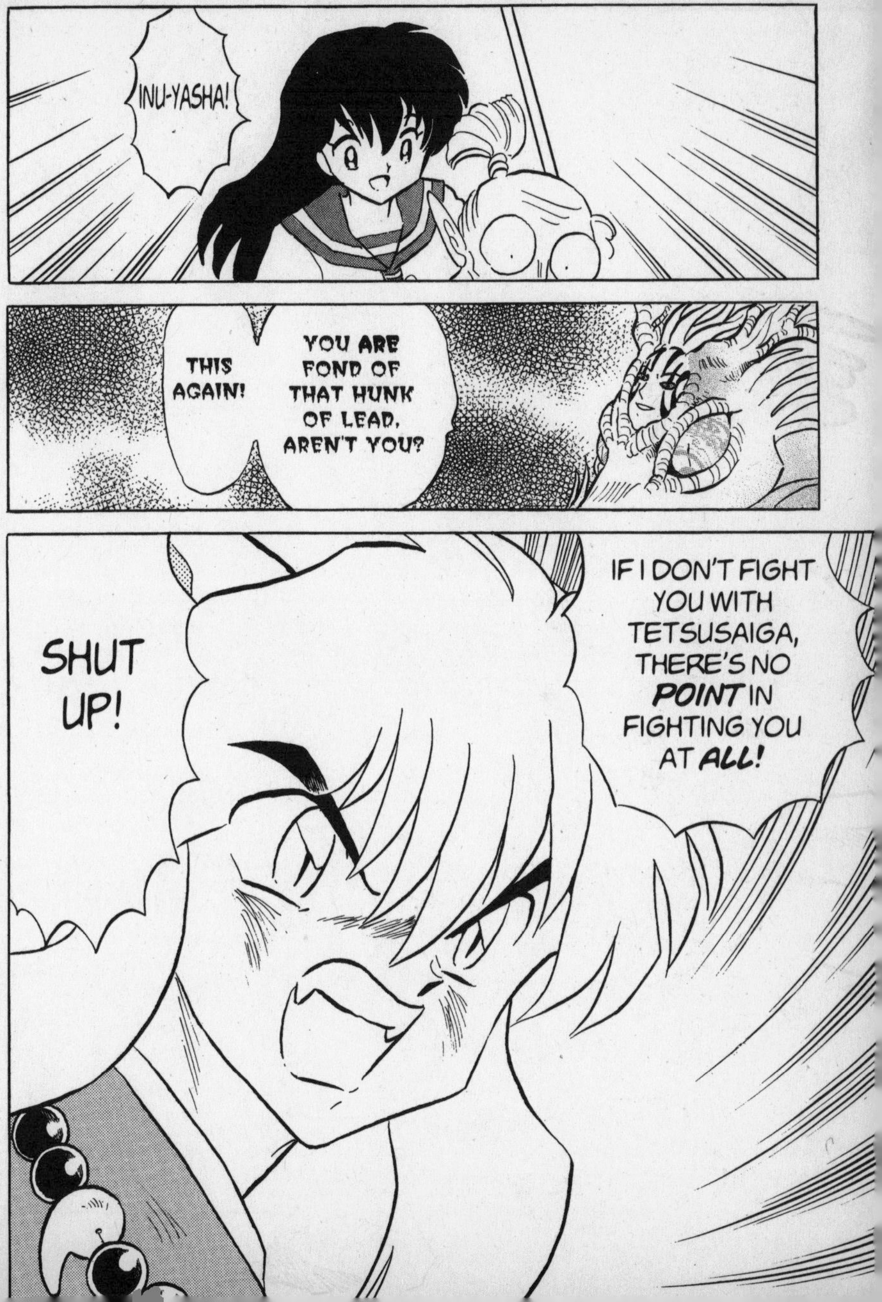
INU-YASHA!
THIS AGAIN!
YOU ARE FOND OF THAT HUNK OF LEAD, AREN'T YOU?
SHUT UP!
IF I DON'T FIGHT YOU WITH TETSUSAIGA, THERE'S NO POINT IN FIGHTING YOU AT ALL!

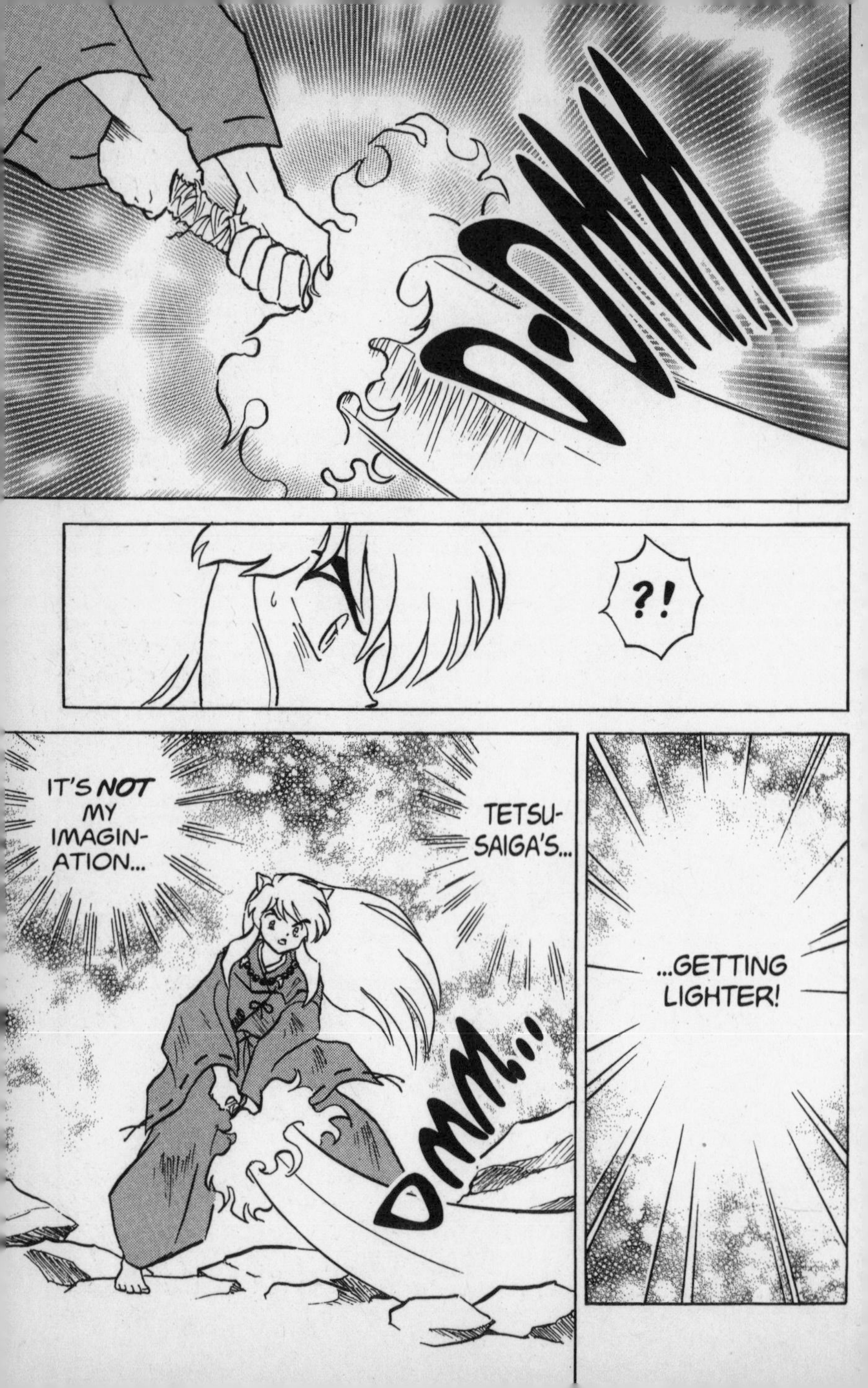
DMM
?!
IT'S NOT MY IMAGINATION...
TETSU-SAIGA'S...
DMM...
...GETTING LIGHTER!

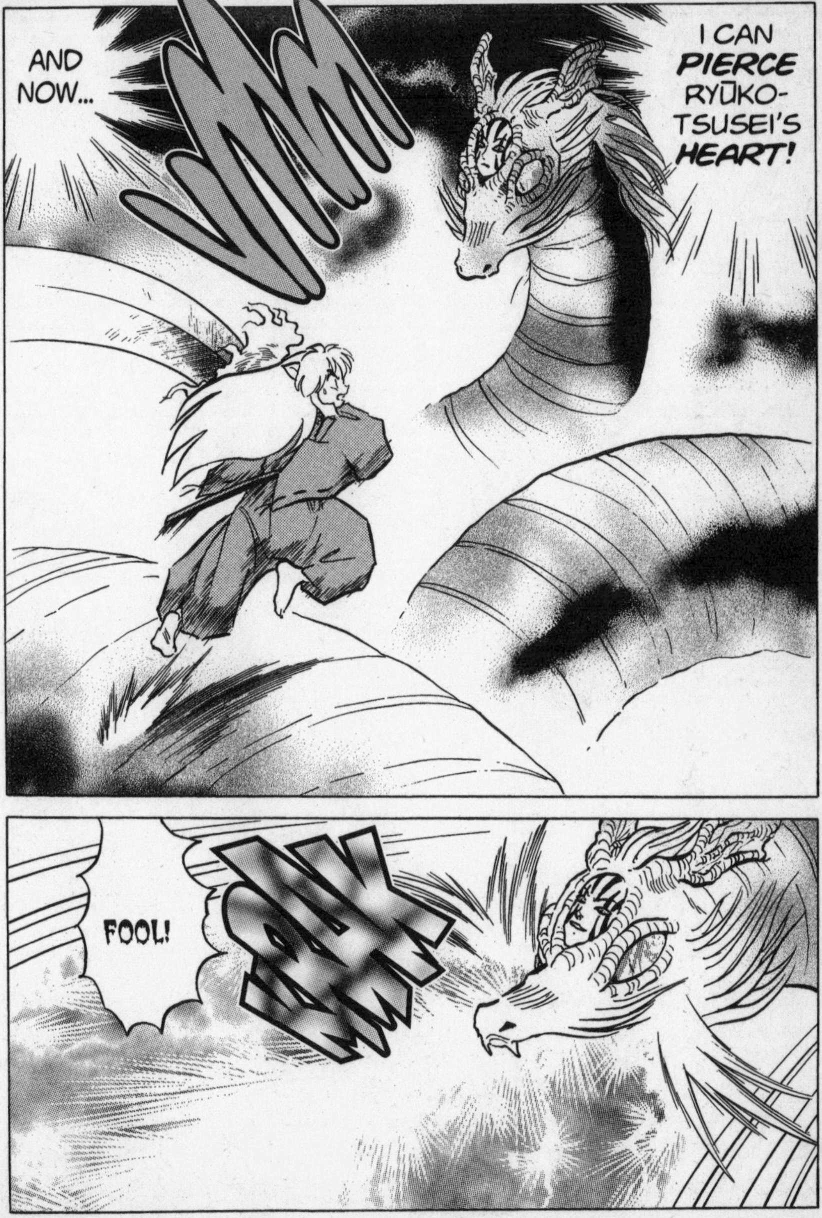
AND NOW...
I CAN PIERCE RYŪKO-TSUSEI'S HEART!
FOOL!

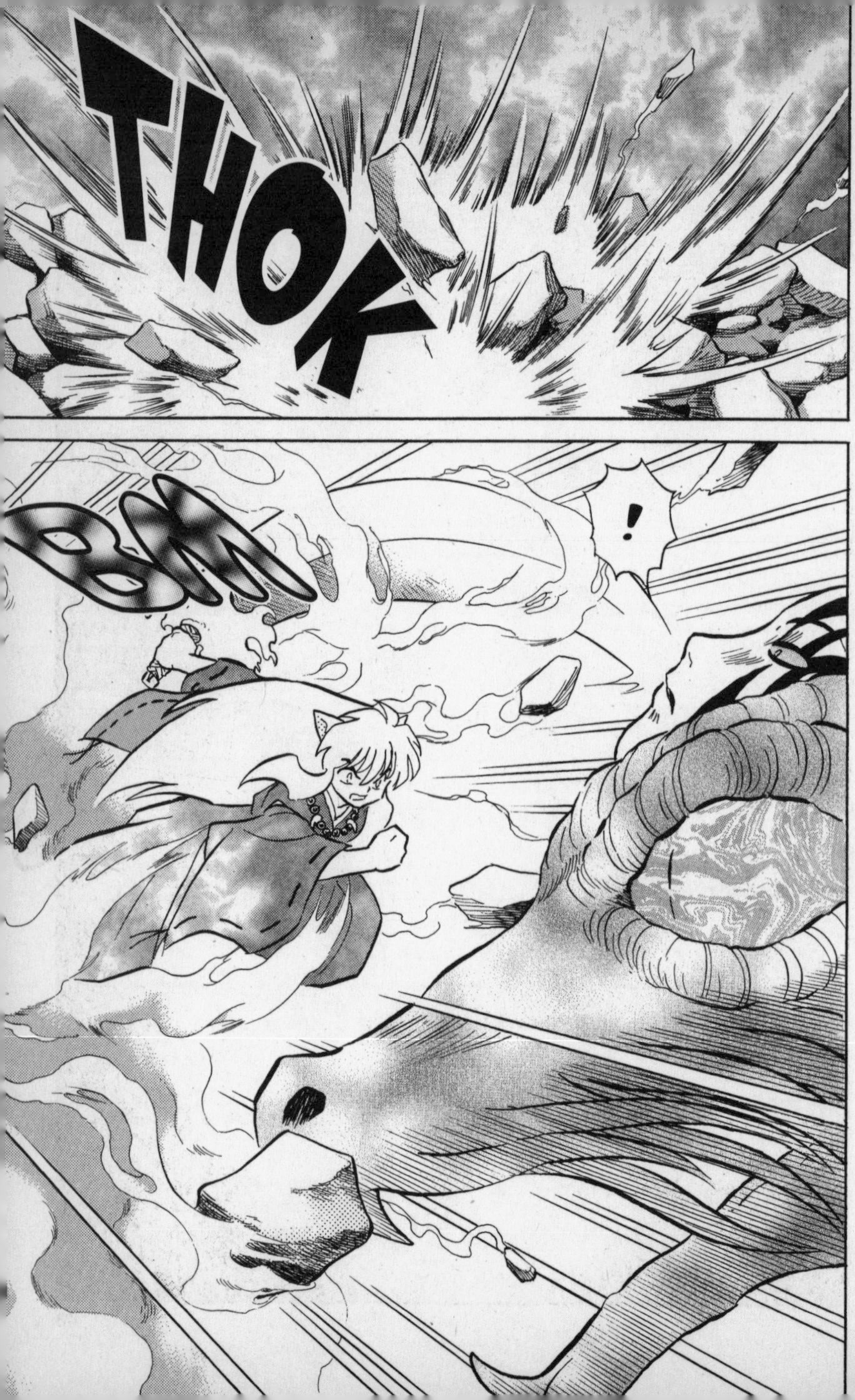
THOK
BAM
!

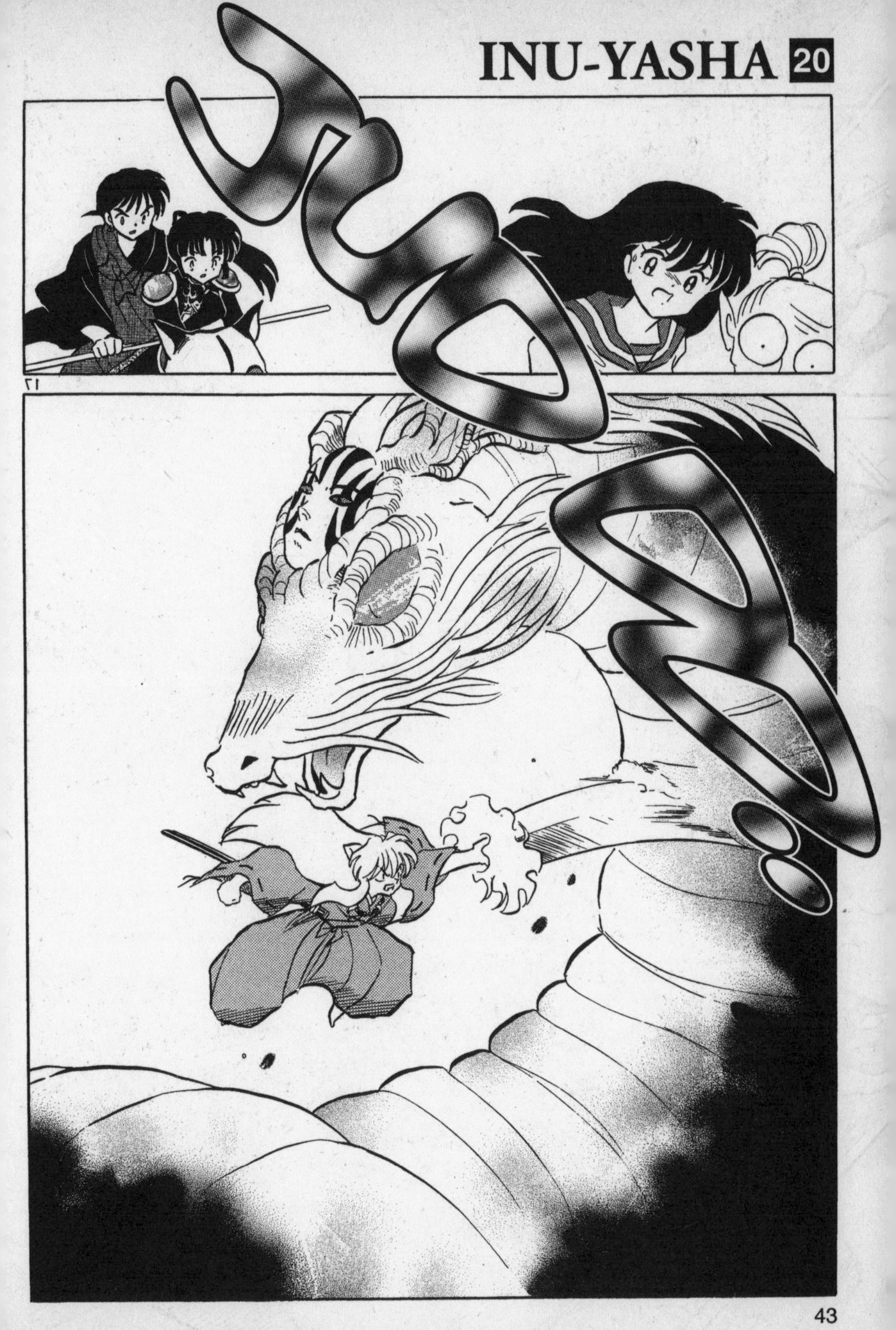

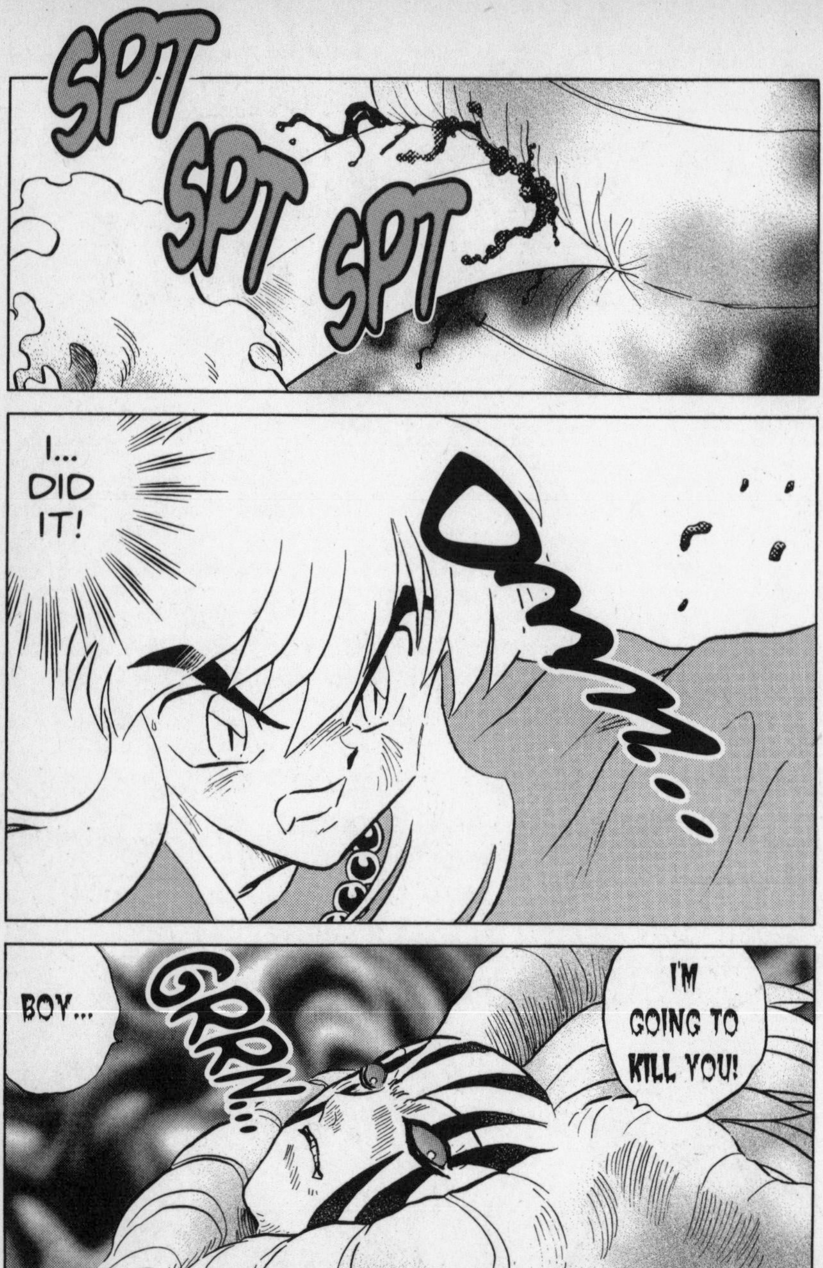
SPT SPT SPT
I... DID IT!
DMM...
BOY...
GRRN...
I'M GOING TO KILL YOU!

SCROLL THREE

THE NEW TETSUSAIGA

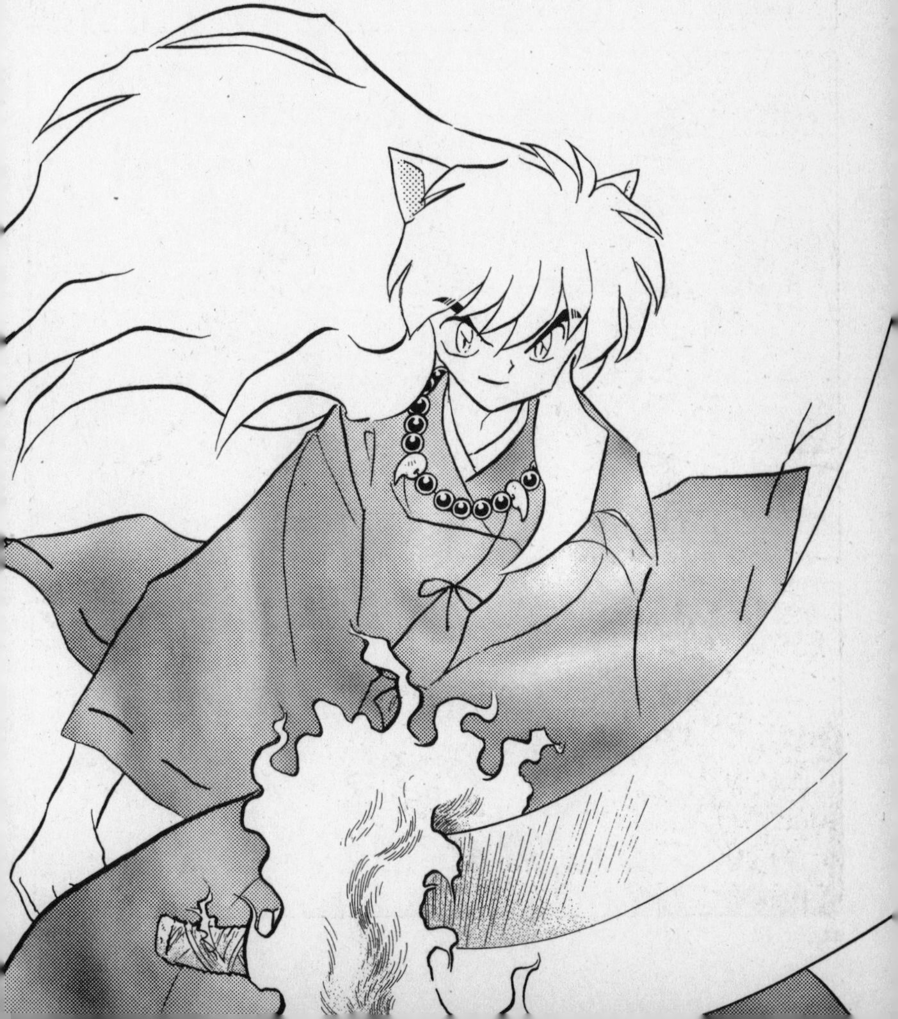

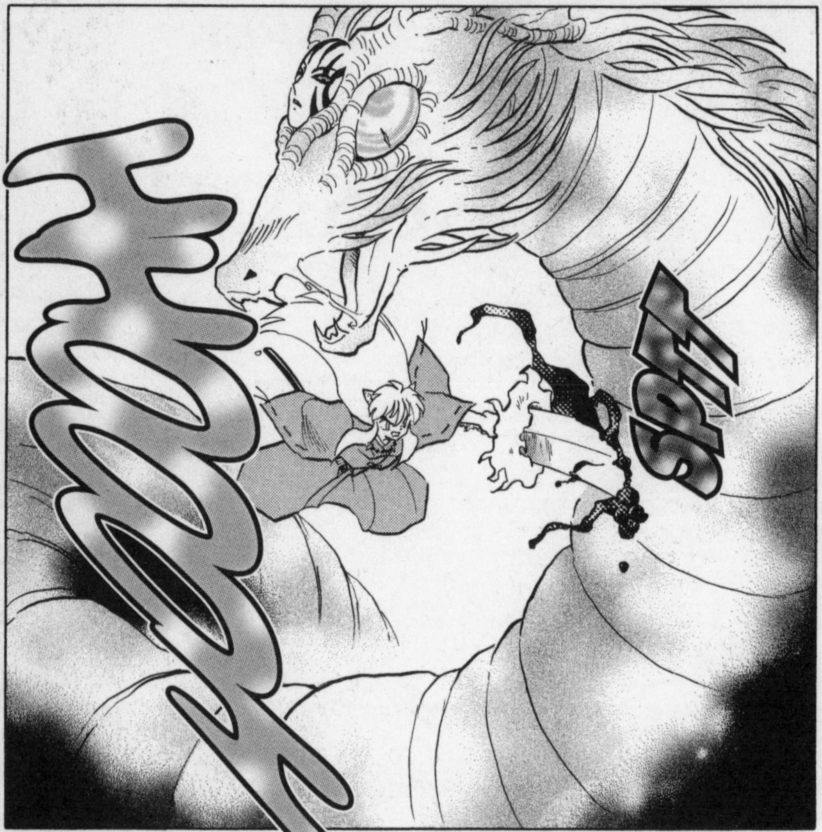

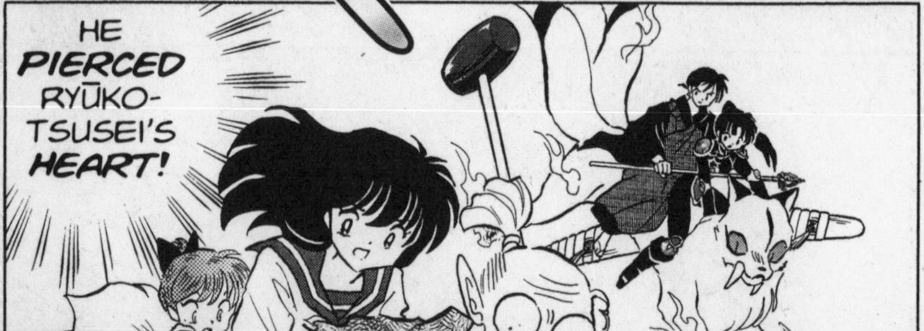
HE PIERCED RYŪKO-TSUSEI'S HEART!

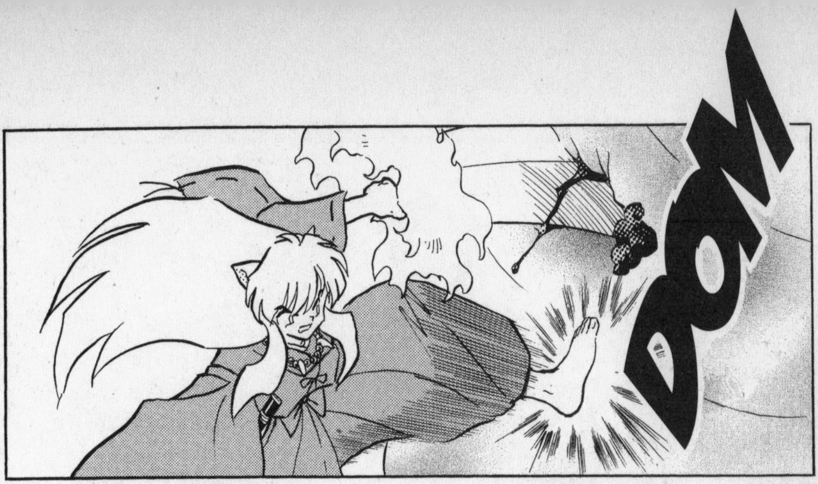
DOOM

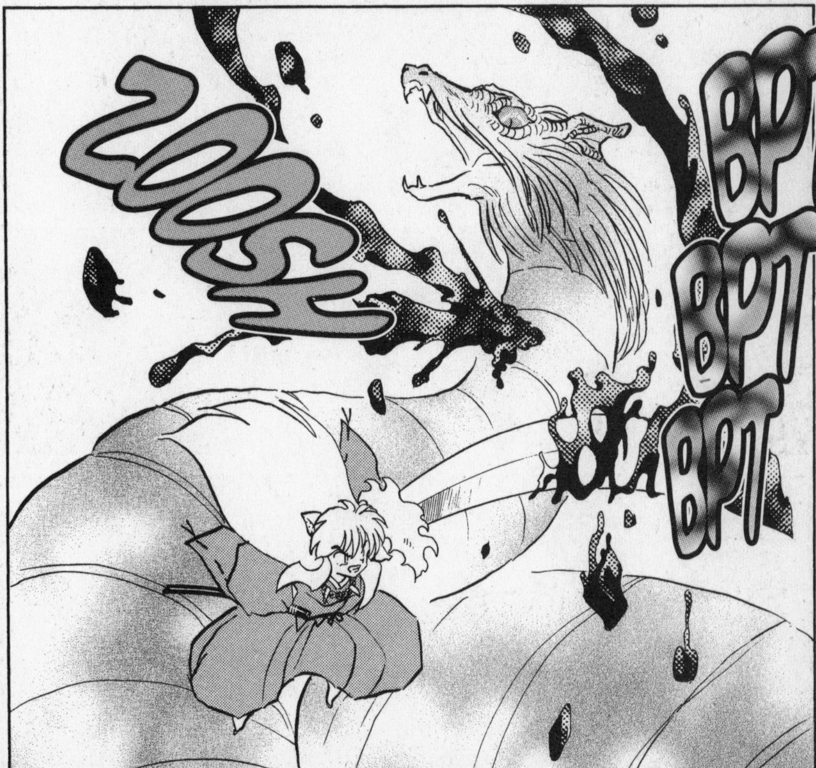
ZOOSH
BPT
BPT
BPT

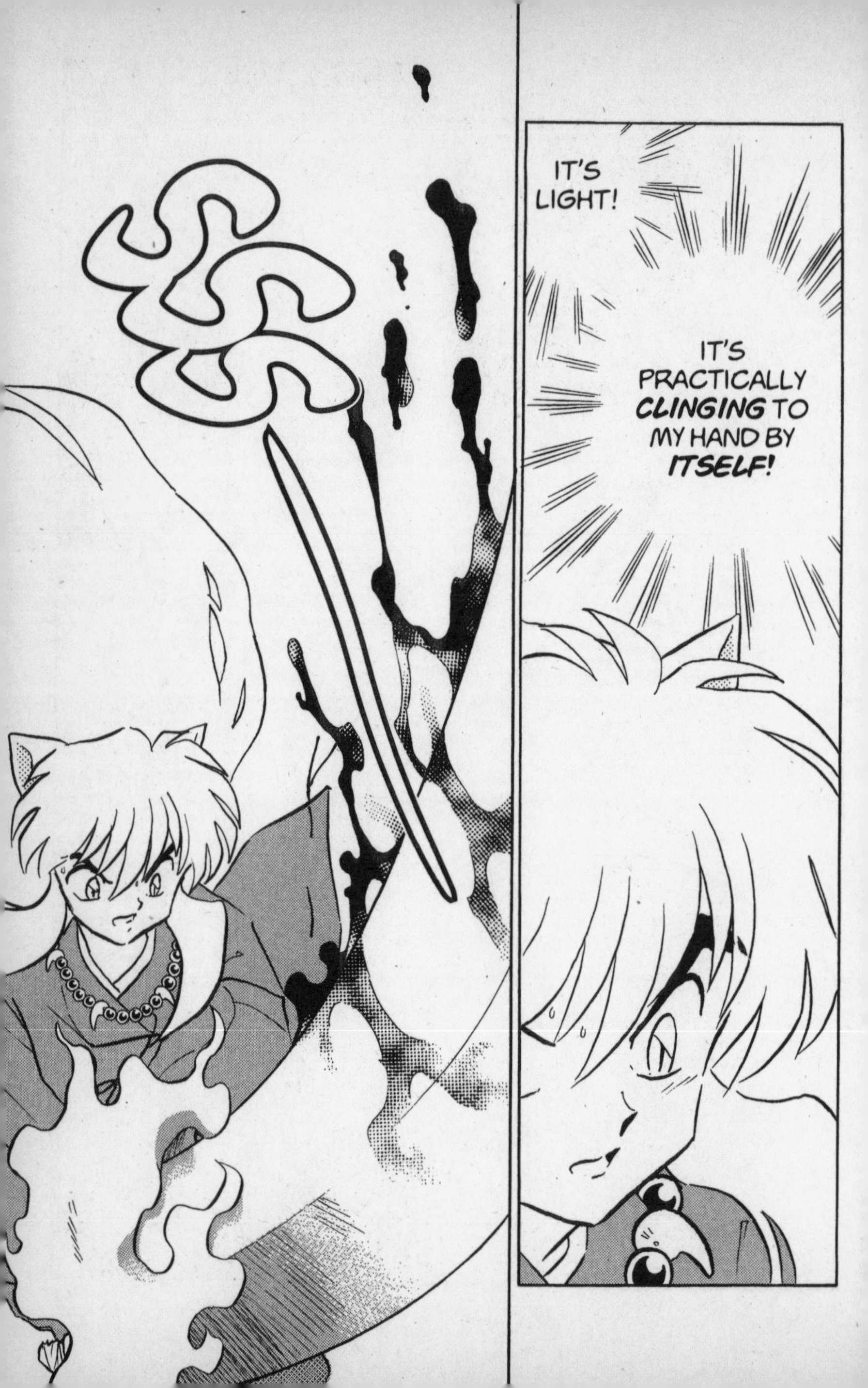
IT'S LIGHT!
IT'S PRACTICALLY **CLINGING** TO MY HAND BY **ITSELF!**

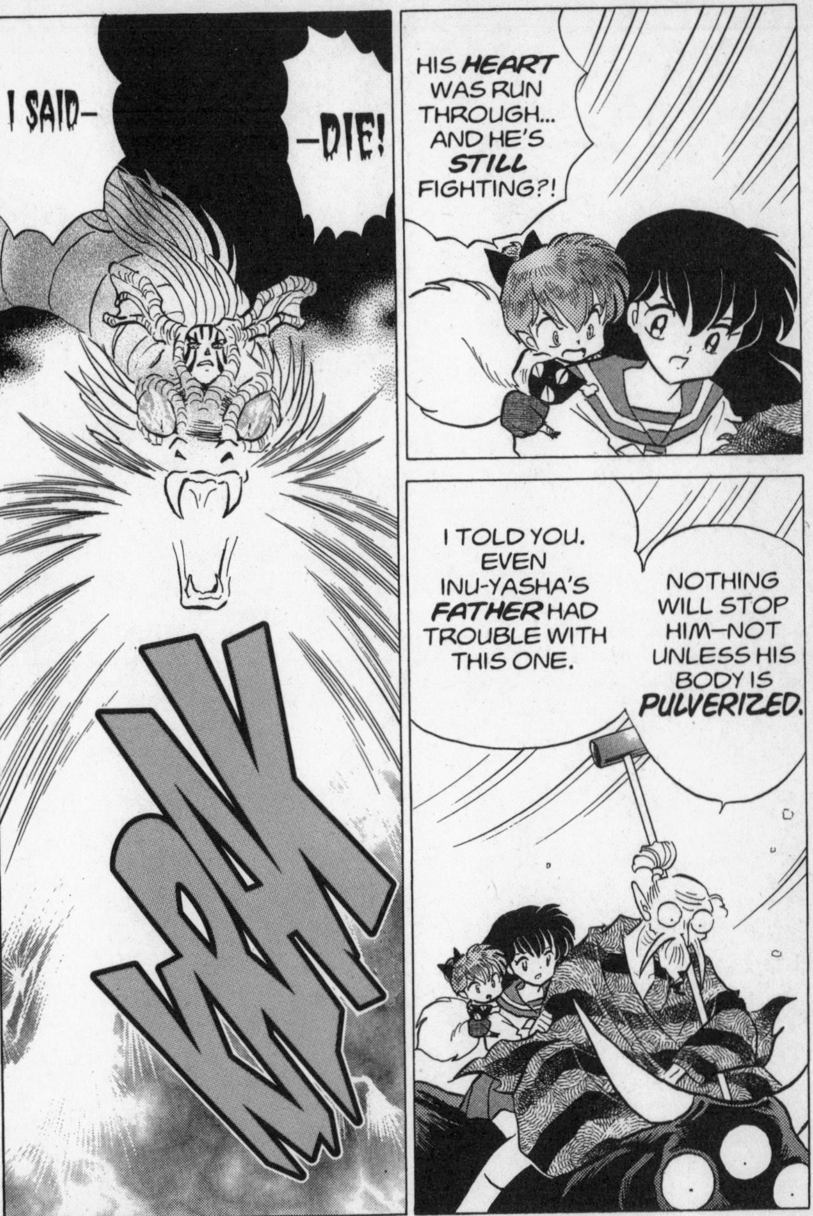
I SAID-
-DIE!
HIS HEART WAS RUN THROUGH... AND HE'S STILL FIGHTING?!
I TOLD YOU. EVEN INU-YASHA'S FATHER HAD TROUBLE WITH THIS ONE.
NOTHING WILL STOP HIM—NOT UNLESS HIS BODY IS PULVERIZED.

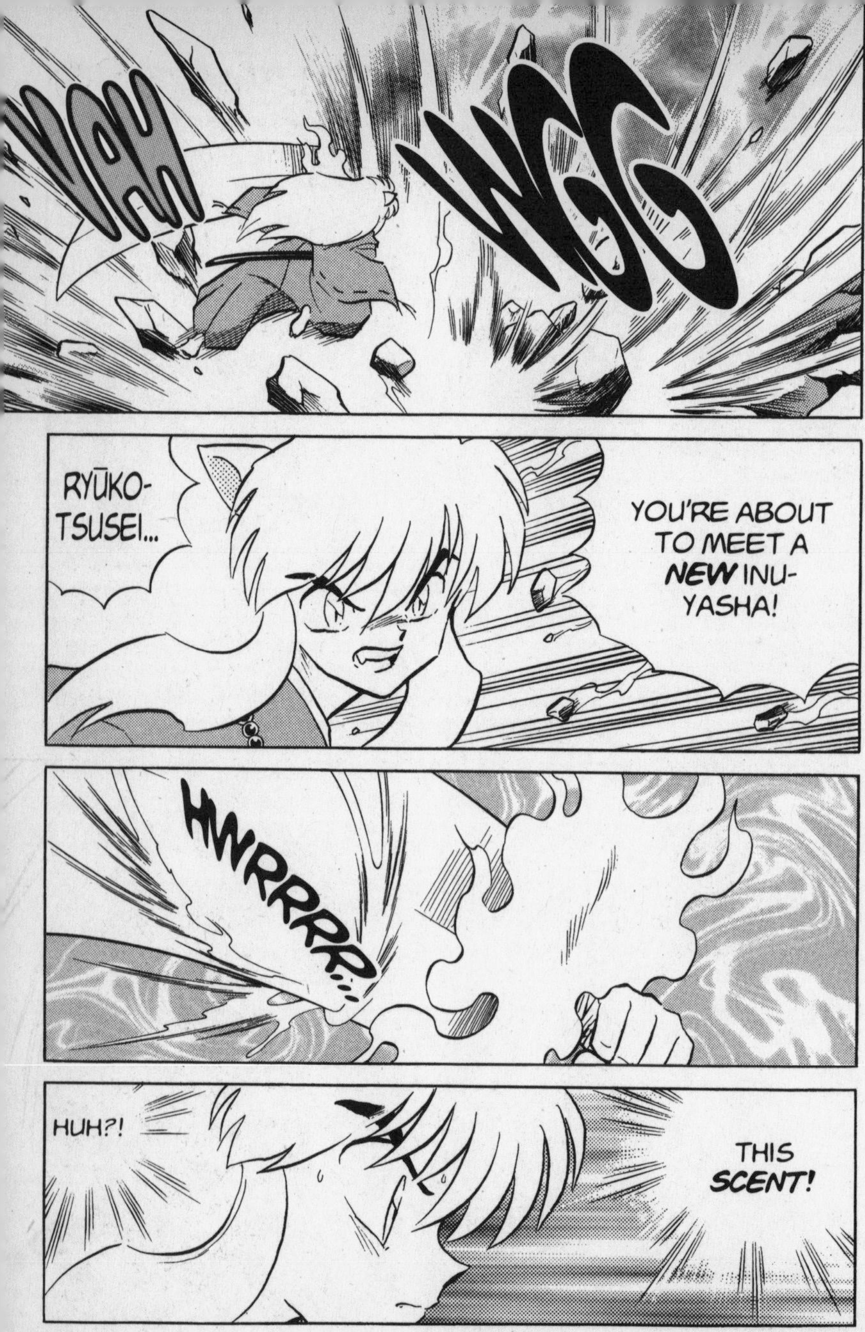
NYAH
WOOO
RYŪKO-TSUSEI...
YOU'RE ABOUT TO MEET A NEW INU-YASHA!
HWRRRR...!!
HUH?!
THIS SCENT!

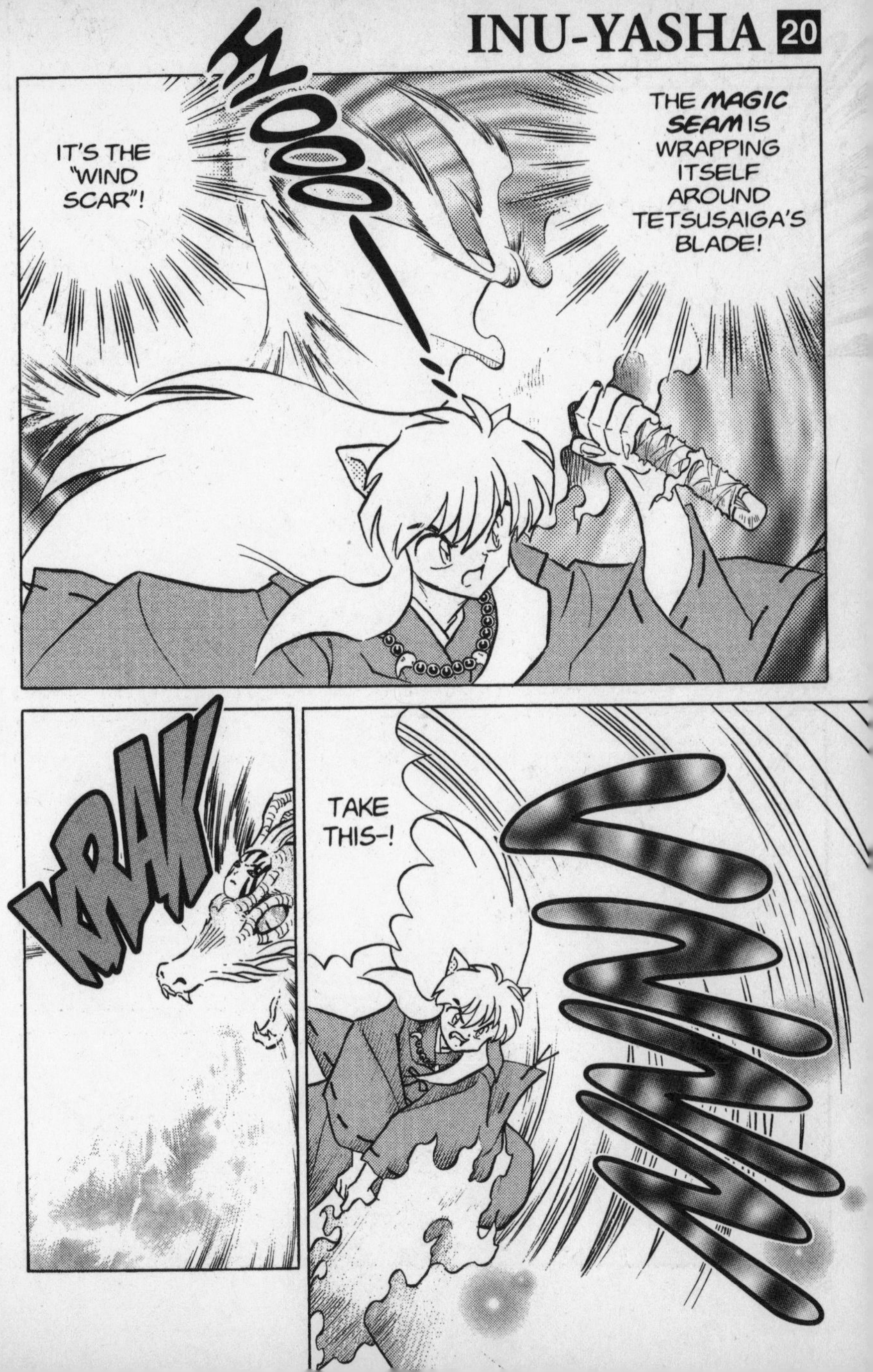
HWOOO
THE MAGIC SEAM IS WRAPPING ITSELF AROUND TETSUSAIGA'S BLADE!
IT'S THE "WIND SCAR"!
TAKE THIS-!
KRAK

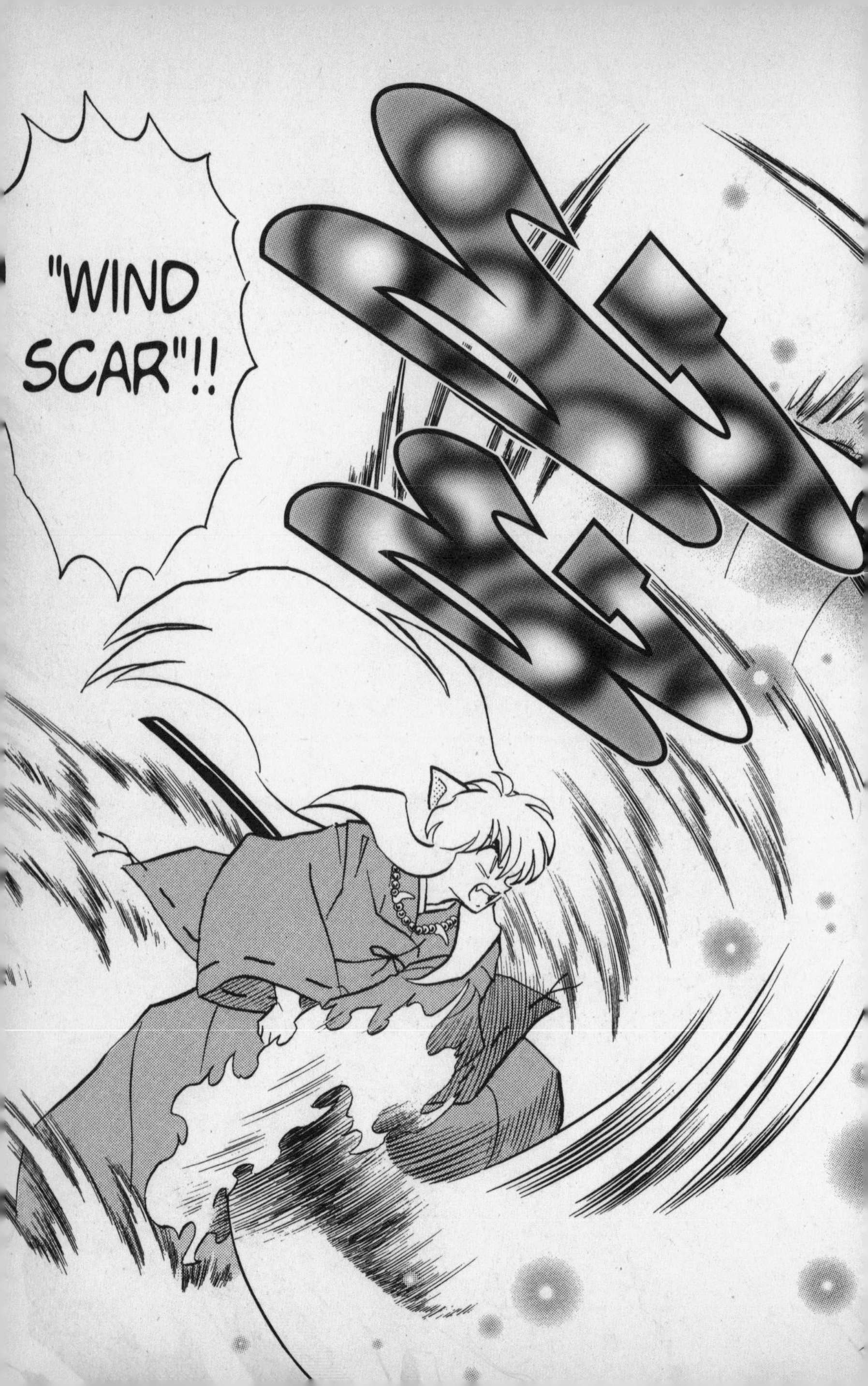
"WIND SCAR"!!

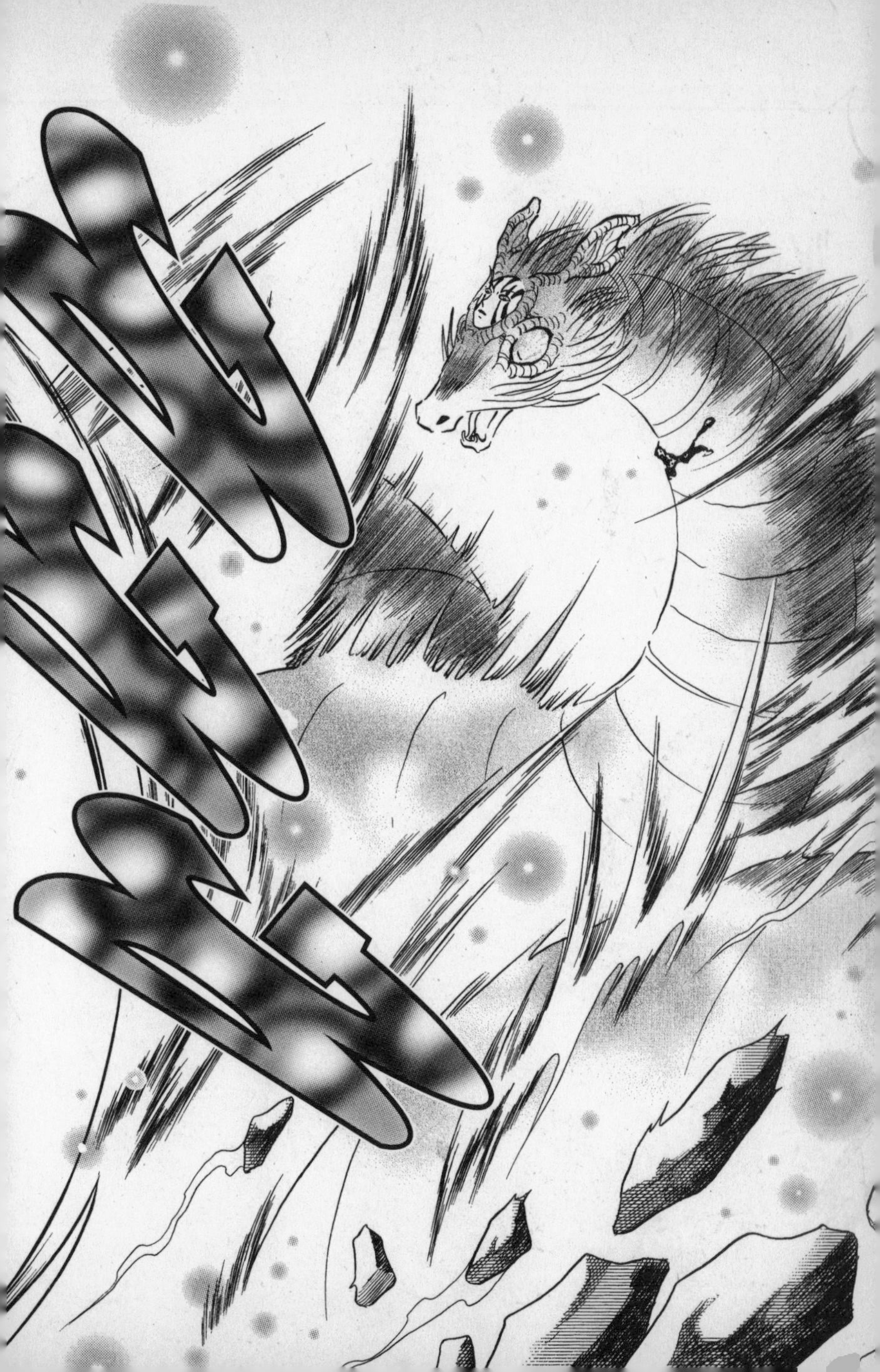

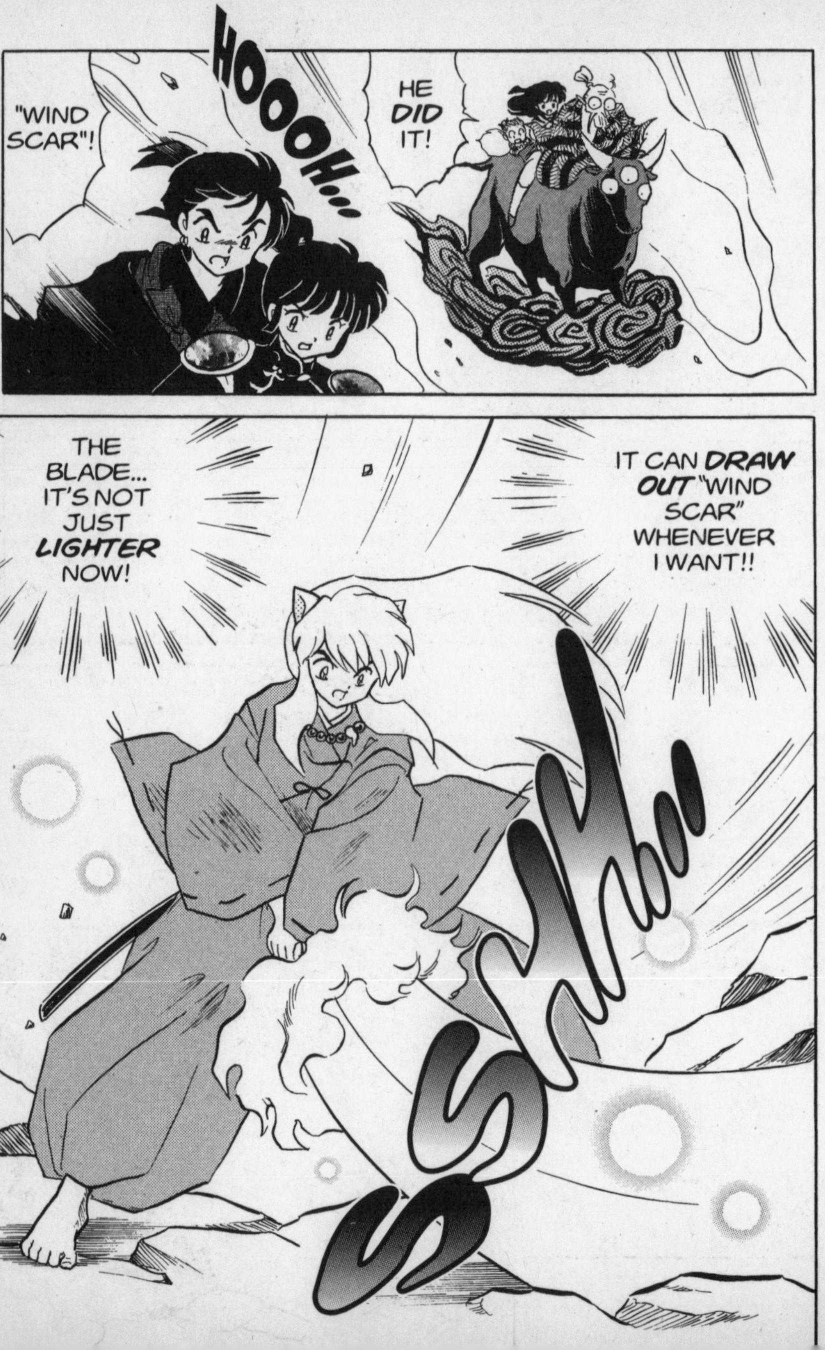
"WIND SCAR"!
HOOOH...
HE DID IT!
THE BLADE... IT'S NOT JUST LIGHTER NOW!
IT CAN DRAW OUT "WIND SCAR" WHENEVER I WANT!!
SSHH...

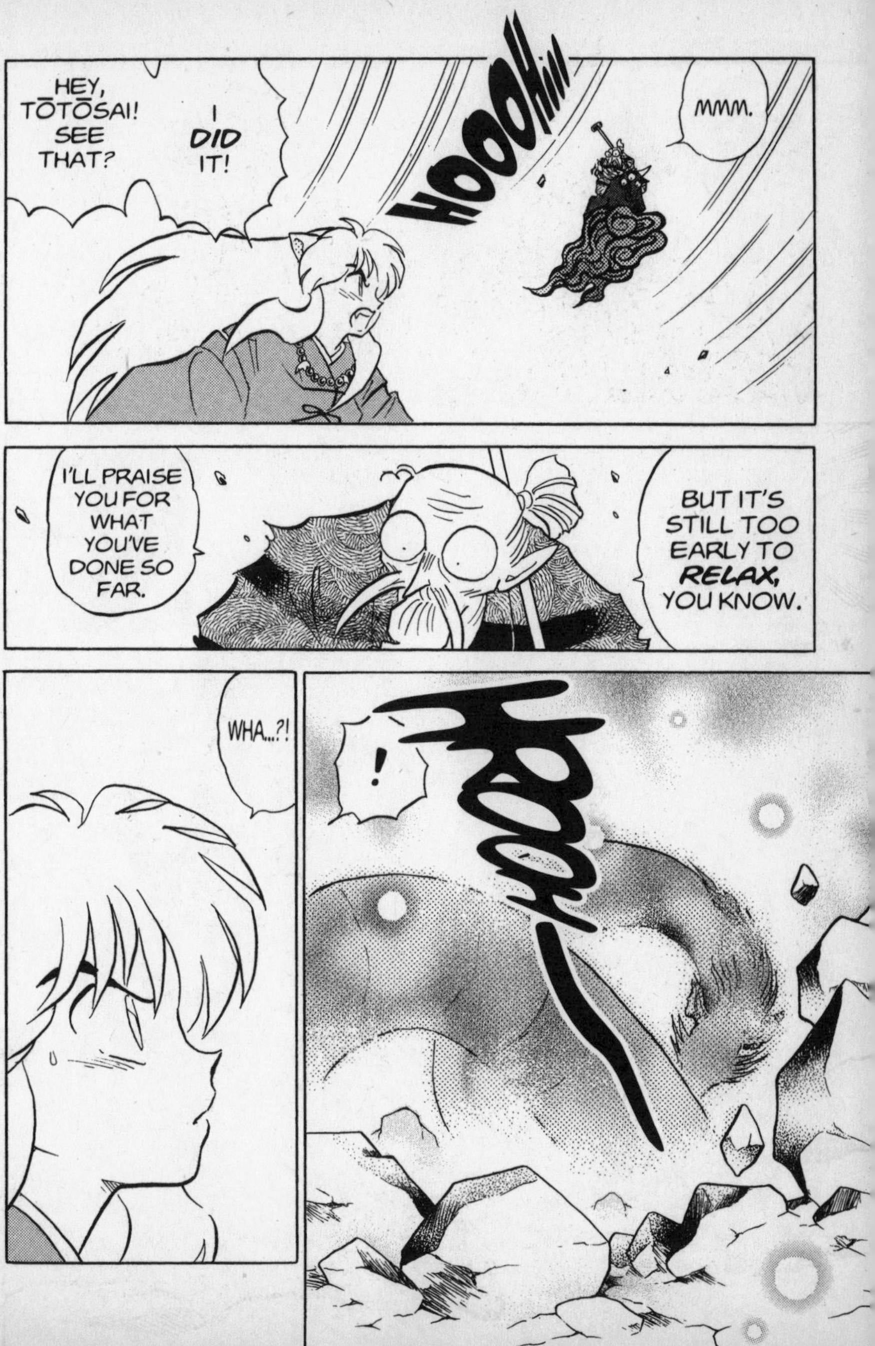
HEY, TŌTŌSAI! SEE THAT?
I DID IT!
HOOOHHHH
MMM.
I'LL PRAISE YOU FOR WHAT YOU'VE DONE SO FAR.
BUT IT'S STILL TOO EARLY TO RELAX, YOU KNOW.
WHA...?!
!

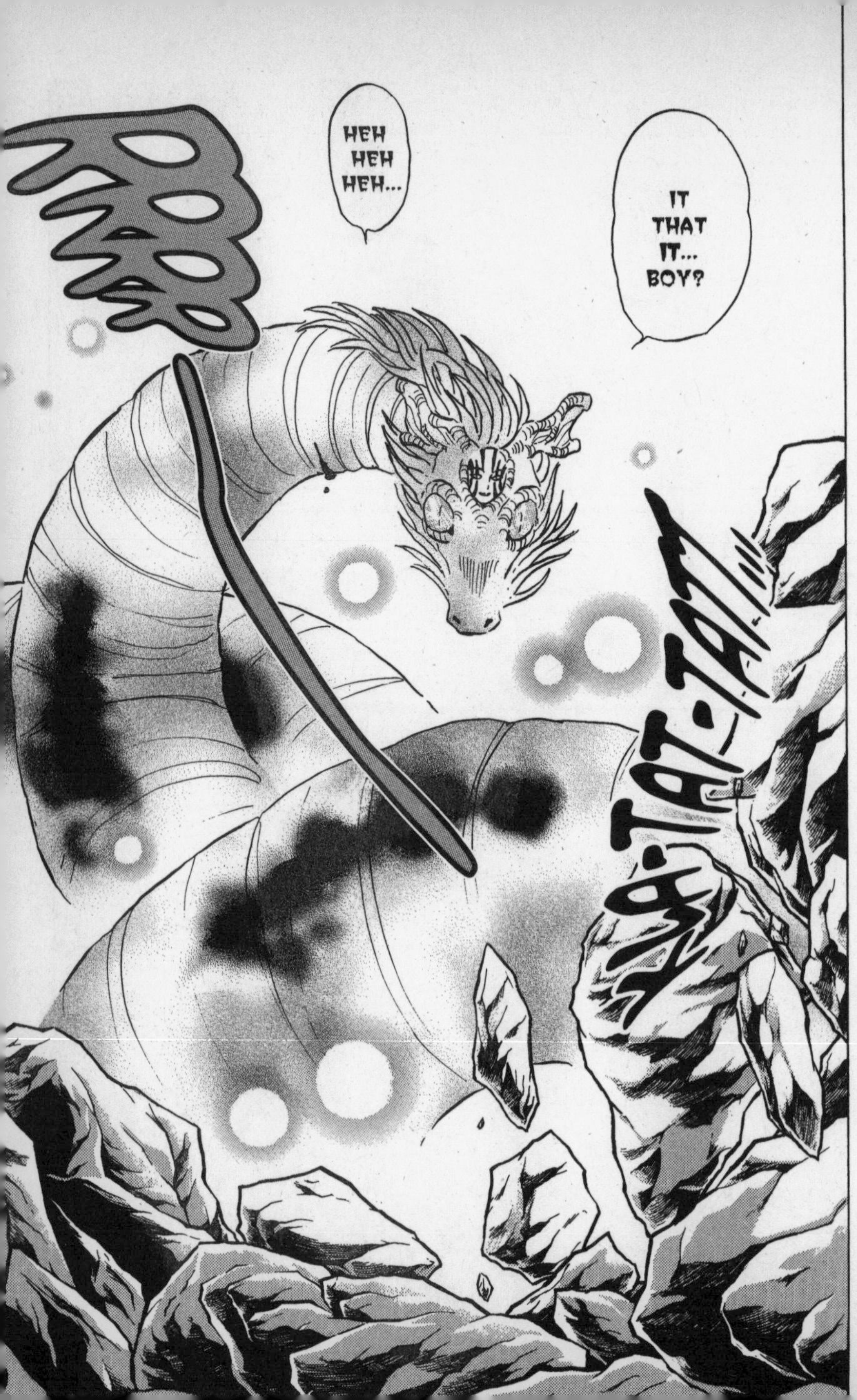
HEH HEH HEH...
IT THAT IT... BOY?

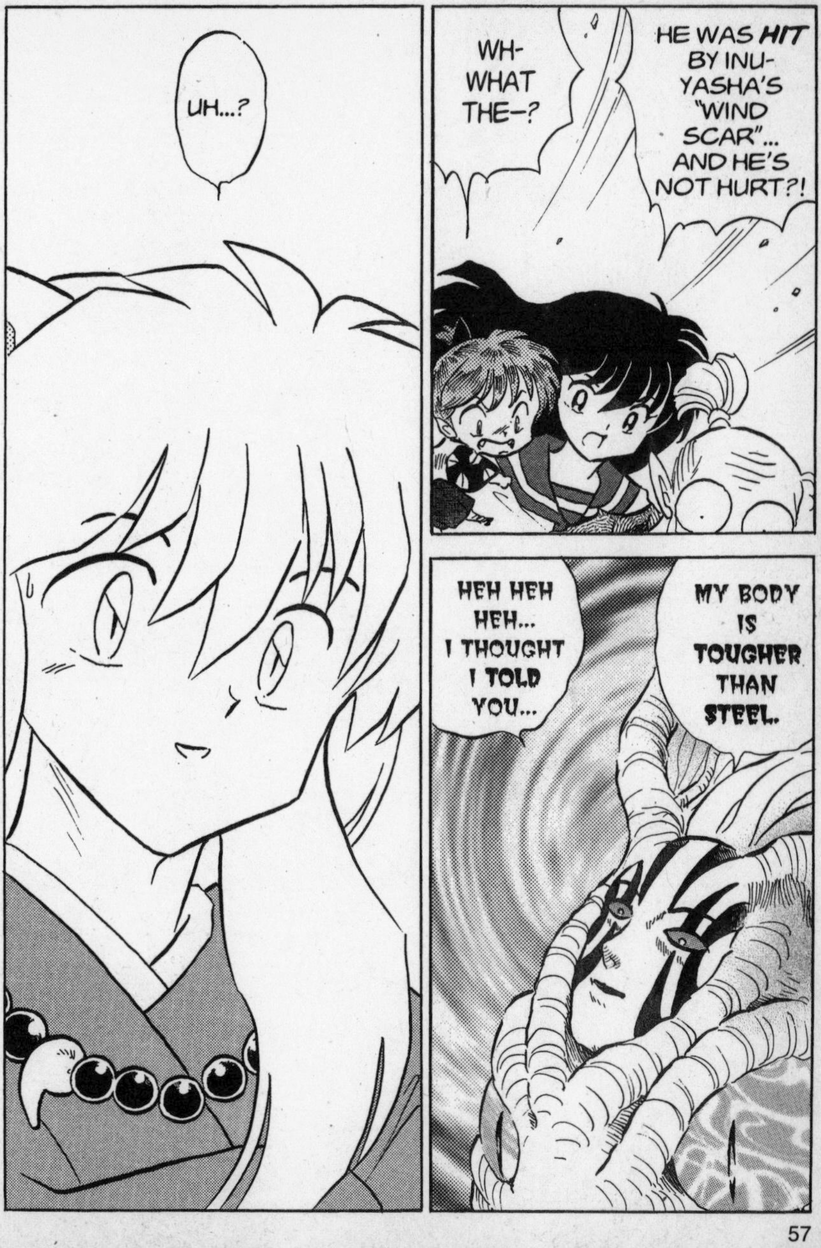
UH...?
WH- WHAT THE–?
HE WAS **HIT** BY INU-YASHA'S "WIND SCAR"... AND HE'S NOT HURT?!
HEH HEH HEH... I THOUGHT I TOLD YOU...
MY BODY IS TOUGHER THAN STEEL.

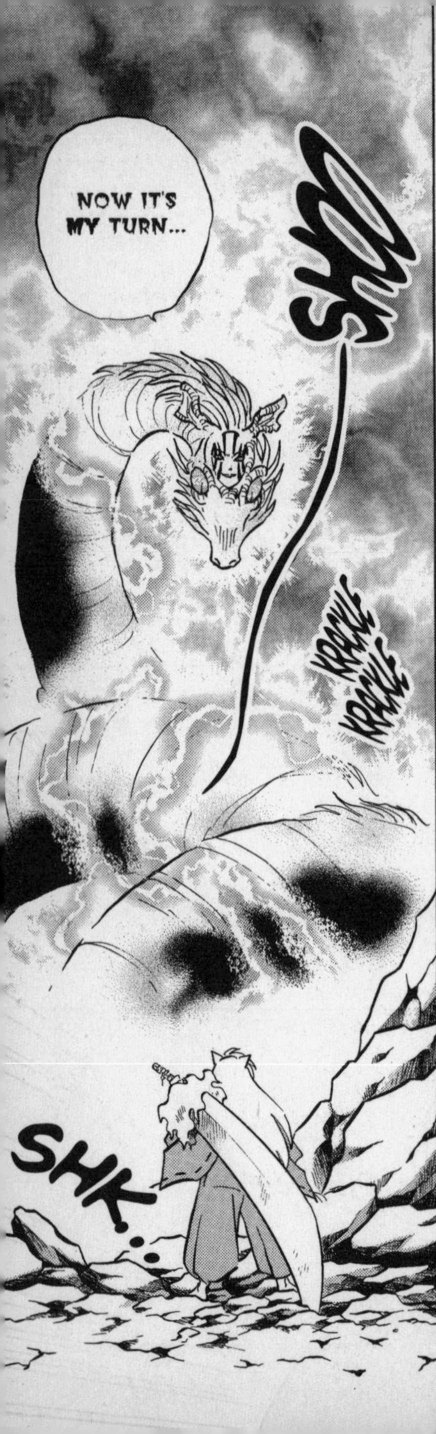
NOW IT'S MY TURN...
SHOO
KRACKLE KRACKLE
SHK...

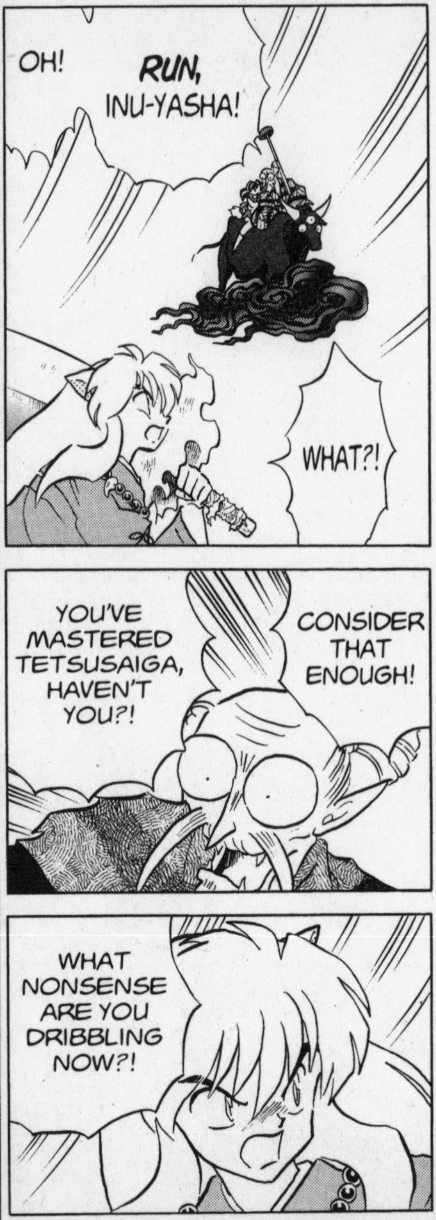
OH!
RUN, INU-YASHA!
WHAT?!
YOU'VE MASTERED TETSUSAIGA, HAVEN'T YOU?!
CONSIDER THAT ENOUGH!
WHAT NONSENSE ARE YOU DRIBBLING NOW?!

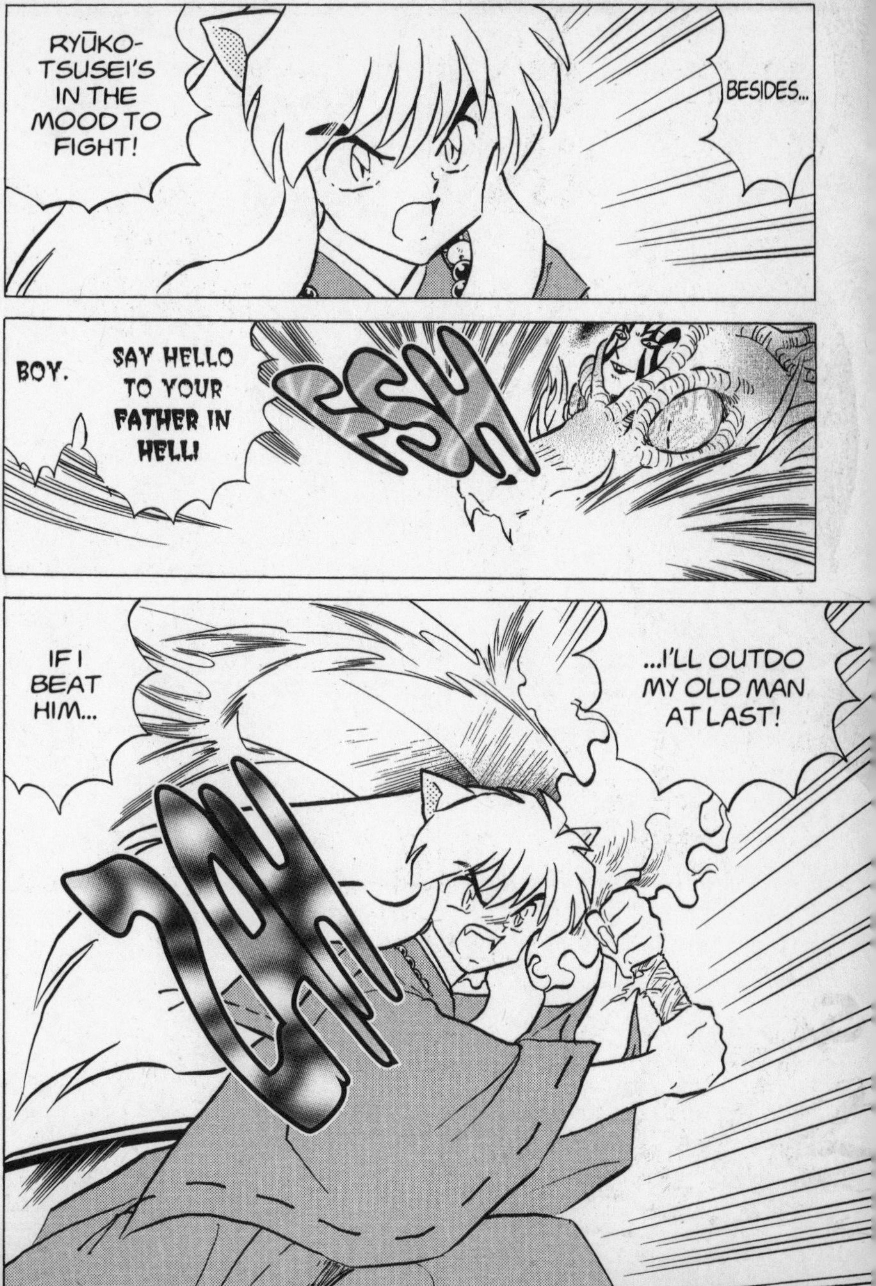
RYŪKO-TSUSEI'S IN THE MOOD TO FIGHT!
BESIDES...
BOY.
SAY HELLO TO YOUR FATHER IN HELL!
IF I BEAT HIM...
...I'LL OUTDO MY OLD MAN AT LAST!

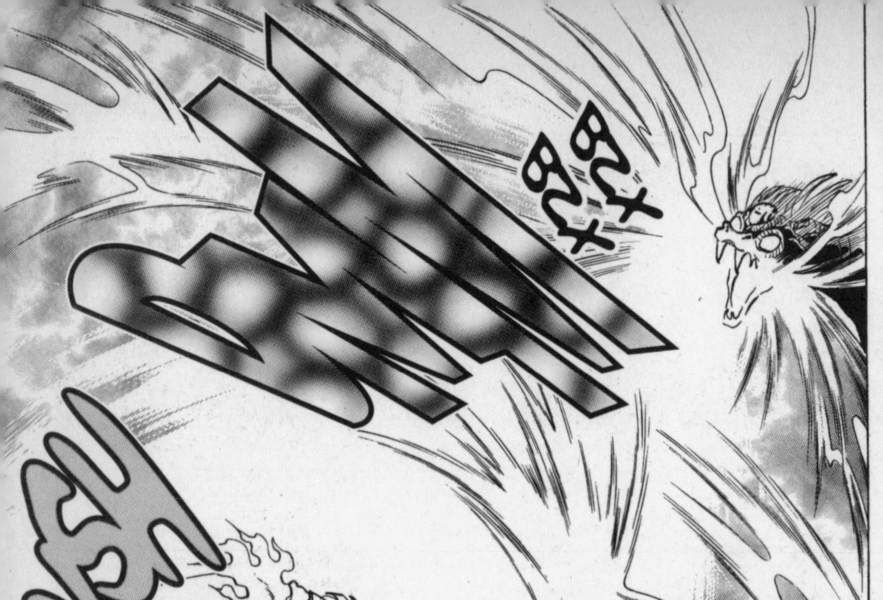
BZT
BZT

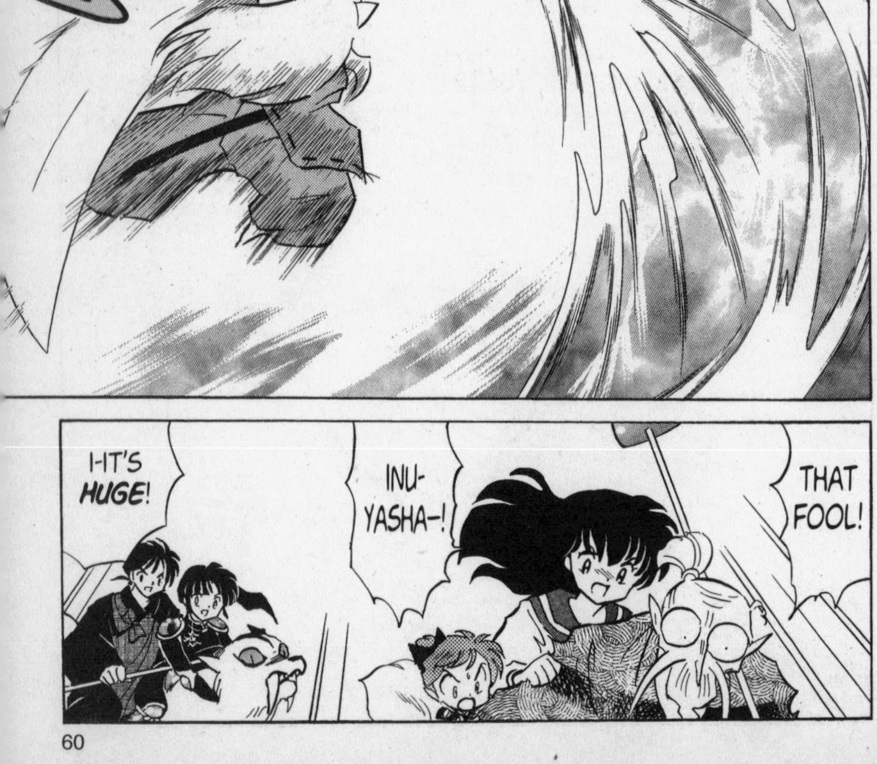
I-IT'S *HUGE*!
INU-YASHA-!
THAT FOOL!

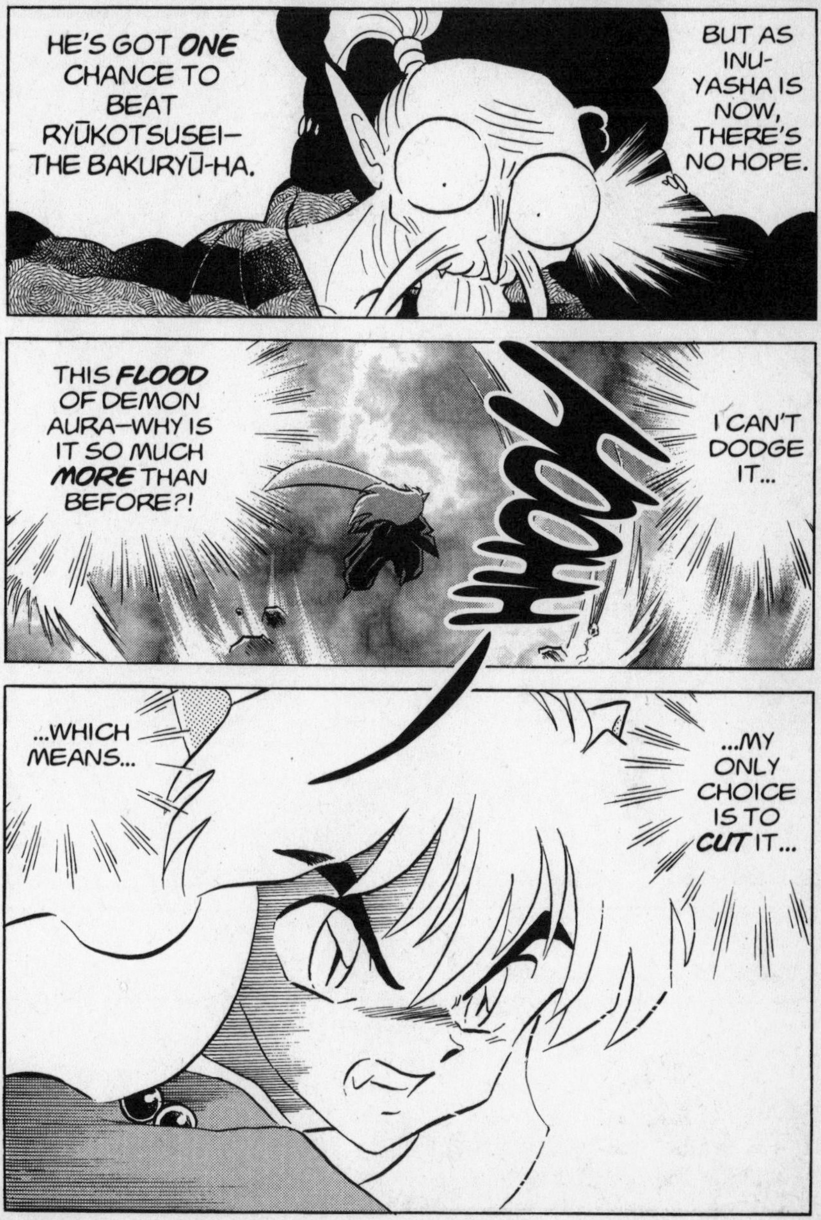
HE'S GOT ONE CHANCE TO BEAT RYŪKOTSUSEI– THE BAKURYŪ-HA.
BUT AS INU-YASHA IS NOW, THERE'S NO HOPE.
THIS FLOOD OF DEMON AURA–WHY IS IT SO MUCH MORE THAN BEFORE?!
WHOOM
I CAN'T DODGE IT...
...WHICH MEANS...
...MY ONLY CHOICE IS TO CUT IT...

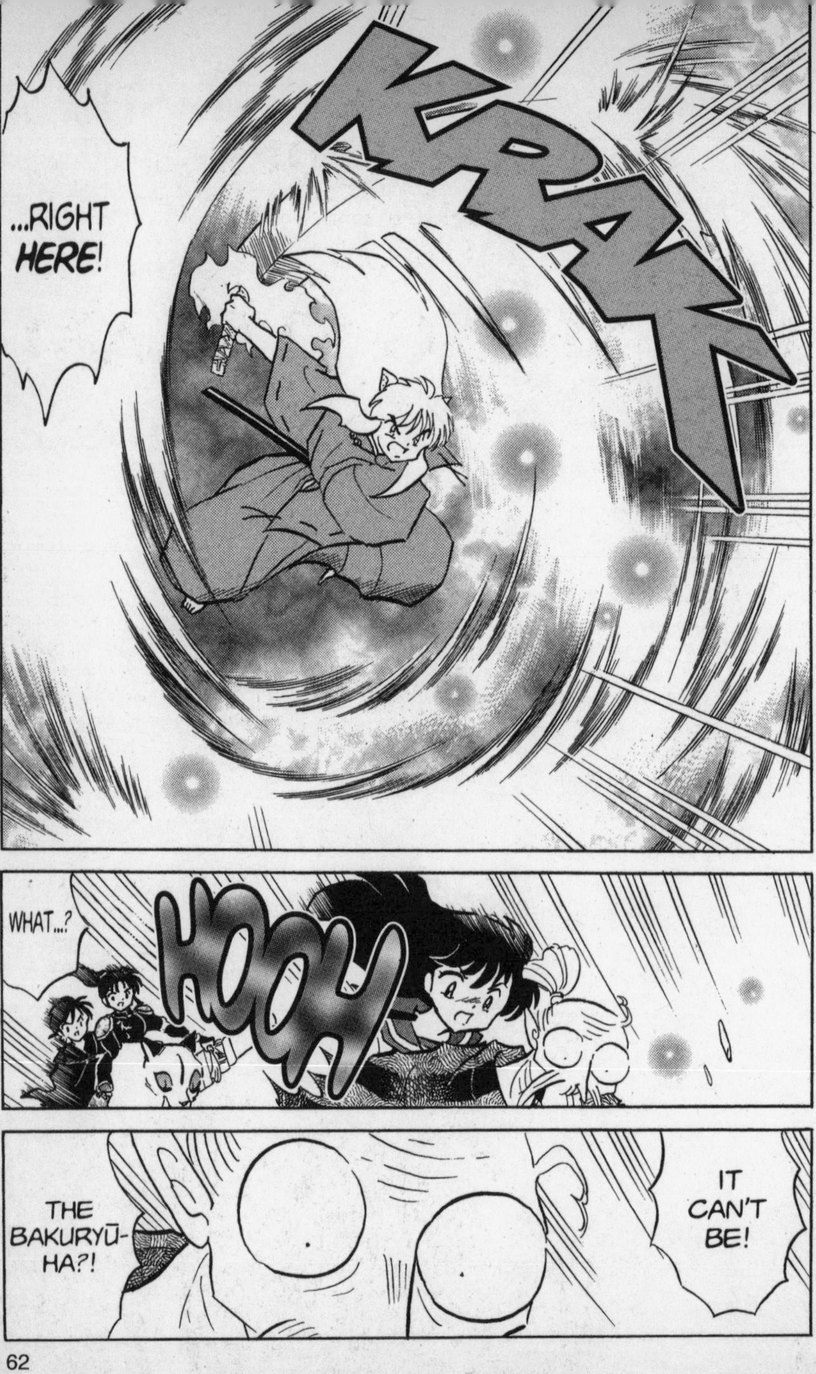

...RIGHT HERE!
KRAK
WHAT...?
HOOH
THE BAKURYŪ-HA?!
IT CAN'T BE!

SCROLL FOUR
THE CRUSHING STREAM

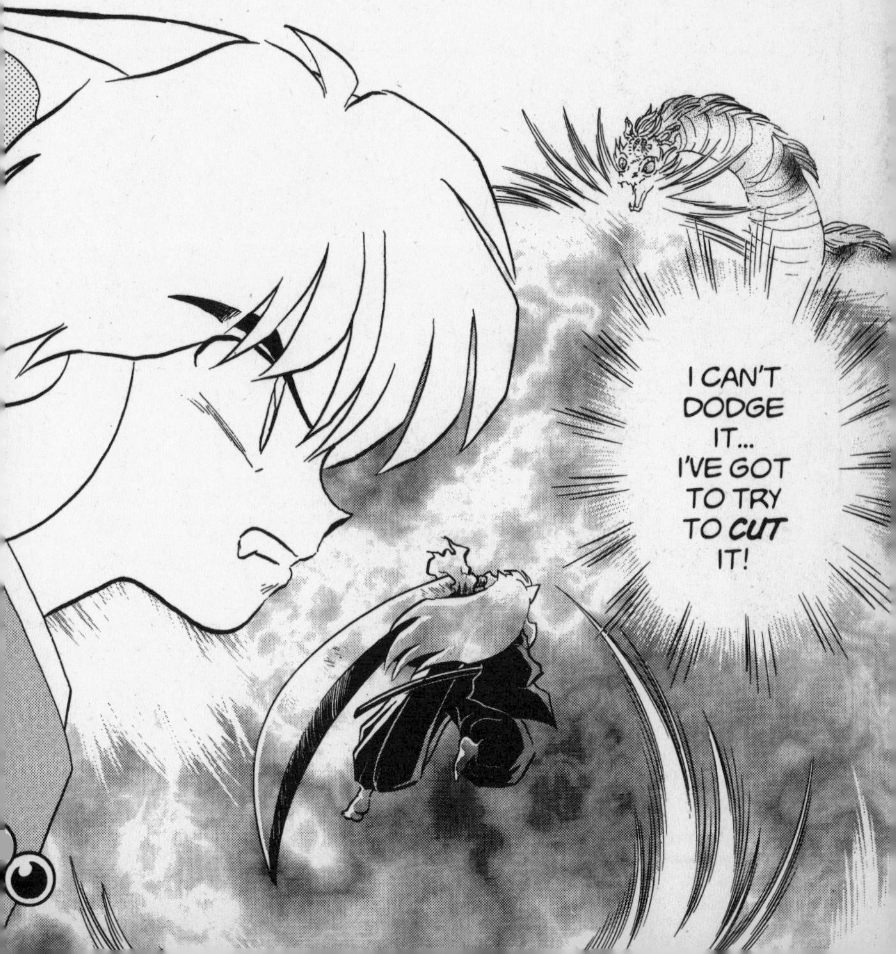
I CAN'T DODGE IT... I'VE GOT TO TRY TO CUT IT!

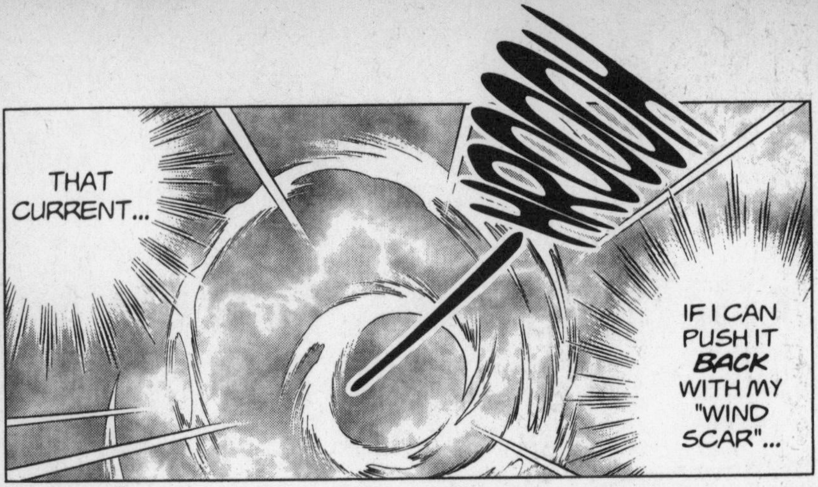
THAT CURRENT...
WOOOSH
IF I CAN PUSH IT **BACK** WITH MY "WIND SCAR"...
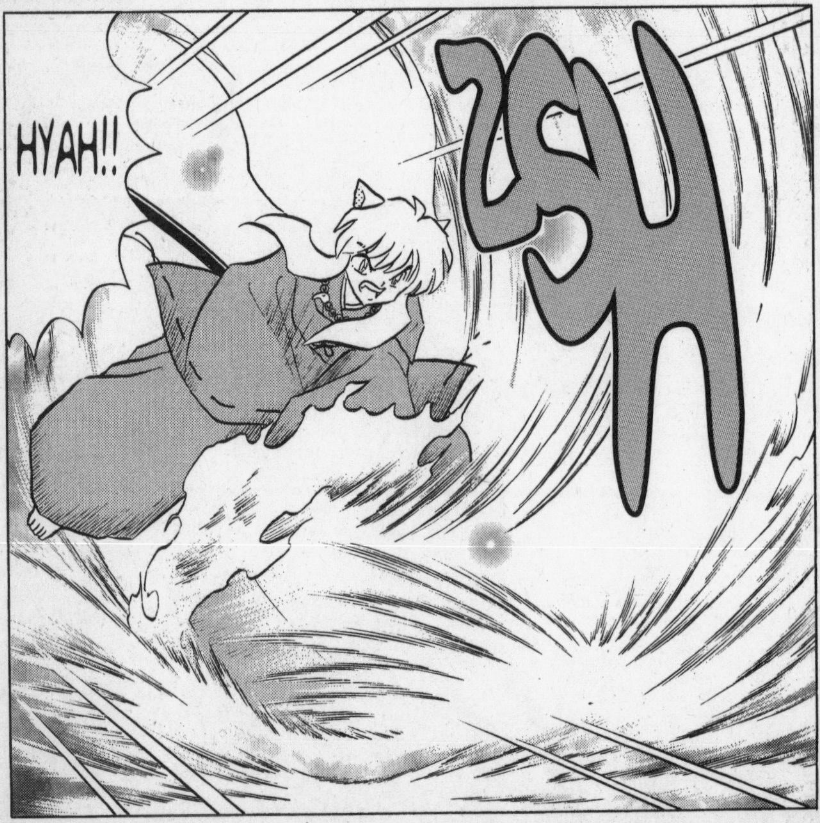
HYAH!!
ZSH

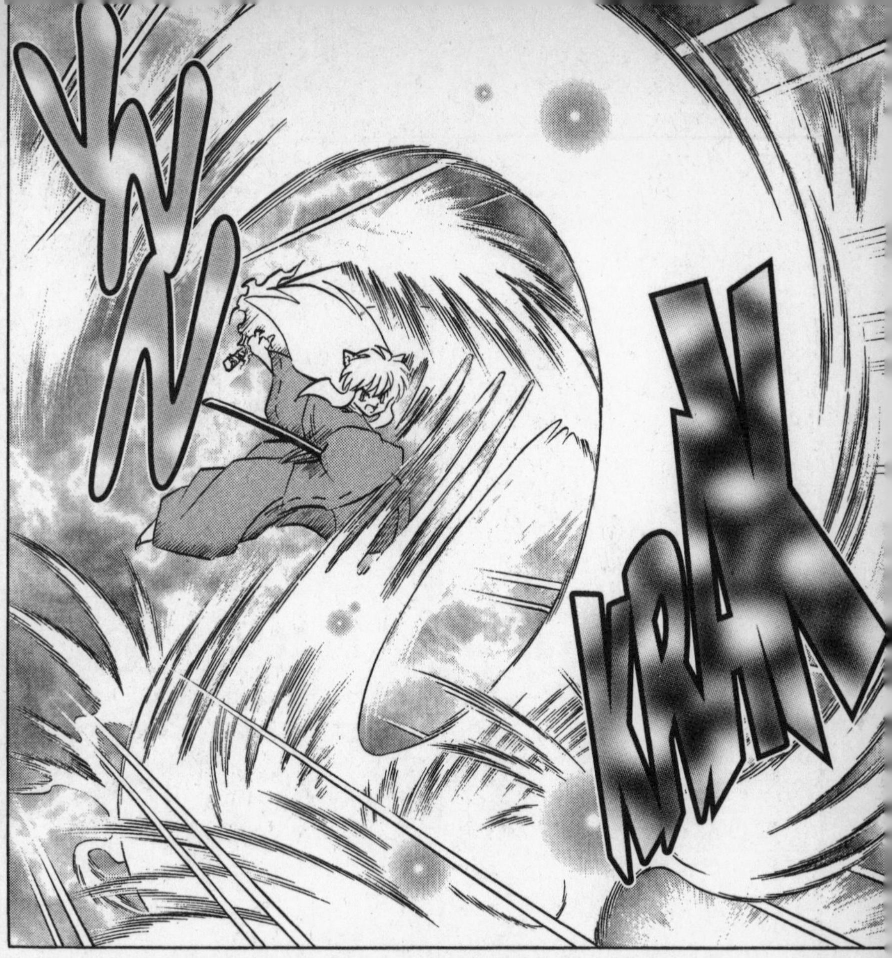
KRAK
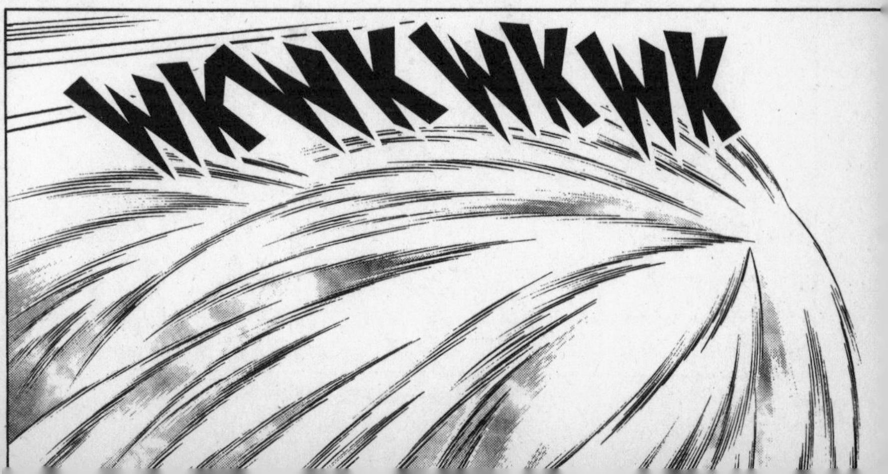
WKWKWKWK

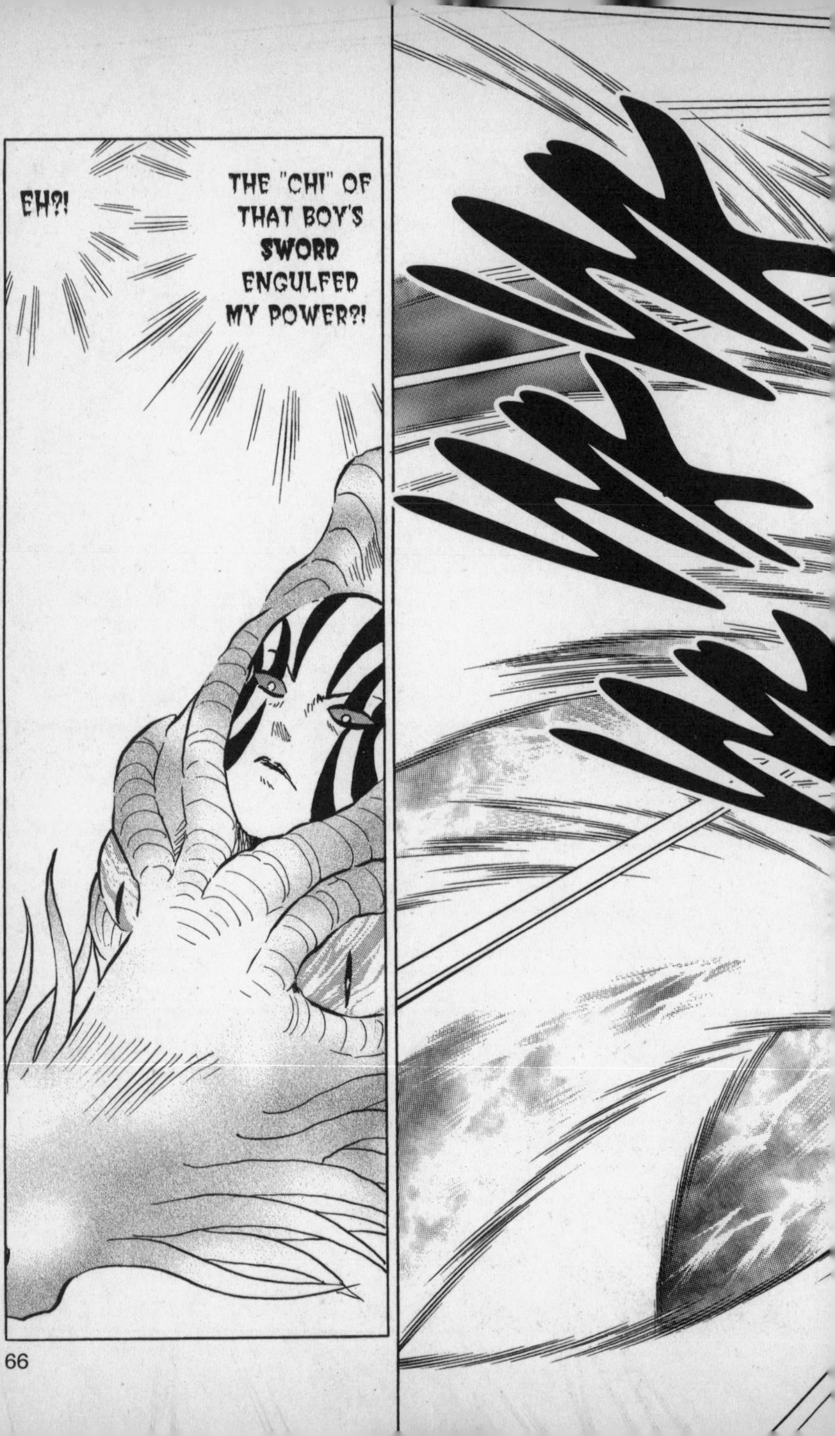
EH?!
THE "CHI" OF THAT BOY'S SWORD ENGULFED MY POWER?!

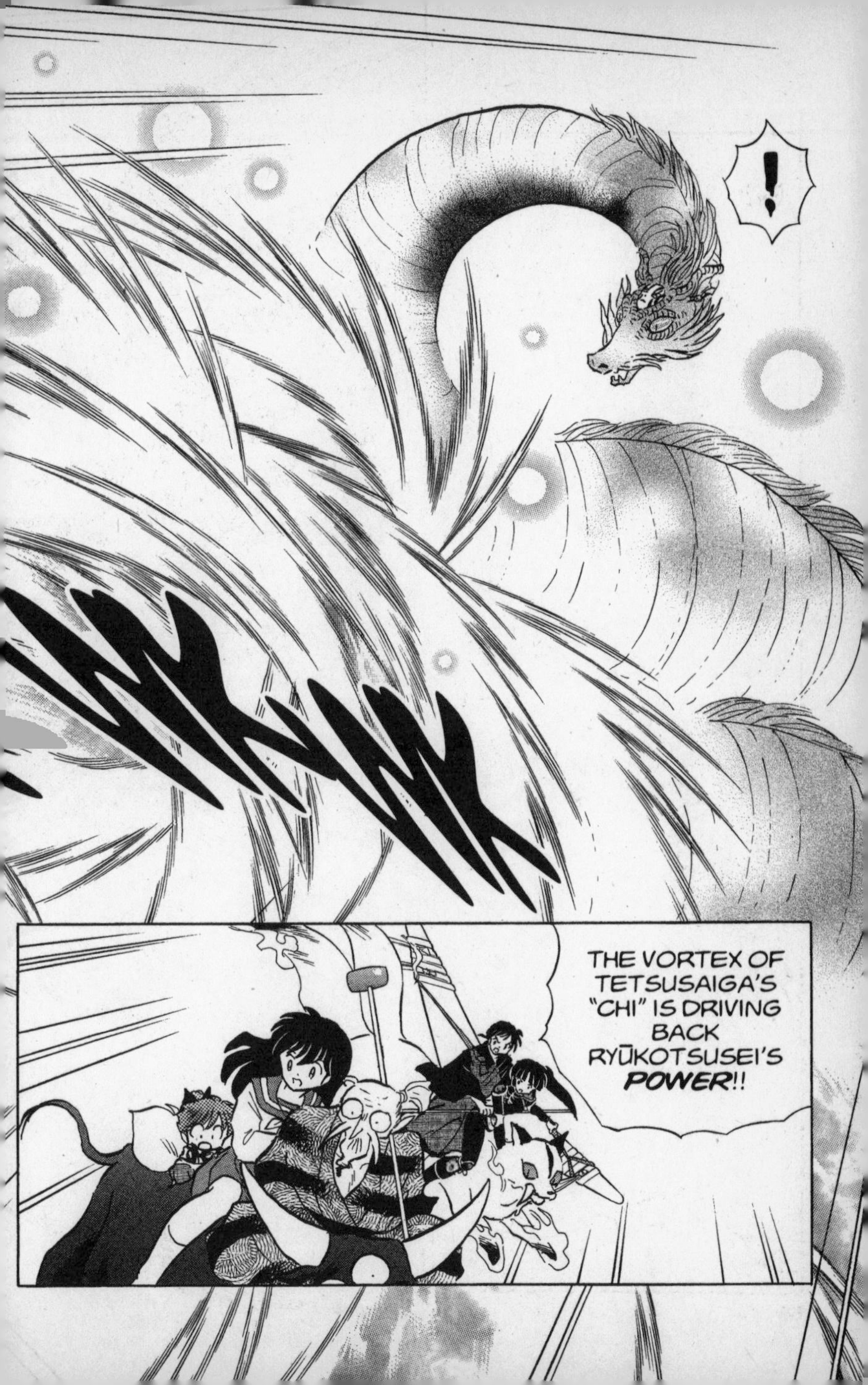
!
THE VORTEX OF TETSUSAIGA'S "CHI" IS DRIVING BACK RYŪKOTSUSEI'S ***POWER***!!

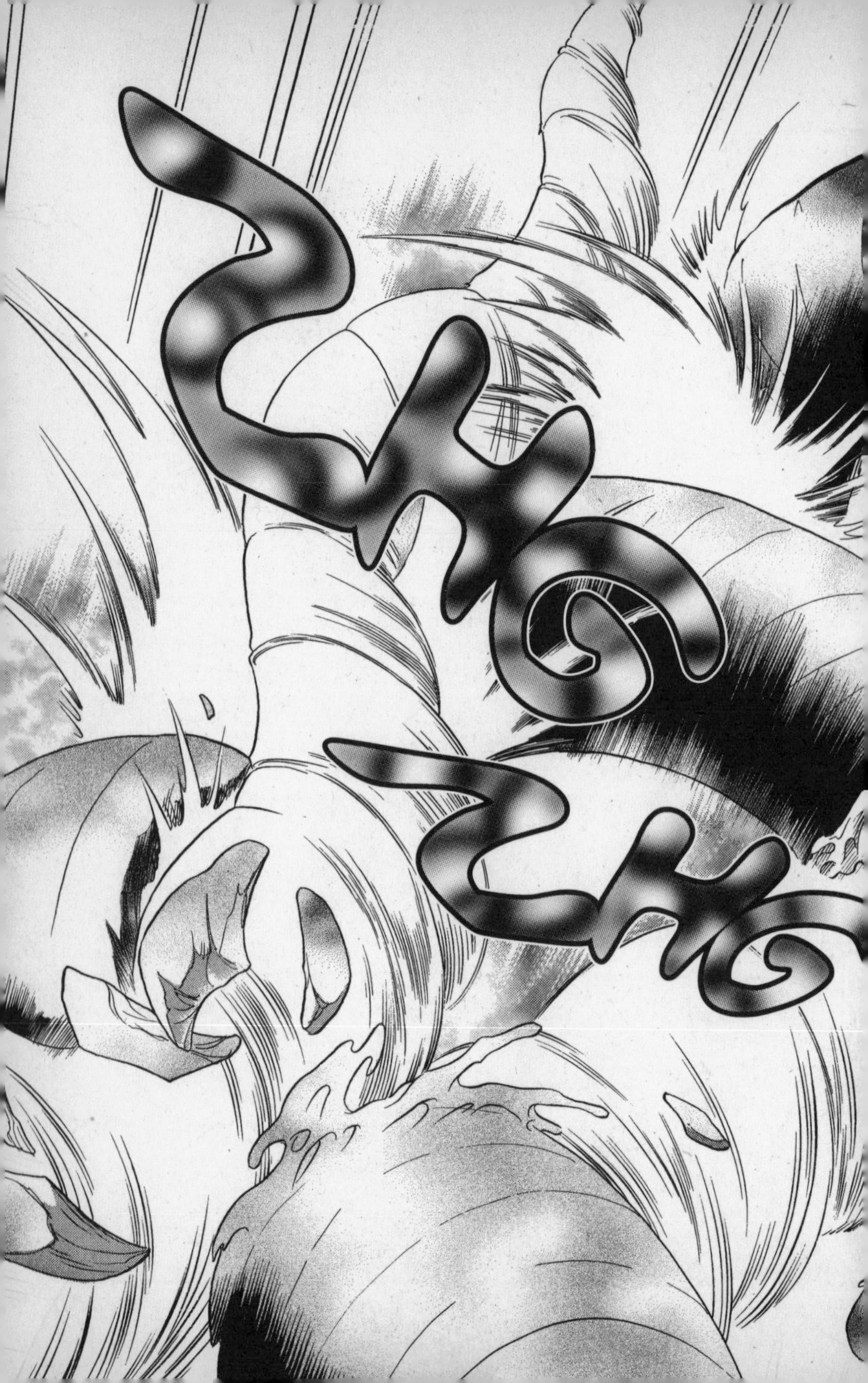

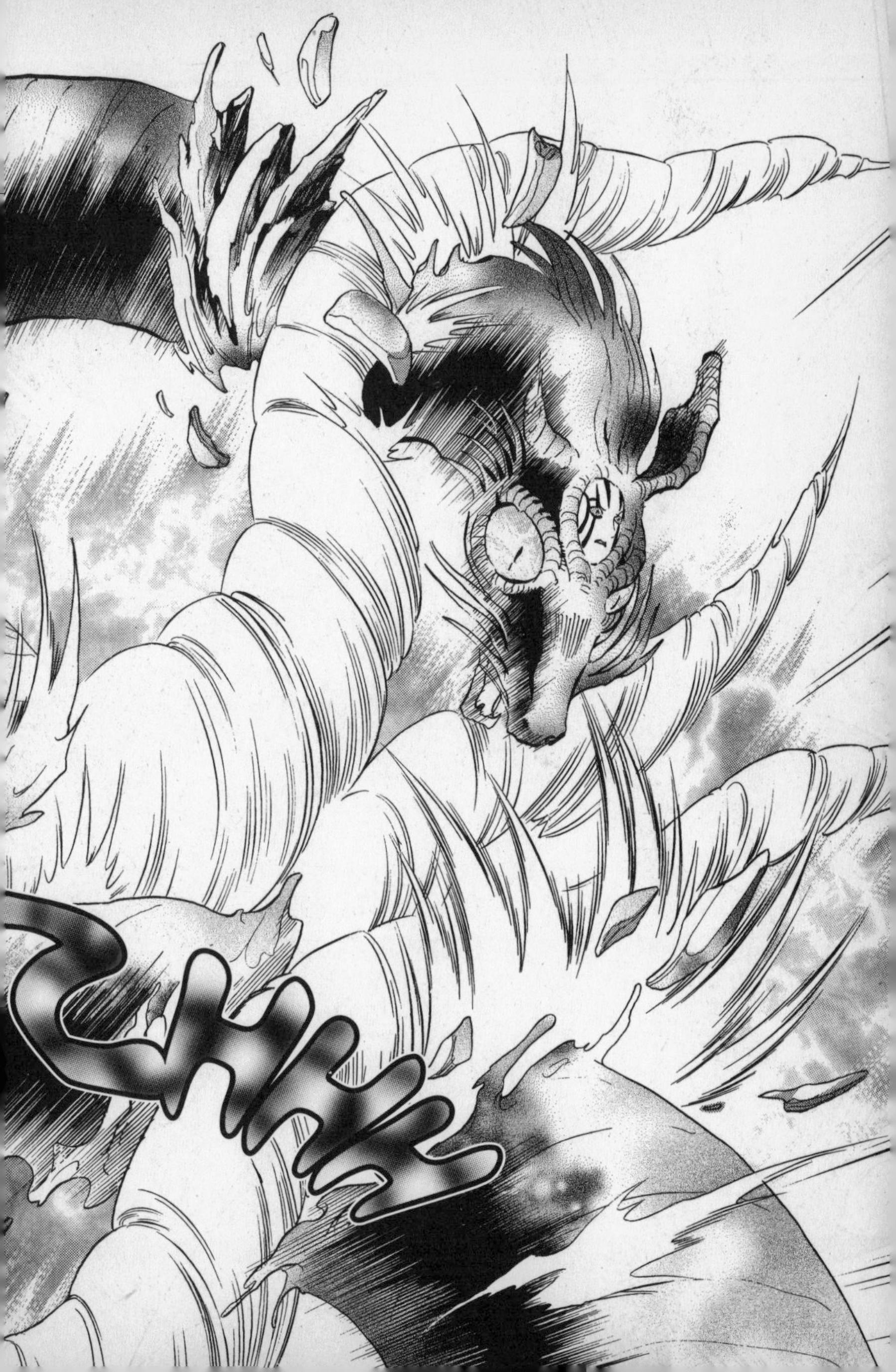

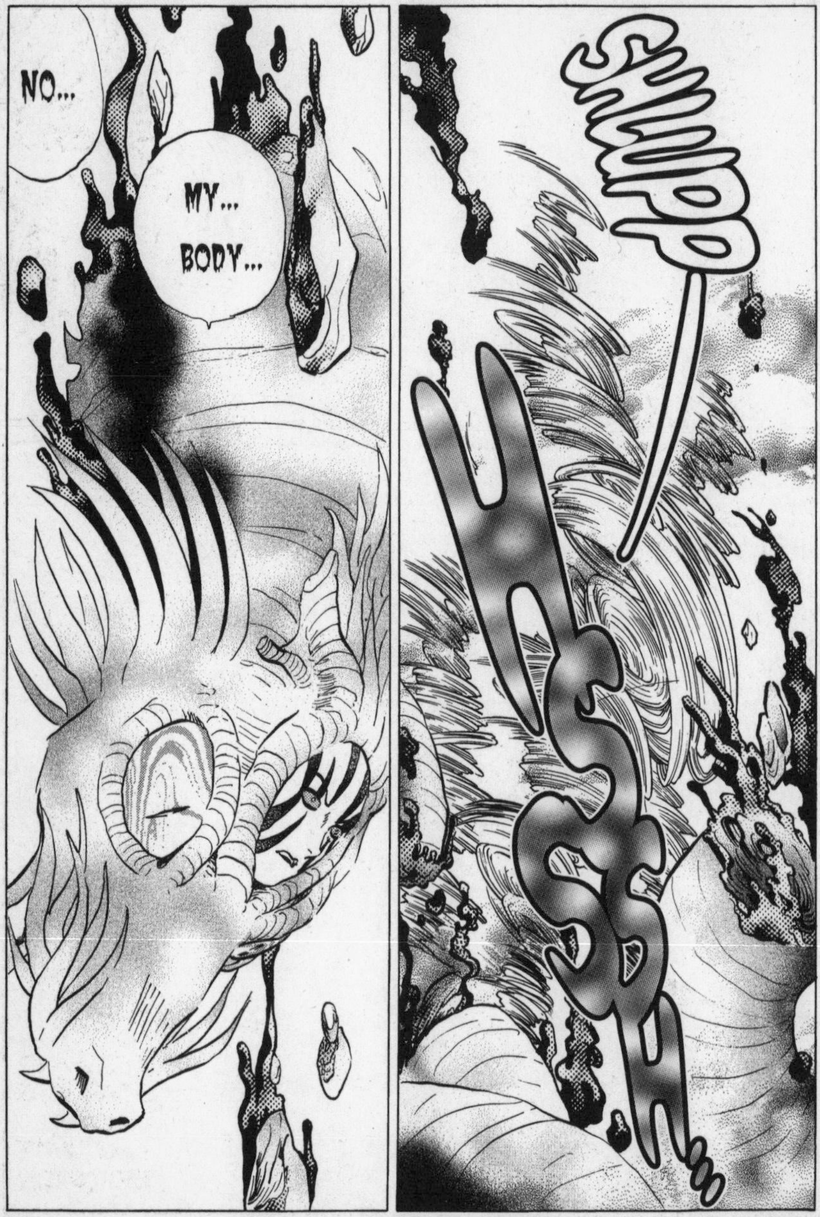
NO...
MY... BODY...
SHLUPP
SSSSH

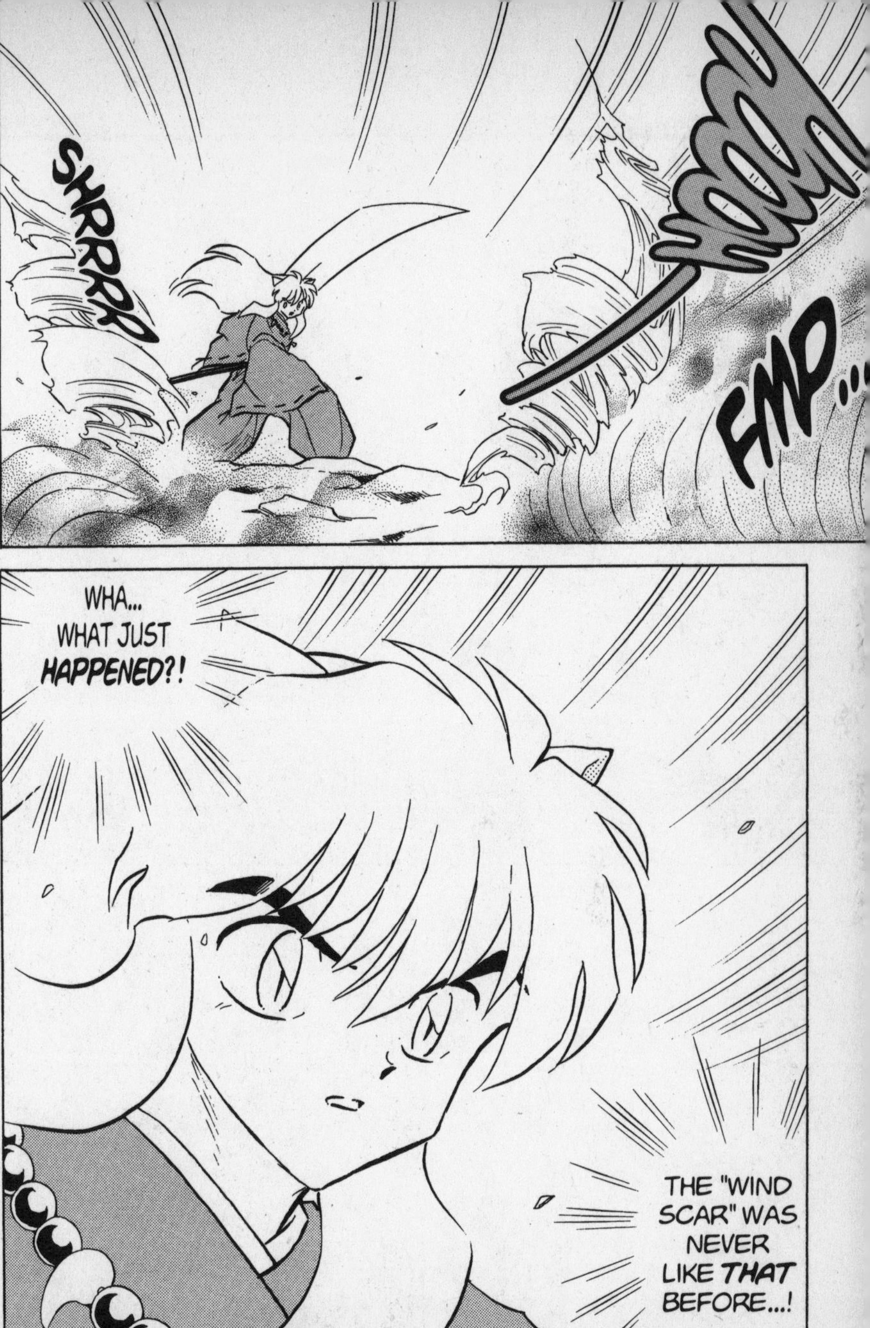
SHRRRR
FMP...
WHA... WHAT JUST HAPPENED?!
THE "WIND SCAR" WAS NEVER LIKE THAT BEFORE...!

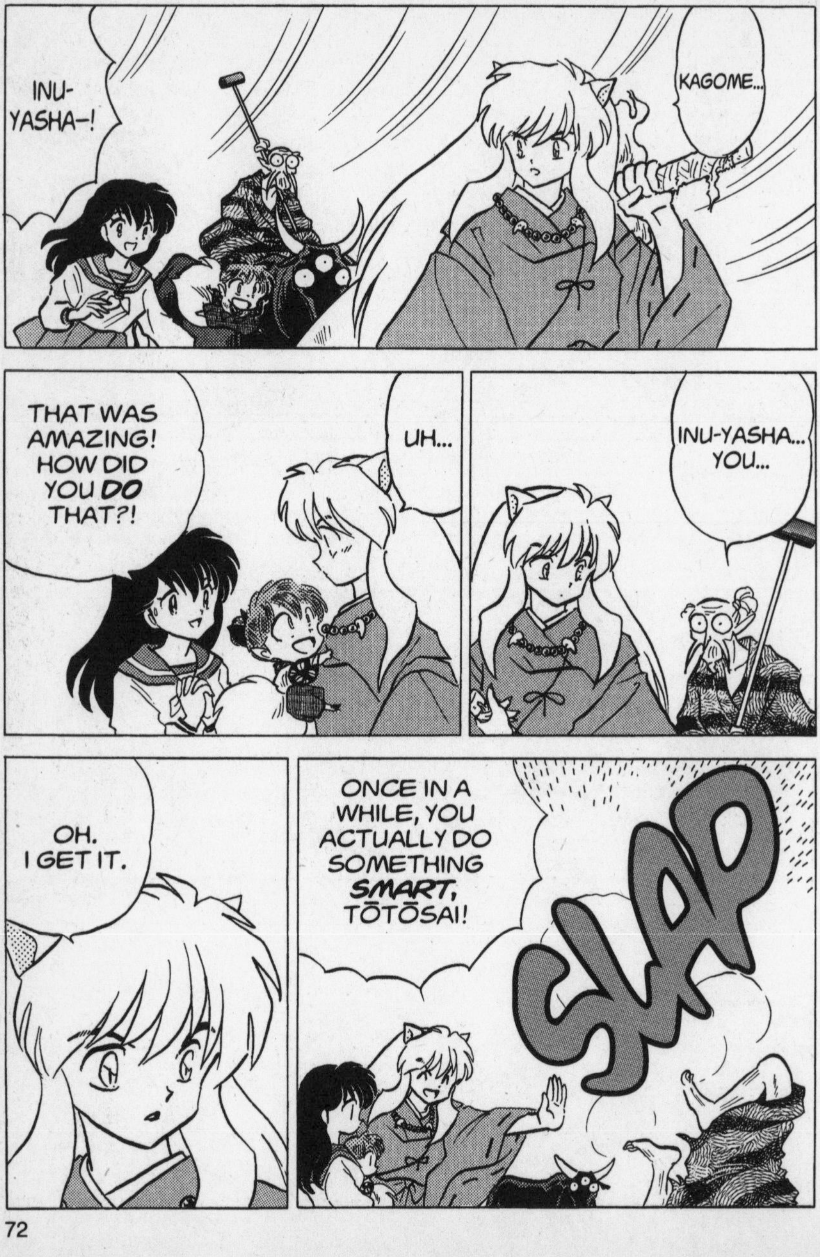
INU-YASHA-!
KAGOME...
THAT WAS AMAZING! HOW DID YOU DO THAT?!
UH...
INU-YASHA... YOU...
OH. I GET IT.
ONCE IN A WHILE, YOU ACTUALLY DO SOMETHING SMART, TŌTŌSAI!
SLAP

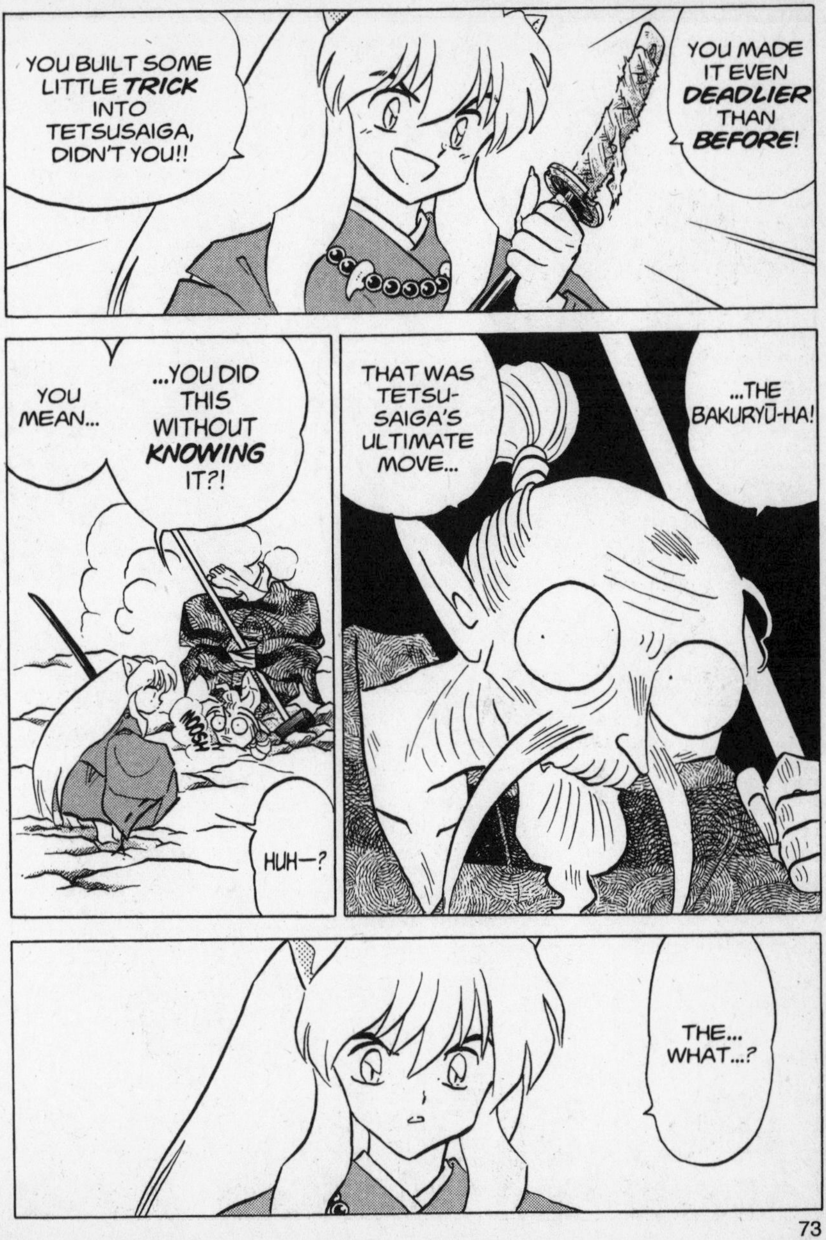
YOU BUILT SOME LITTLE TRICK INTO TETSUSAIGA, DIDN'T YOU!!
YOU MADE IT EVEN DEADLIER THAN BEFORE!
YOU MEAN...
...YOU DID THIS WITHOUT KNOWING IT?!
WOOSH
HUH—?
THAT WAS TETSU-SAIGA'S ULTIMATE MOVE...
...THE BAKURYŪ-HA!
THE... WHAT...?

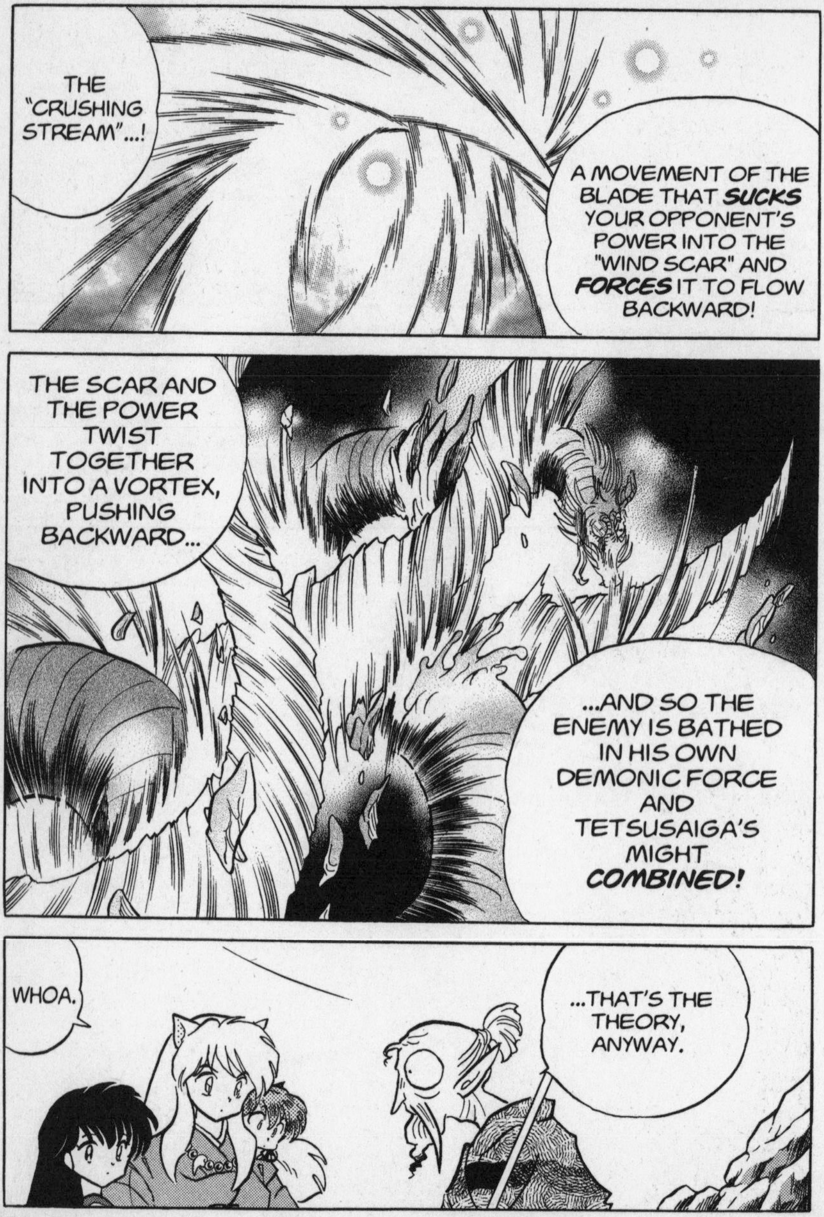
THE "CRUSHING STREAM"...!
A MOVEMENT OF THE BLADE THAT **SUCKS** YOUR OPPONENT'S POWER INTO THE "WIND SCAR" AND **FORCES** IT TO FLOW BACKWARD!
THE SCAR AND THE POWER TWIST TOGETHER INTO A VORTEX, PUSHING BACKWARD...
...AND SO THE ENEMY IS BATHED IN HIS OWN DEMONIC FORCE AND TETSUSAIGA'S MIGHT **COMBINED!**
WHOA.
...THAT'S THE THEORY, ANYWAY.

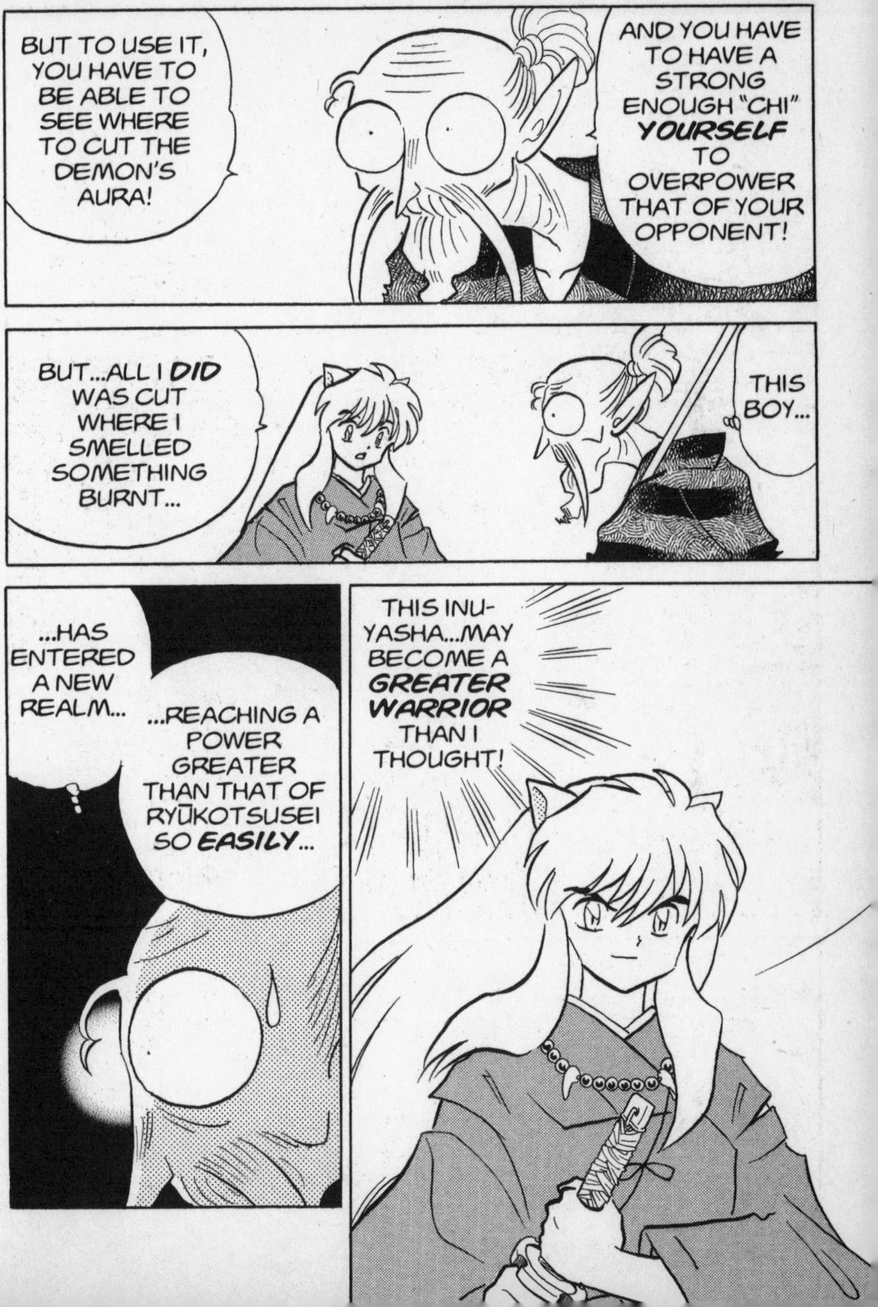
BUT TO USE IT, YOU HAVE TO BE ABLE TO SEE WHERE TO CUT THE DEMON'S AURA!
AND YOU HAVE TO HAVE A STRONG ENOUGH "CHI" YOURSELF TO OVERPOWER THAT OF YOUR OPPONENT!
BUT...ALL I DID WAS CUT WHERE I SMELLED SOMETHING BURNT...
THIS BOY...
...HAS ENTERED A NEW REALM...
...REACHING A POWER GREATER THAN THAT OF RYŪKOTSUSEI SO EASILY...
THIS INU-YASHA...MAY BECOME A GREATER WARRIOR THAN I THOUGHT!

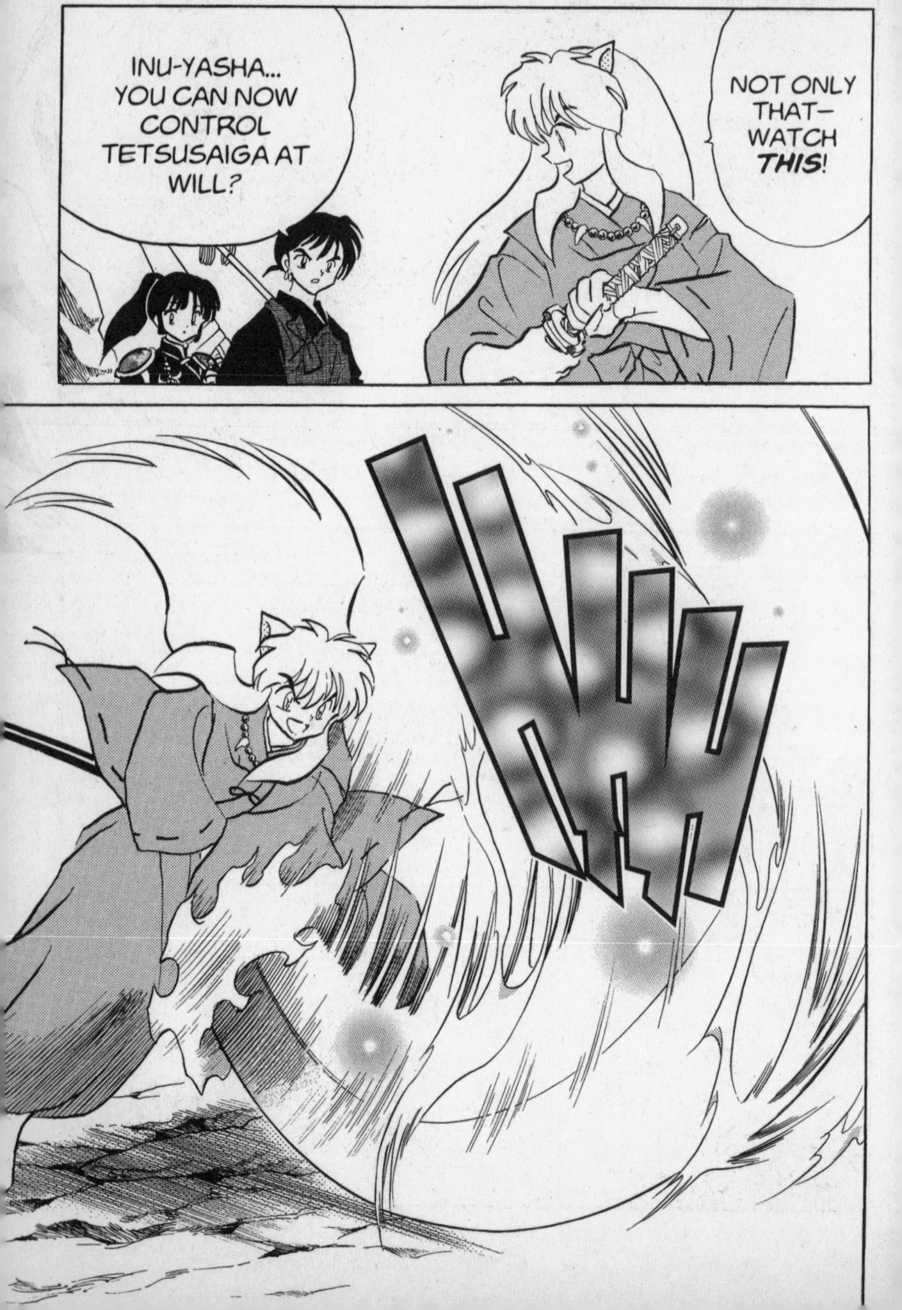
INU-YASHA... YOU CAN NOW CONTROL TETSUSAIGA AT WILL?
NOT ONLY THAT— WATCH **THIS**!

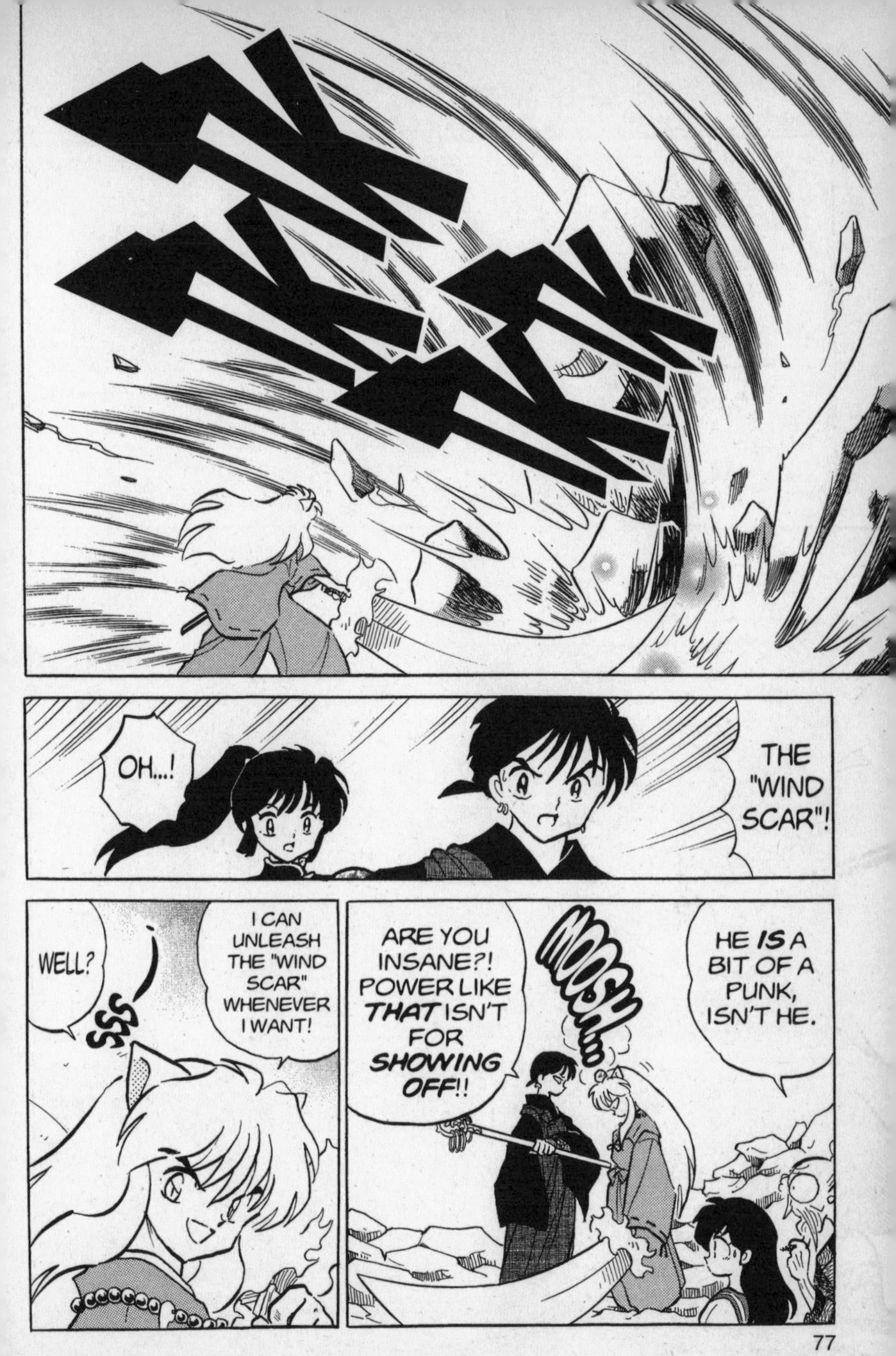
OH...!
THE "WIND SCAR"!
WELL?
SSS
I CAN UNLEASH THE "WIND SCAR" WHENEVER I WANT!
ARE YOU INSANE?! POWER LIKE **THAT** ISN'T FOR **SHOWING OFF**!!
WOOSH...
HE **IS** A BIT OF A PUNK, ISN'T HE.

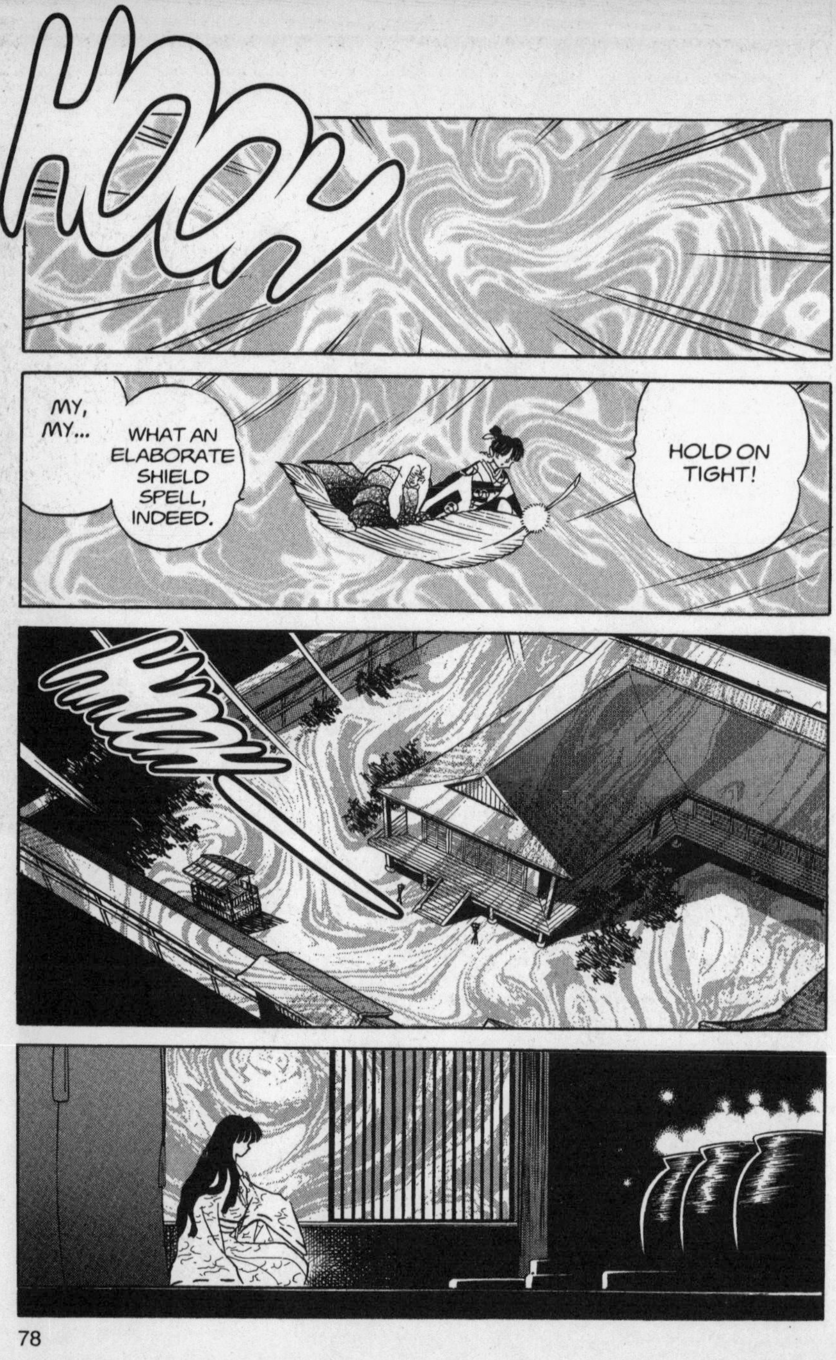
MY, MY...
WHAT AN ELABORATE SHIELD SPELL, INDEED.
HOLD ON TIGHT!

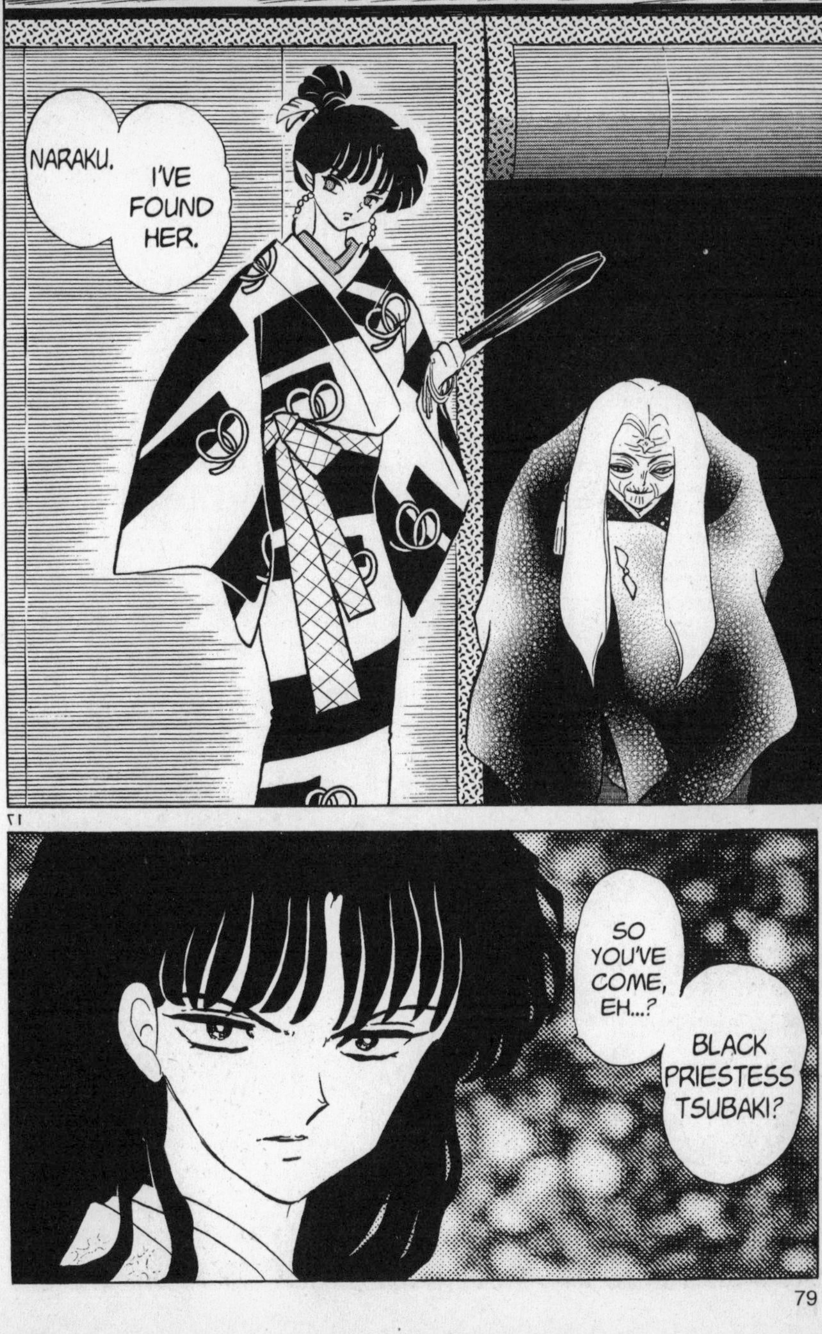
NARAKU.
I'VE FOUND HER.
SO YOU'VE COME, EH...?
BLACK PRIESTESS TSUBAKI?

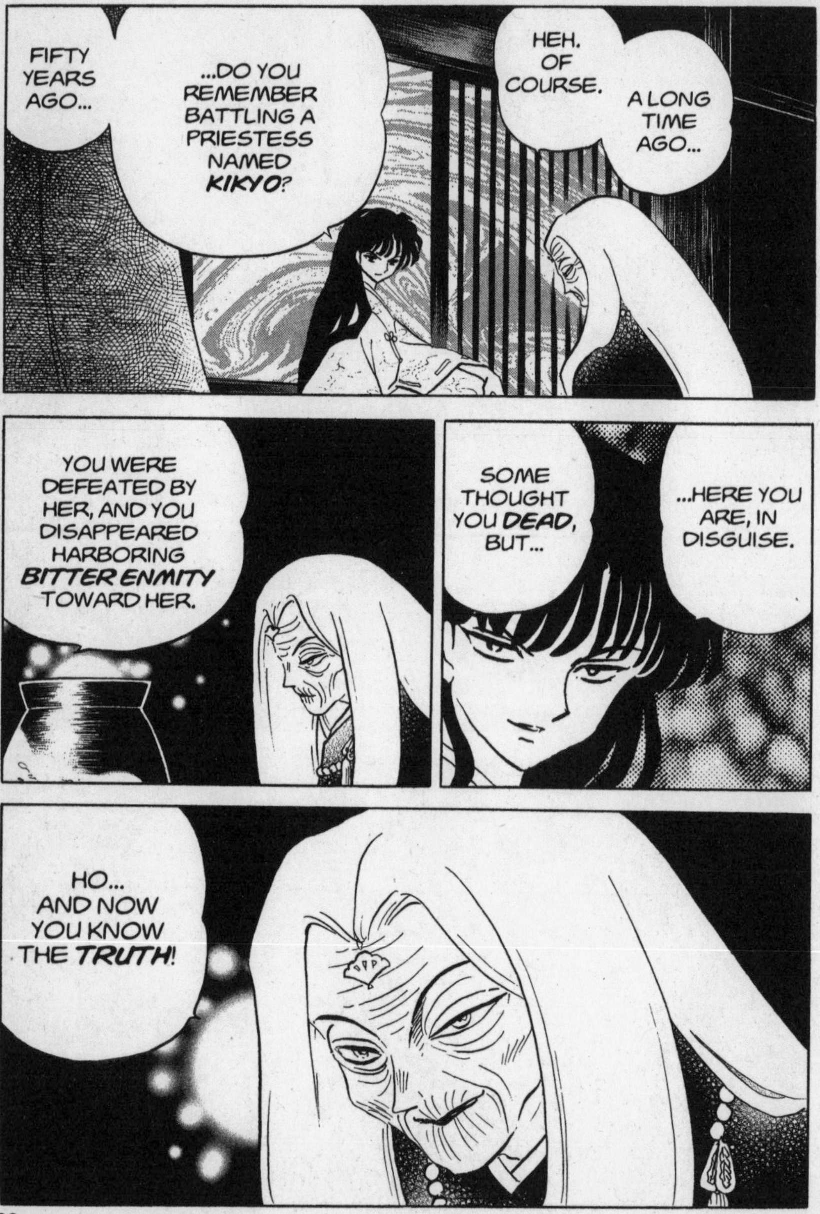
FIFTY YEARS AGO...
...DO YOU REMEMBER BATTLING A PRIESTESS NAMED **KIKYO**?
HEH. OF COURSE.
A LONG TIME AGO...
YOU WERE DEFEATED BY HER, AND YOU DISAPPEARED HARBORING **BITTER ENMITY** TOWARD HER.
SOME THOUGHT YOU **DEAD**, BUT...
...HERE YOU ARE, IN DISGUISE.
HO... AND NOW YOU KNOW THE **TRUTH**!

SCROLL FIVE

TSUBAKI, THE BLACK PRIESTESS

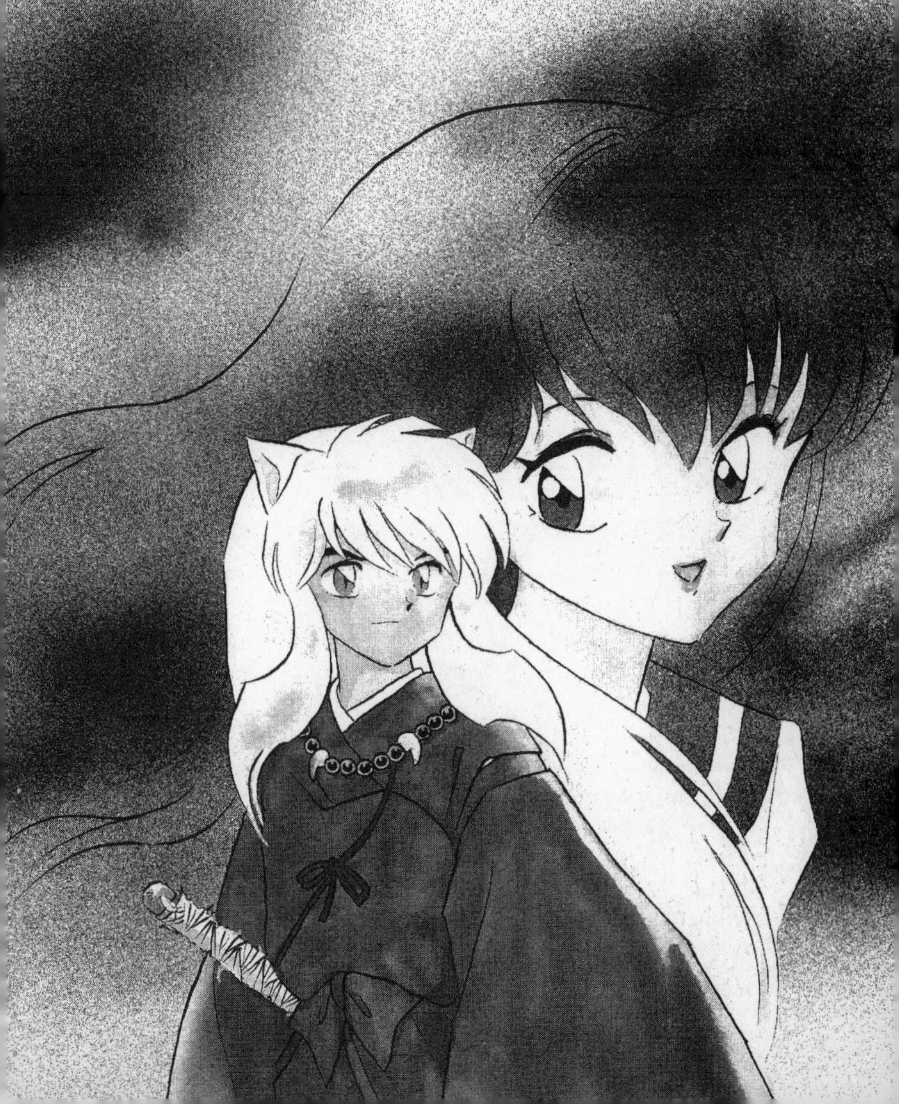

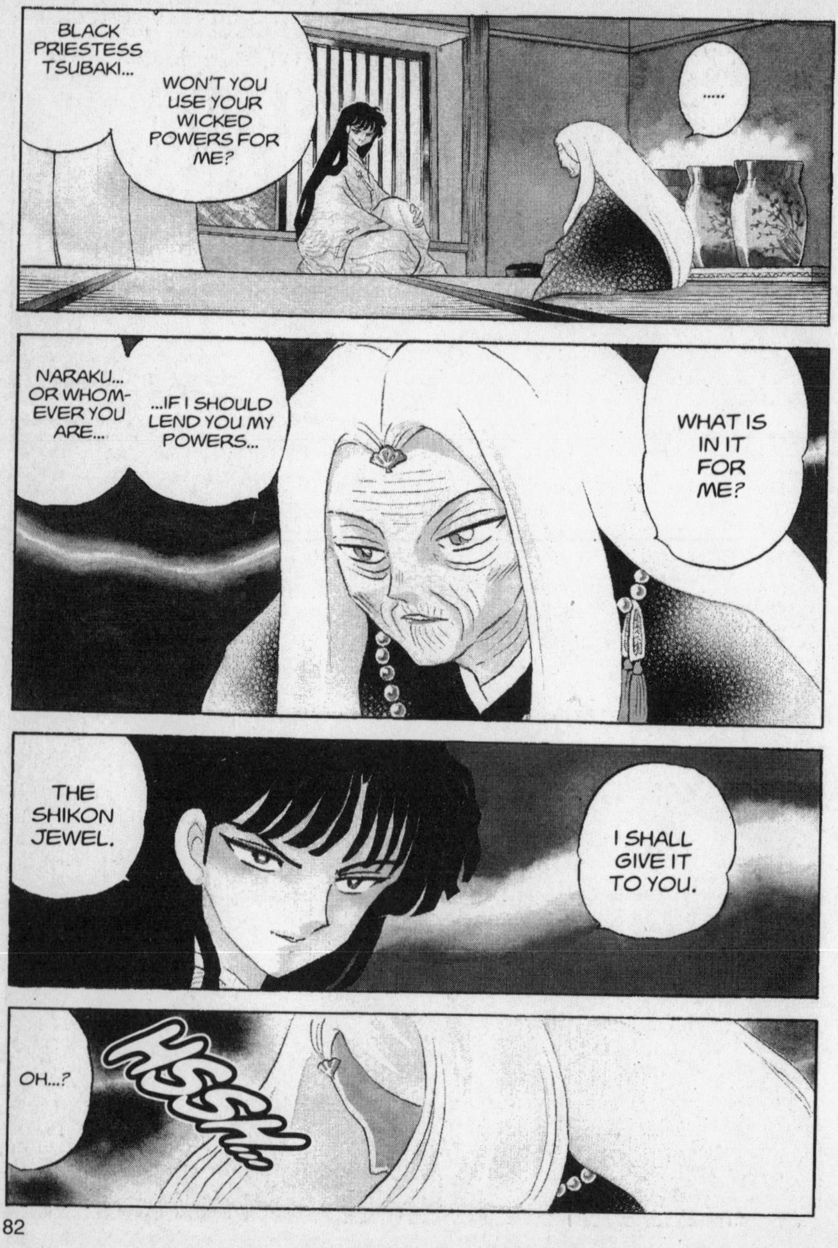
BLACK PRIESTESS TSUBAKI...
WON'T YOU USE YOUR WICKED POWERS FOR ME?
.....
NARAKU... OR WHOM-EVER YOU ARE...
...IF I SHOULD LEND YOU MY POWERS...
WHAT IS IN IT FOR ME?
THE SHIKON JEWEL.
I SHALL GIVE IT TO YOU.
OH...?
HSSH...

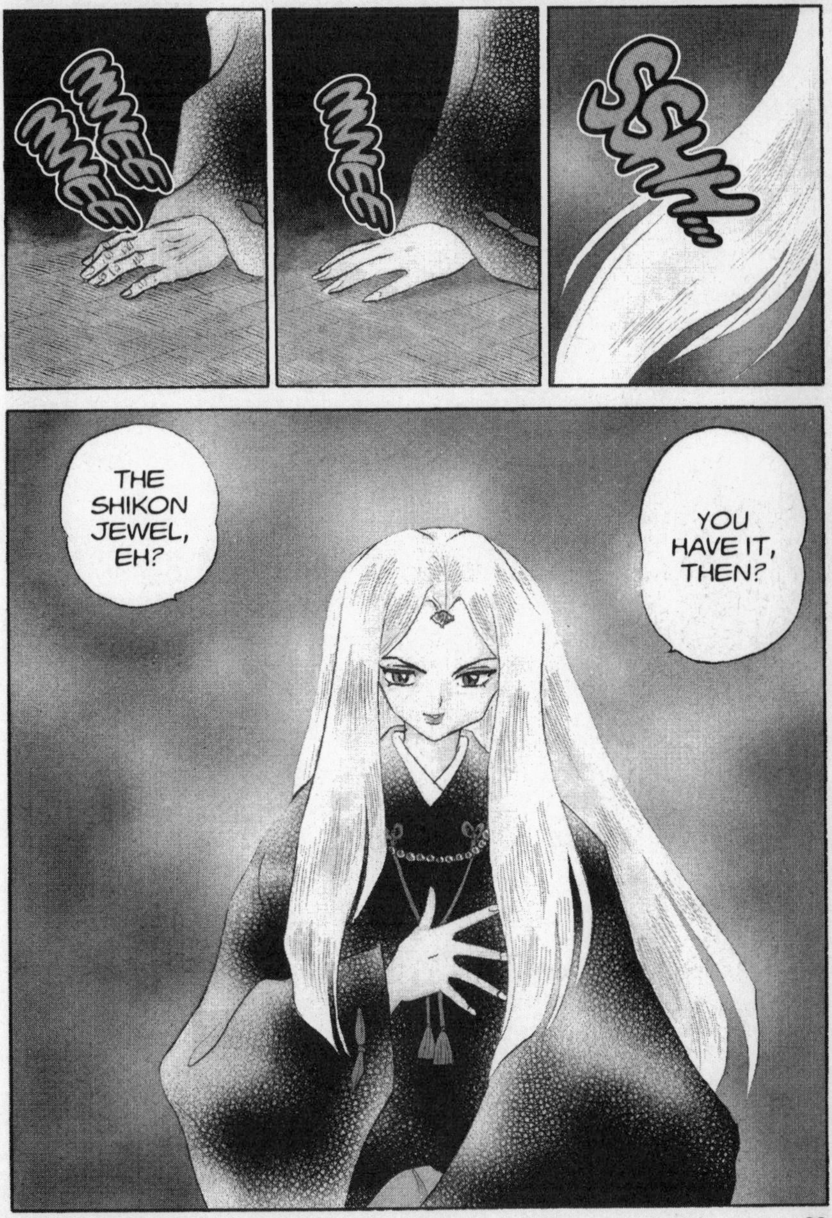
MNEE
MNEE
MNEE
SSH...
THE SHIKON JEWEL, EH?
YOU HAVE IT, THEN?

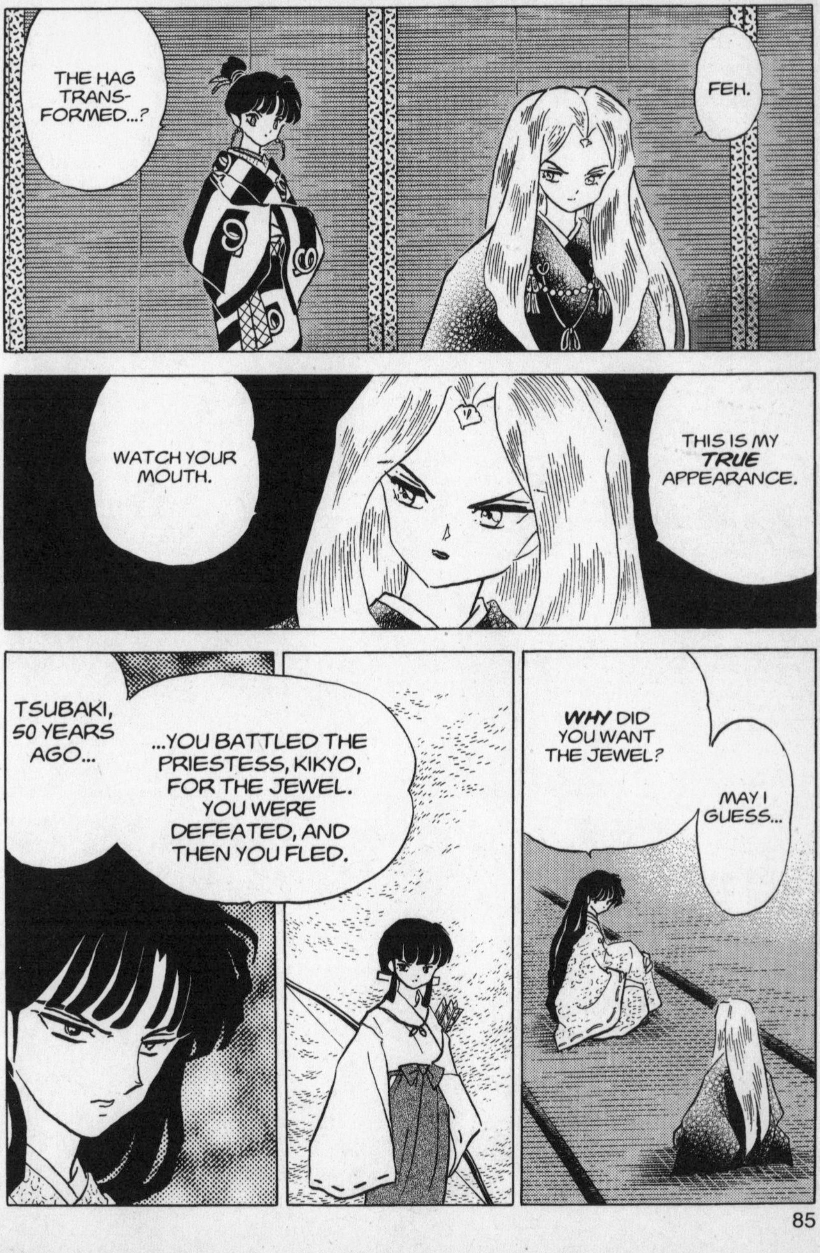
THE HAG TRANS-FORMED...?
FEH.
WATCH YOUR MOUTH.
THIS IS MY *TRUE* APPEARANCE.
TSUBAKI, 50 YEARS AGO...
...YOU BATTLED THE PRIESTESS, KIKYO, FOR THE JEWEL. YOU WERE DEFEATED, AND THEN YOU FLED.
WHY DID YOU WANT THE JEWEL?
MAY I GUESS...

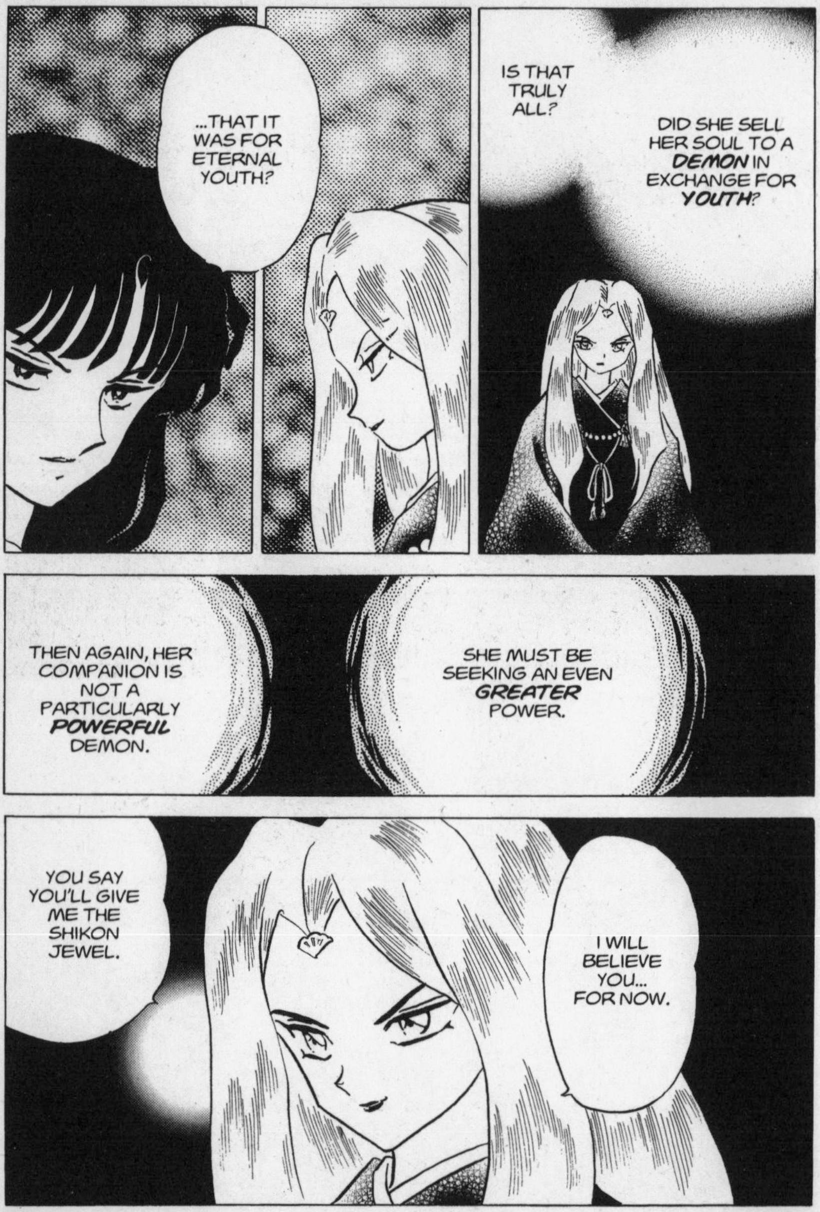
...THAT IT WAS FOR ETERNAL YOUTH?
IS THAT TRULY ALL?
DID SHE SELL HER SOUL TO A ***DEMON*** IN EXCHANGE FOR ***YOUTH***?
THEN AGAIN, HER COMPANION IS NOT A PARTICULARLY ***POWERFUL*** DEMON.
SHE MUST BE SEEKING AN EVEN ***GREATER*** POWER.
YOU SAY YOU'LL GIVE ME THE SHIKON JEWEL.
I WILL BELIEVE YOU... FOR NOW.

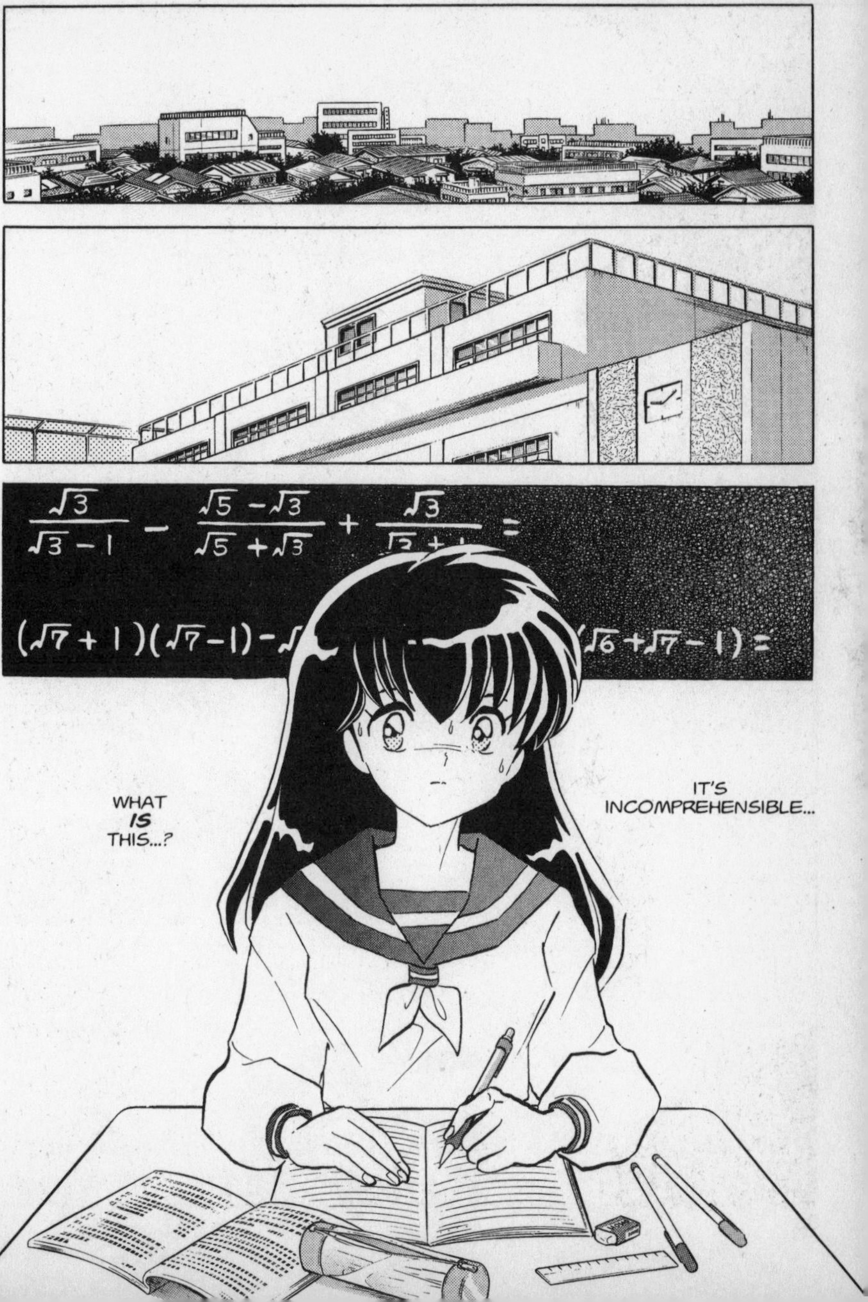
WHAT *IS* THIS...?
IT'S INCOMPREHENSIBLE...

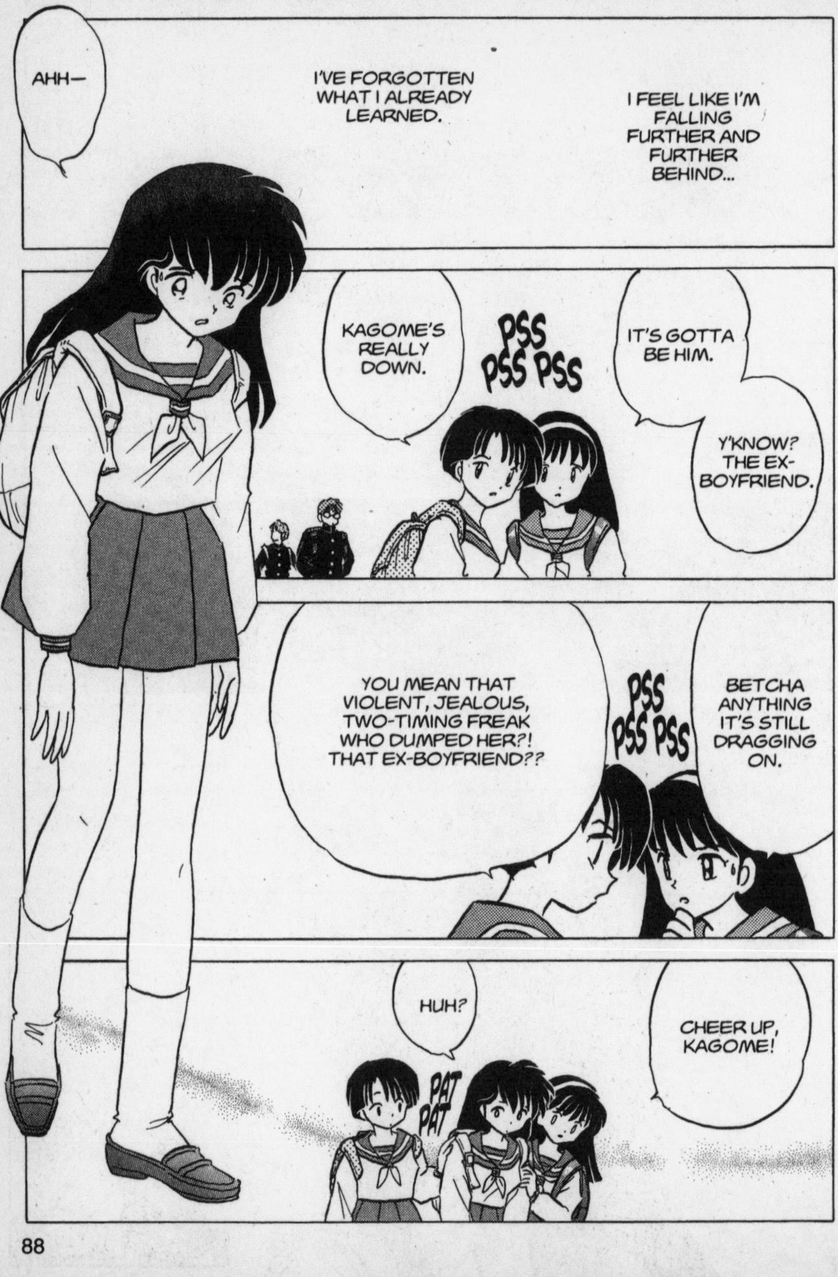
AHH—
I'VE FORGOTTEN WHAT I ALREADY LEARNED.
I FEEL LIKE I'M FALLING FURTHER AND FURTHER BEHIND...
KAGOME'S REALLY DOWN.
PSS PSS PSS
IT'S GOTTA BE HIM.
Y'KNOW? THE EX-BOYFRIEND.
YOU MEAN THAT VIOLENT, JEALOUS, TWO-TIMING FREAK WHO DUMPED HER?! THAT EX-BOYFRIEND??
PSS PSS PSS
BETCHA ANYTHING IT'S STILL DRAGGING ON.
HUH?
PAT PAT
CHEER UP, KAGOME!

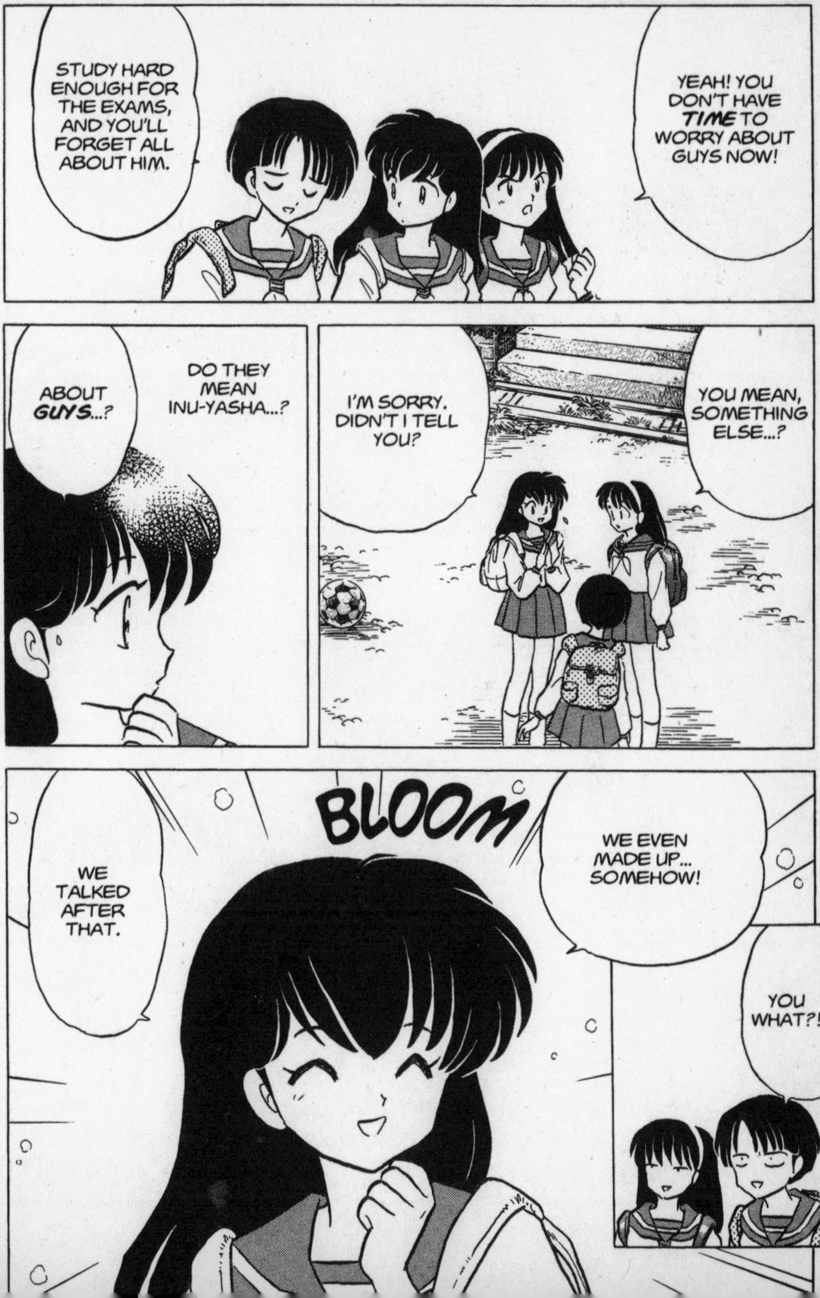
STUDY HARD ENOUGH FOR THE EXAMS, AND YOU'LL FORGET ALL ABOUT HIM.
YEAH! YOU DON'T HAVE *TIME* TO WORRY ABOUT GUYS NOW!
ABOUT *GUYS*...?
DO THEY MEAN INU-YASHA...?
I'M SORRY. DIDN'T I TELL YOU?
YOU MEAN, SOMETHING ELSE...?
BLOOM
WE TALKED AFTER THAT.
WE EVEN MADE UP... SOMEHOW!
YOU WHAT?!

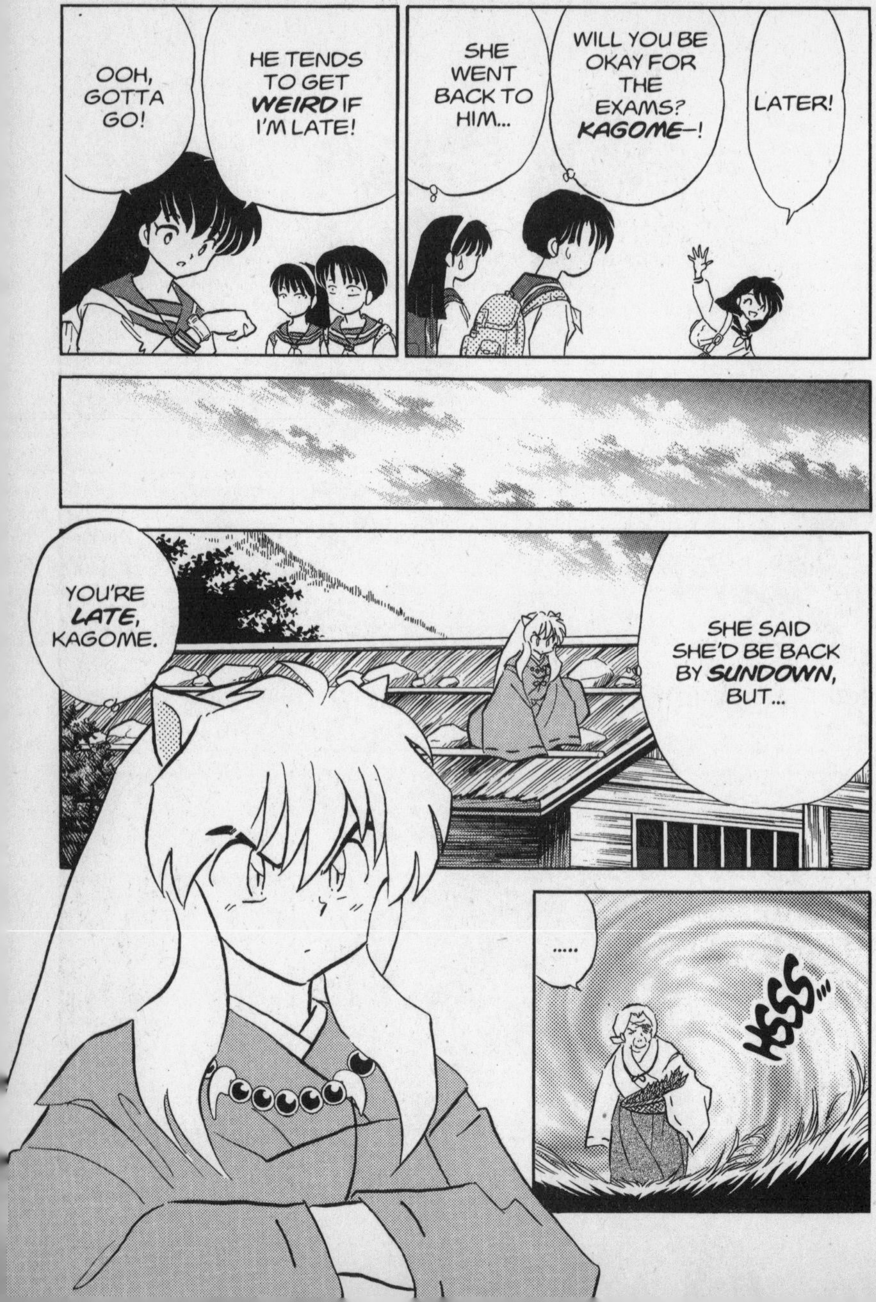

OOH, GOTTA GO!
HE TENDS TO GET **WEIRD** IF I'M LATE!
SHE WENT BACK TO HIM...
WILL YOU BE OKAY FOR THE EXAMS? **KAGOME**—!
LATER!
YOU'RE **LATE**, KAGOME.
SHE SAID SHE'D BE BACK BY **SUNDOWN**, BUT...
.....
HSSS...

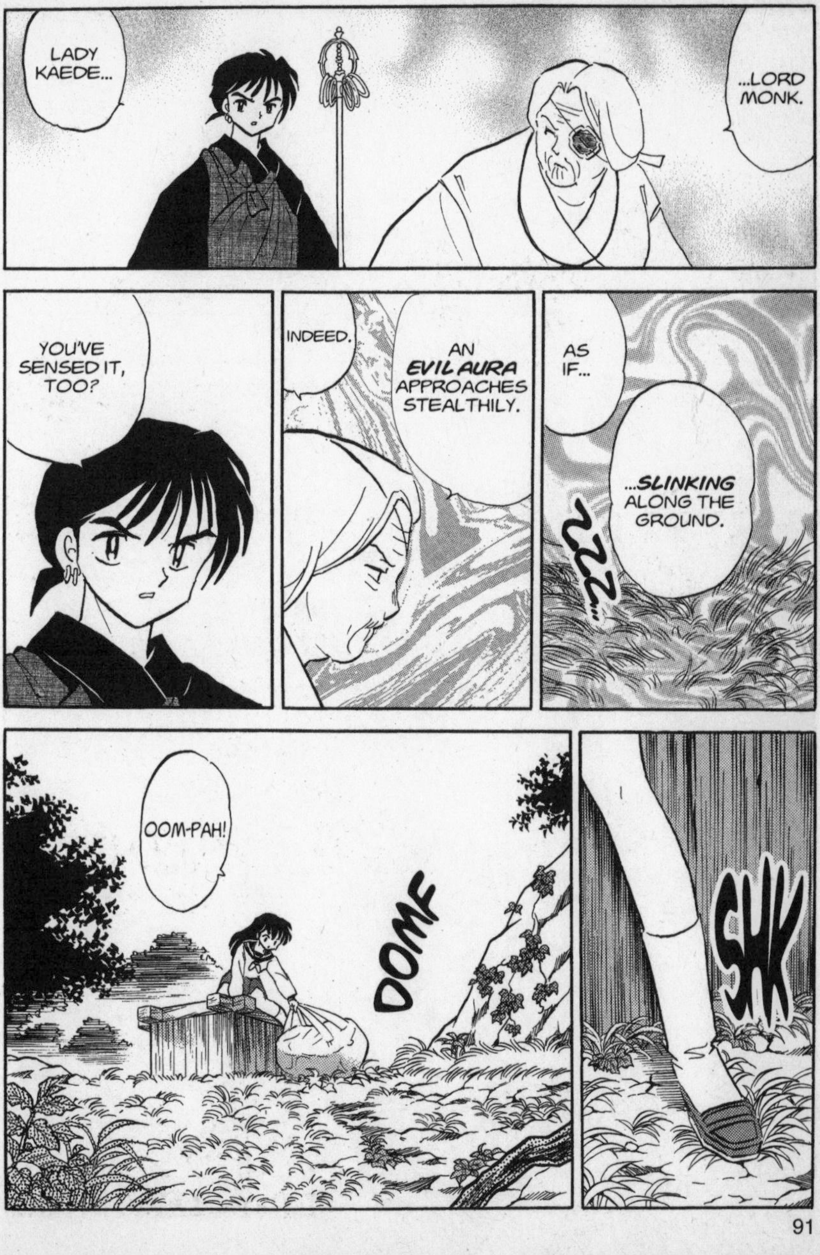
LADY KAEDE...
...LORD MONK.
YOU'VE SENSED IT, TOO?
INDEED.
AN EVIL AURA APPROACHES STEALTHILY.
AS IF...
...SLINKING ALONG THE GROUND.
ZZZ...
OOM-PAH!
DOMF
SHK

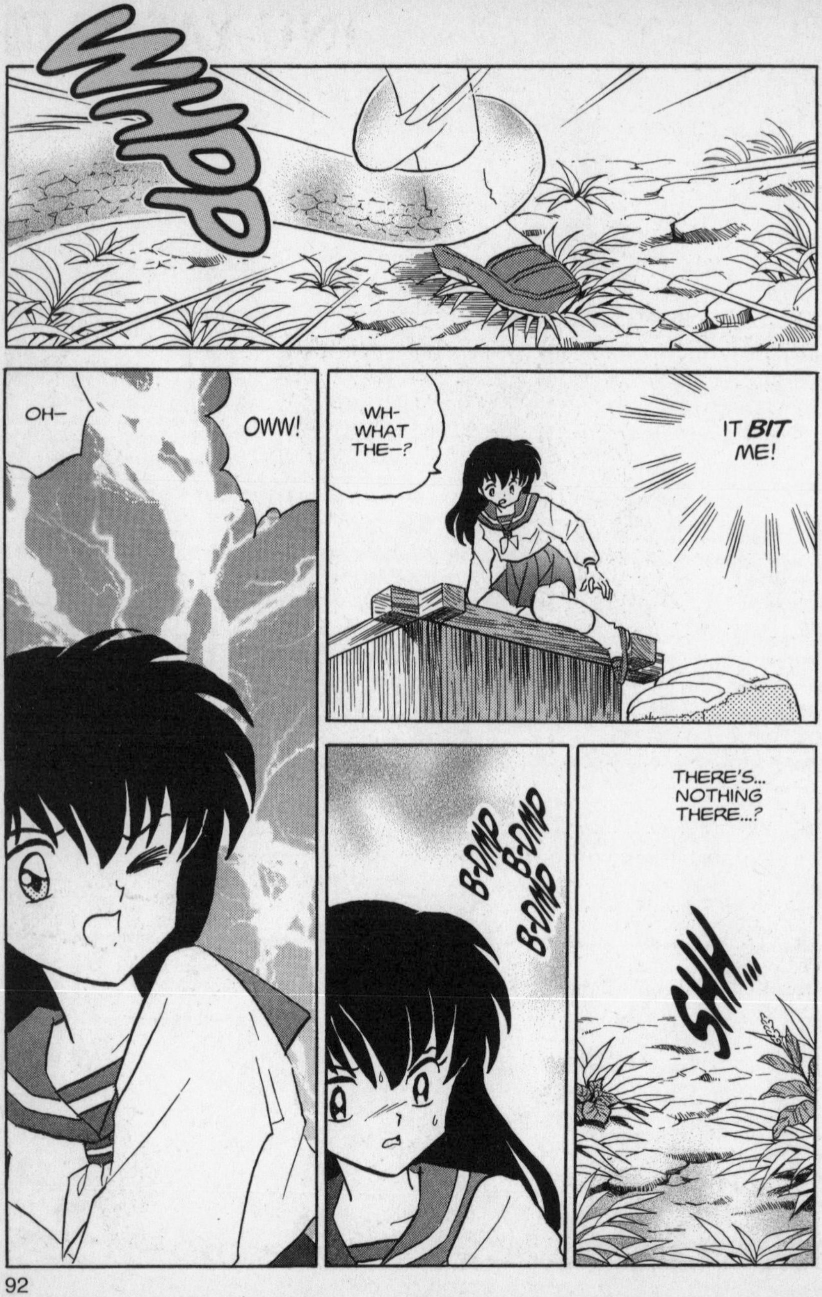
WHPP
OH–
OWW!
WH-
WHAT
THE–?
IT BIT
ME!
B-DMP
B-DMP
B-DMP
THERE'S...
NOTHING
THERE...?
SHH...

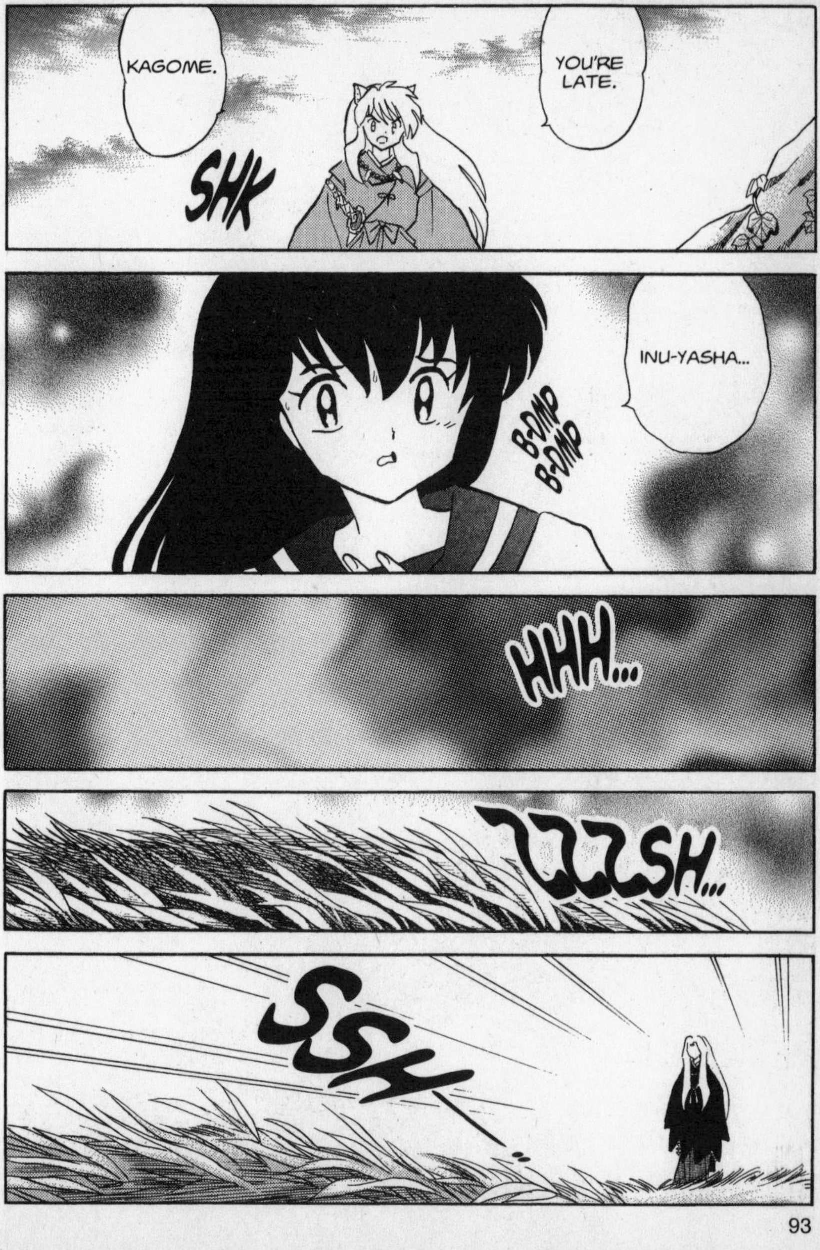
KAGOME.
YOU'RE LATE.
SHK
INU-YASHA...
B-DMP B-DMP
HHH...
ZZZSH...
SSH

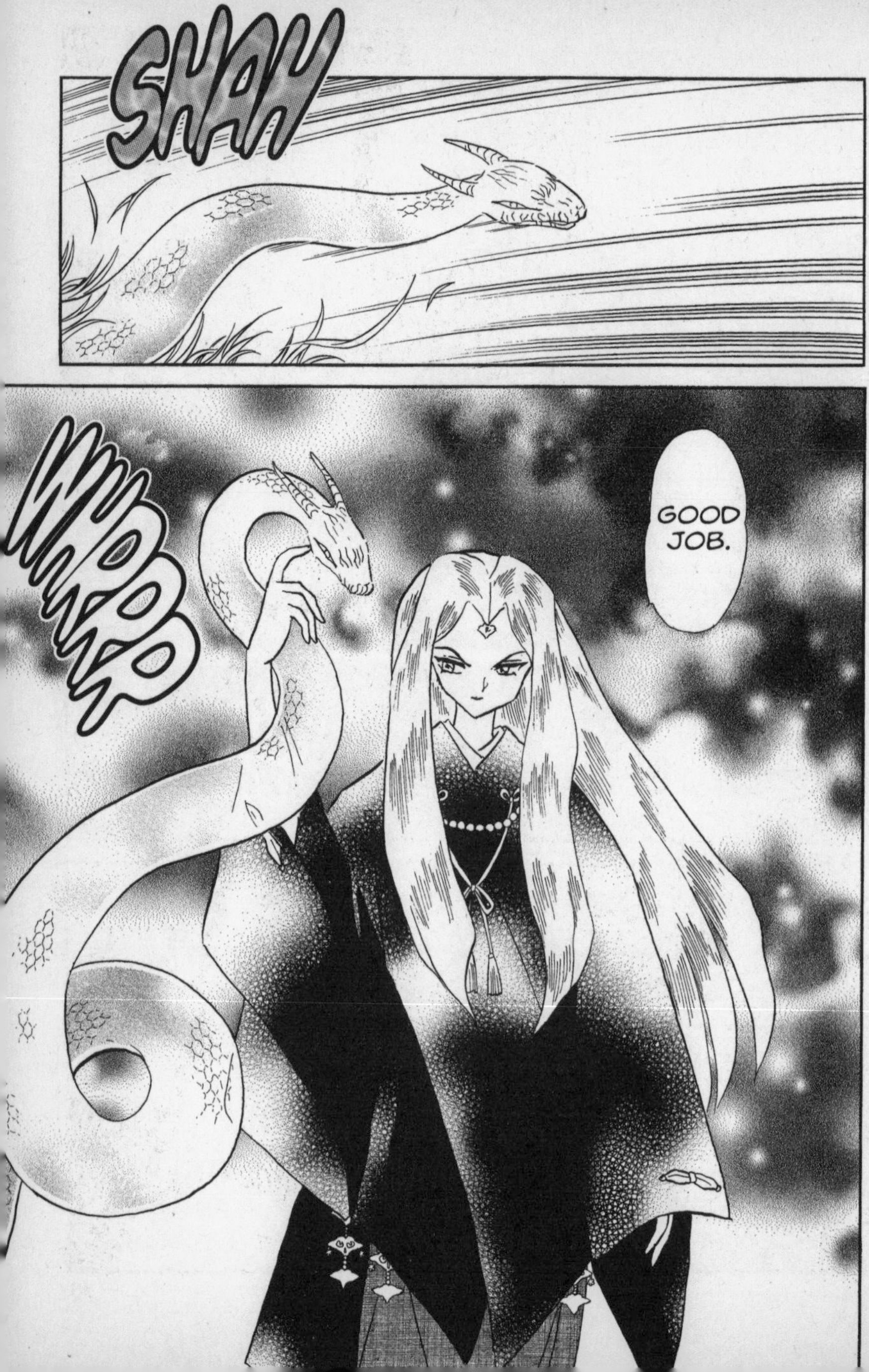
SHAH
WHRRR
GOOD JOB.

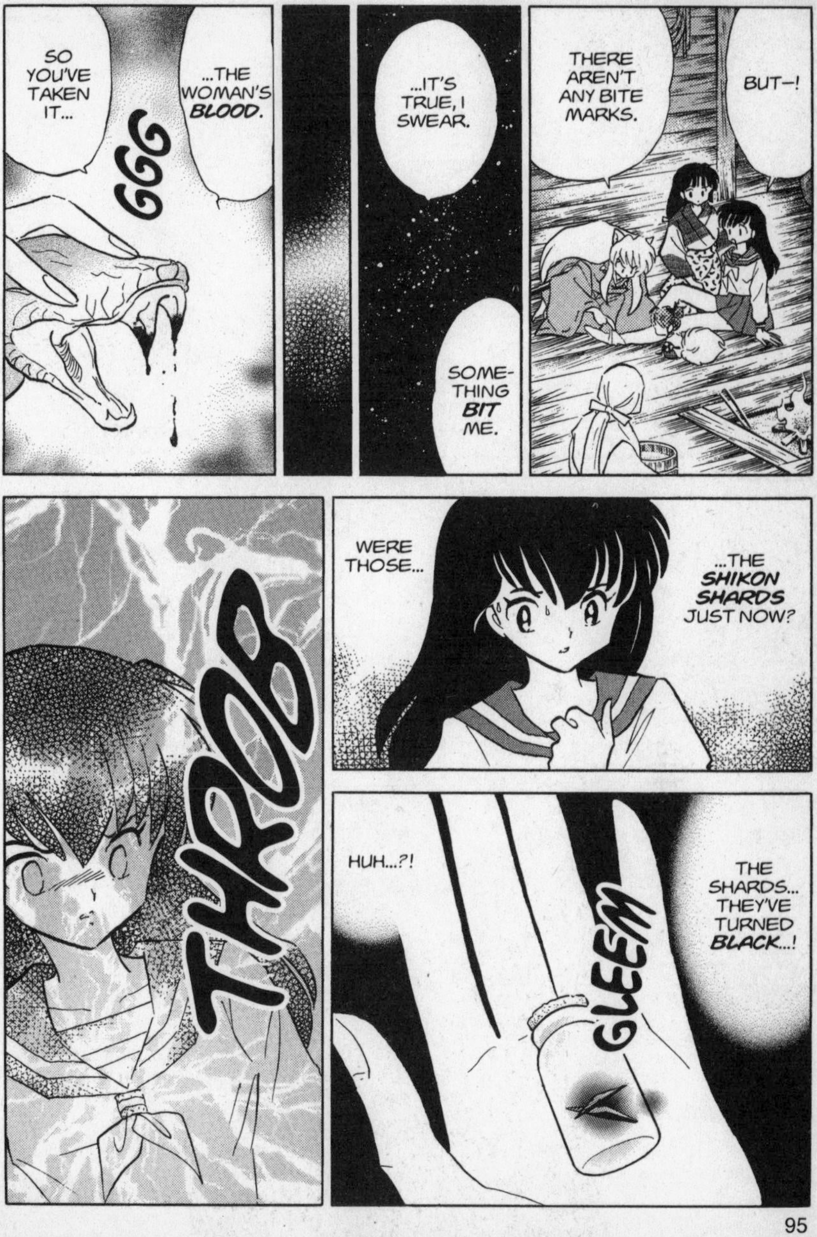
SO YOU'VE TAKEN IT...
...THE WOMAN'S **BLOOD**.
GGG
...IT'S TRUE, I SWEAR.
SOME-THING **BIT** ME.
THERE AREN'T ANY BITE MARKS.
BUT—!
THROB
WERE THOSE...
...THE **SHIKON SHARDS** JUST NOW?
HUH...?!
GLEEM
THE SHARDS... THEY'VE TURNED **BLACK**...!

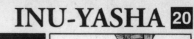

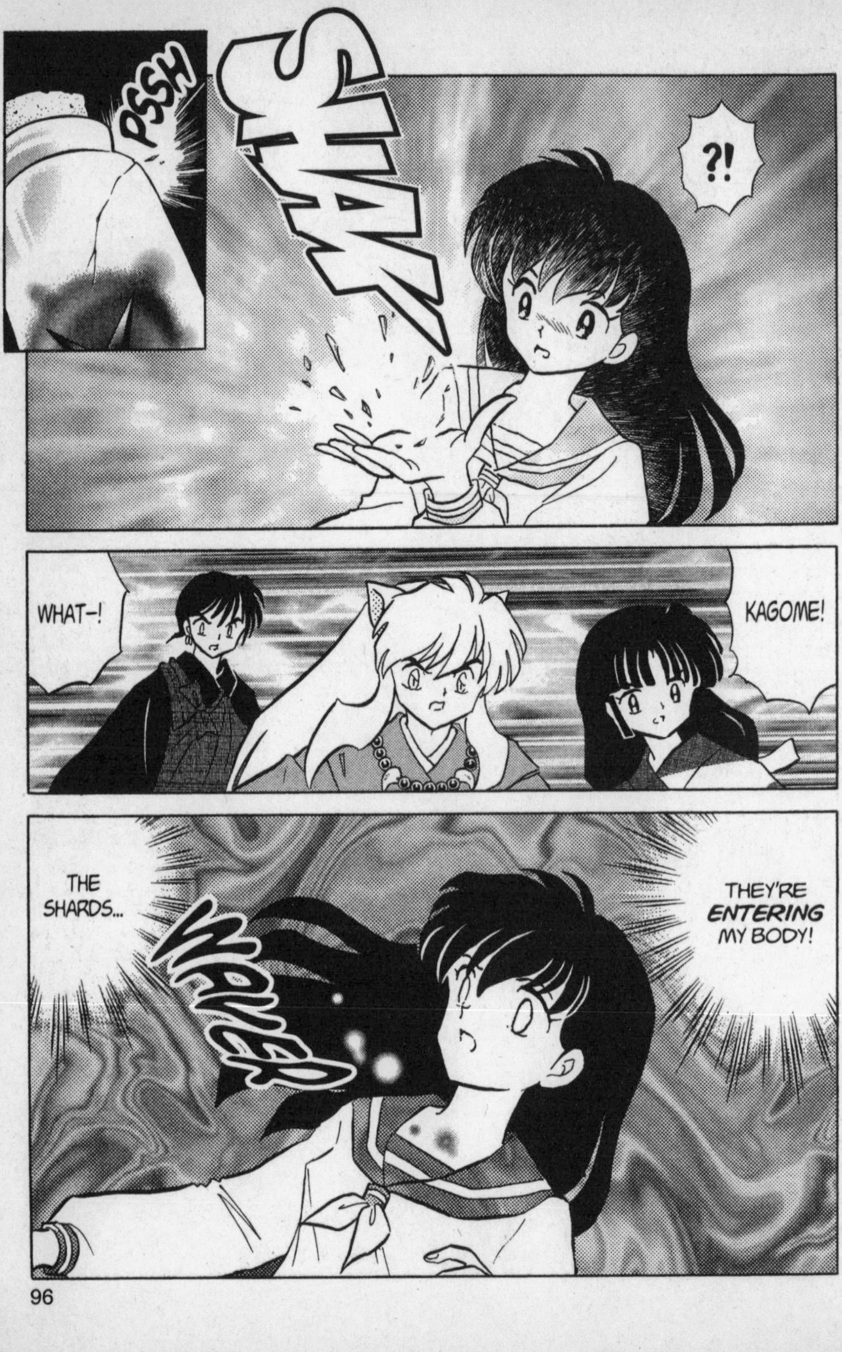
PSSH
SHAK
?!
WHAT-!
KAGOME!
THE SHARDS...
WAVER
THEY'RE *ENTERING* MY BODY!

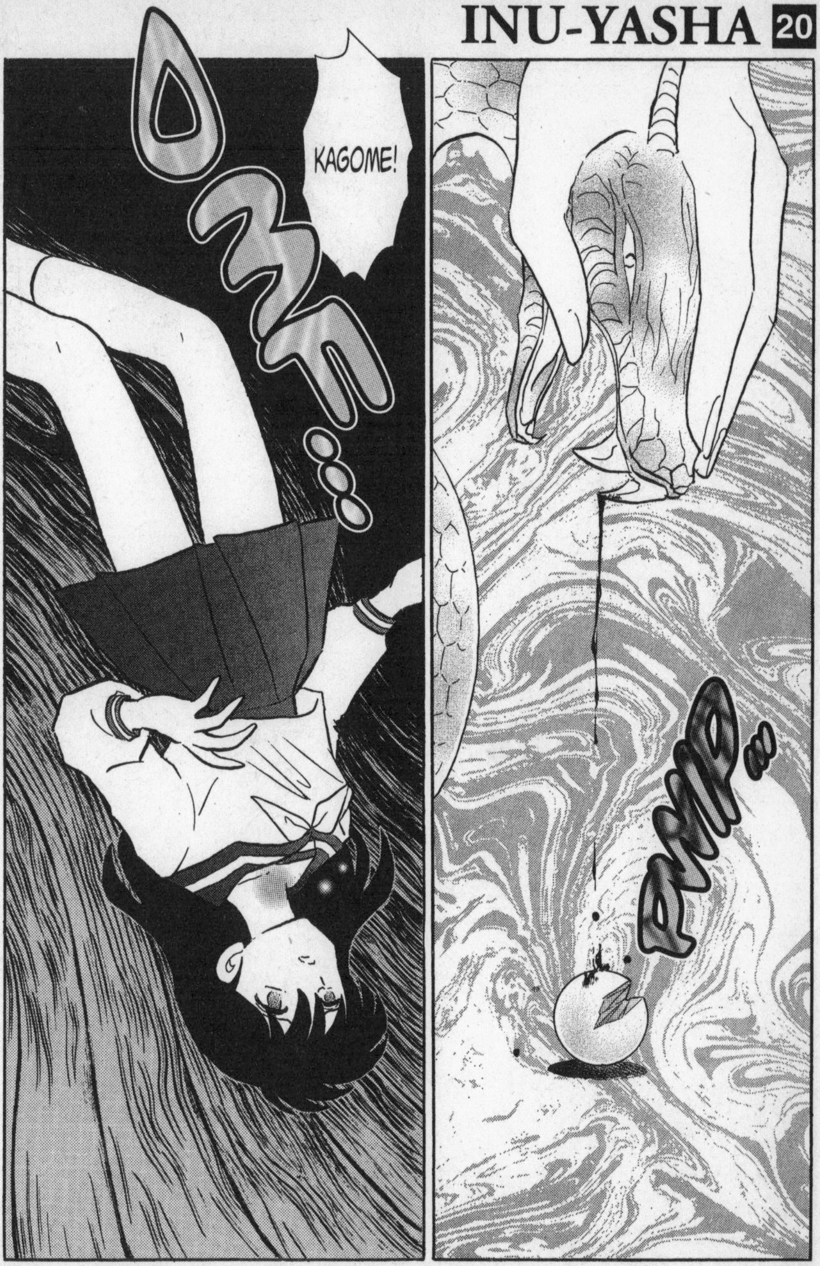
KAGOME!

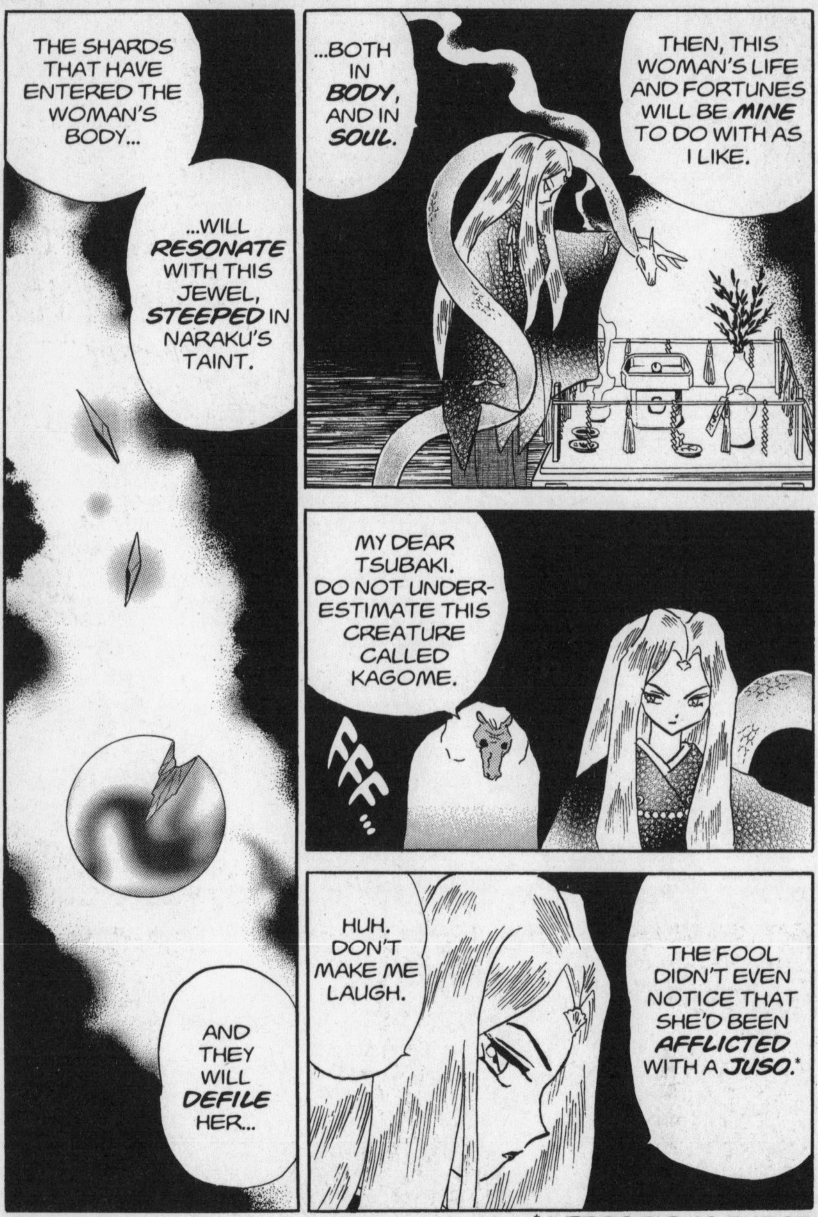
THE SHARDS THAT HAVE ENTERED THE WOMAN'S BODY...
...WILL RESONATE WITH THIS JEWEL, STEEPED IN NARAKU'S TAINT.
AND THEY WILL DEFILE HER...
...BOTH IN BODY, AND IN SOUL.
THEN, THIS WOMAN'S LIFE AND FORTUNES WILL BE MINE TO DO WITH AS I LIKE.
MY DEAR TSUBAKI. DO NOT UNDER-ESTIMATE THIS CREATURE CALLED KAGOME.
FFF...
HUH. DON'T MAKE ME LAUGH.
THE FOOL DIDN'T EVEN NOTICE THAT SHE'D BEEN AFFLICTED WITH A JUSO.*

*A FEROCIOUS CURSE.

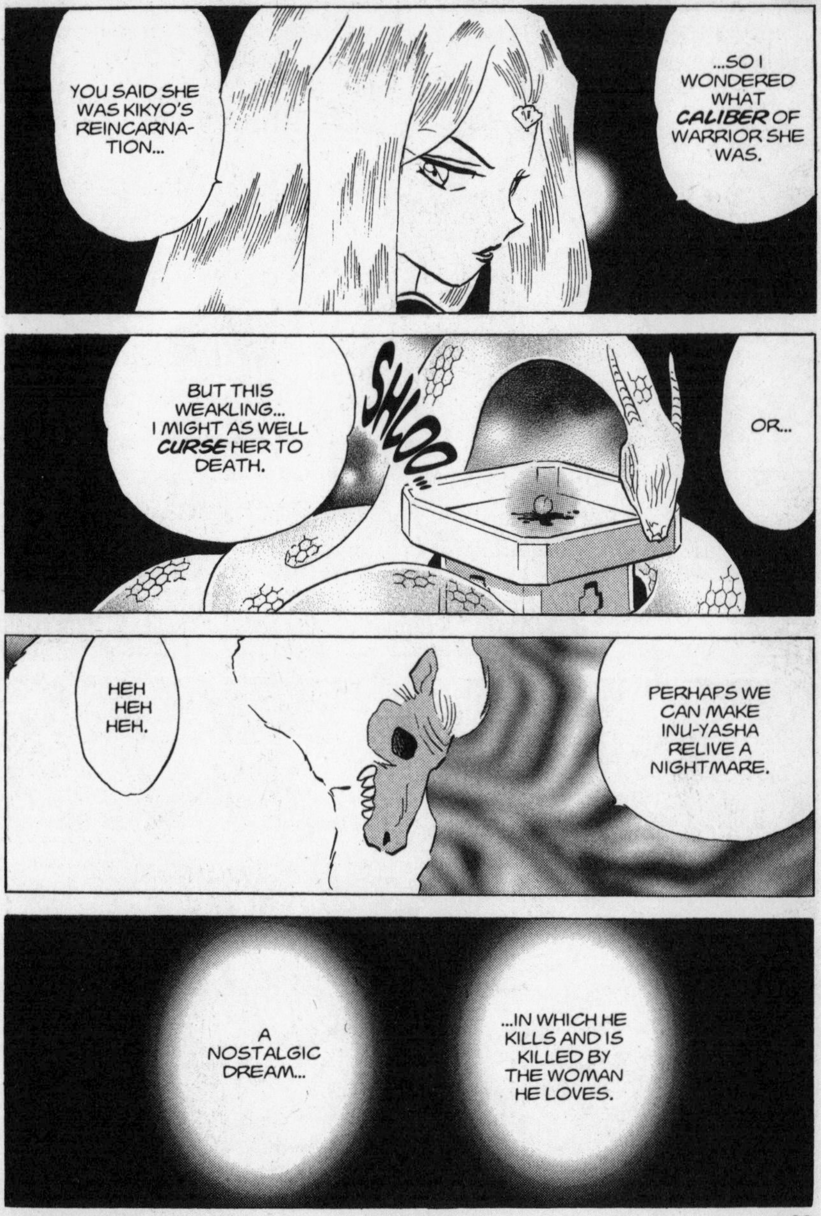
YOU SAID SHE WAS KIKYO'S REINCARNATION...
...SO I WONDERED WHAT CALIBER OF WARRIOR SHE WAS.
BUT THIS WEAKLING... I MIGHT AS WELL CURSE HER TO DEATH.
SHLOO
OR...
HEH HEH HEH.
PERHAPS WE CAN MAKE INU-YASHA RELIVE A NIGHTMARE.
A NOSTALGIC DREAM...
...IN WHICH HE KILLS AND IS KILLED BY THE WOMAN HE LOVES.

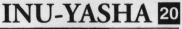

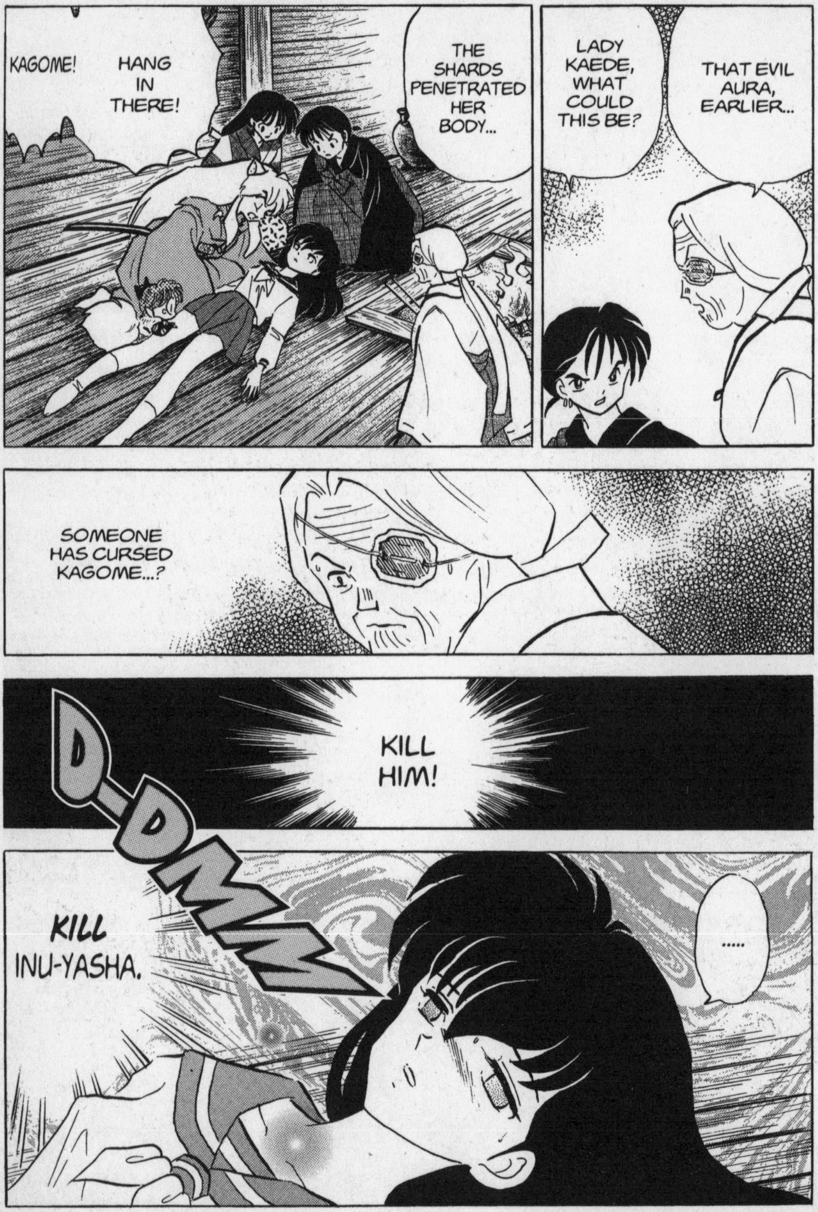
KAGOME!
HANG IN THERE!
THE SHARDS PENETRATED HER BODY...
LADY KAEDE, WHAT COULD THIS BE?
THAT EVIL AURA, EARLIER...
SOMEONE HAS CURSED KAGOME...?
KILL HIM!
D-DMMM
KILL INU-YASHA.
.....

SCROLL SIX
THE CURSE

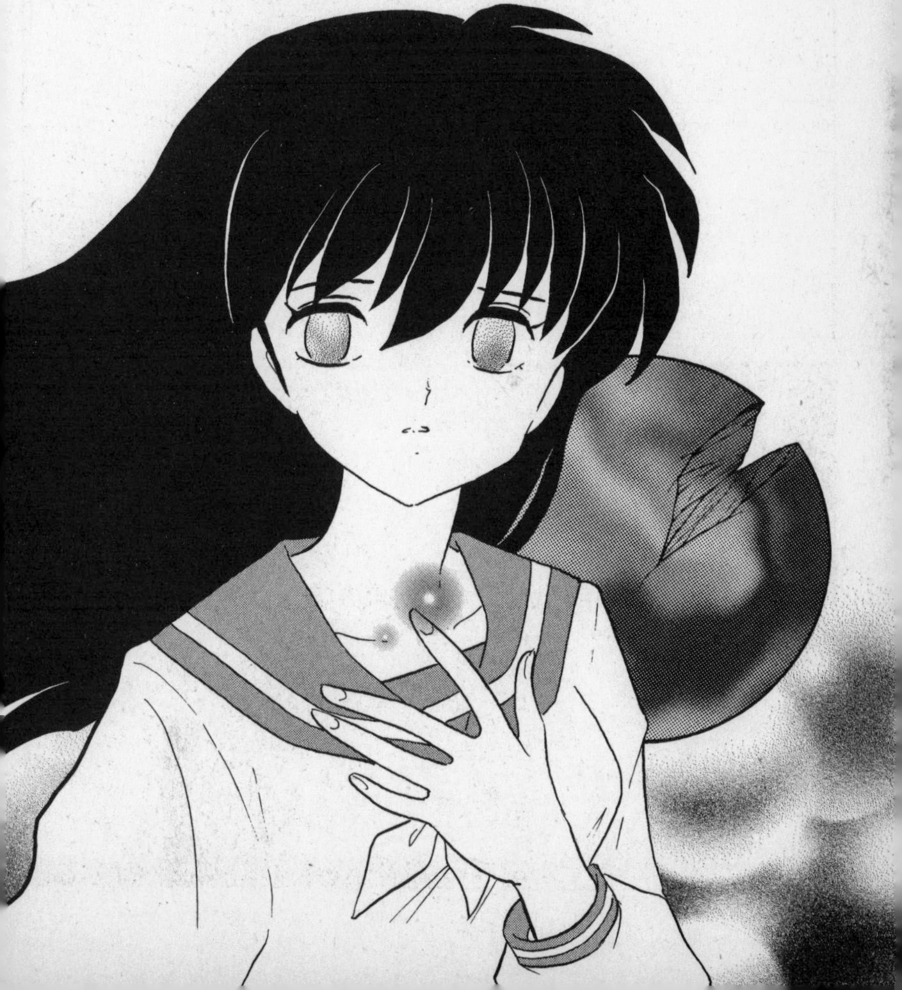

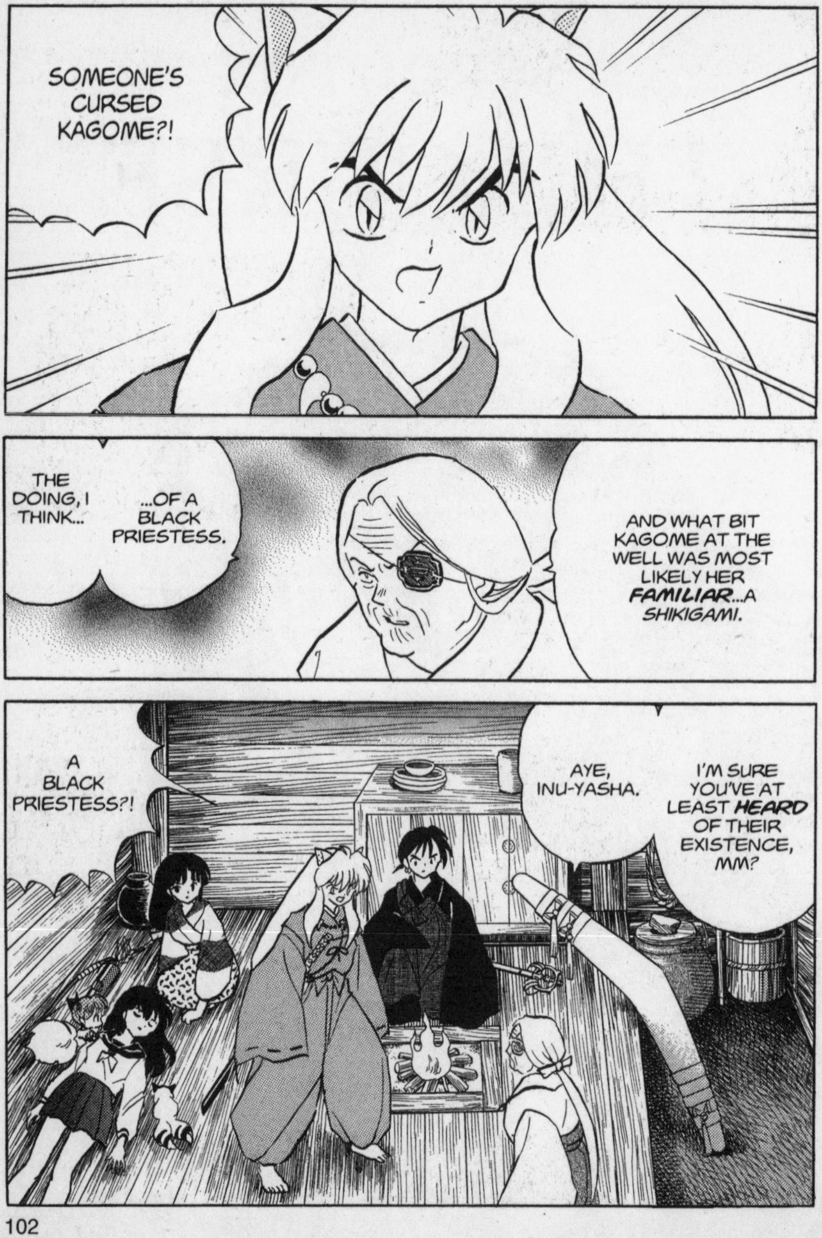
SOMEONE'S CURSED KAGOME?!
THE DOING, I THINK...
...OF A BLACK PRIESTESS.
AND WHAT BIT KAGOME AT THE WELL WAS MOST LIKELY HER FAMILIAR...A SHIKIGAMI.
A BLACK PRIESTESS?!
AYE, INU-YASHA.
I'M SURE YOU'VE AT LEAST HEARD OF THEIR EXISTENCE, MM?

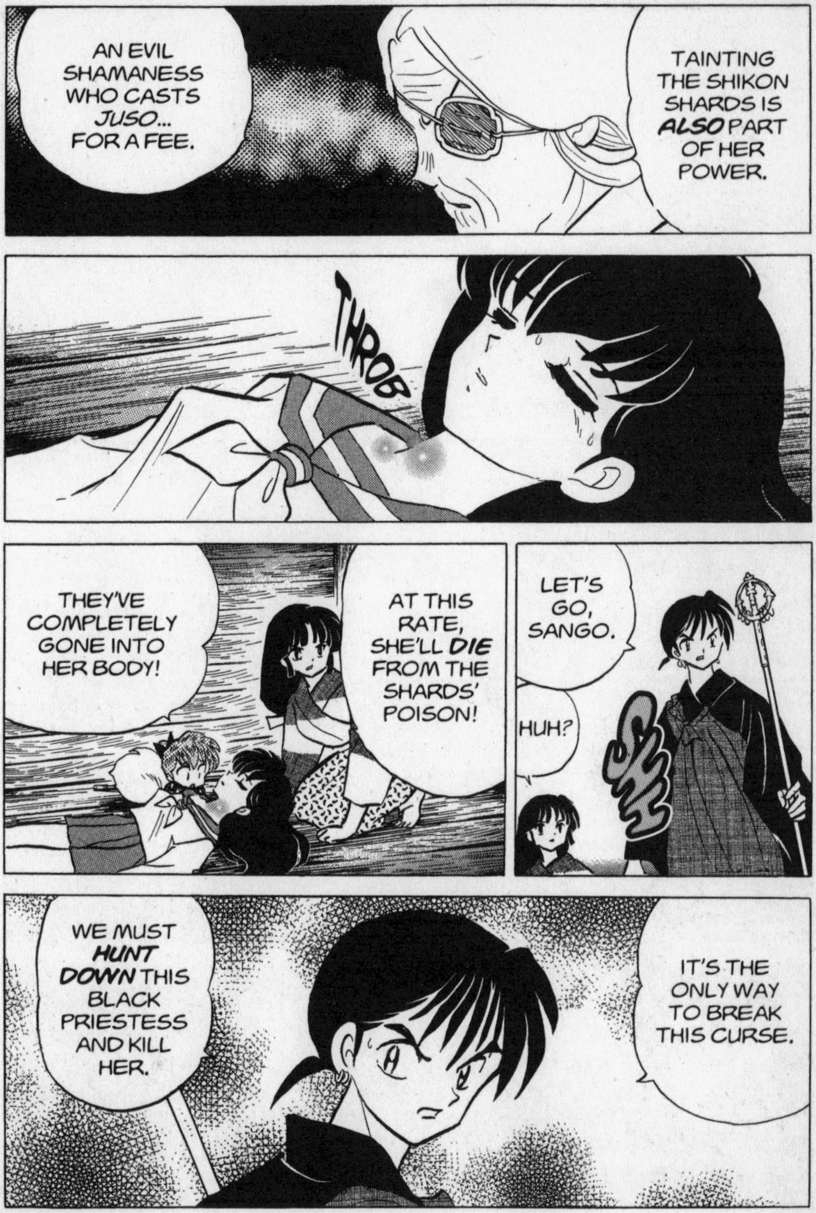
AN EVIL SHAMANESS WHO CASTS JUSO... FOR A FEE.
TAINTING THE SHIKON SHARDS IS ALSO PART OF HER POWER.
THROB
THEY'VE COMPLETELY GONE INTO HER BODY!
AT THIS RATE, SHE'LL DIE FROM THE SHARDS' POISON!
LET'S GO, SANGO.
HUH?
WE MUST HUNT DOWN THIS BLACK PRIESTESS AND KILL HER.
IT'S THE ONLY WAY TO BREAK THIS CURSE.

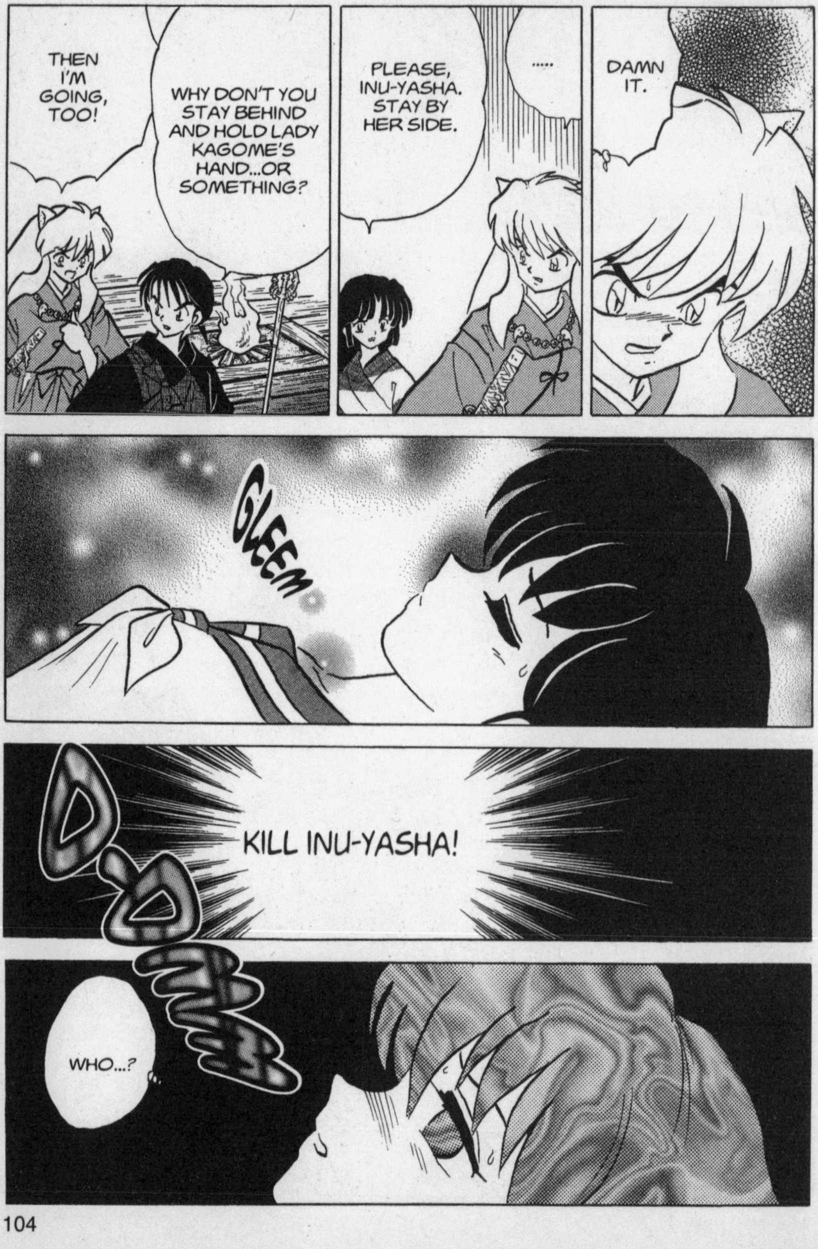
THEN I'M GOING, TOO!
WHY DON'T YOU STAY BEHIND AND HOLD LADY KAGOME'S HAND...OR SOMETHING?
PLEASE, INU-YASHA. STAY BY HER SIDE.
.....
DAMN IT.
GLEEM
KILL INU-YASHA!
D-DMMM
WHO...?

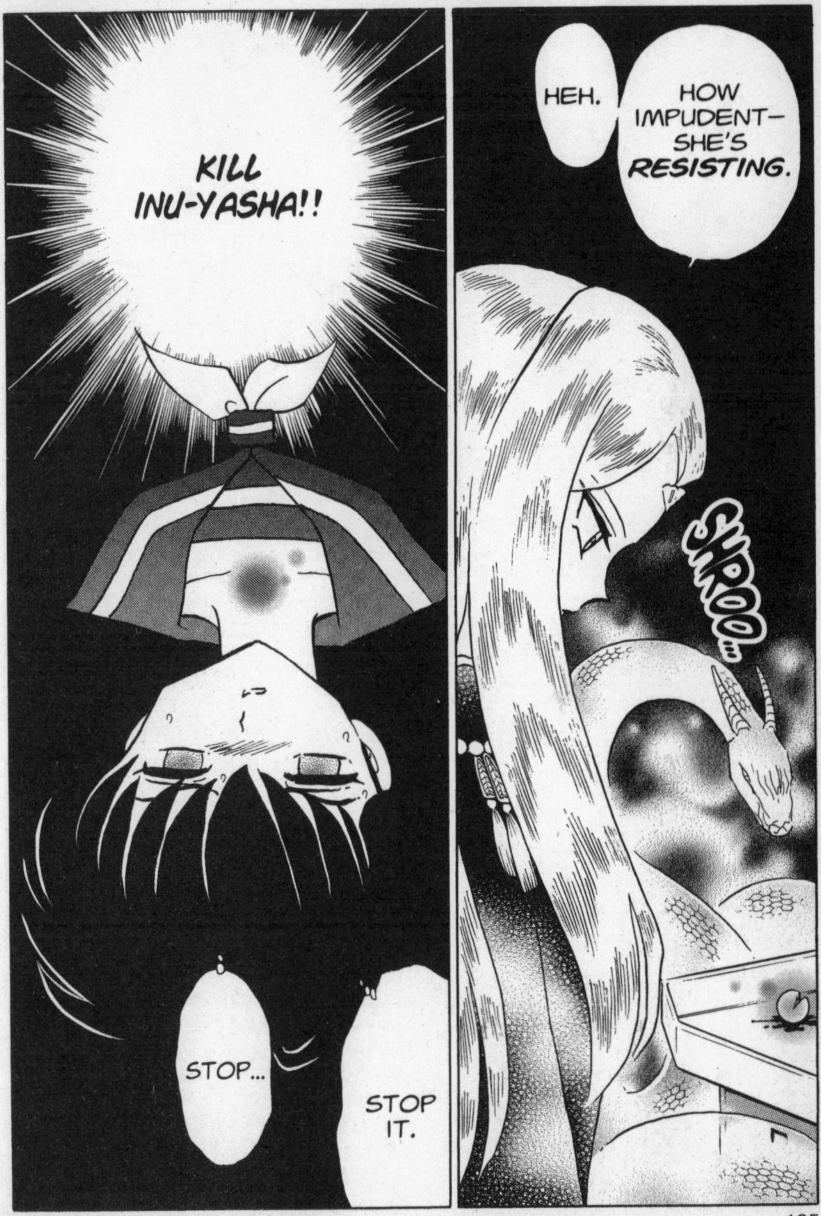
KILL INU-YASHA!!
STOP...
STOP IT.
HEH.
HOW IMPUDENT—SHE'S RESISTING.
SHROO...

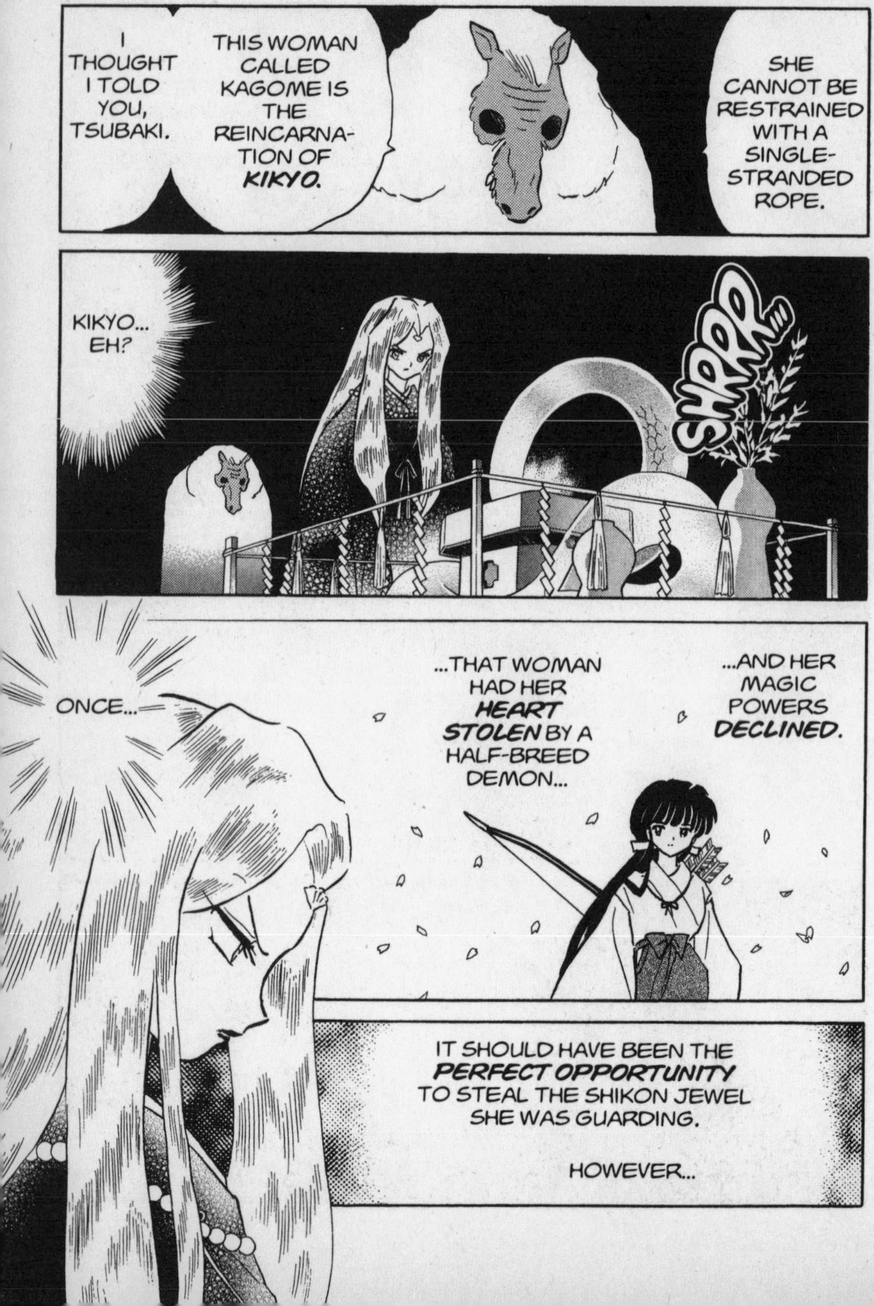
I THOUGHT I TOLD YOU, TSUBAKI.
THIS WOMAN CALLED KAGOME IS THE REINCARNATION OF ***KIKYO.***
SHE CANNOT BE RESTRAINED WITH A SINGLE-STRANDED ROPE.
KIKYO... EH?
SHRRR...
ONCE...
...THAT WOMAN HAD HER ***HEART STOLEN*** BY A HALF-BREED DEMON...
...AND HER MAGIC POWERS ***DECLINED.***
IT SHOULD HAVE BEEN THE ***PERFECT OPPORTUNITY*** TO STEAL THE SHIKON JEWEL SHE WAS GUARDING.
HOWEVER...

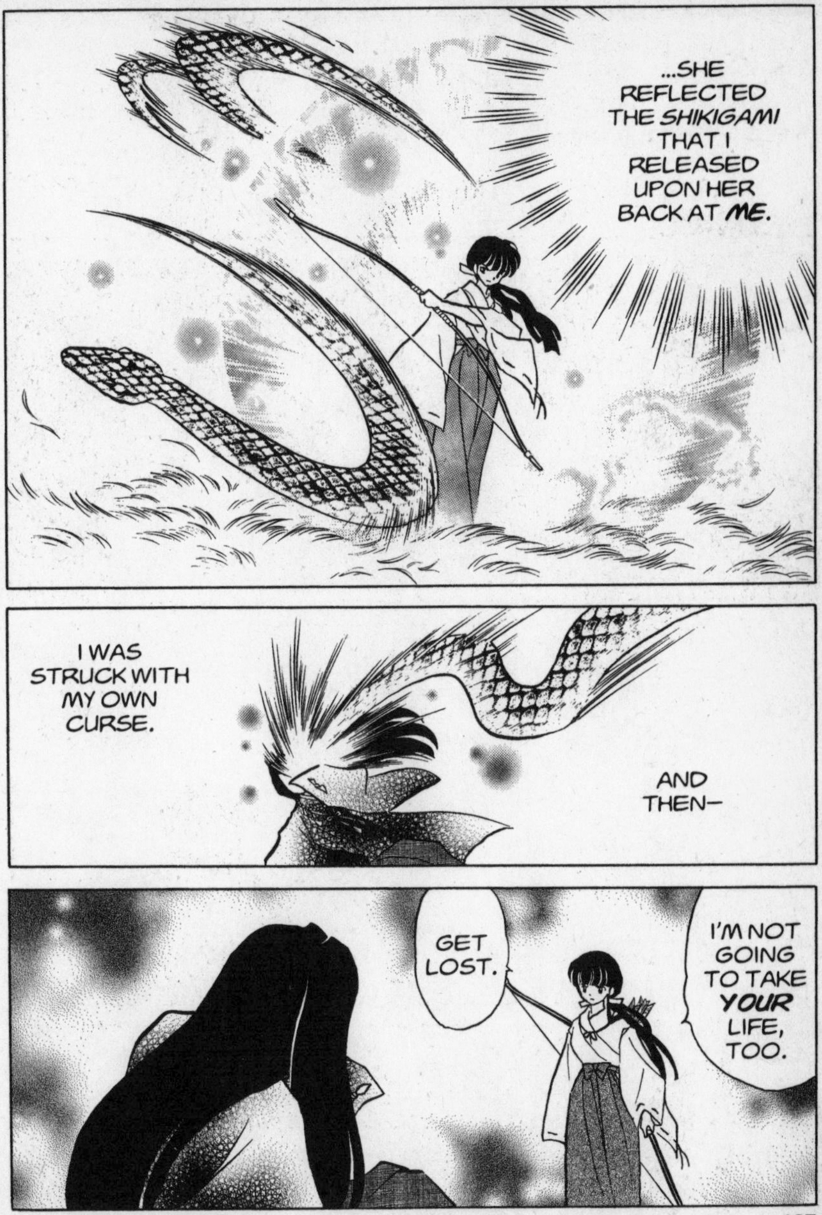
...SHE REFLECTED THE SHIKIGAMI THAT I RELEASED UPON HER BACK AT ME.
I WAS STRUCK WITH MY OWN CURSE.
AND THEN–
GET LOST.
I'M NOT GOING TO TAKE YOUR LIFE, TOO.

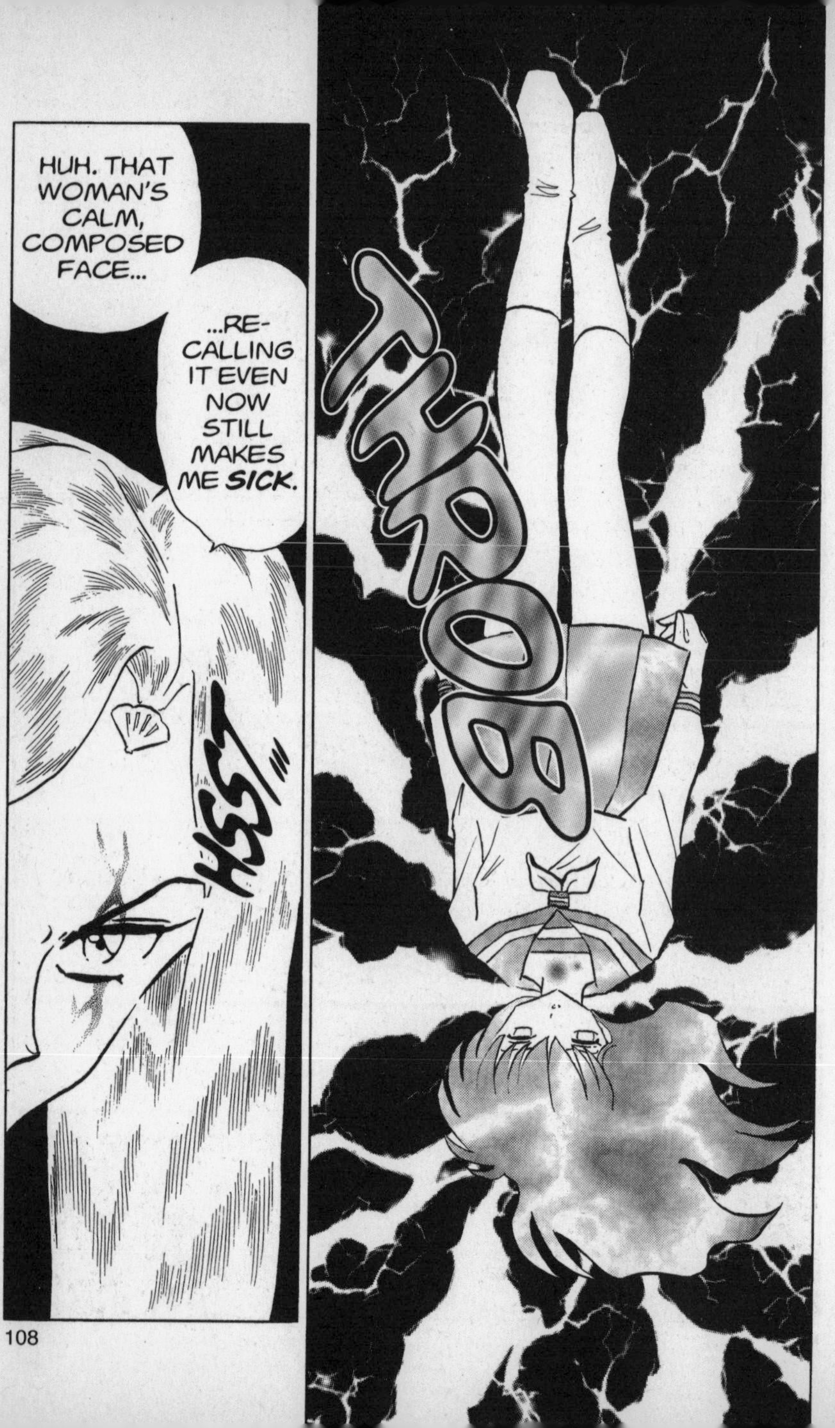
HUH. THAT WOMAN'S CALM, COMPOSED FACE...
...RE-CALLING IT EVEN NOW STILL MAKES ME **SICK**.
HSSST!!!
THROB

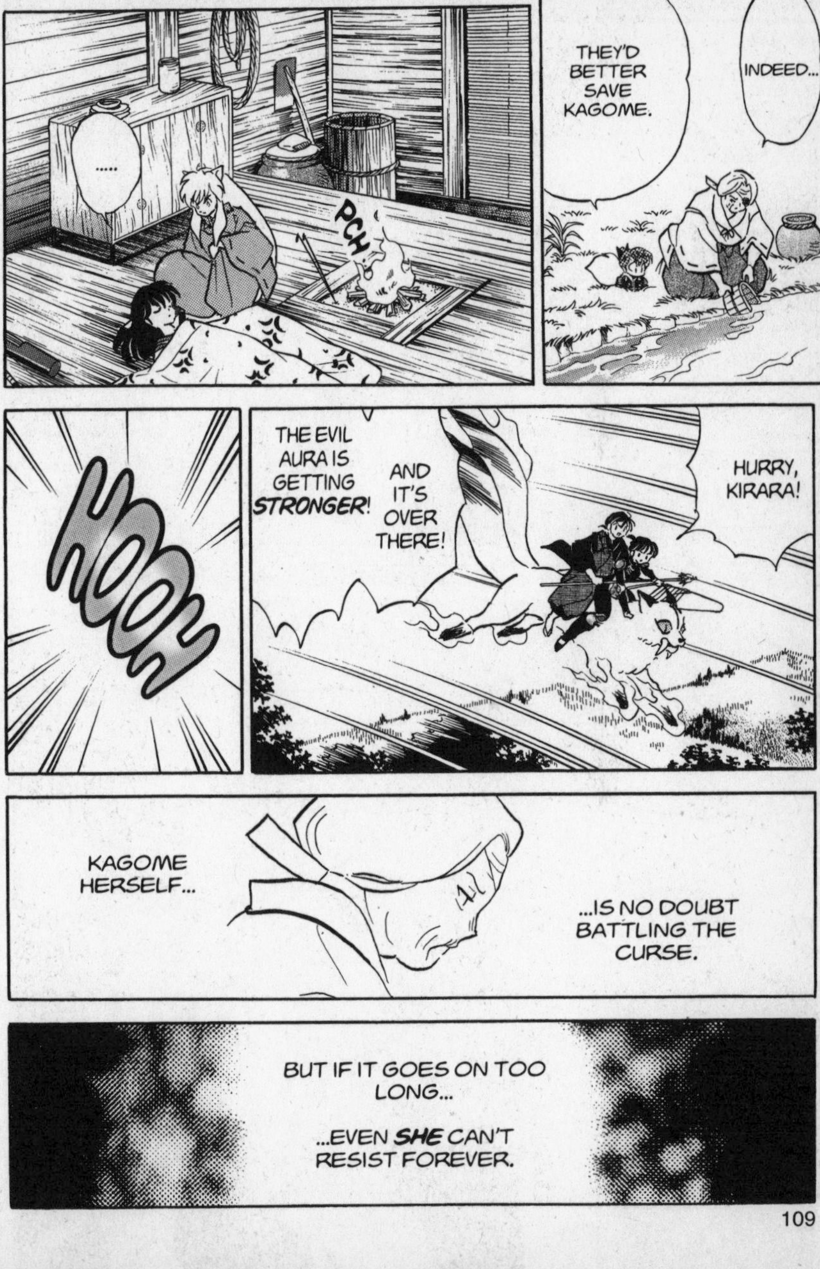
.....
PCH
THEY'D BETTER SAVE KAGOME.
INDEED...
HOOOH
THE EVIL AURA IS GETTING STRONGER!
AND IT'S OVER THERE!
HURRY, KIRARA!
KAGOME HERSELF...
...IS NO DOUBT BATTLING THE CURSE.
BUT IF IT GOES ON TOO LONG...
...EVEN SHE CAN'T RESIST FOREVER.

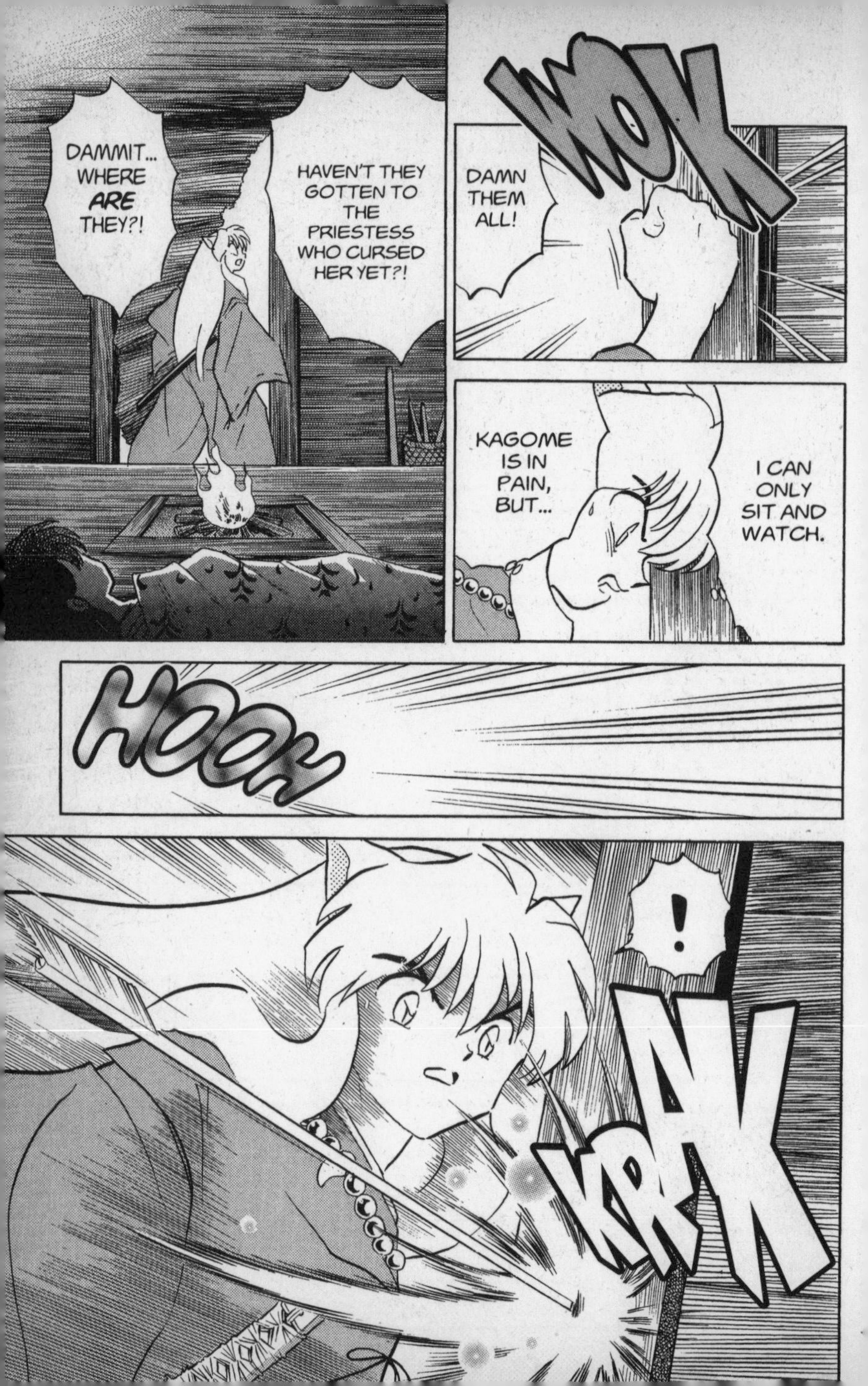
DAMMIT... WHERE ARE THEY?!
HAVEN'T THEY GOTTEN TO THE PRIESTESS WHO CURSED HER YET?!
WOK
DAMN THEM ALL!
KAGOME IS IN PAIN, BUT...
I CAN ONLY SIT AND WATCH.
HOOH
!
KRAK

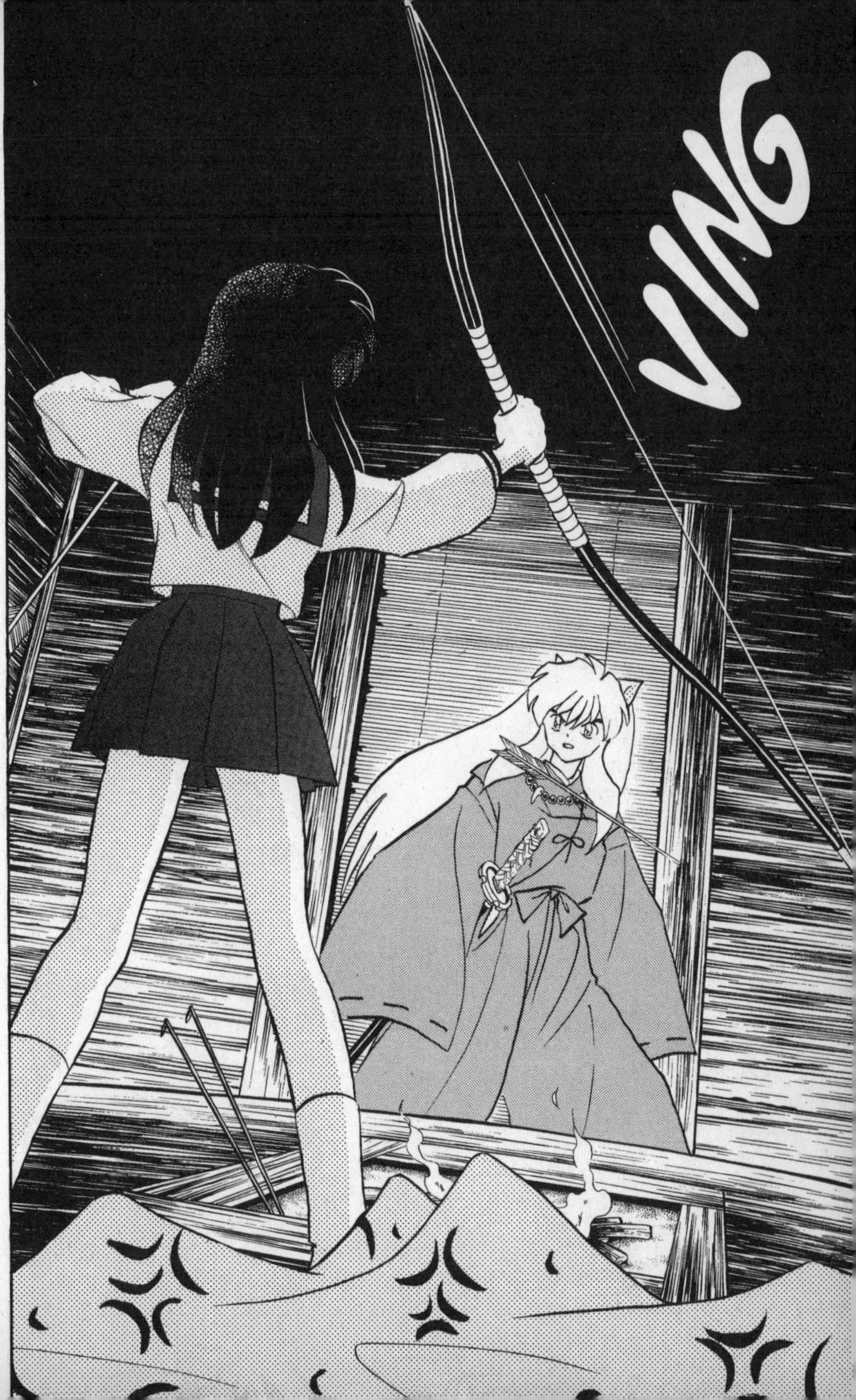
VING

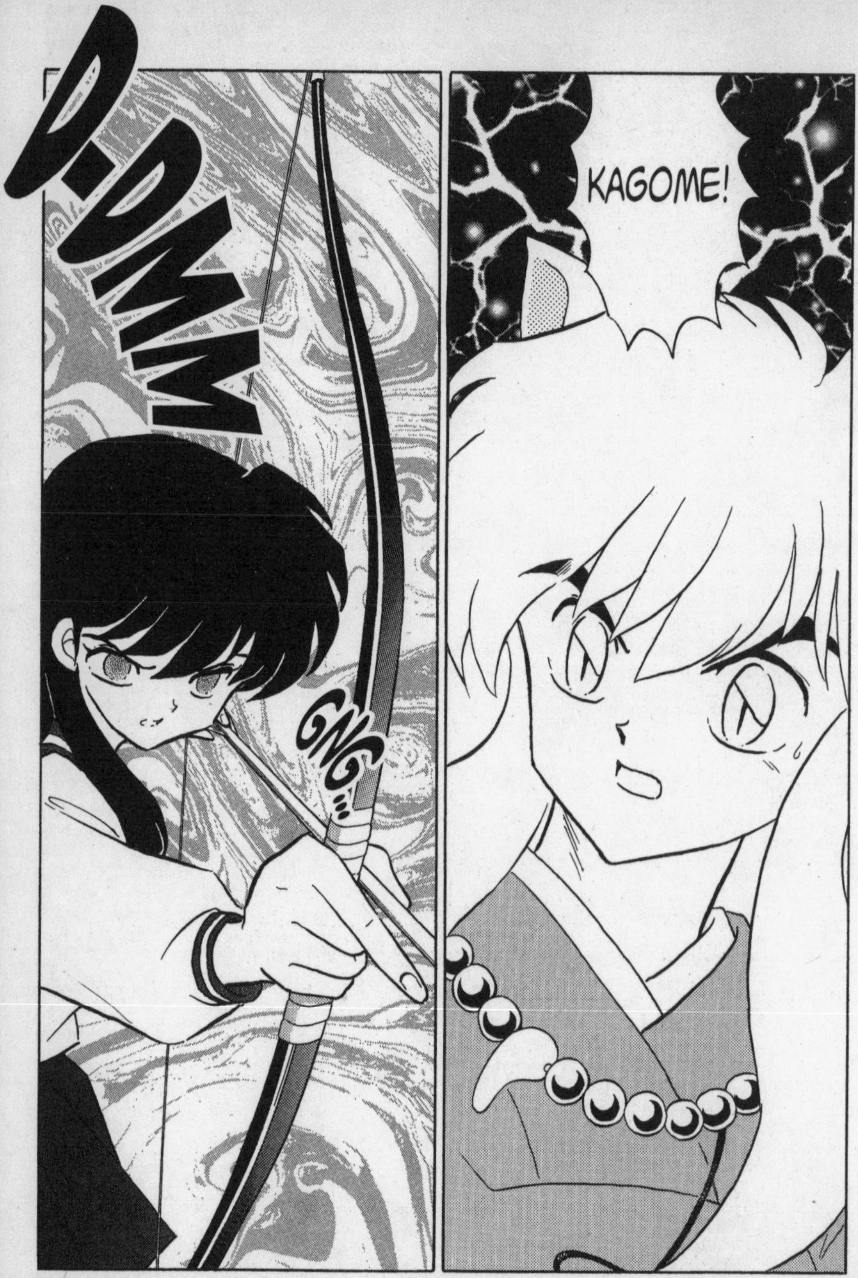
D-DMM!
GNG...
KAGOME!

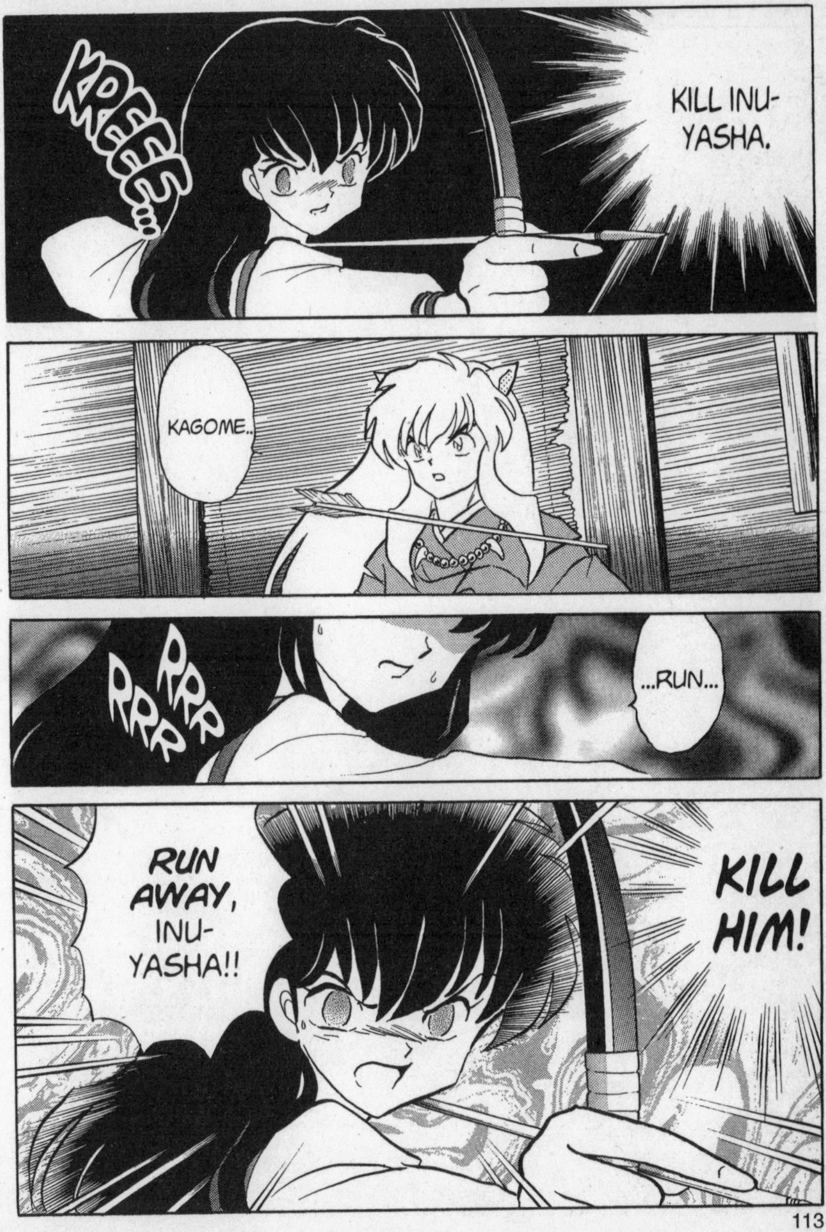
KREEE...
KILL INU-
YASHA.
KAGOME...
RRR
RRR
...RUN...
RUN
AWAY,
INU-
YASHA!!
KILL
HIM!

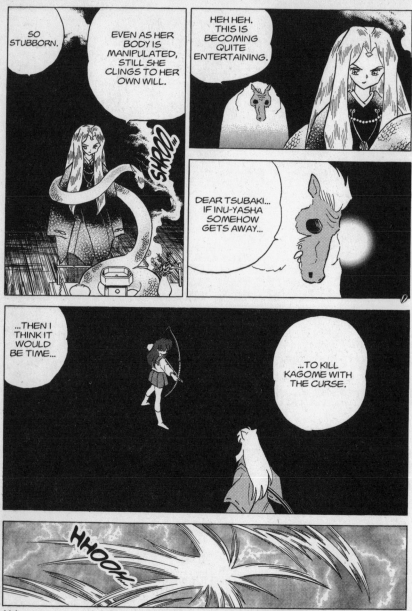

SO STUBBORN.

EVEN AS HER BODY IS MANIPULATED, STILL SHE CLINGS TO HER OWN WILL.

HEH HEH. THIS IS BECOMING QUITE ENTERTAINING.

SHROO...

DEAR TSUBAKI... IF INU-YASHA SOMEHOW GETS AWAY...

...THEN I THINK IT WOULD BE TIME...

...TO KILL KAGOME WITH THE CURSE.

HHOOH!

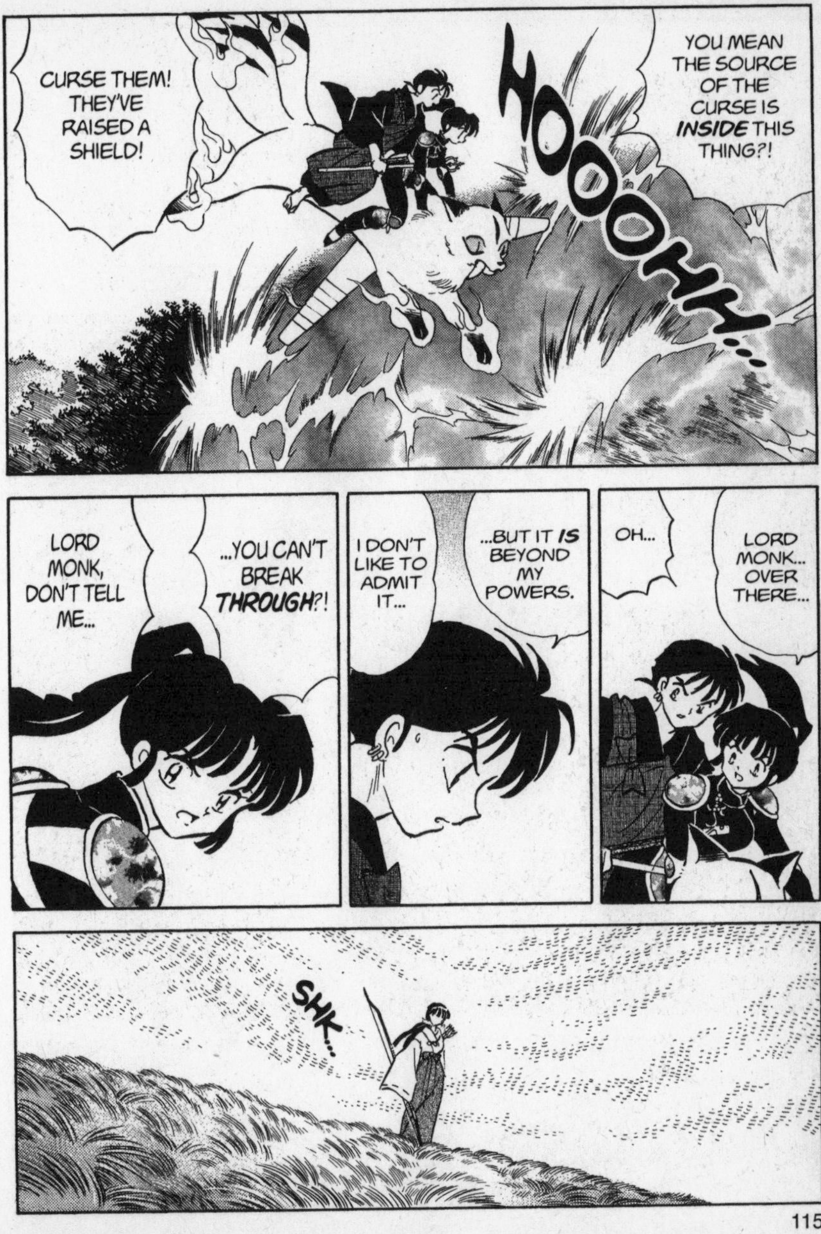
CURSE THEM! THEY'VE RAISED A SHIELD!
HOOOOHH...
YOU MEAN THE SOURCE OF THE CURSE IS **INSIDE** THIS THING?!
LORD MONK, DON'T TELL ME...
...YOU CAN'T BREAK **THROUGH**?!
I DON'T LIKE TO ADMIT IT...
...BUT IT **IS** BEYOND MY POWERS.
OH...
LORD MONK... OVER THERE...
SHK...

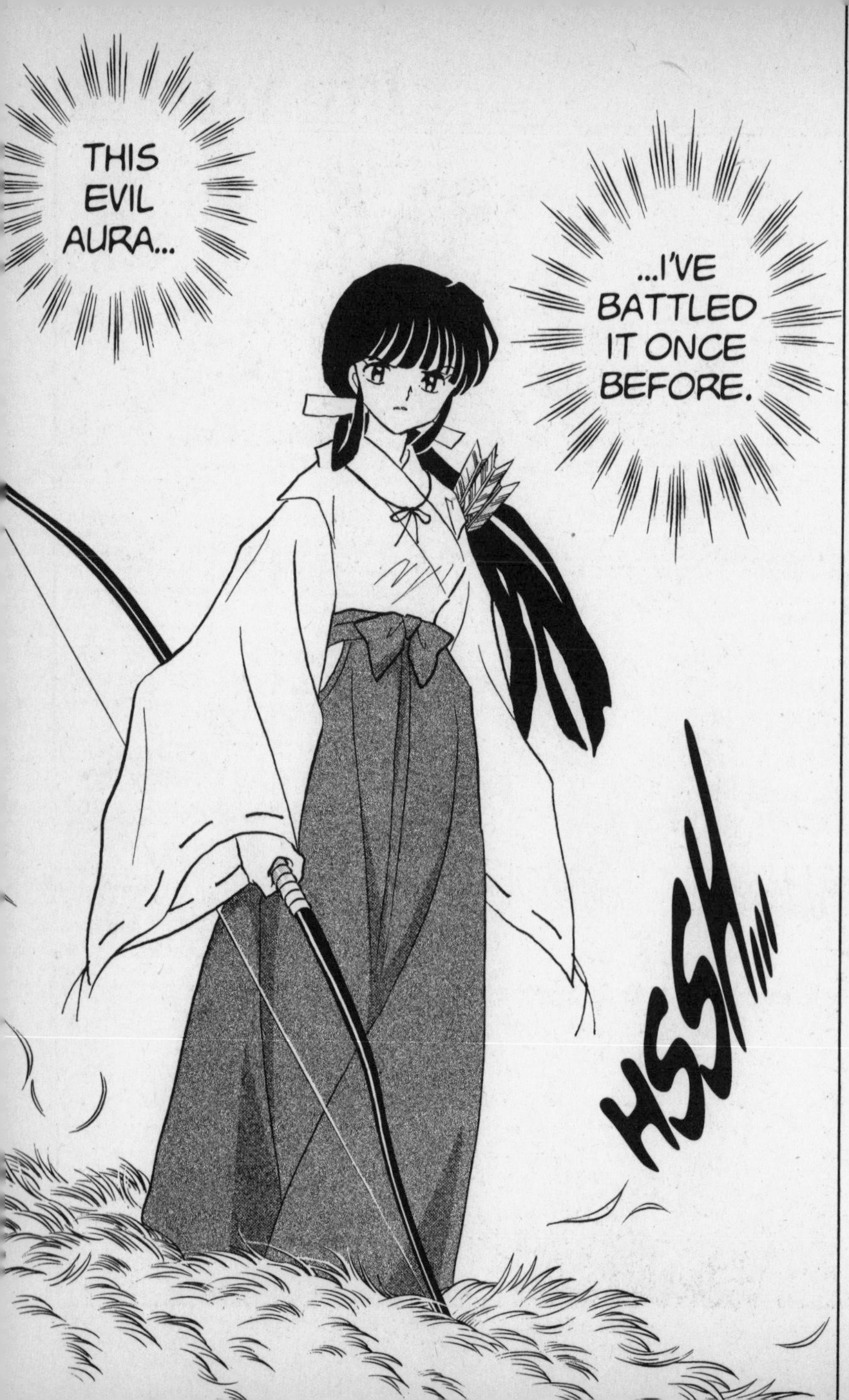
THIS EVIL AURA...
...I'VE BATTLED IT ONCE BEFORE.
HSSH

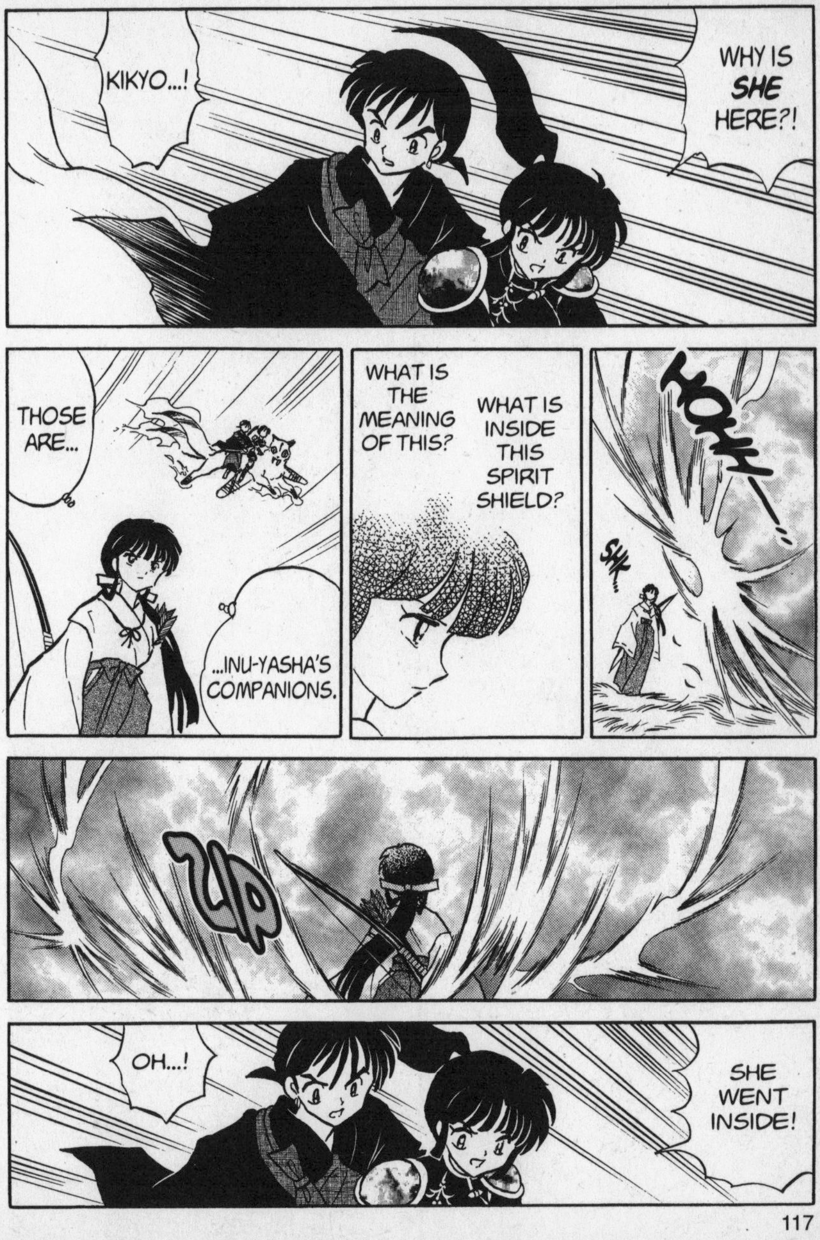
KIKYO...!
WHY IS SHE HERE?!
THOSE ARE...
...INU-YASHA'S COMPANIONS.
WHAT IS THE MEANING OF THIS?
WHAT IS INSIDE THIS SPIRIT SHIELD?
HOMM—!?
SHK...
ZIP
OH...!
SHE WENT INSIDE!

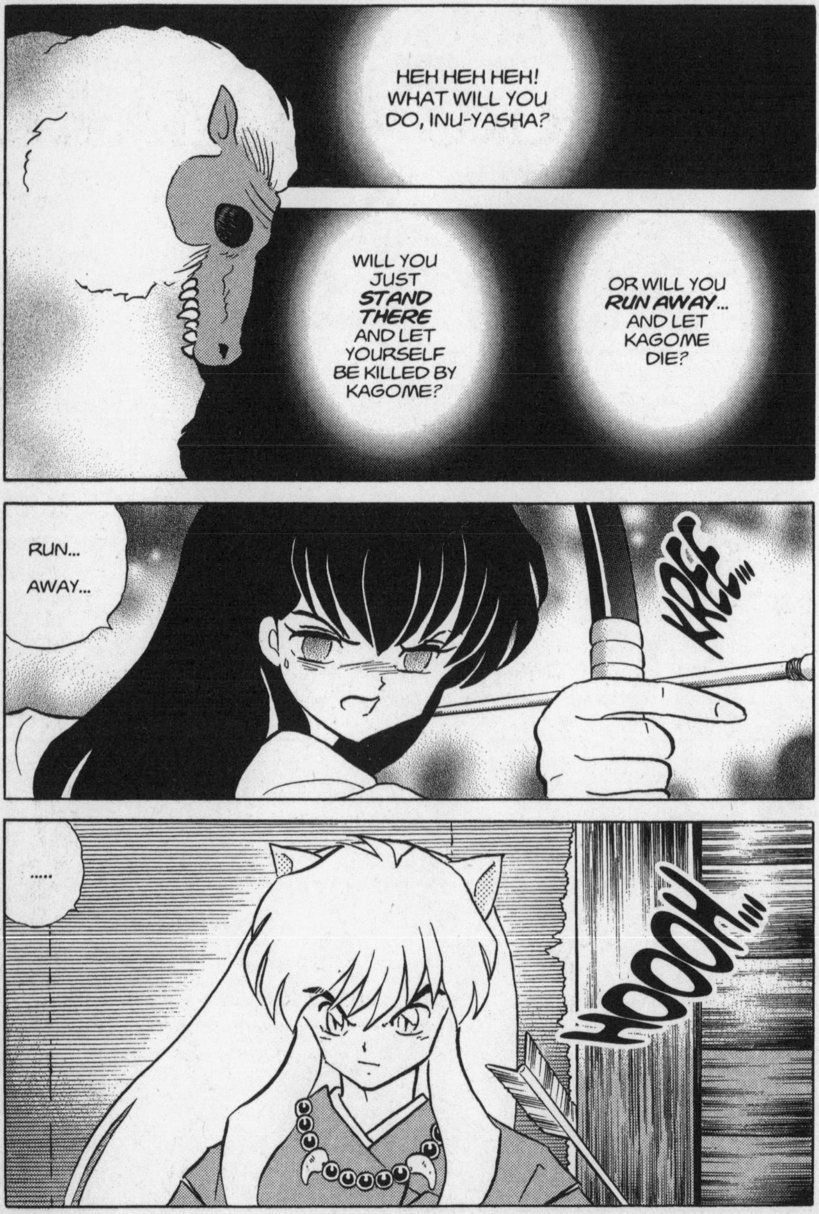
HEH HEH HEH! WHAT WILL YOU DO, INU-YASHA?
WILL YOU JUST STAND THERE AND LET YOURSELF BE KILLED BY KAGOME?
OR WILL YOU RUN AWAY... AND LET KAGOME DIE?
RUN... AWAY...
KREE...
.....
HOOOH...

SCROLL SEVEN
THE ARROW'S MARK

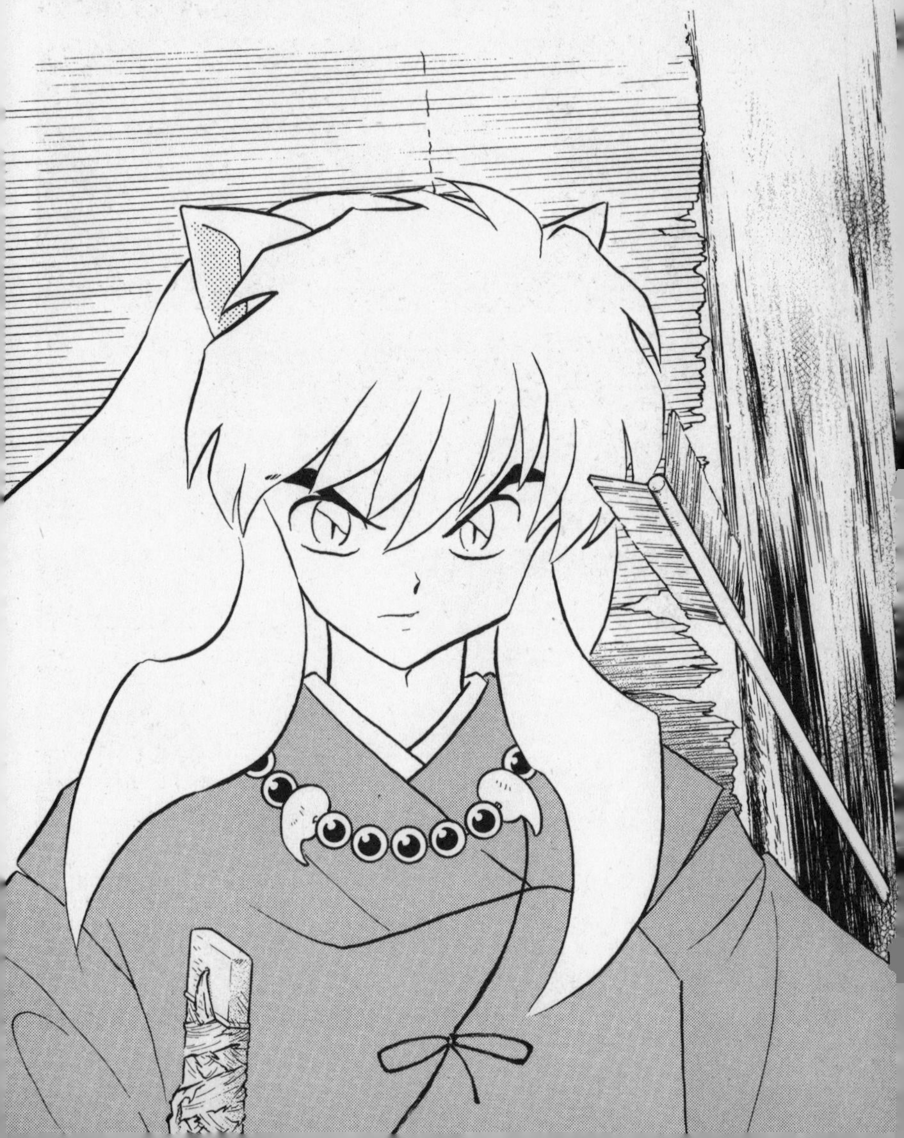

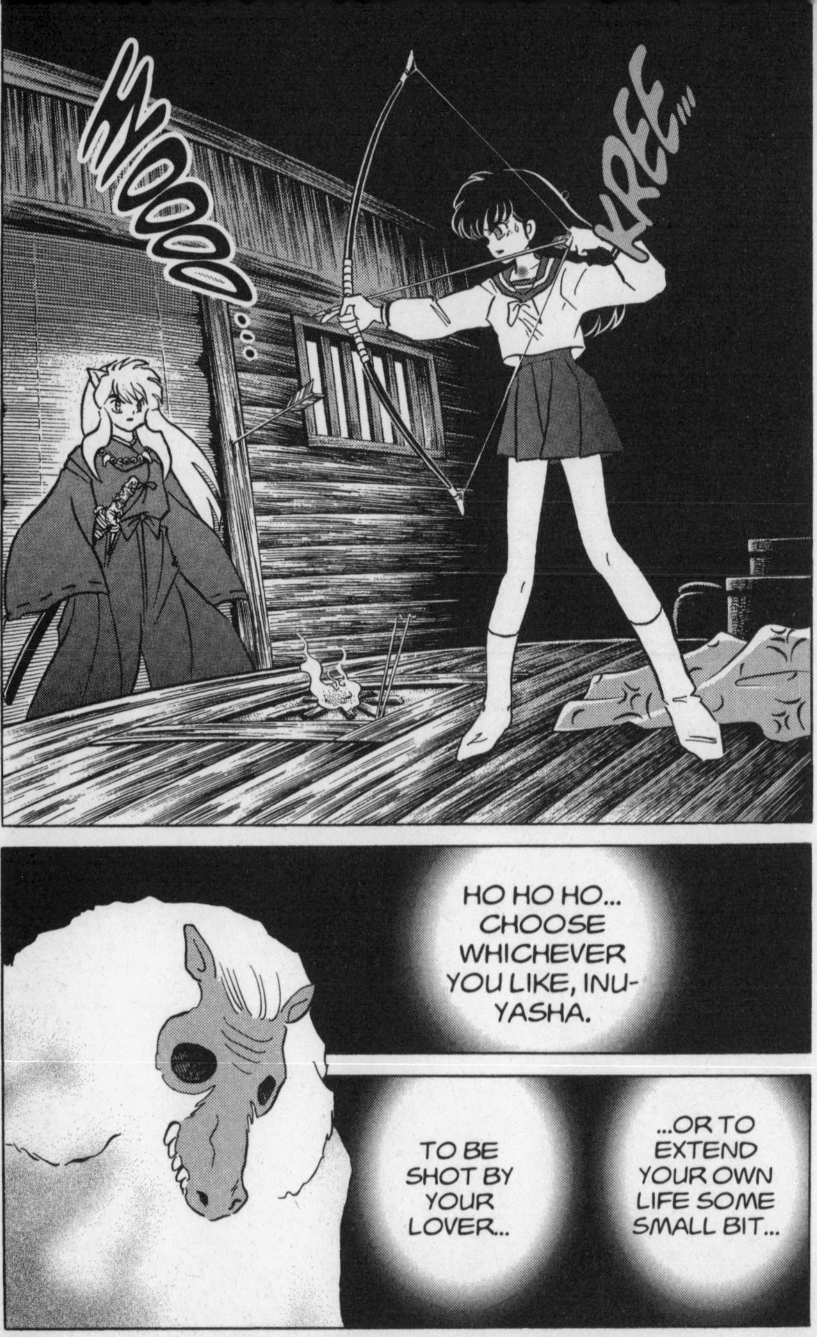
HYOOOO
KREE...
HO HO HO... CHOOSE WHICHEVER YOU LIKE, INU-YASHA.
TO BE SHOT BY YOUR LOVER...
...OR TO EXTEND YOUR OWN LIFE SOME SMALL BIT...

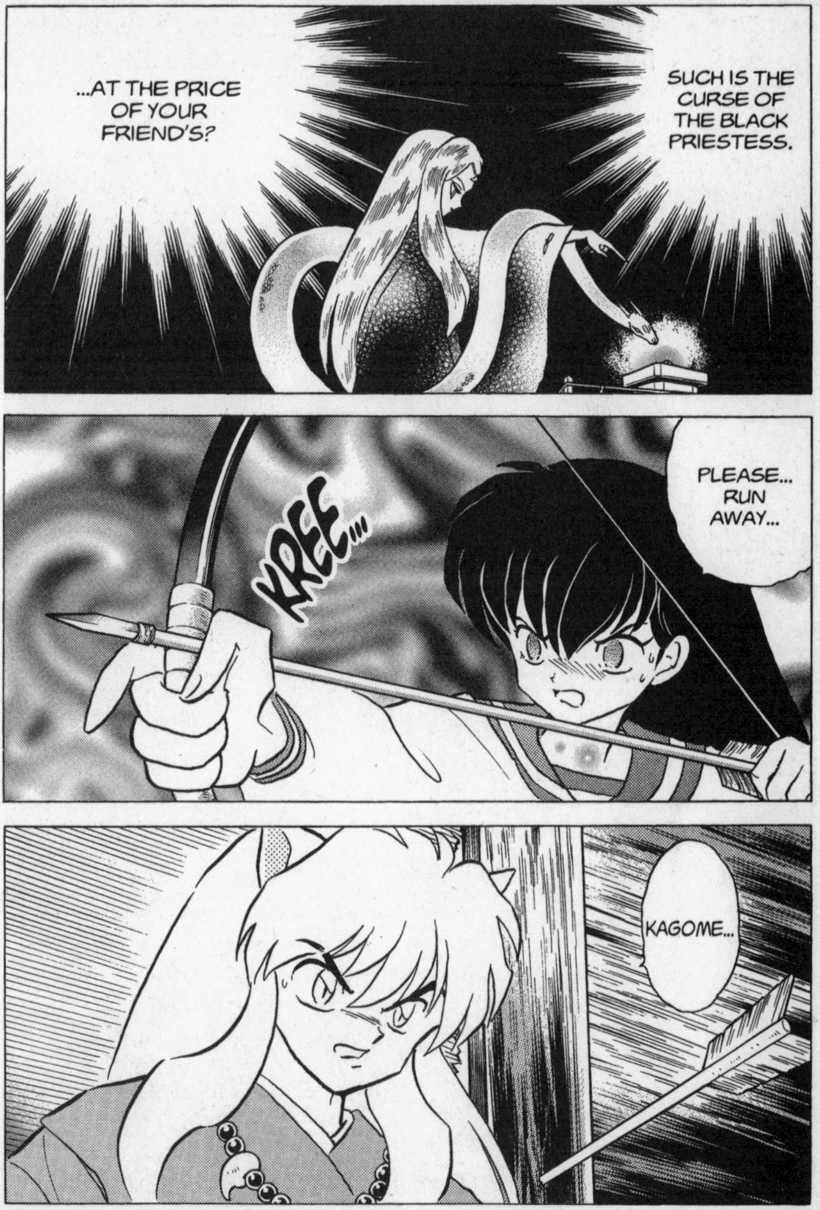
...AT THE PRICE OF YOUR FRIEND'S?
SUCH IS THE CURSE OF THE BLACK PRIESTESS.
KREE...
PLEASE... RUN AWAY...
KAGOME...

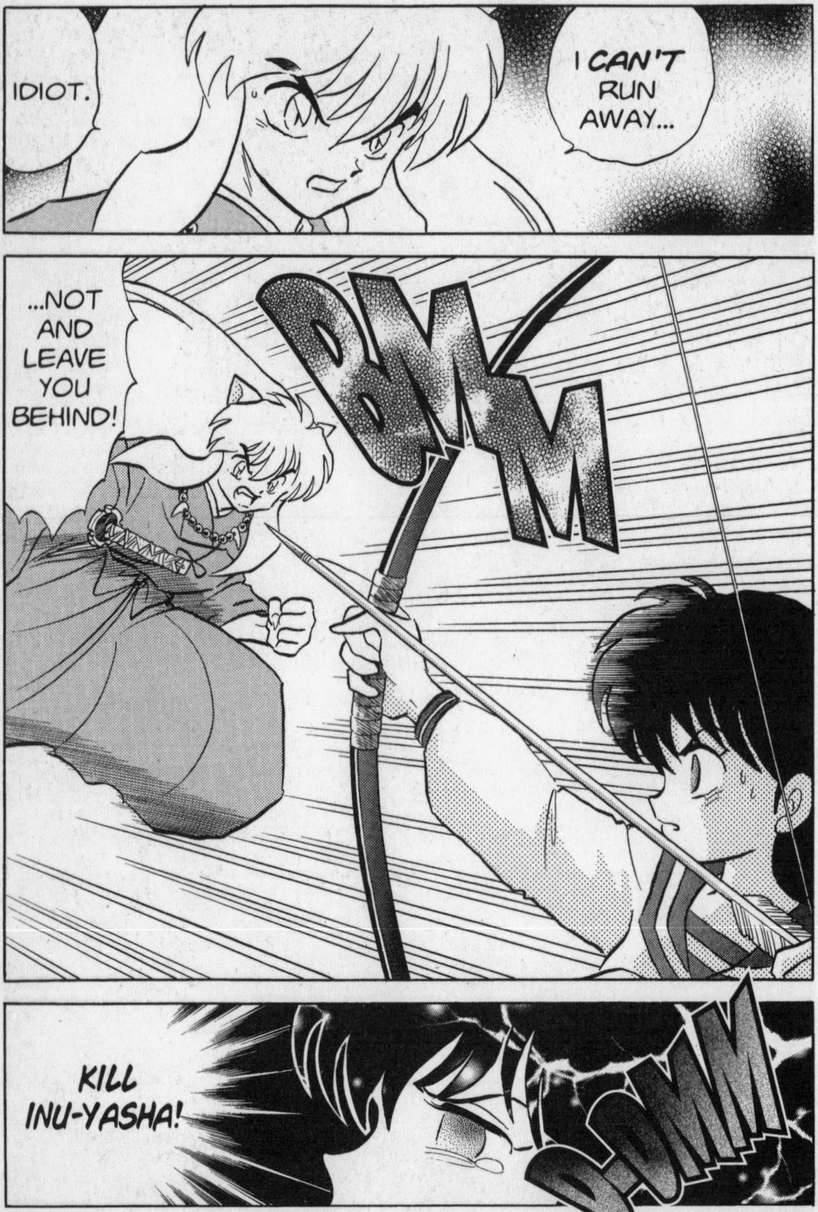
IDIOT.
I CAN'T RUN AWAY...
...NOT AND LEAVE YOU BEHIND!
KILL INU-YASHA!

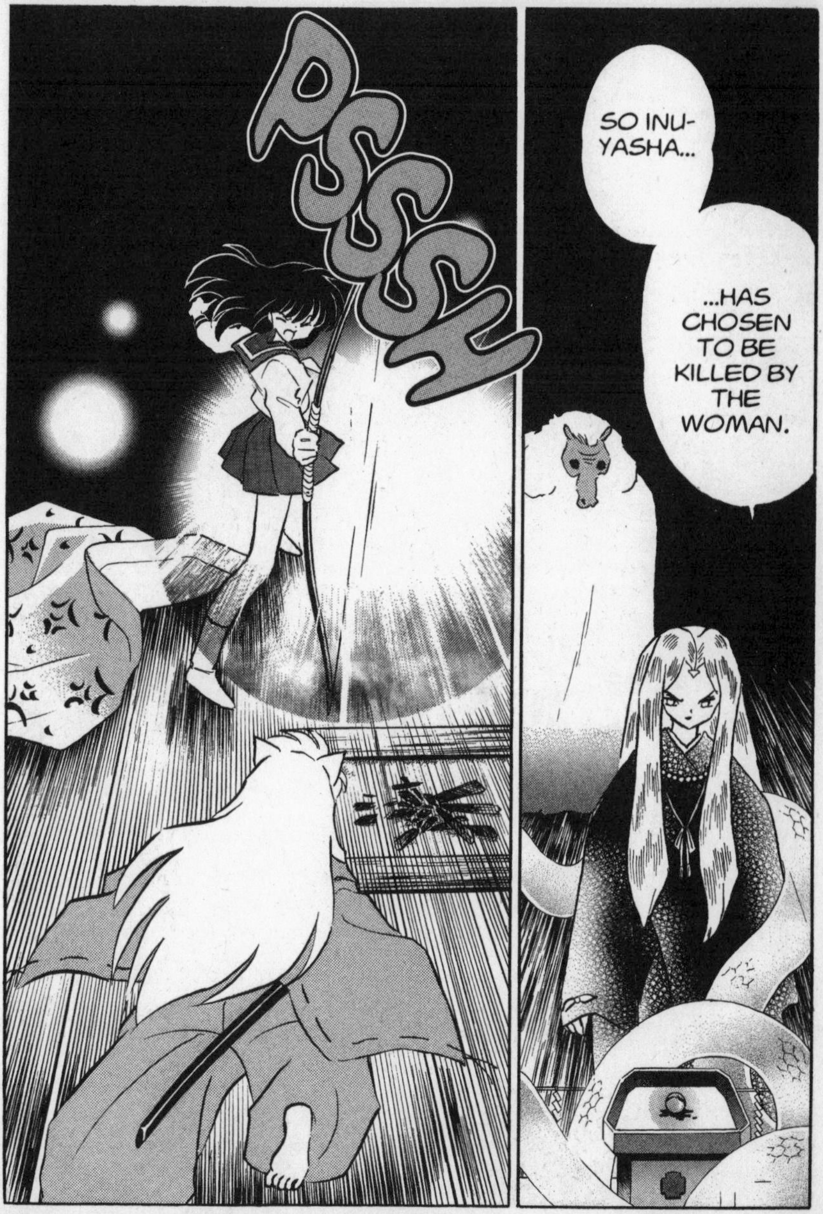
PSSSH
SO INU-YASHA...
...HAS CHOSEN TO BE KILLED BY THE WOMAN.

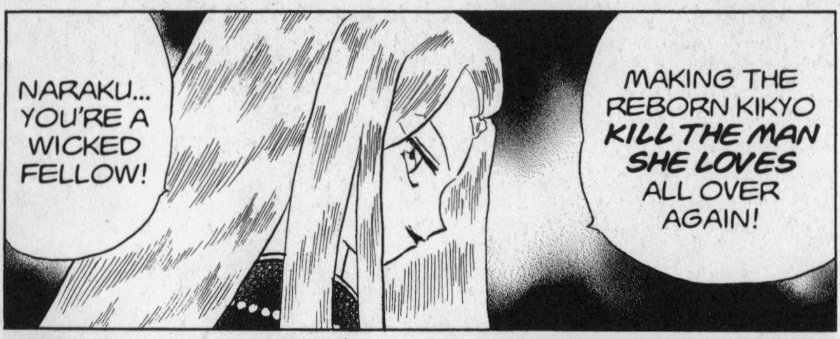
NARAKU... YOU'RE A WICKED FELLOW!
MAKING THE REBORN KIKYO **KILL THE MAN SHE LOVES** ALL OVER AGAIN!

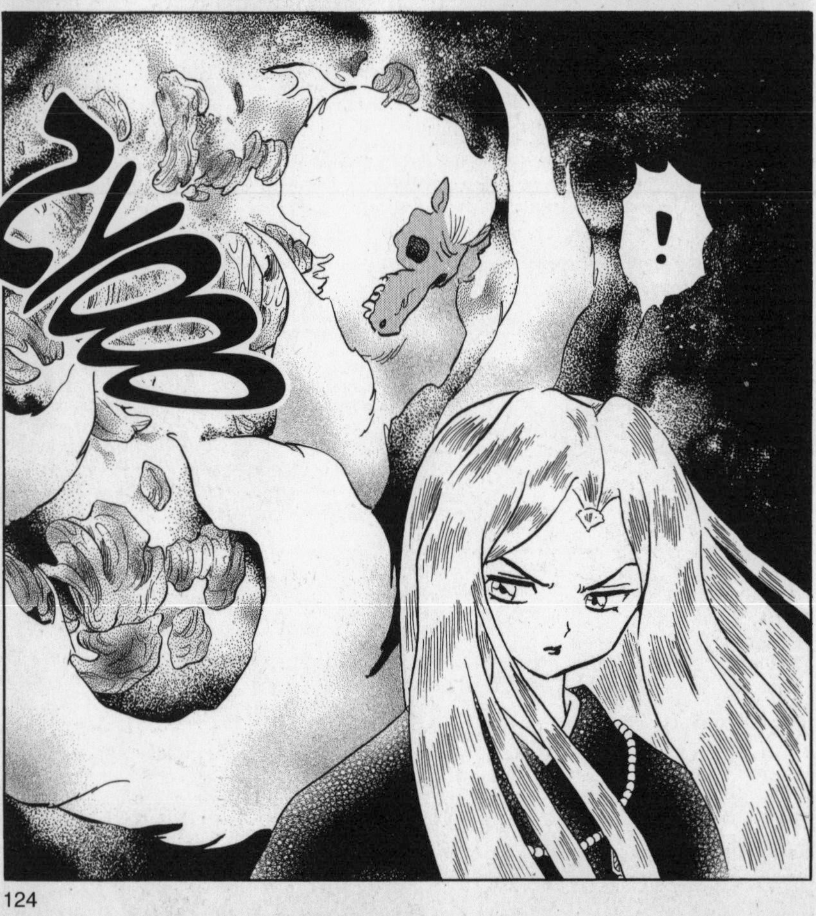
ZYOO
!

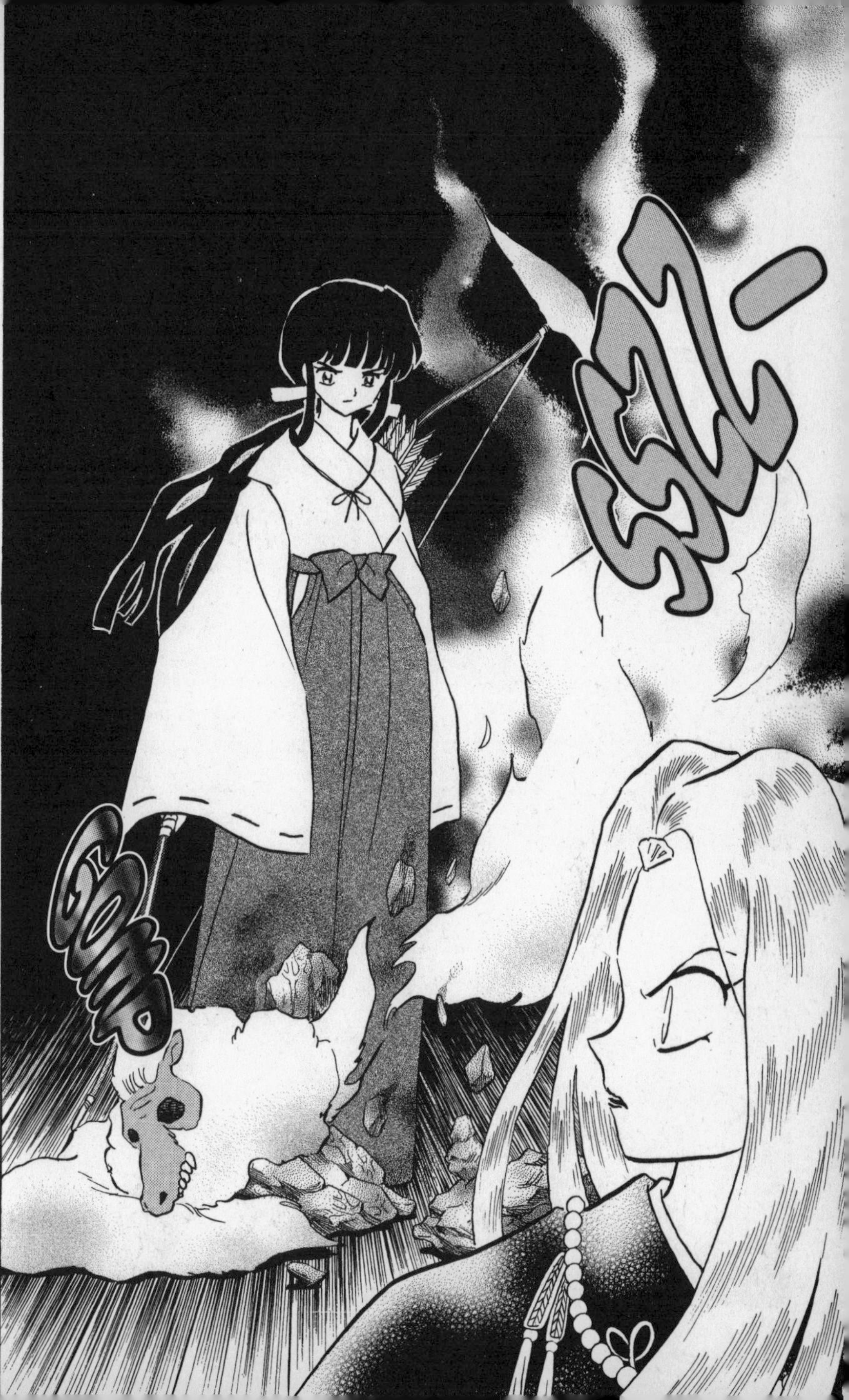
SSZZ-

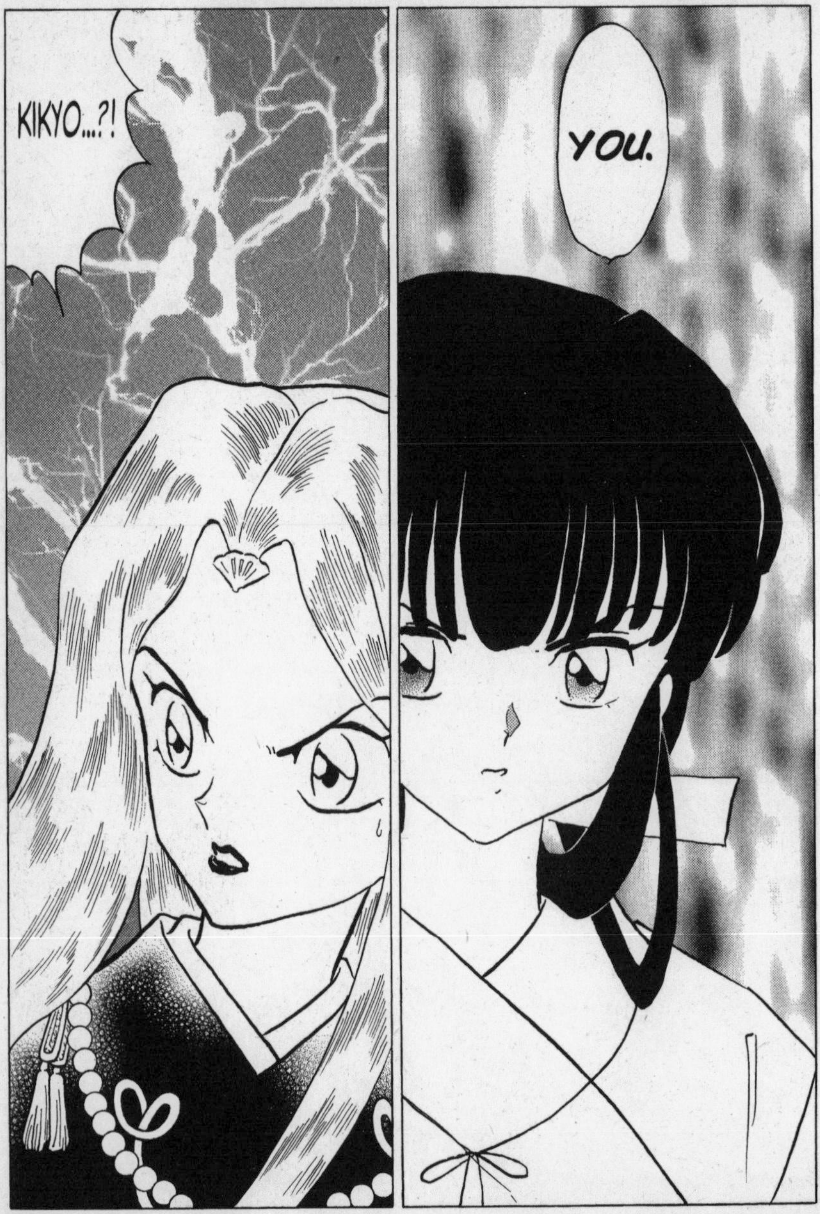
KIKYO...?!
YOU.

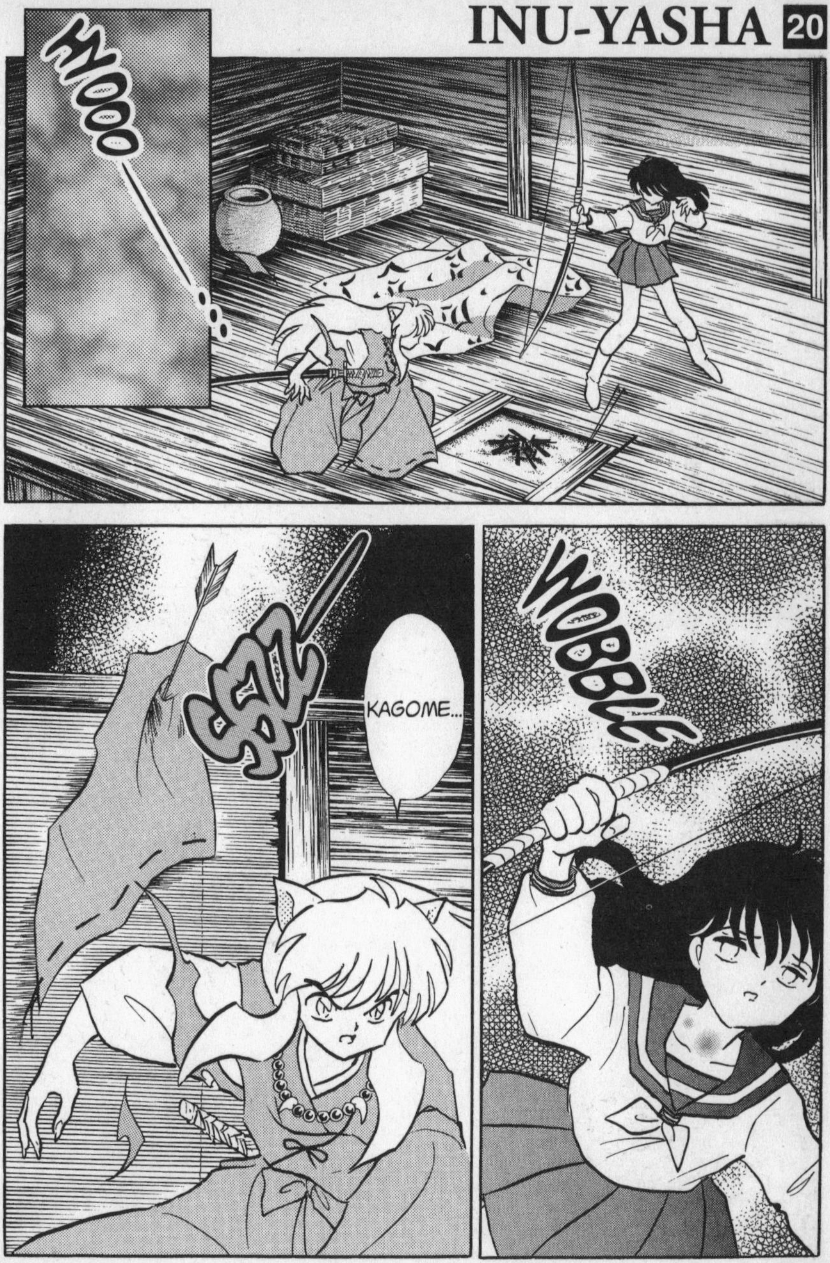
HYOOO
..
SSSZ
KAGOME...
WOBBLE

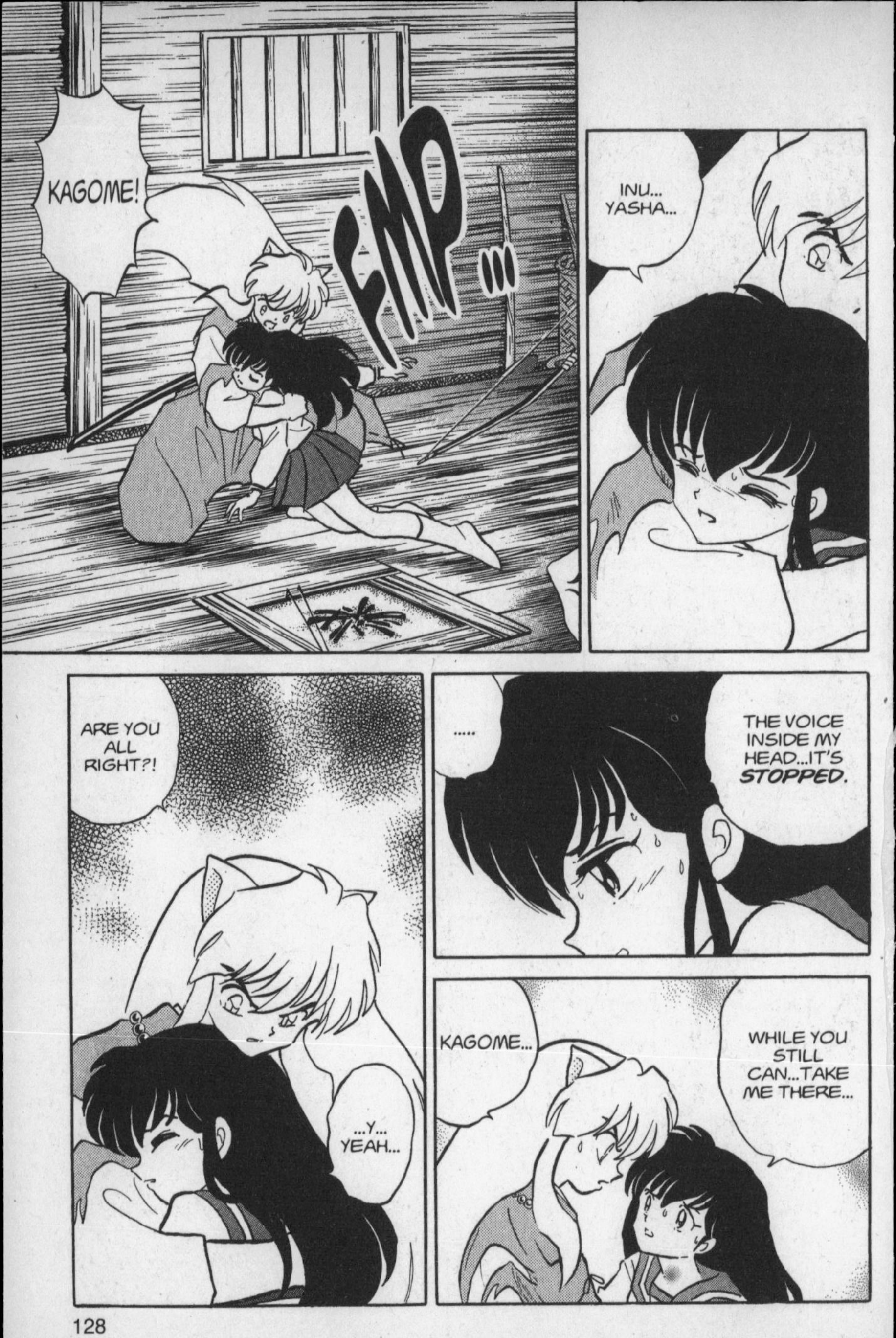
KAGOME!
FMP...
INU... YASHA...
ARE YOU ALL RIGHT?!
...Y... YEAH...
.....
THE VOICE INSIDE MY HEAD...IT'S *STOPPED*.
KAGOME...
WHILE YOU STILL CAN...TAKE ME THERE...

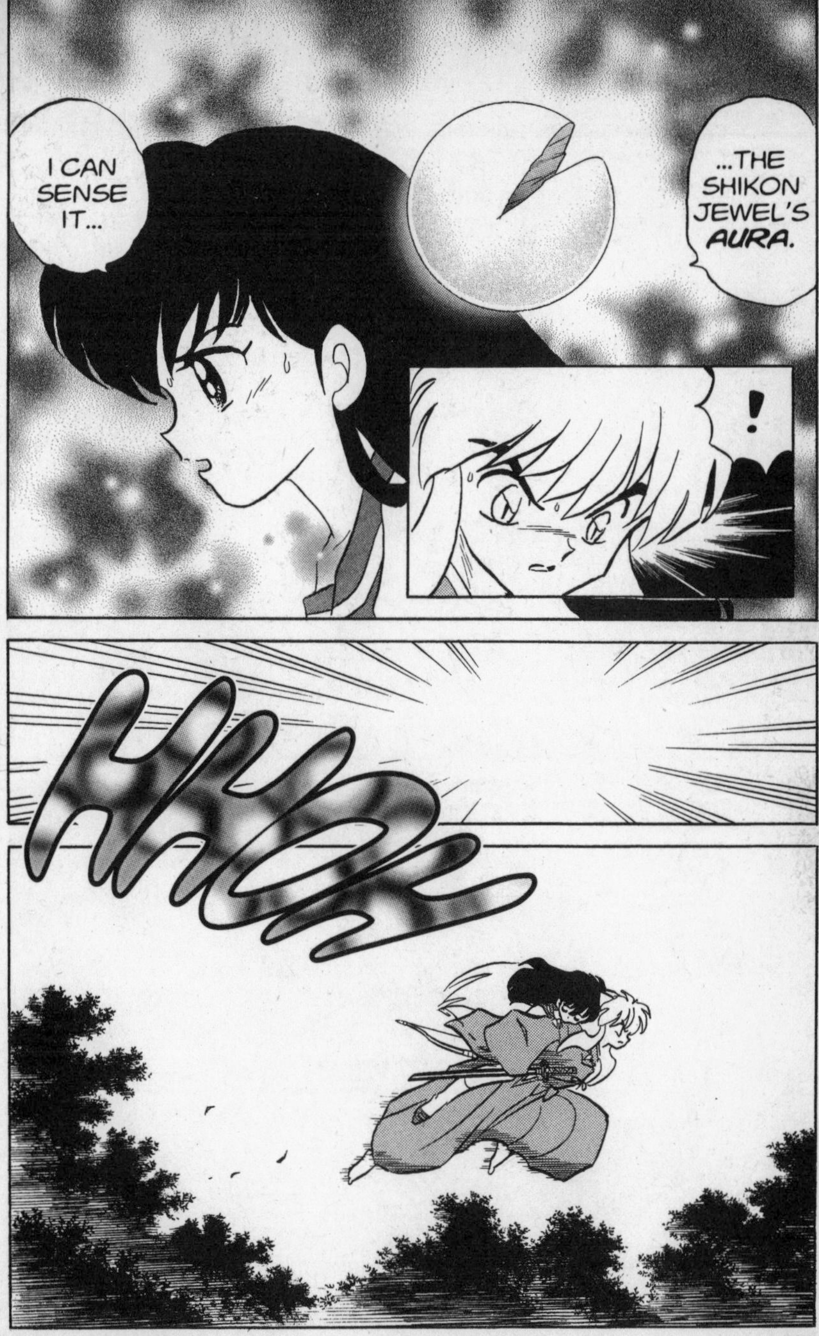
I CAN SENSE IT...
...THE SHIKON JEWEL'S AURA.
!

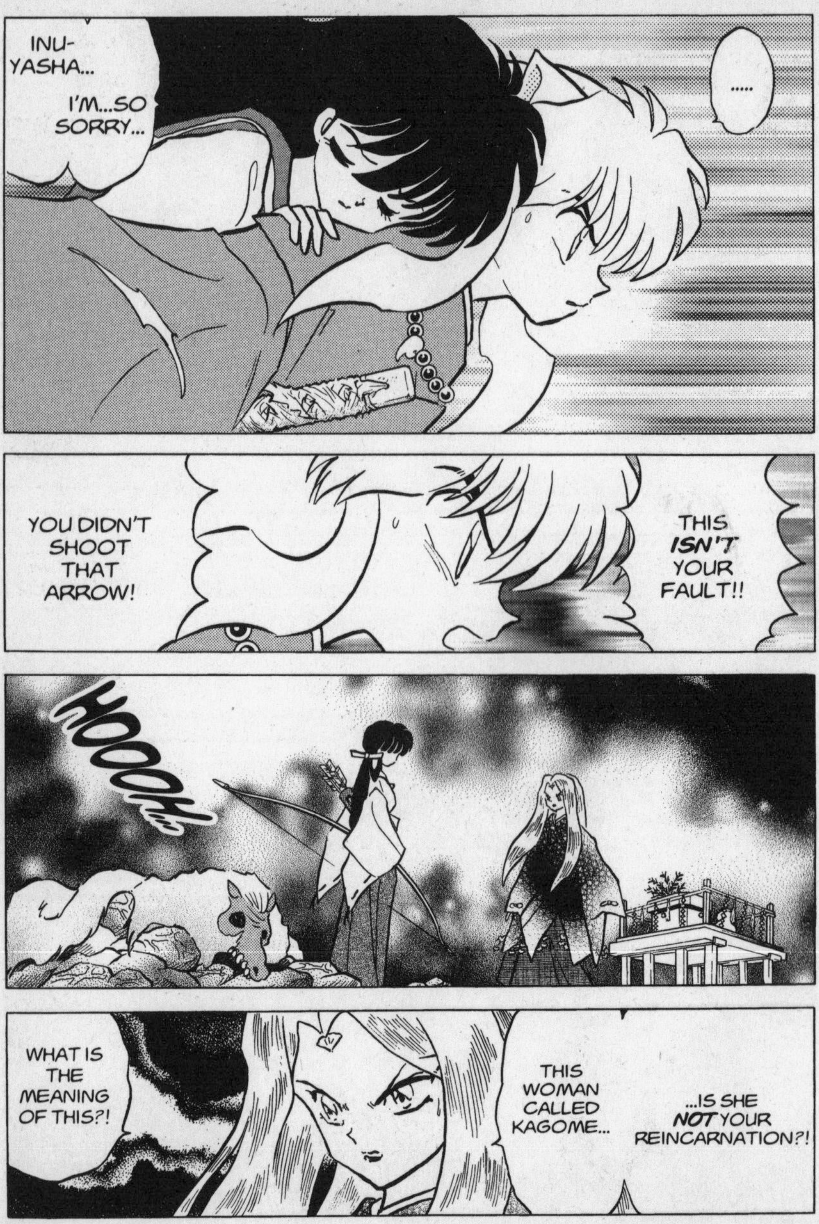
INU-
YASHA...
I'M...SO
SORRY...
.....
YOU DIDN'T
SHOOT
THAT
ARROW!
THIS
ISN'T
YOUR
FAULT!!
HOOOH...
WHAT IS
THE
MEANING
OF THIS?!
THIS
WOMAN
CALLED
KAGOME...
...IS SHE
NOT YOUR
REINCARNATION?!

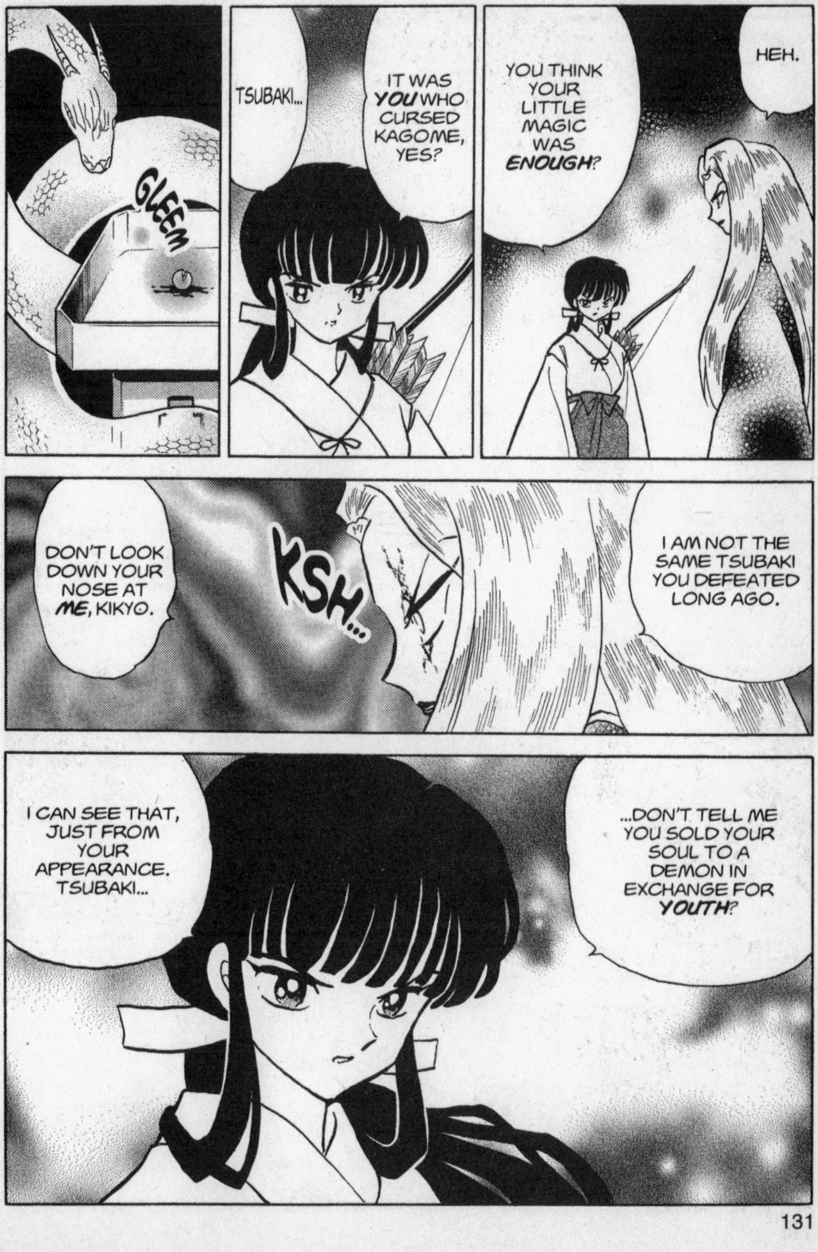
GLEEM
TSUBAKI...
IT WAS YOU WHO CURSED KAGOME, YES?
YOU THINK YOUR LITTLE MAGIC WAS ENOUGH?
HEH.
DON'T LOOK DOWN YOUR NOSE AT ME, KIKYO.
KSH...
I AM NOT THE SAME TSUBAKI YOU DEFEATED LONG AGO.
I CAN SEE THAT, JUST FROM YOUR APPEARANCE. TSUBAKI...
...DON'T TELL ME YOU SOLD YOUR SOUL TO A DEMON IN EXCHANGE FOR YOUTH?

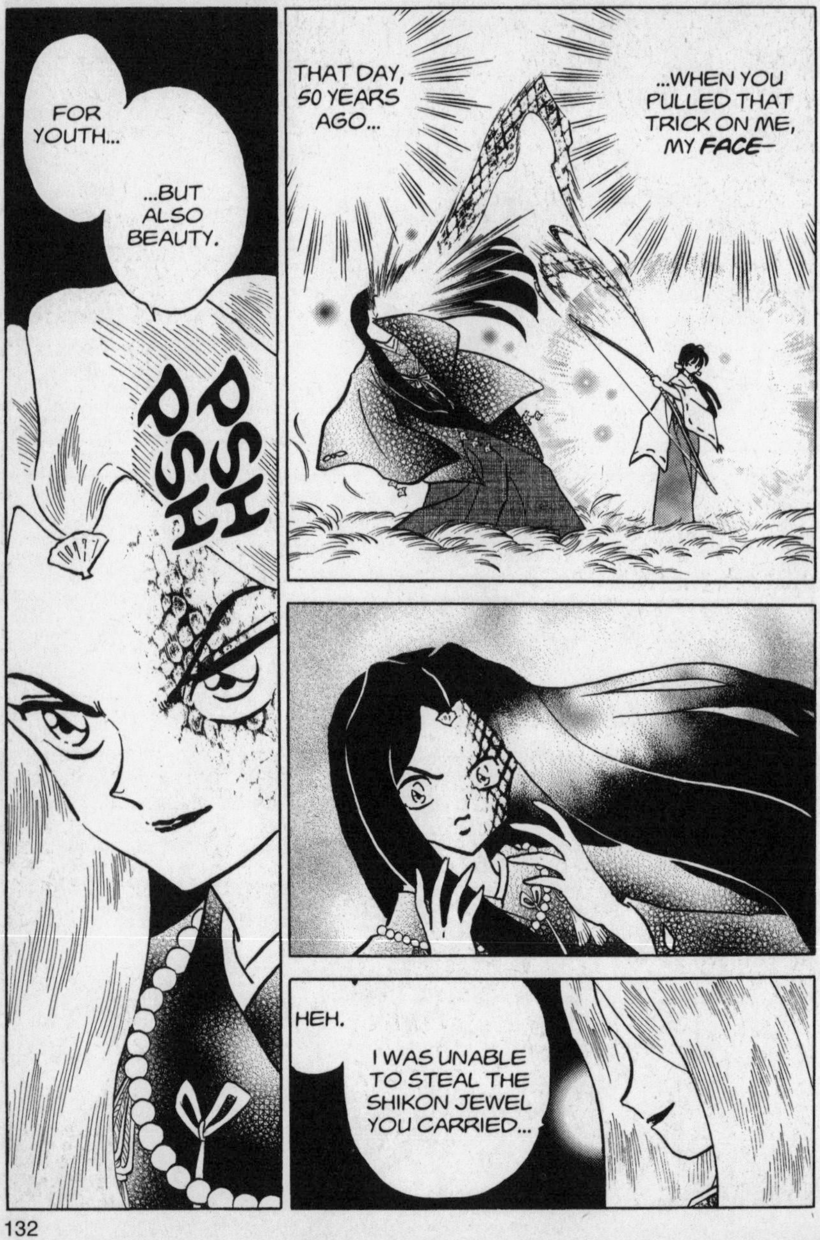
FOR YOUTH...
...BUT ALSO BEAUTY.
PSH PSH
THAT DAY, 50 YEARS AGO...
...WHEN YOU PULLED THAT TRICK ON ME, MY *FACE*—
HEH.
I WAS UNABLE TO STEAL THE SHIKON JEWEL YOU CARRIED...

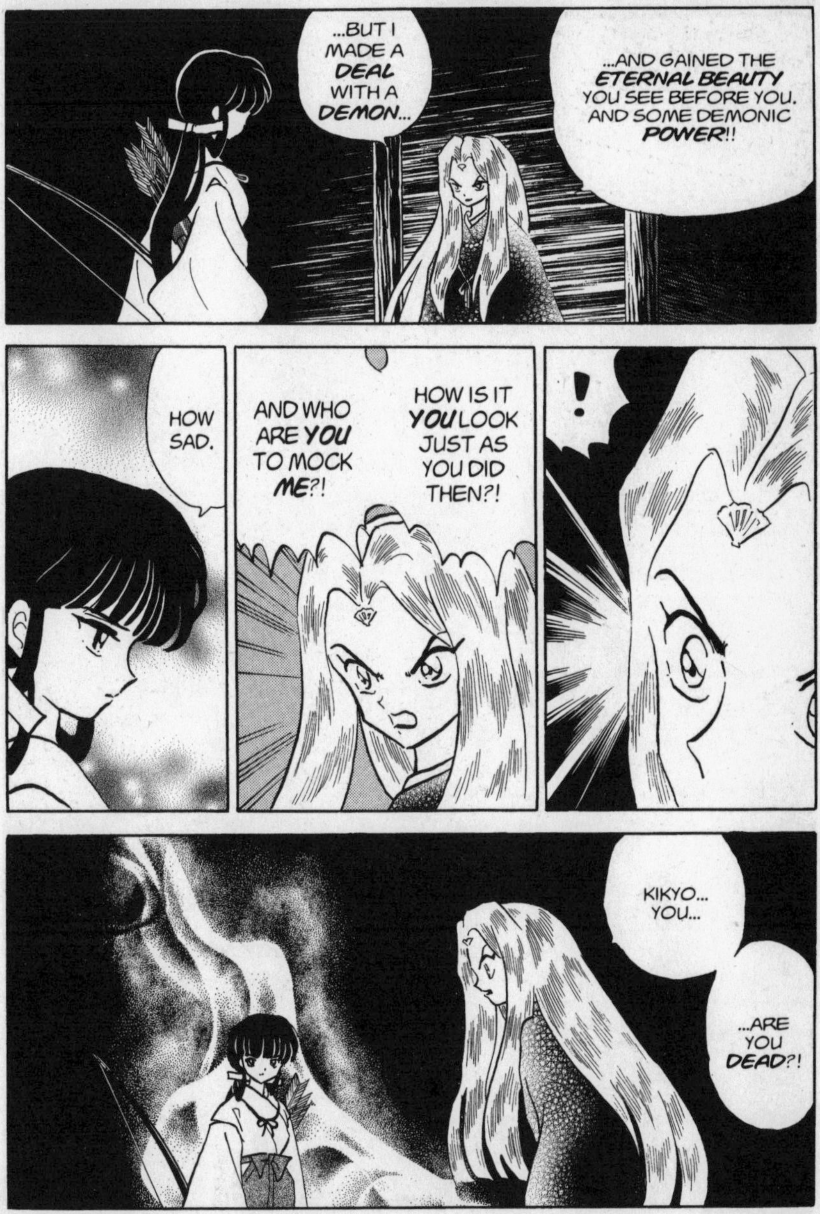
...BUT I MADE A DEAL WITH A DEMON...
...AND GAINED THE ETERNAL BEAUTY YOU SEE BEFORE YOU. AND SOME DEMONIC POWER!!
HOW SAD.
AND WHO ARE YOU TO MOCK ME?!
HOW IS IT YOU LOOK JUST AS YOU DID THEN?!
!
KIKYO... YOU...
...ARE YOU DEAD?!

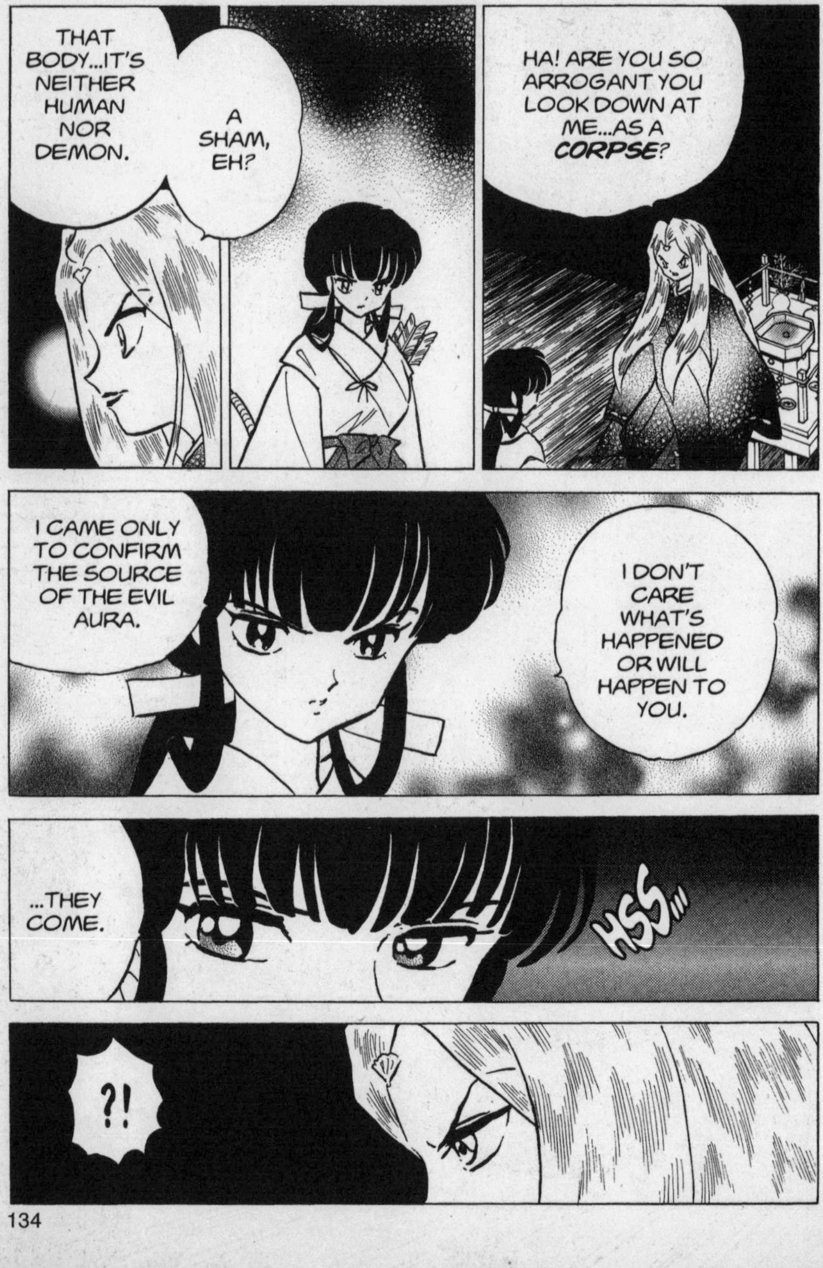
THAT BODY...IT'S NEITHER HUMAN NOR DEMON.
A SHAM, EH?
HA! ARE YOU SO ARROGANT YOU LOOK DOWN AT ME...AS A *CORPSE*?
I CAME ONLY TO CONFIRM THE SOURCE OF THE EVIL AURA.
I DON'T CARE WHAT'S HAPPENED OR WILL HAPPEN TO YOU.
...THEY COME.
HSS...
?!

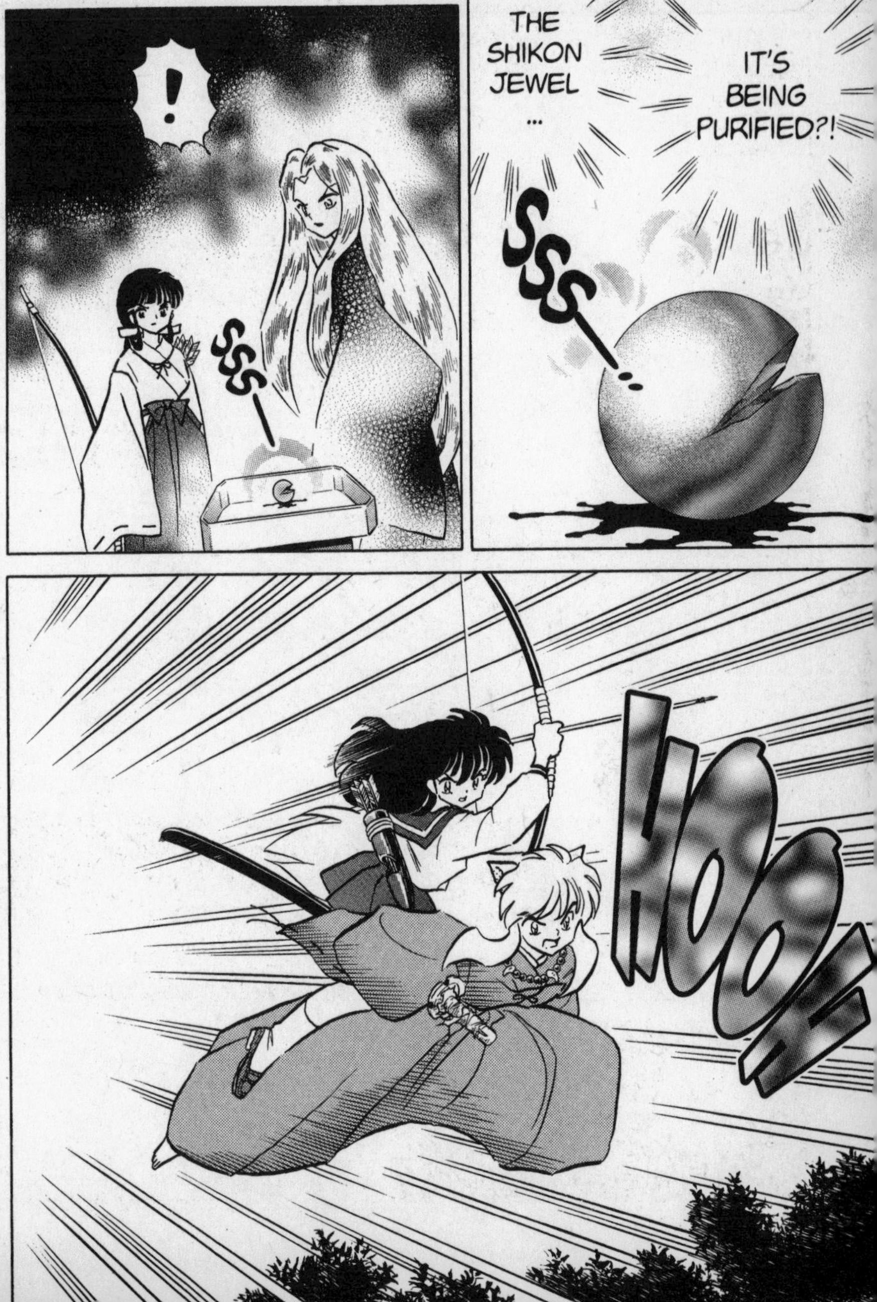

THE SHIKON JEWEL ...
IT'S BEING PURIFIED?!
SSS—!!
!
SSS—

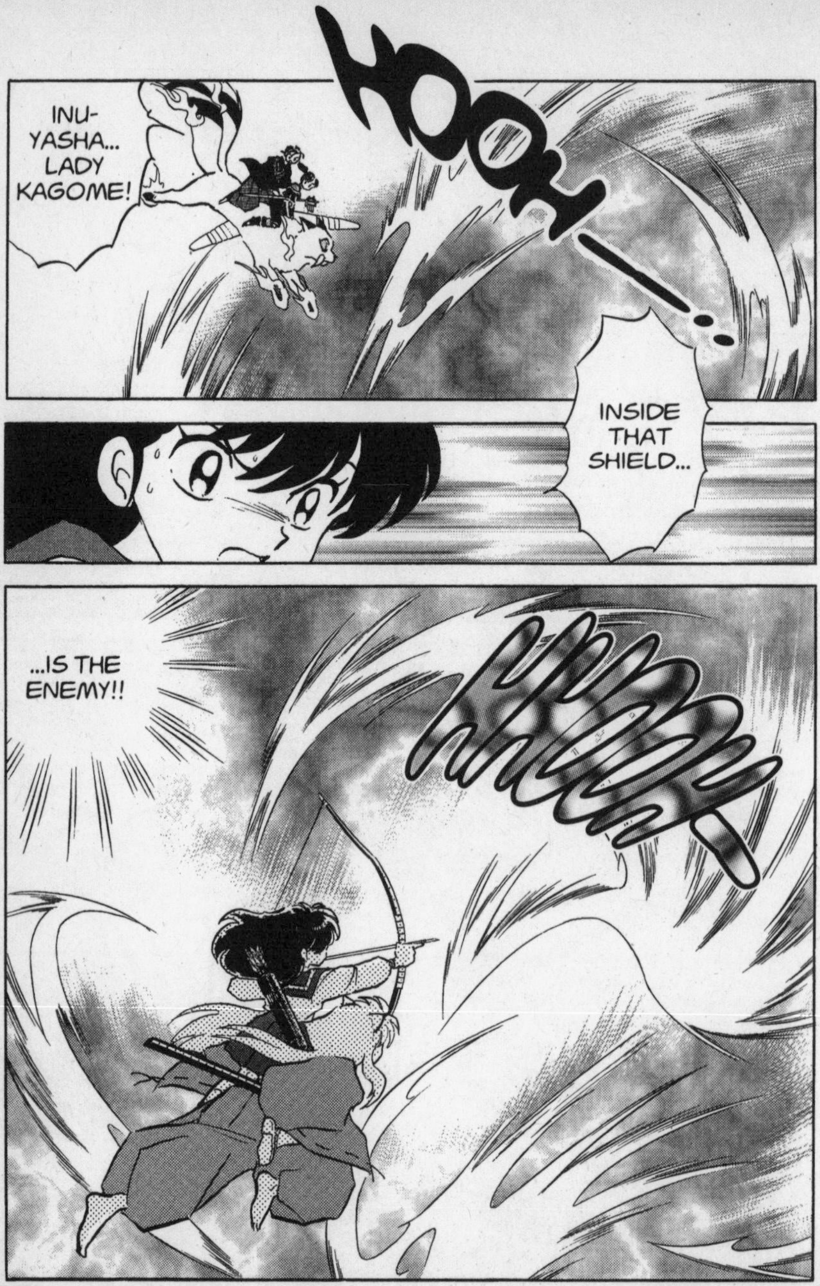
INU-YASHA... LADY KAGOME!
HOOH!!
INSIDE THAT SHIELD...
...IS THE ENEMY!!

SCROLL EIGHT

TSUBAKI'S SHRINE

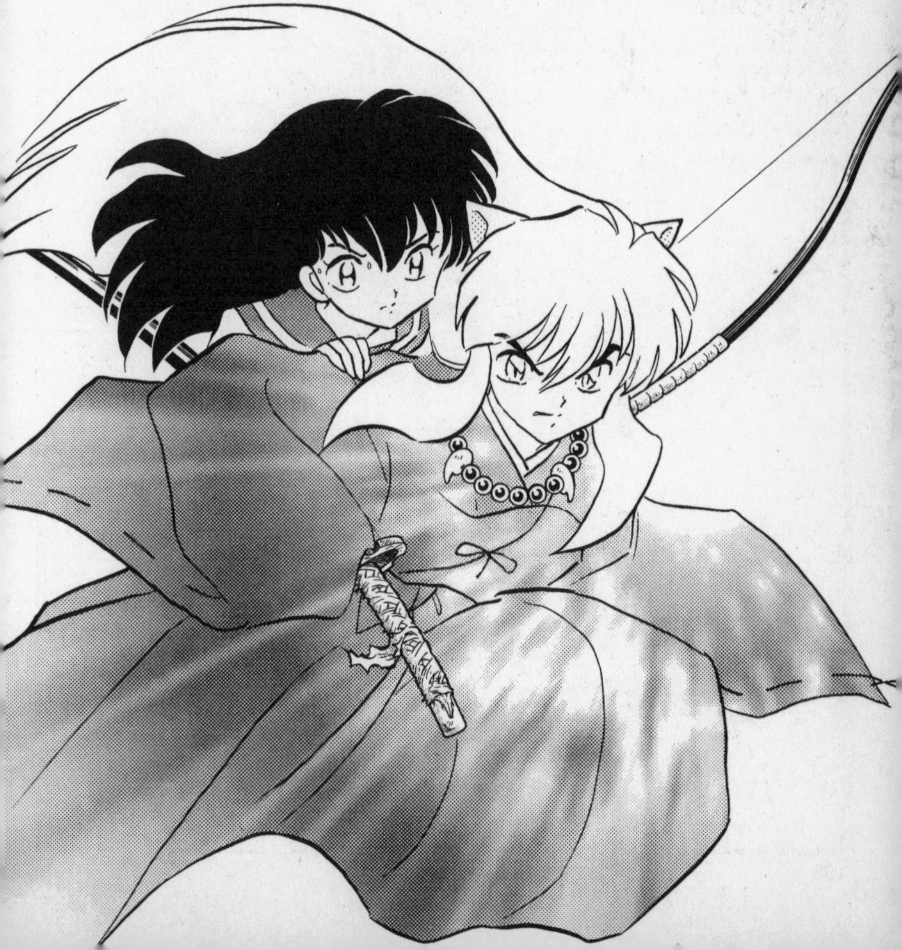

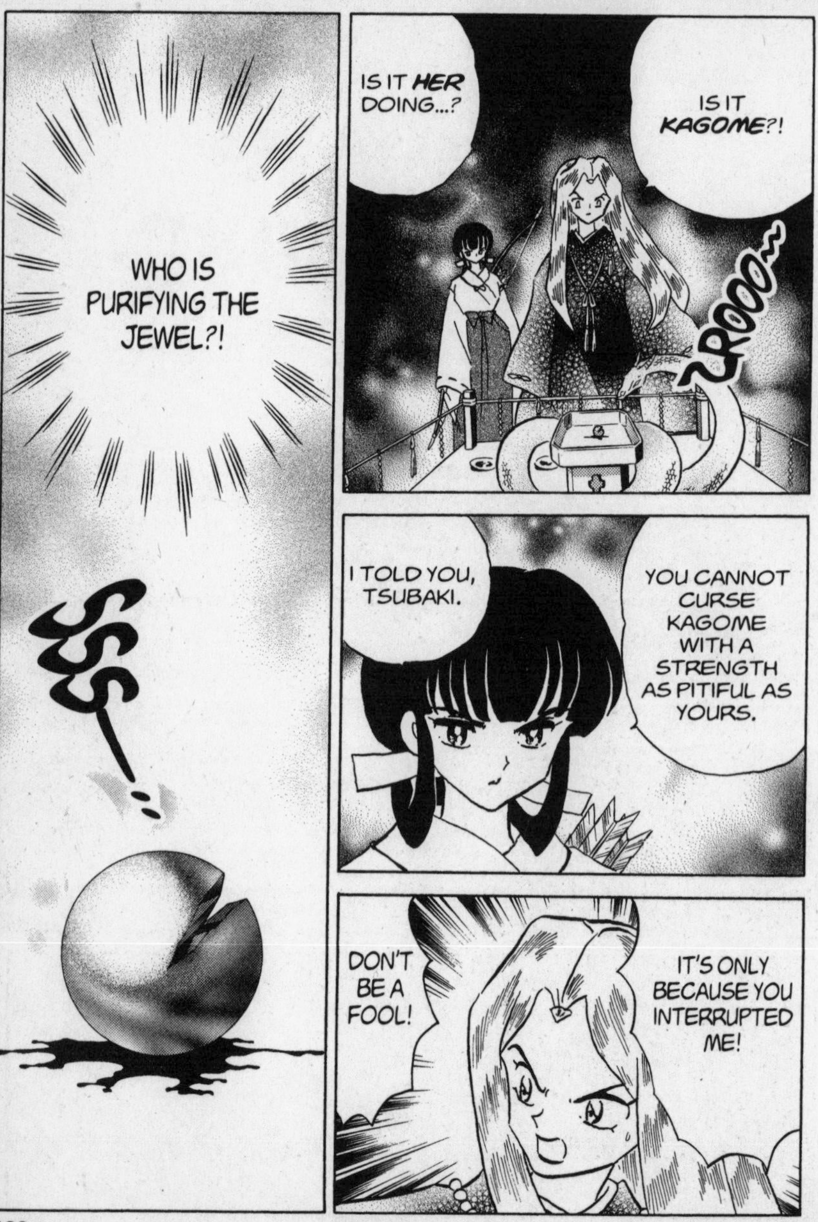
WHO IS PURIFYING THE JEWEL?!
SSS—
IS IT HER DOING...?
IS IT KAGOME?!
ZROOO...
I TOLD YOU, TSUBAKI.
YOU CANNOT CURSE KAGOME WITH A STRENGTH AS PITIFUL AS YOURS.
DON'T BE A FOOL!
IT'S ONLY BECAUSE YOU INTERRUPTED ME!

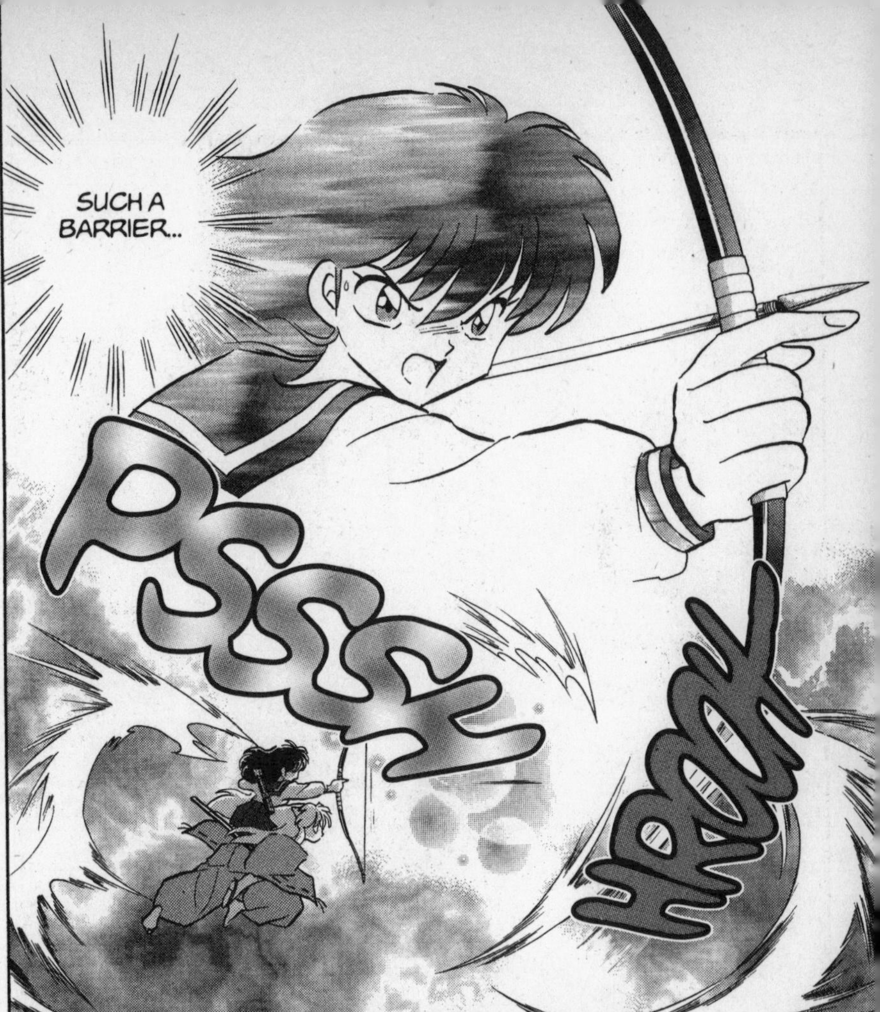
SUCH A BARRIER...

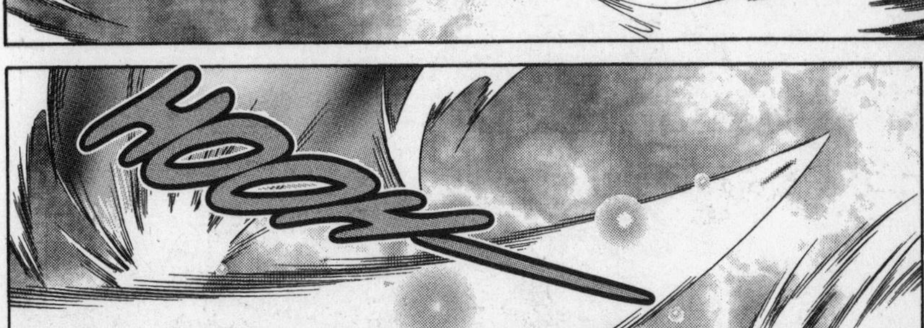

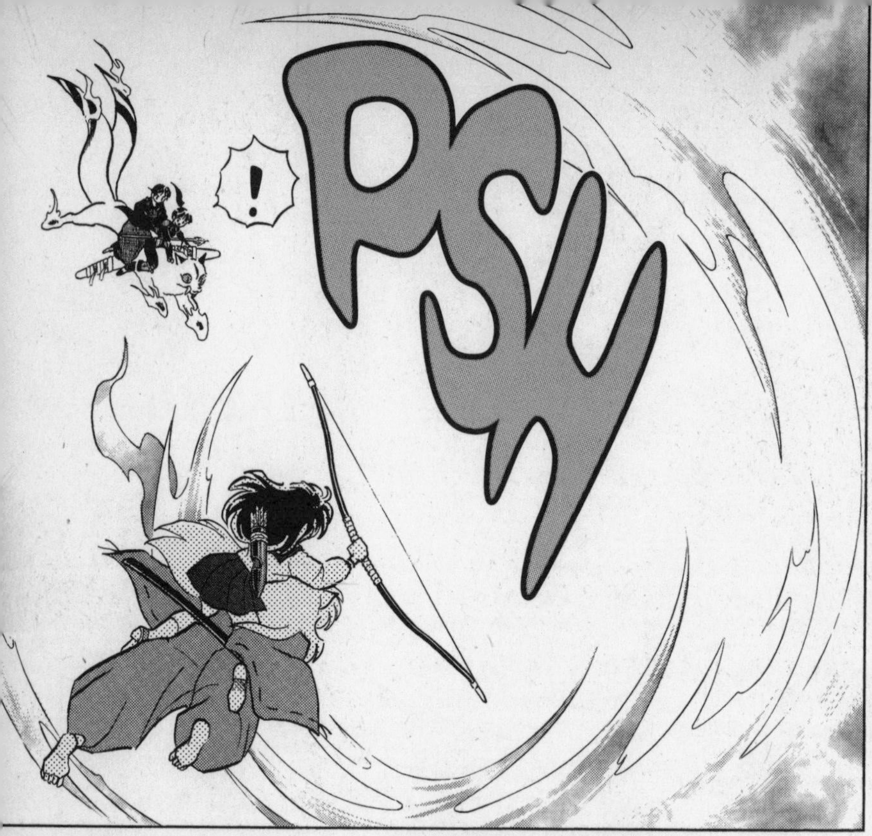
!
PSH

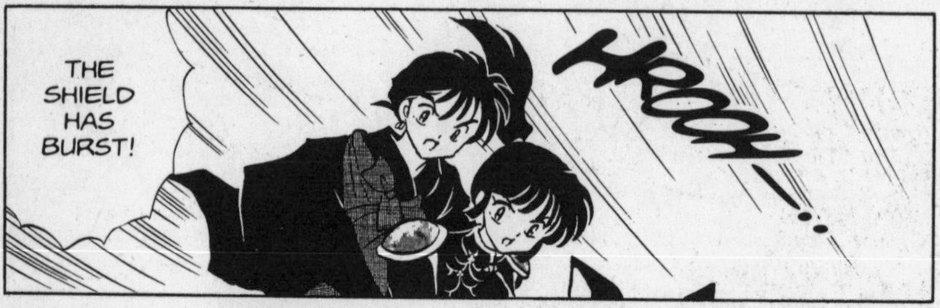
THE SHIELD HAS BURST!
HROOH

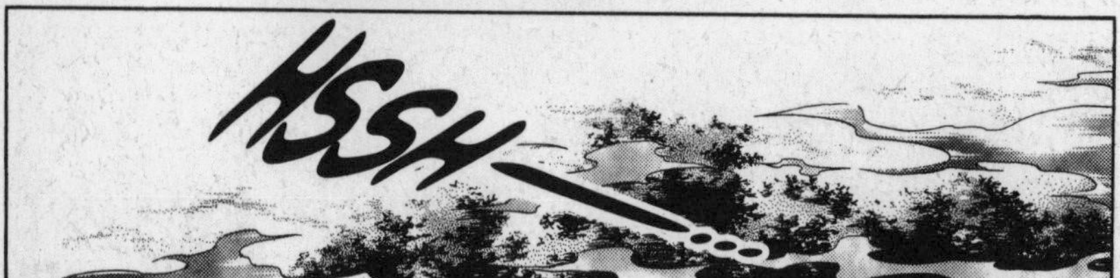
HSSH

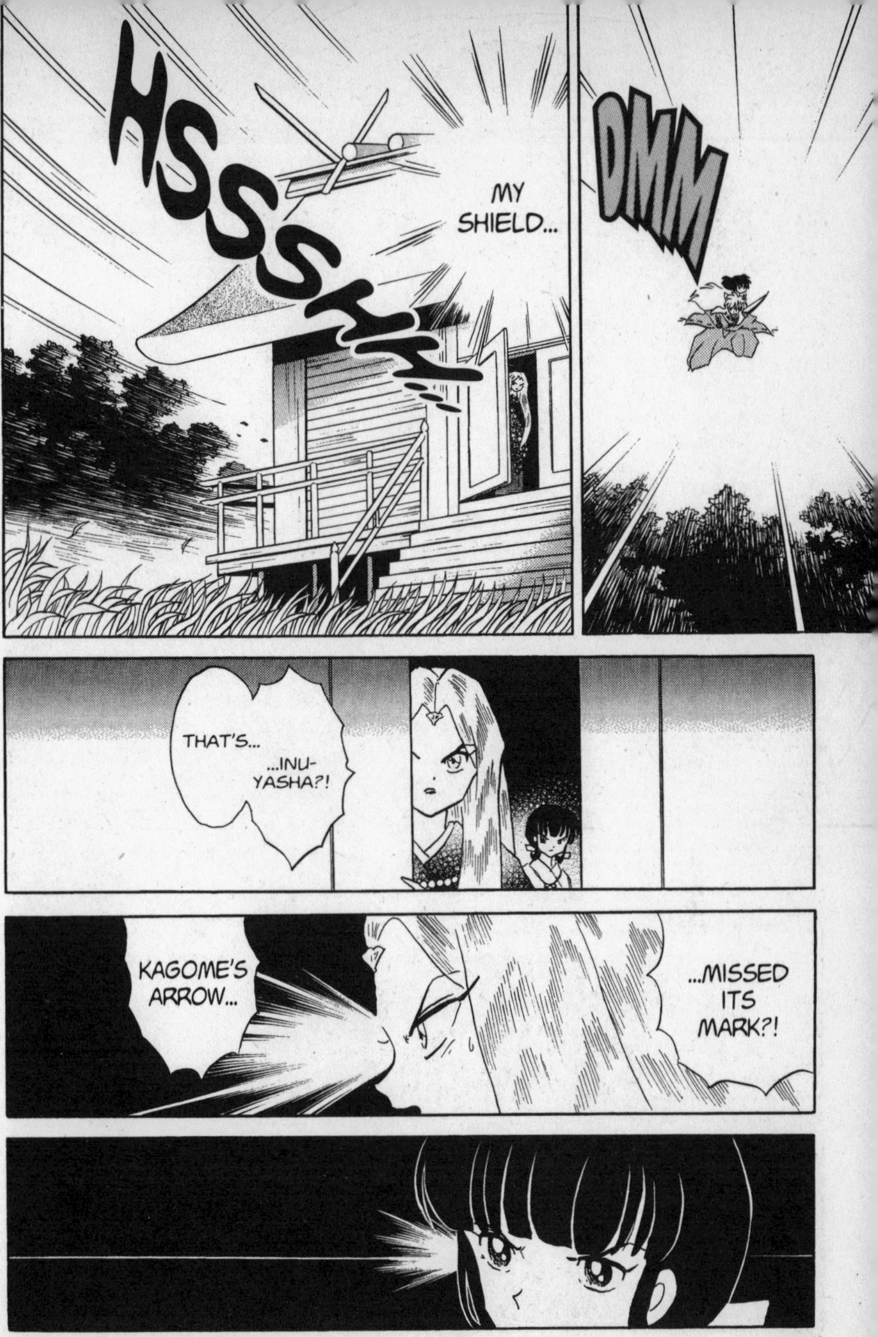
HSSSH
MY SHIELD...
DMM
THAT'S...
...INU-YASHA?!
KAGOME'S ARROW...
...MISSED ITS MARK?!

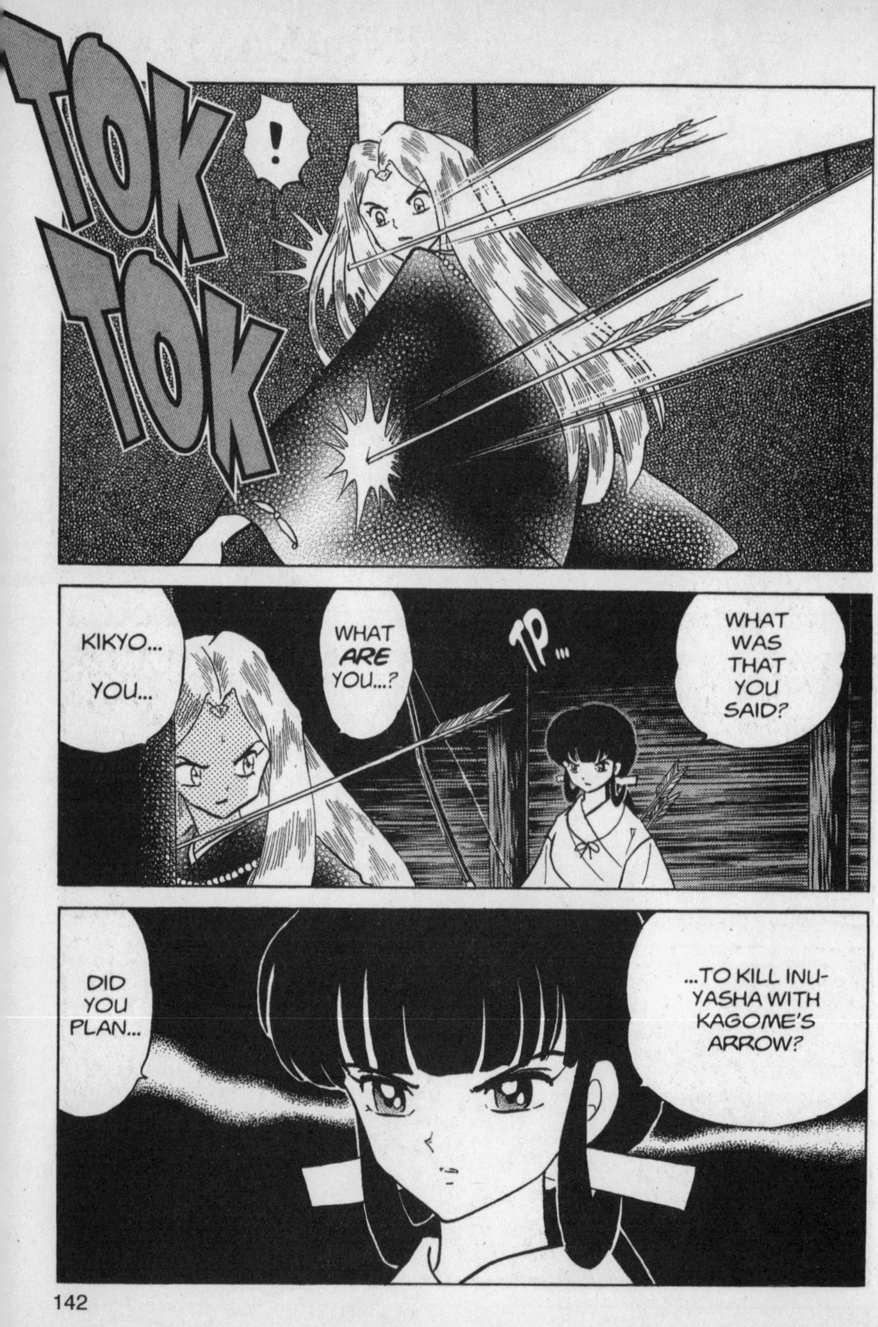

TOK TOK
!
KIKYO... YOU...
WHAT ARE YOU...?
TP...
WHAT WAS THAT YOU SAID?
DID YOU PLAN...
...TO KILL INU-YASHA WITH KAGOME'S ARROW?

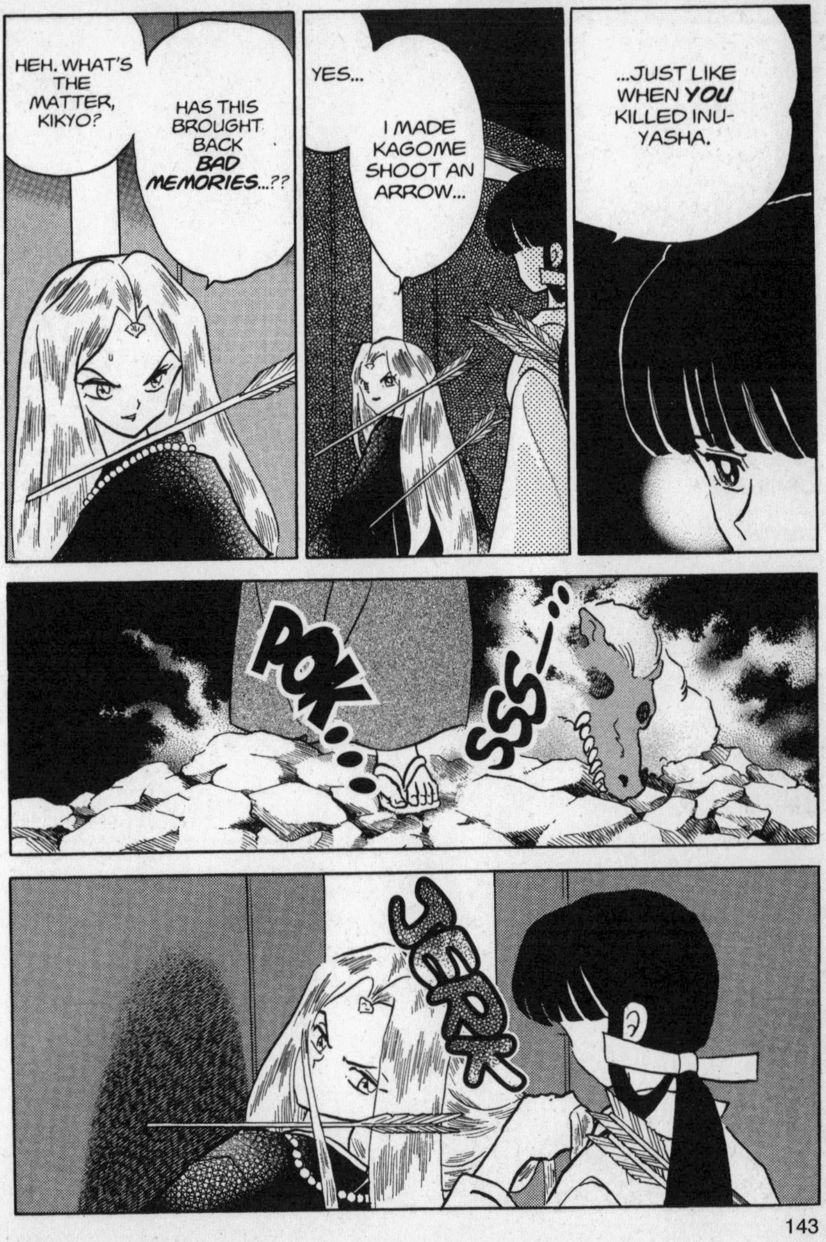
HEH. WHAT'S THE MATTER, KIKYO?
HAS THIS BROUGHT BACK BAD MEMORIES...??
YES...
I MADE KAGOME SHOOT AN ARROW...
...JUST LIKE WHEN YOU KILLED INU-YASHA.
POK...
SSS—!!
JERK

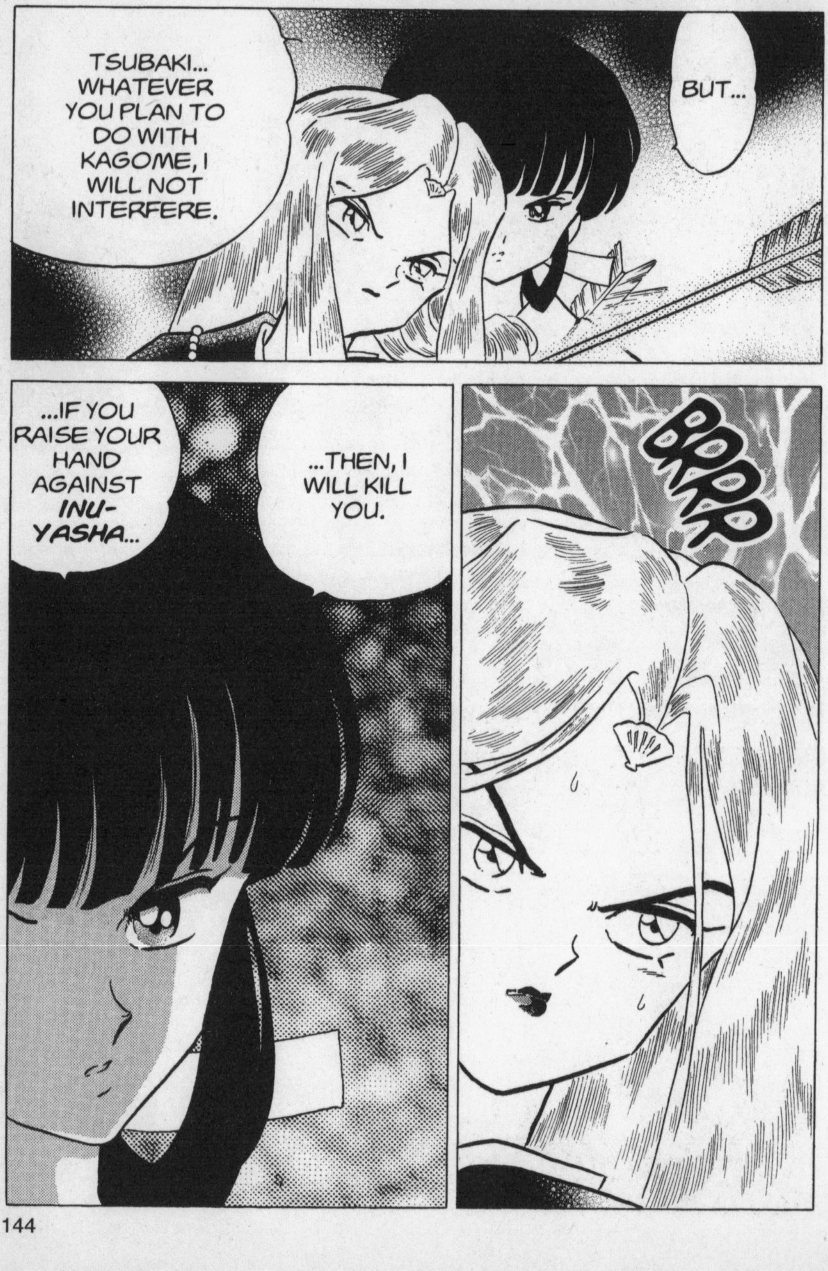

TSUBAKI... WHATEVER YOU PLAN TO DO WITH KAGOME, I WILL NOT INTERFERE.
BUT...
...IF YOU RAISE YOUR HAND AGAINST *INU-YASHA*...
...THEN, I WILL KILL YOU.
BRRR

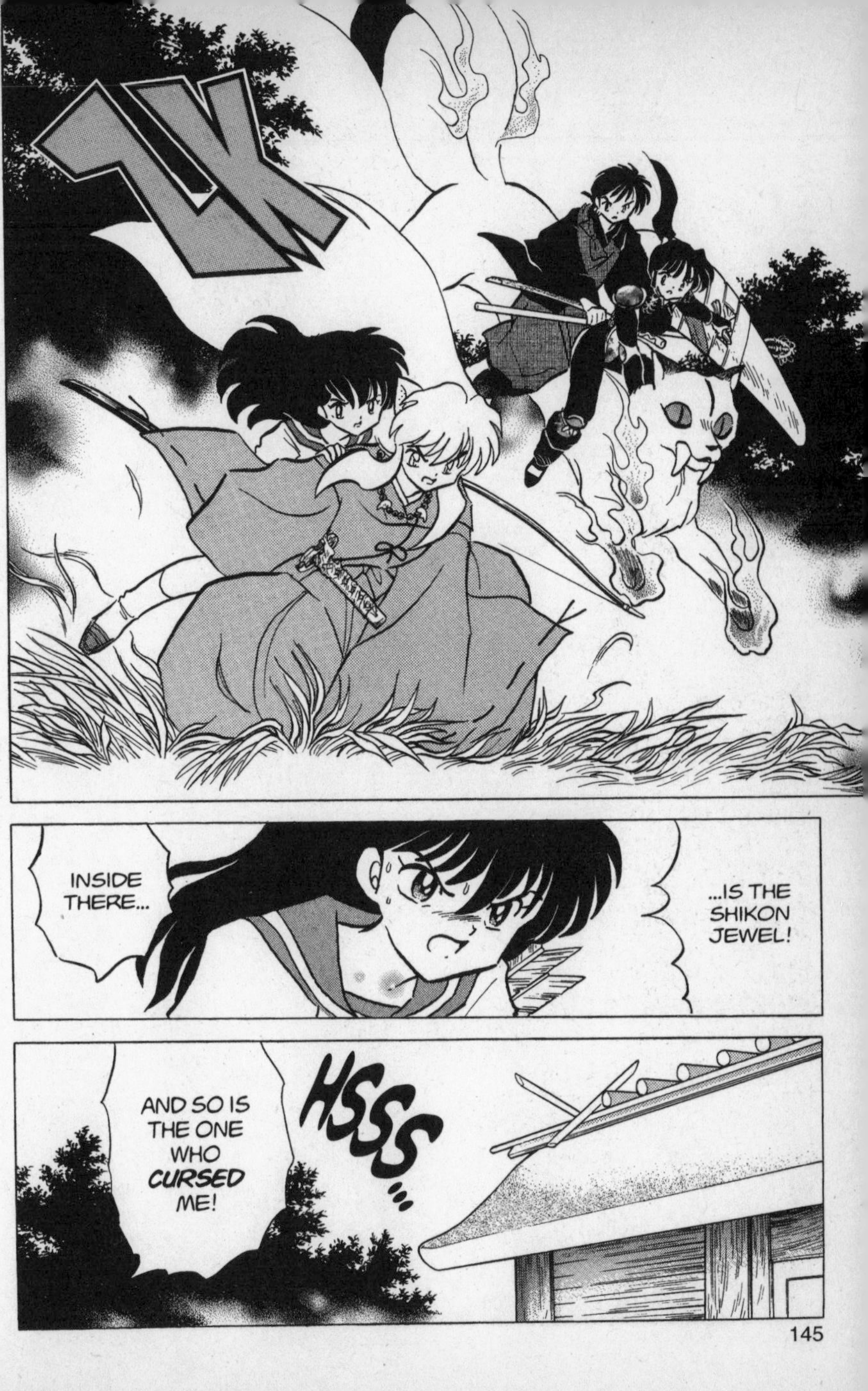

INSIDE THERE...
...IS THE SHIKON JEWEL!
AND SO IS THE ONE WHO **CURSED** ME!
HSSS...

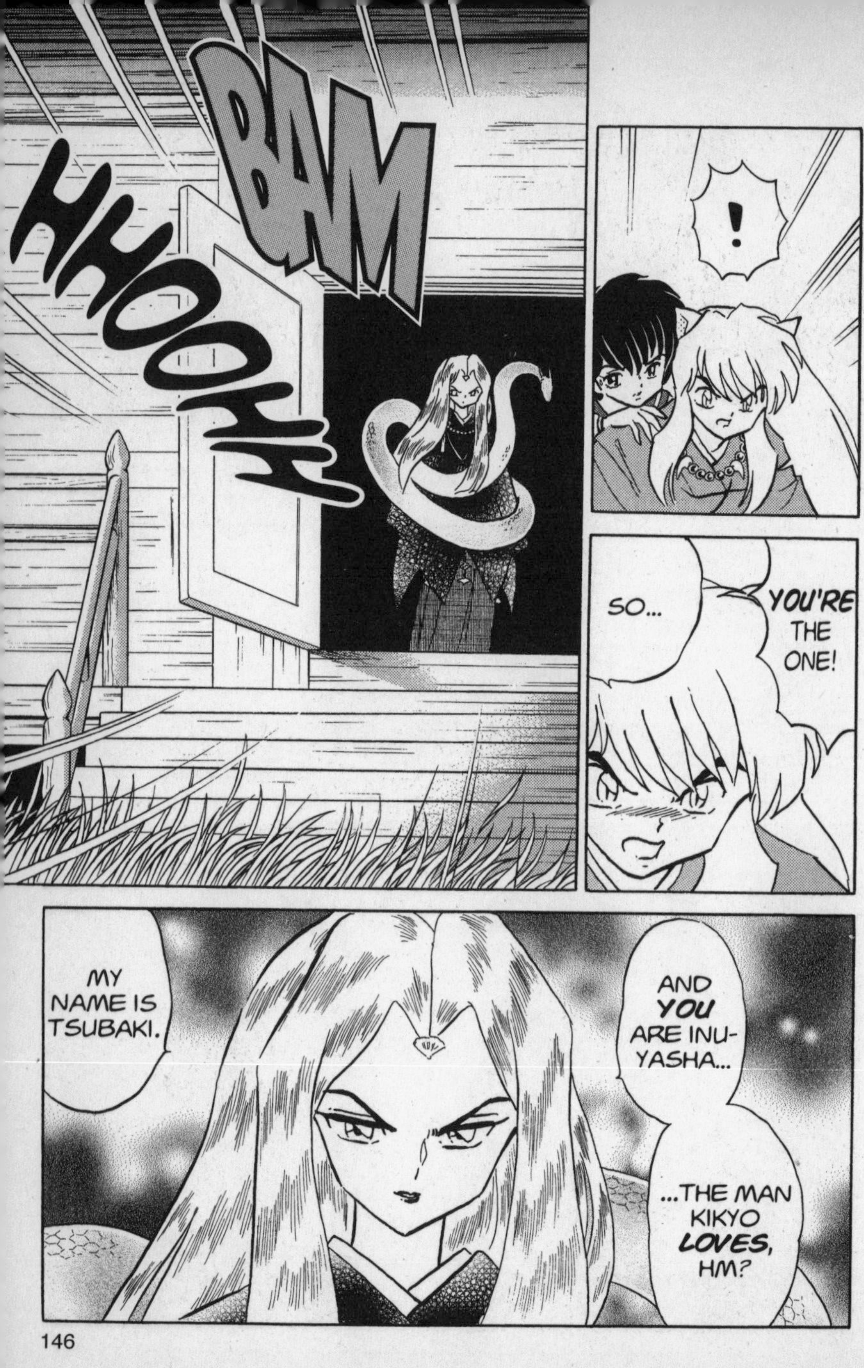
BAM
HHOOHH
!
SO...
YOU'RE THE ONE!
MY NAME IS TSUBAKI.
AND YOU ARE INU-YASHA...
...THE MAN KIKYO LOVES, HM?

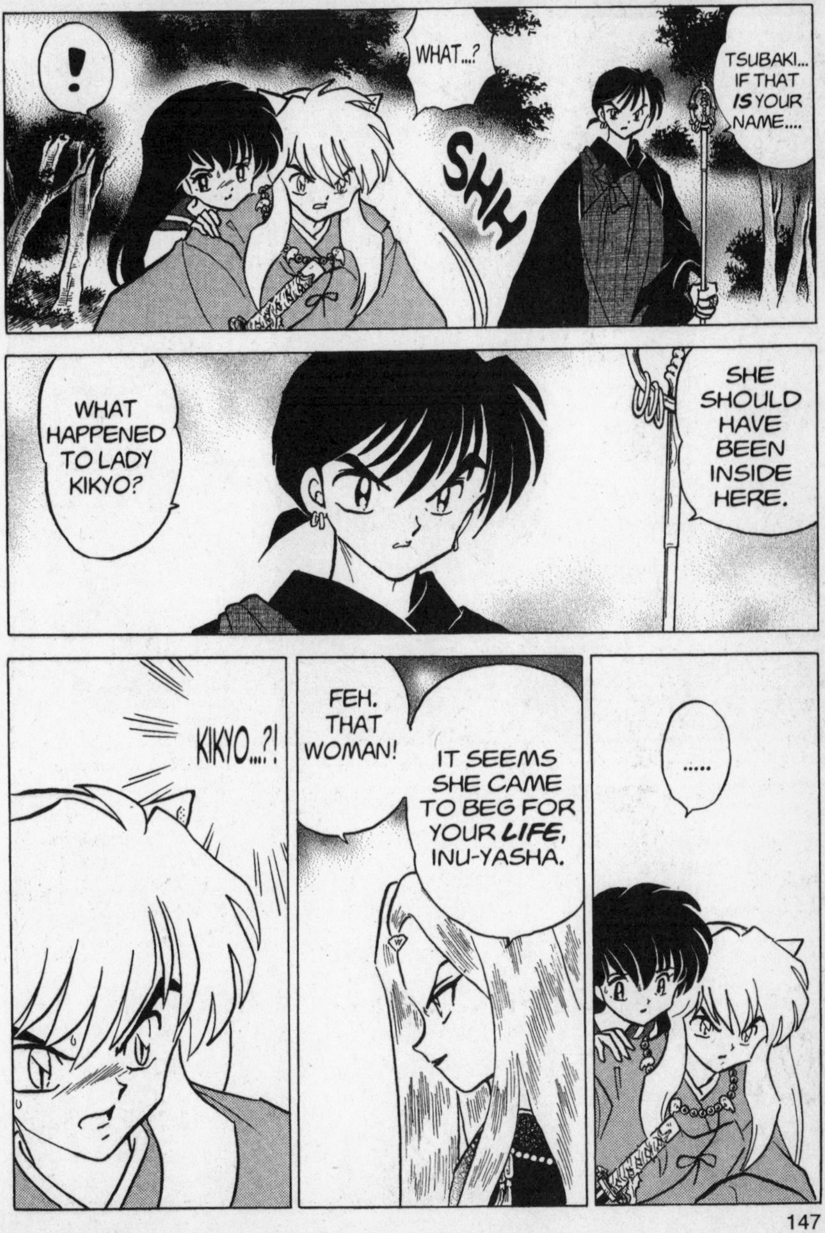
!
WHAT...?
SHH
TSUBAKI... IF THAT *IS* YOUR NAME....
WHAT HAPPENED TO LADY KIKYO?
SHE SHOULD HAVE BEEN INSIDE HERE.
KIKYO...?!
FEH. THAT WOMAN!
IT SEEMS SHE CAME TO BEG FOR YOUR *LIFE*, INU-YASHA.
.....

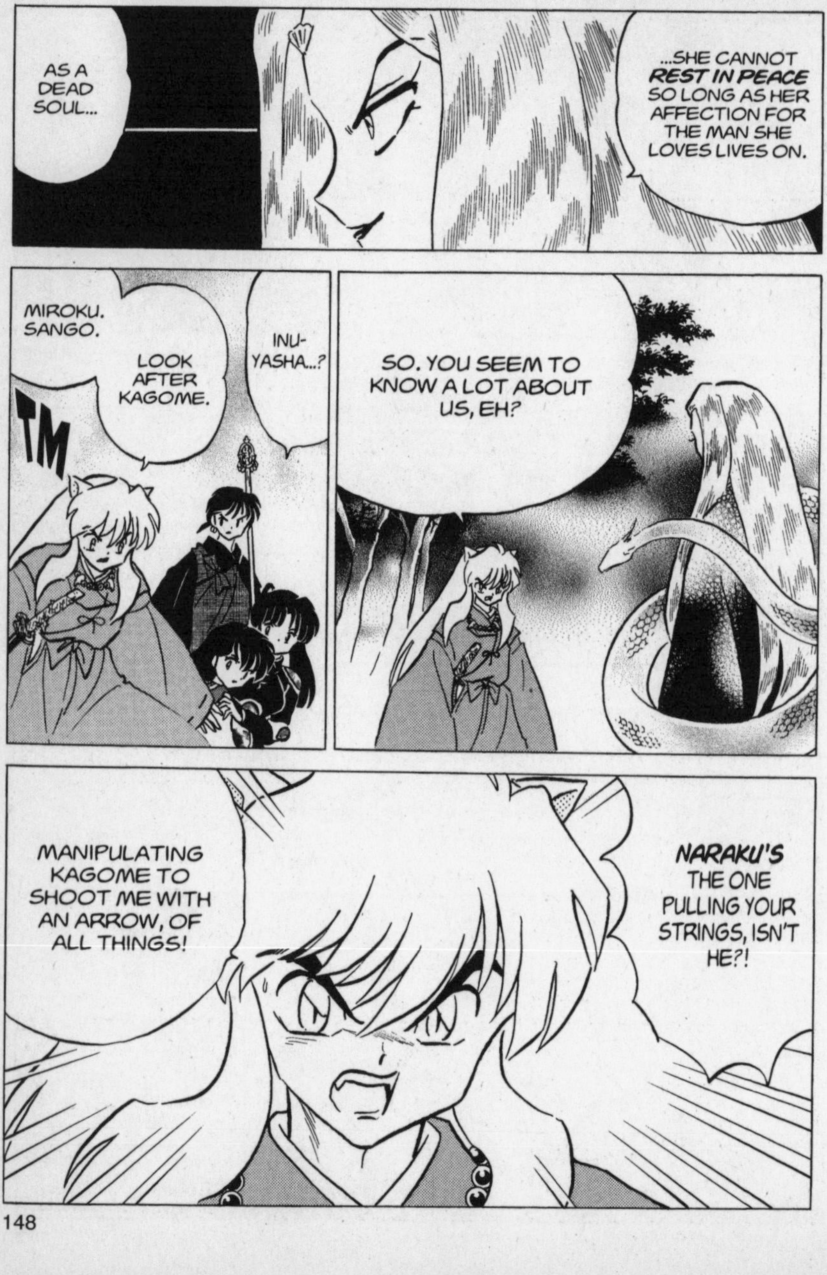
AS A DEAD SOUL...
...SHE CANNOT **REST IN PEACE** SO LONG AS HER AFFECTION FOR THE MAN SHE LOVES LIVES ON.
MIROKU. SANGO.
LOOK AFTER KAGOME.
TM
INU-YASHA...?
SO. YOU SEEM TO KNOW A LOT ABOUT US, EH?
MANIPULATING KAGOME TO SHOOT ME WITH AN ARROW, OF ALL THINGS!
NARAKU'S THE ONE PULLING YOUR STRINGS, ISN'T HE?!

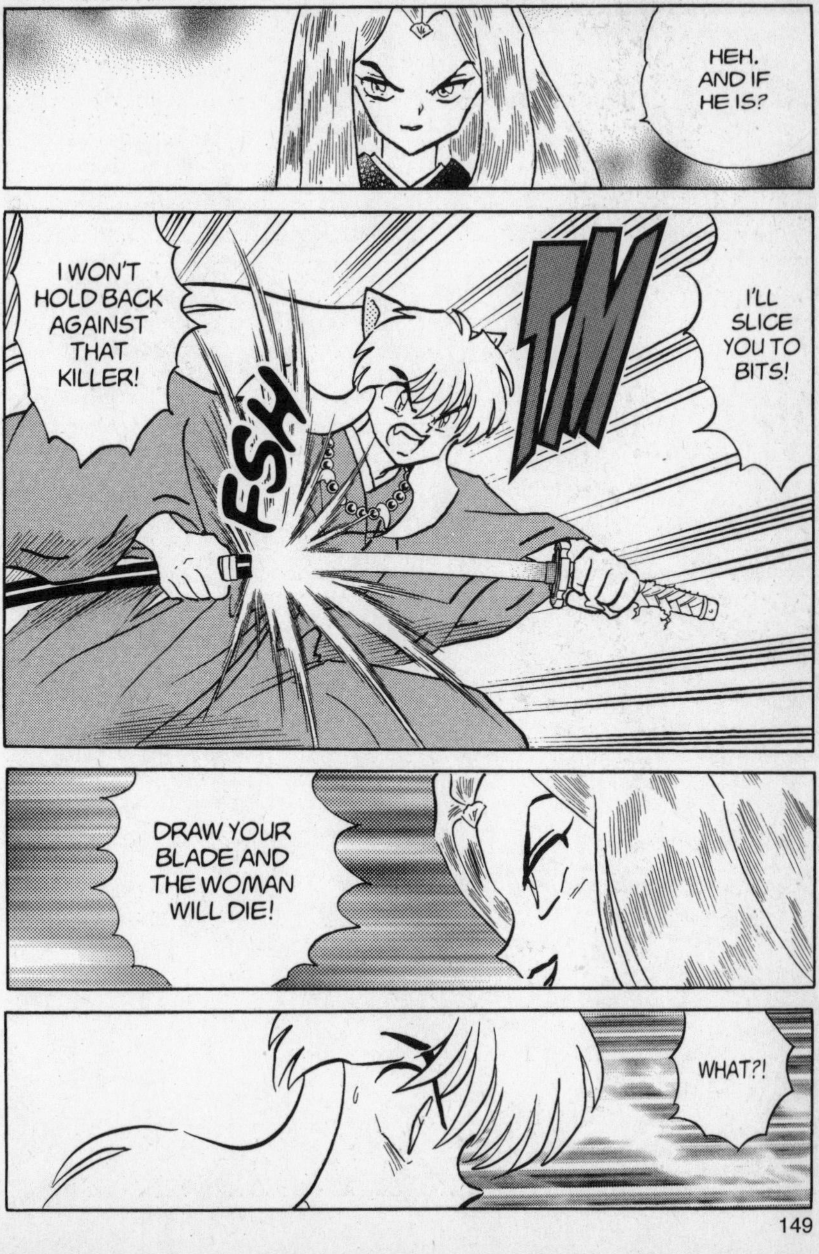
HEH. AND IF HE IS?
I WON'T HOLD BACK AGAINST THAT KILLER!
FSH
TM
I'LL SLICE YOU TO BITS!
DRAW YOUR BLADE AND THE WOMAN WILL DIE!
WHAT?!

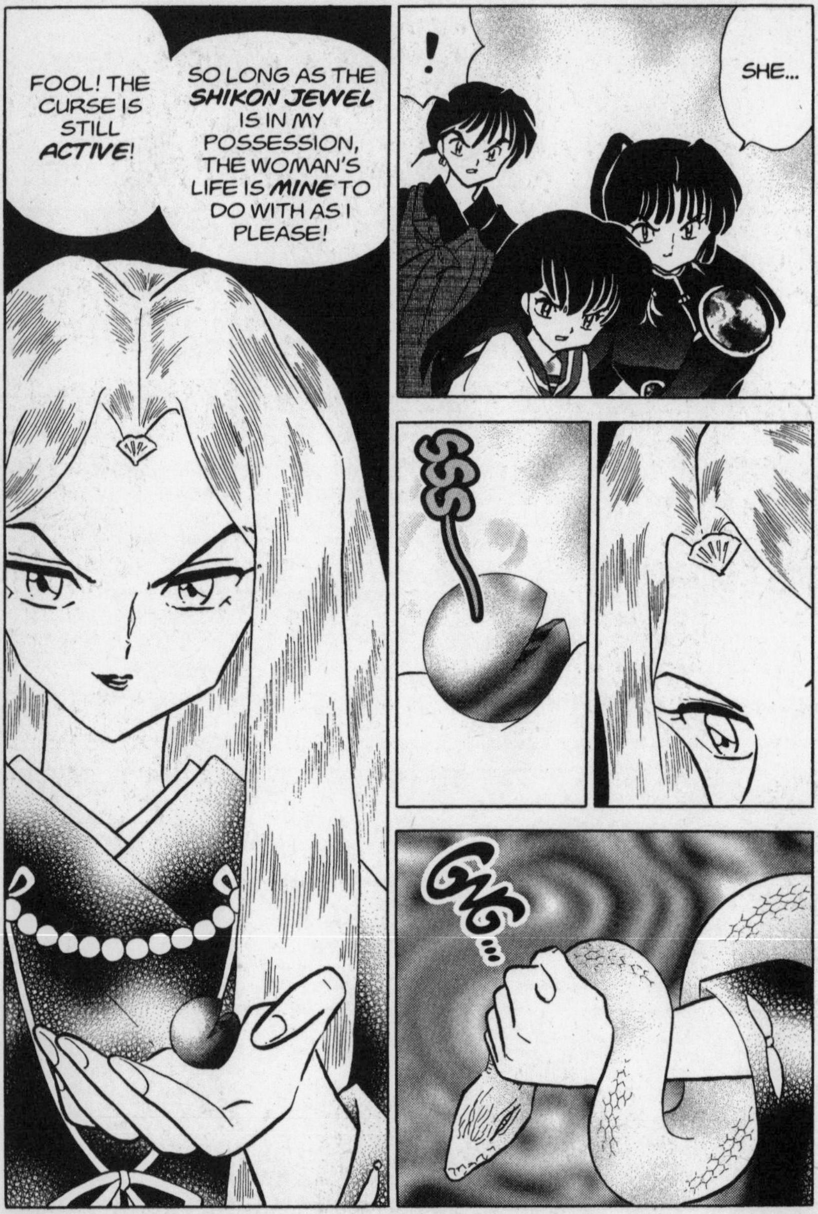
FOOL! THE CURSE IS STILL ACTIVE!
SO LONG AS THE SHIKON JEWEL IS IN MY POSSESSION, THE WOMAN'S LIFE IS MINE TO DO WITH AS I PLEASE!
!
SHE...
SSS
GNG...

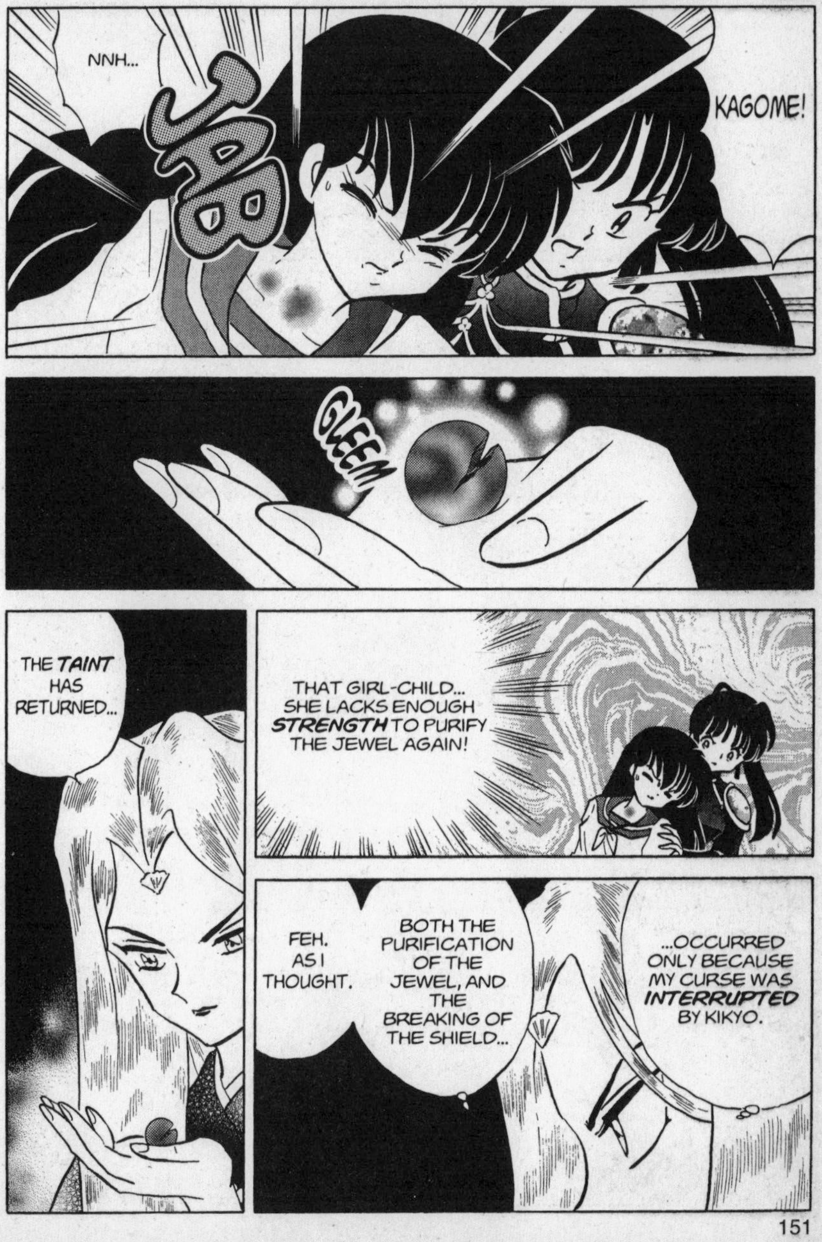
NNH...
JAB
KAGOME!
GLEEM
THE TAINT HAS RETURNED...
THAT GIRL-CHILD... SHE LACKS ENOUGH STRENGTH TO PURIFY THE JEWEL AGAIN!
FEH. AS I THOUGHT.
BOTH THE PURIFICATION OF THE JEWEL, AND THE BREAKING OF THE SHIELD...
...OCCURRED ONLY BECAUSE MY CURSE WAS INTERRUPTED BY KIKYO.

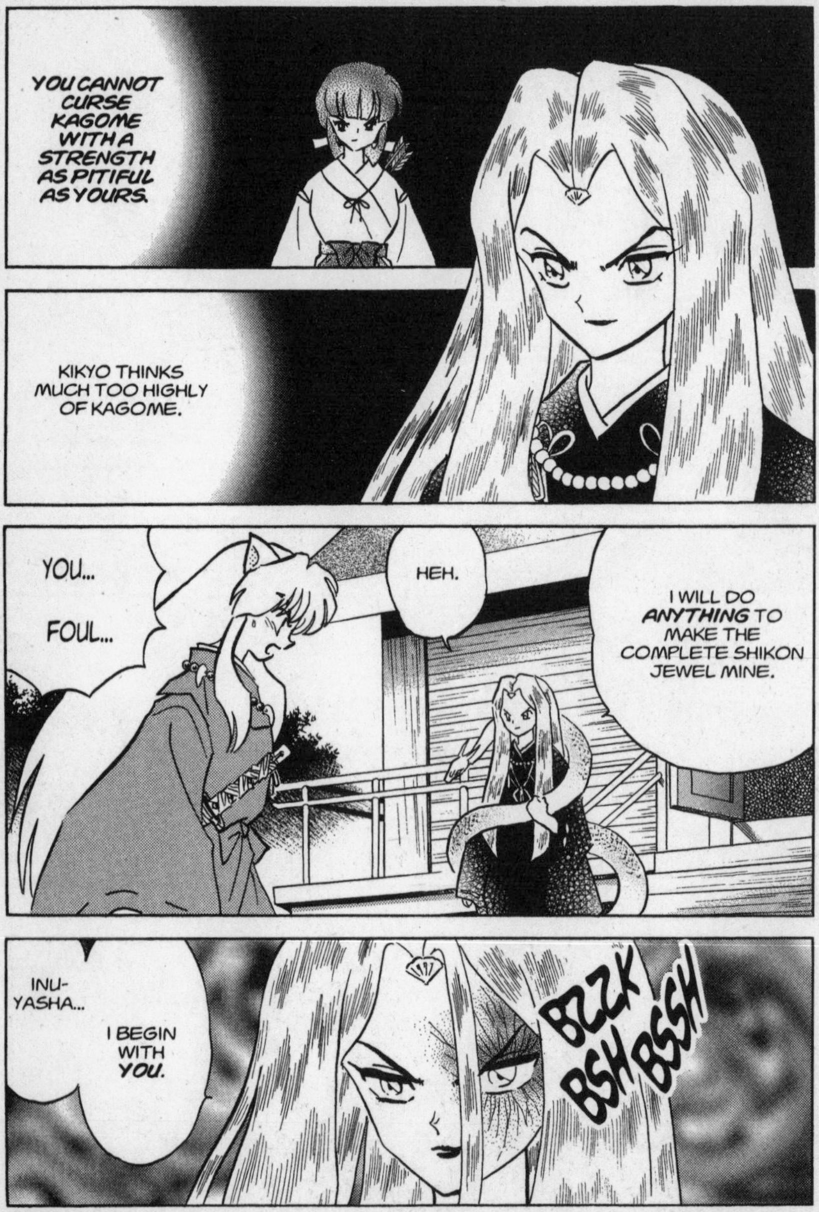
YOU CANNOT CURSE KAGOME WITH A STRENGTH AS PITIFUL AS YOURS.
KIKYO THINKS MUCH TOO HIGHLY OF KAGOME.
I WILL DO ANYTHING TO MAKE THE COMPLETE SHIKON JEWEL MINE.
HEH.
YOU... FOUL...
BZZK BSH BSSH
INU-YASHA... I BEGIN WITH YOU.

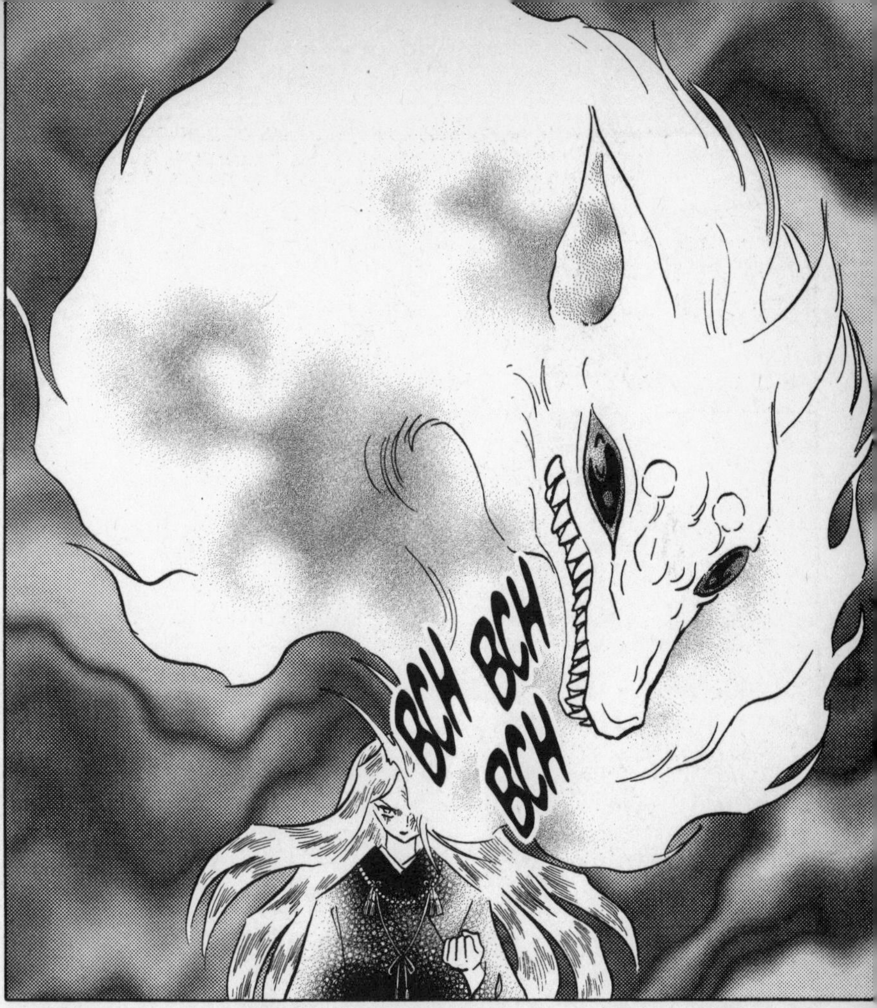
BCH BCH BCH BCH

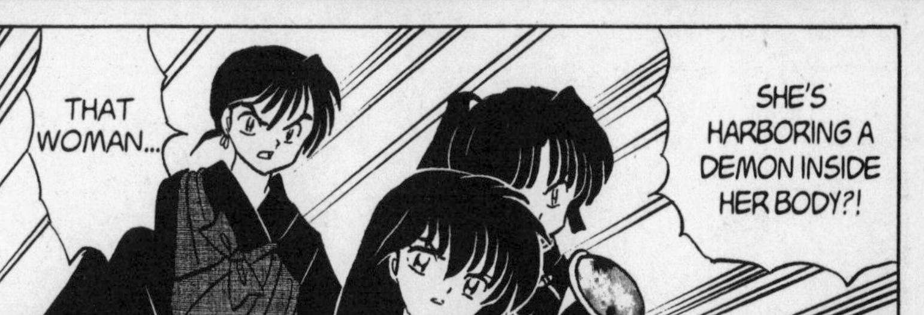
THAT WOMAN...
SHE'S HARBORING A DEMON INSIDE HER BODY?!

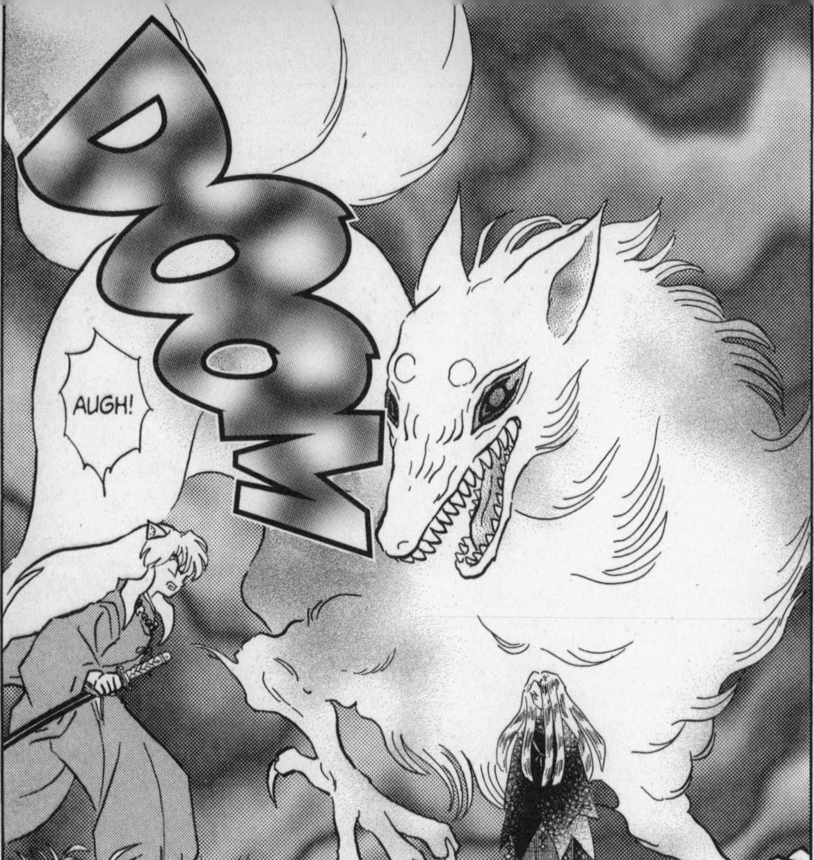
DOOM
AUGH!
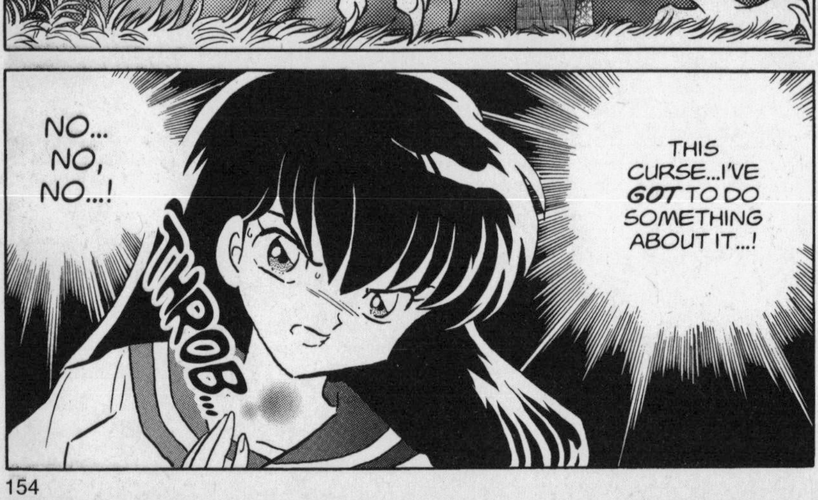
NO... NO, NO...!
THIS CURSE...I'VE **GOT** TO DO SOMETHING ABOUT IT...!
THROB...

SCROLL NINE
THE SHIKIGAMI

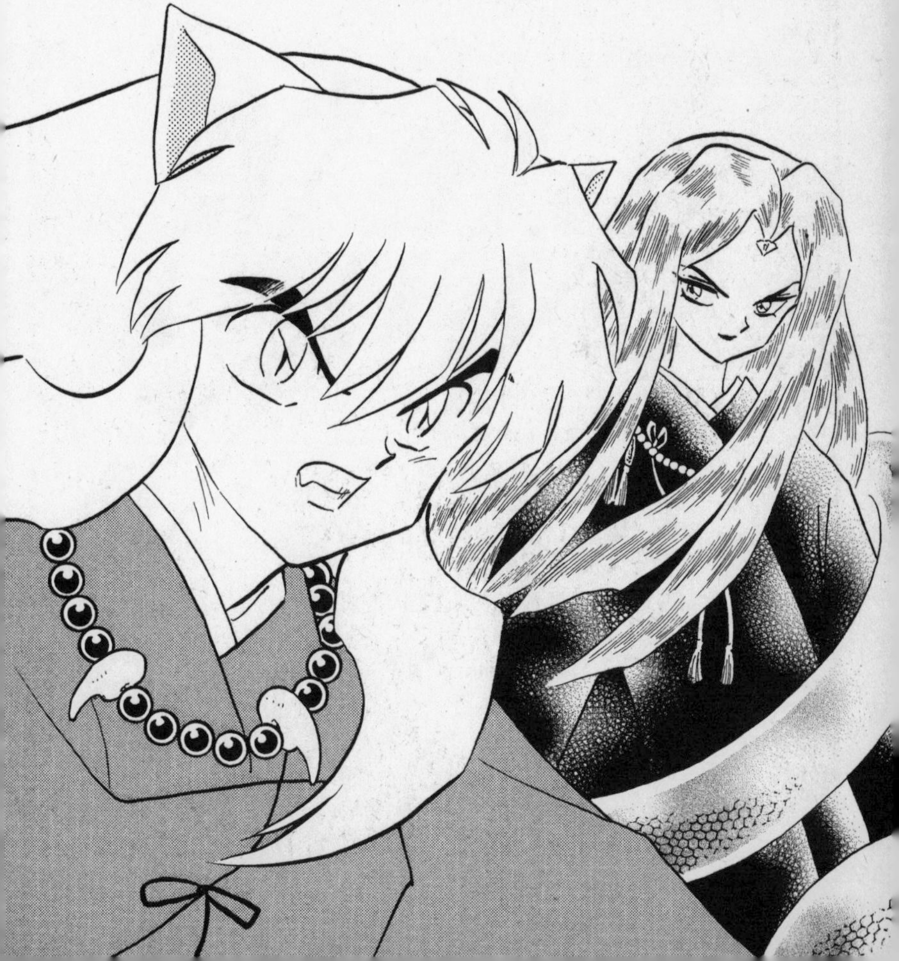

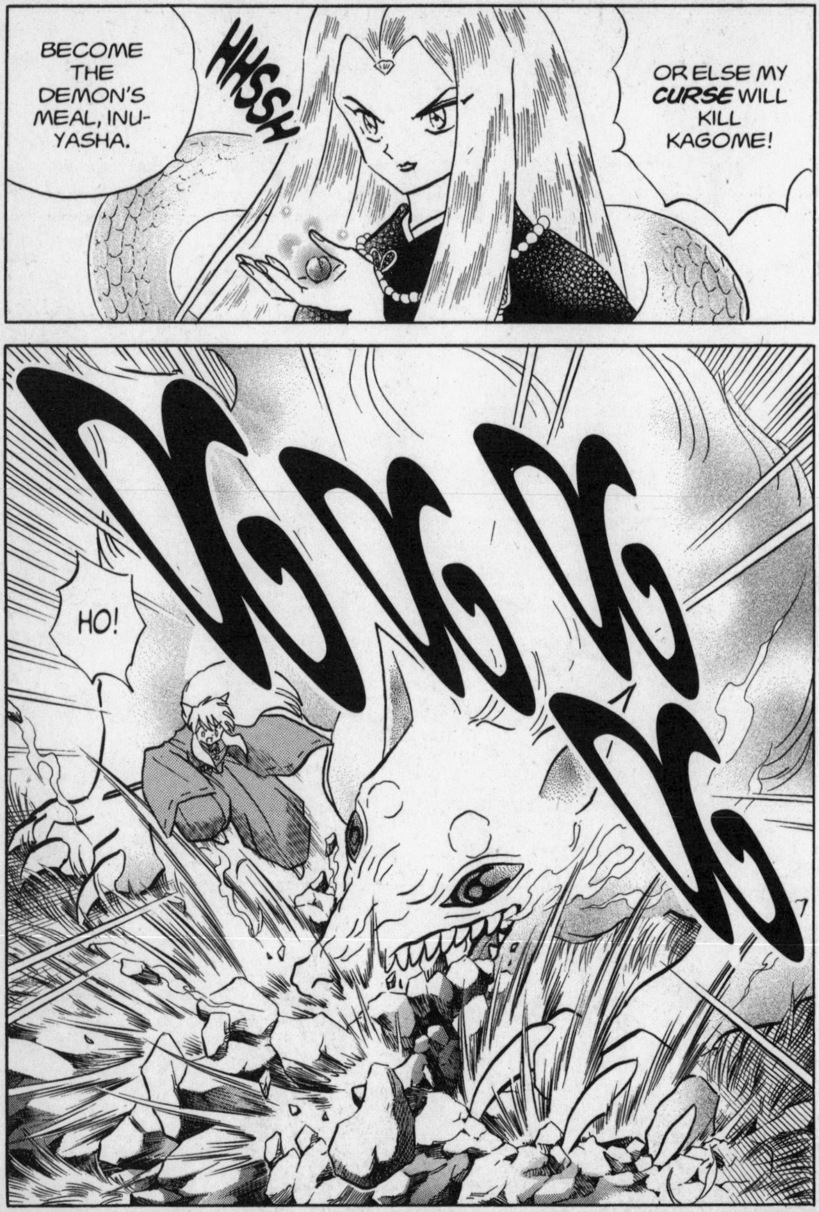
BECOME THE DEMON'S MEAL, INU-YASHA.
HHSSH
OR ELSE MY **CURSE** WILL KILL KAGOME!
HO!

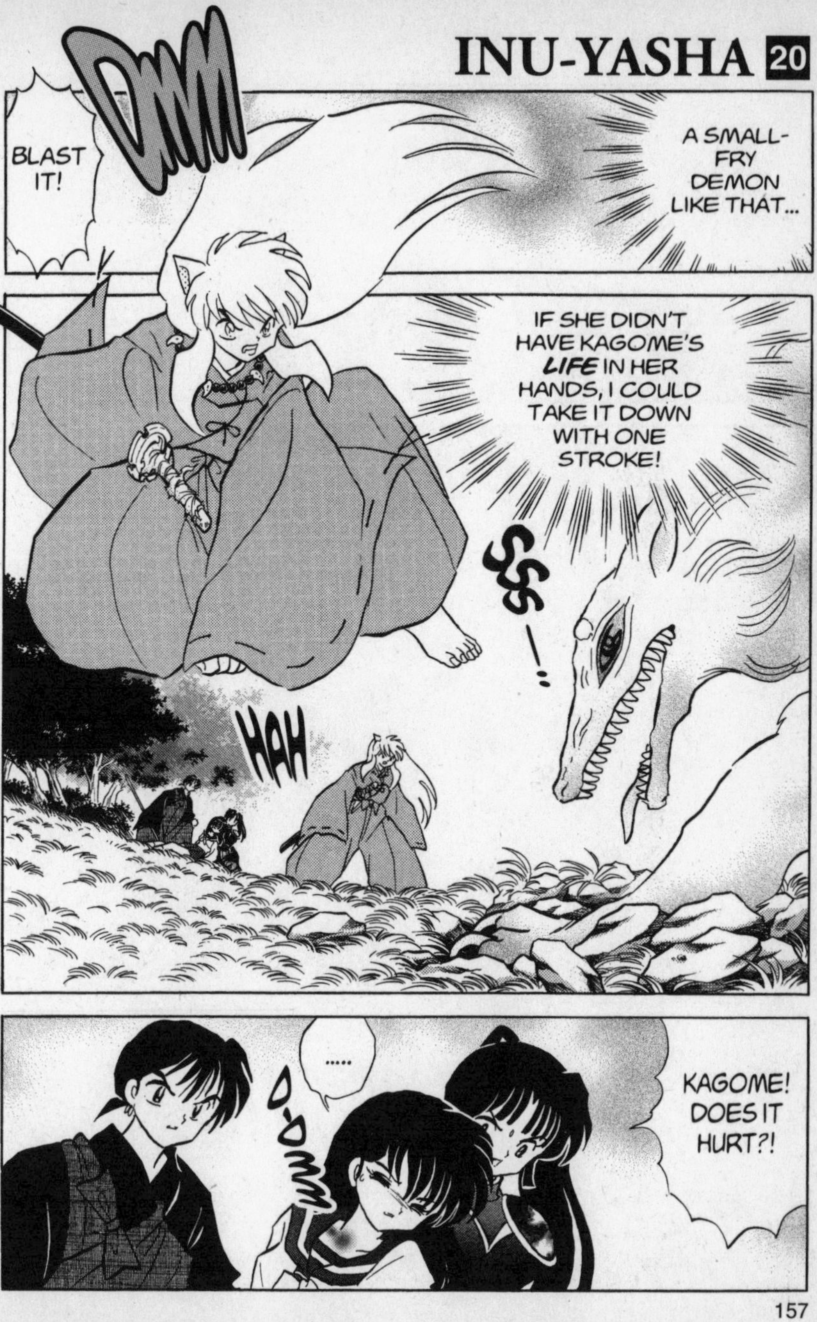
DMM
BLAST IT!
A SMALL-FRY DEMON LIKE THAT...
IF SHE DIDN'T HAVE KAGOME'S *LIFE* IN HER HANDS, I COULD TAKE IT DOWN WITH ONE STROKE!
SSS--!!
HAH
......
D-DMM
KAGOME! DOES IT HURT?!

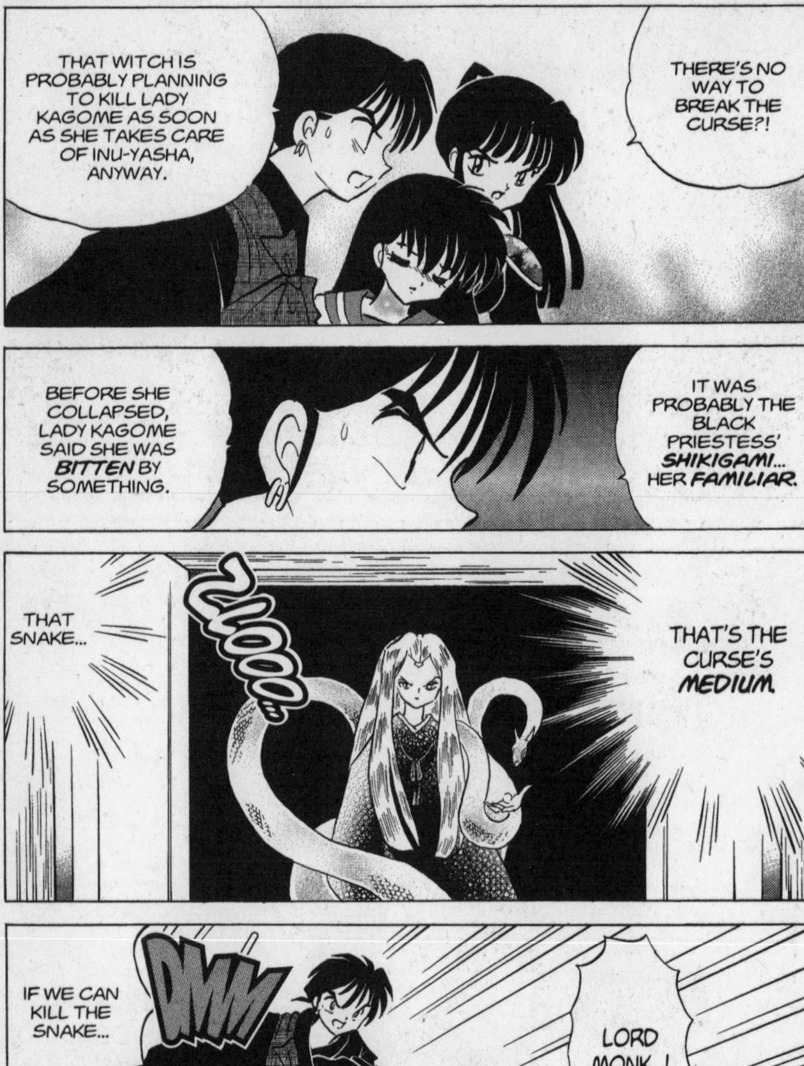
THAT WITCH IS PROBABLY PLANNING TO KILL LADY KAGOME AS SOON AS SHE TAKES CARE OF INU-YASHA, ANYWAY.
THERE'S NO WAY TO BREAK THE CURSE?!
BEFORE SHE COLLAPSED, LADY KAGOME SAID SHE WAS BITTEN BY SOMETHING.
IT WAS PROBABLY THE BLACK PRIESTESS' SHIKIGAMI... HER FAMILIAR.
THAT SNAKE...
ZLOOO...
THAT'S THE CURSE'S MEDIUM.
IF WE CAN KILL THE SNAKE...
DMM
LORD MONK...!

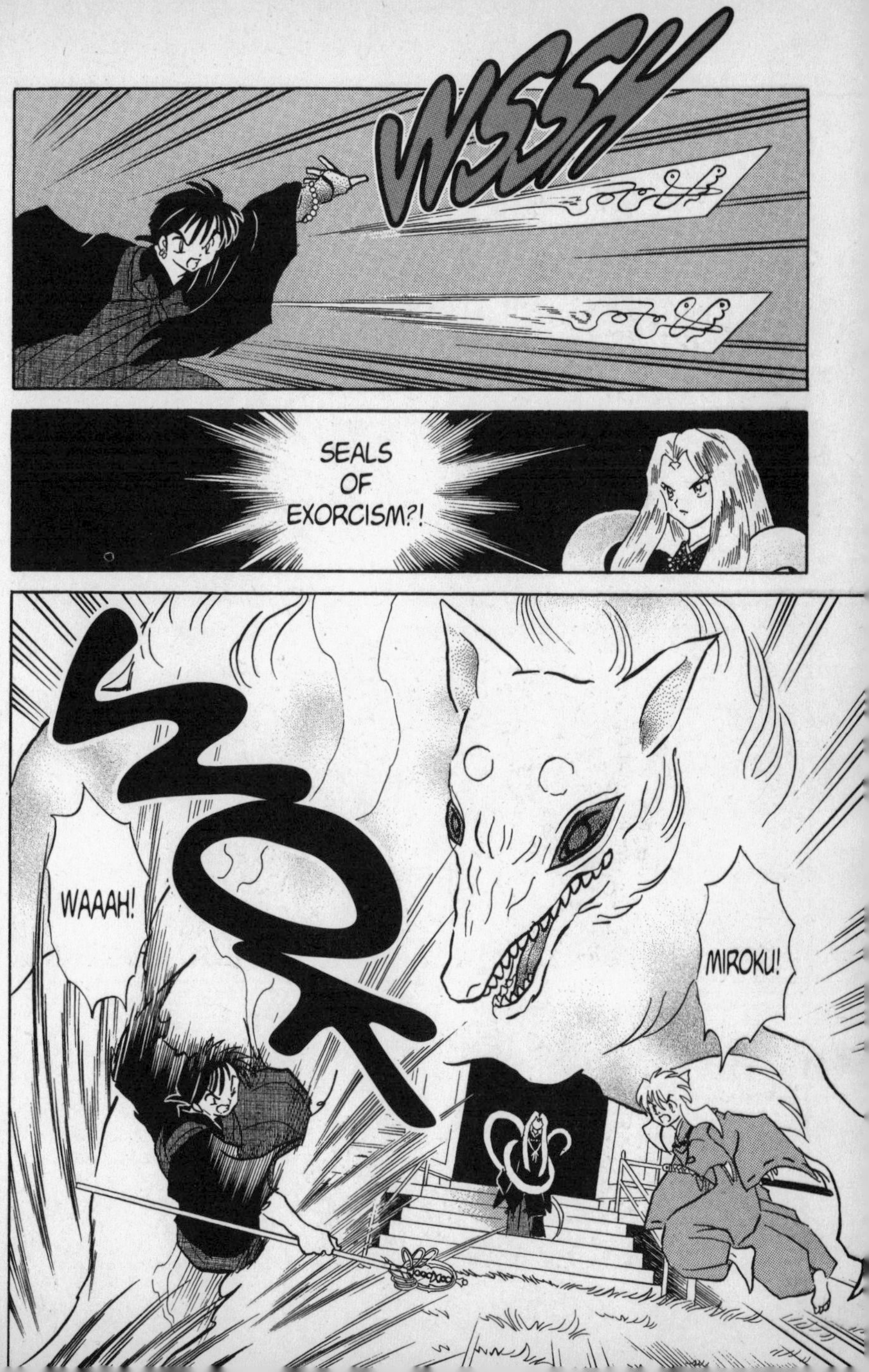
WSSH
SEALS OF EXORCISM?!
WAAAH!
MIROKU!

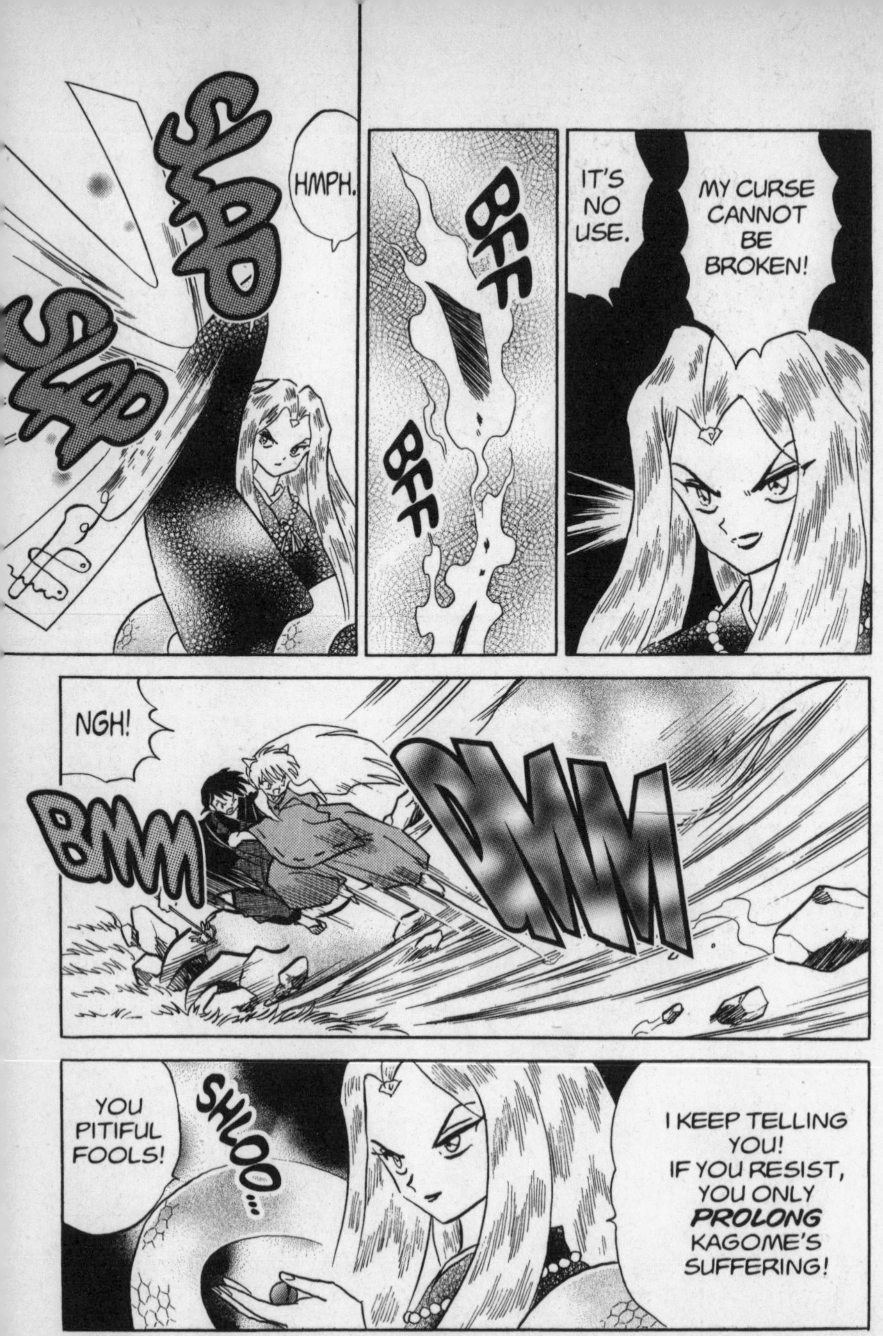
SLAP
SLAP
HMPH.
BFF
BFF
IT'S NO USE.
MY CURSE CANNOT BE BROKEN!
NGH!
BMM
DMM
YOU PITIFUL FOOLS!
SHLOO...
I KEEP TELLING YOU! IF YOU RESIST, YOU ONLY ***PROLONG*** KAGOME'S SUFFERING!

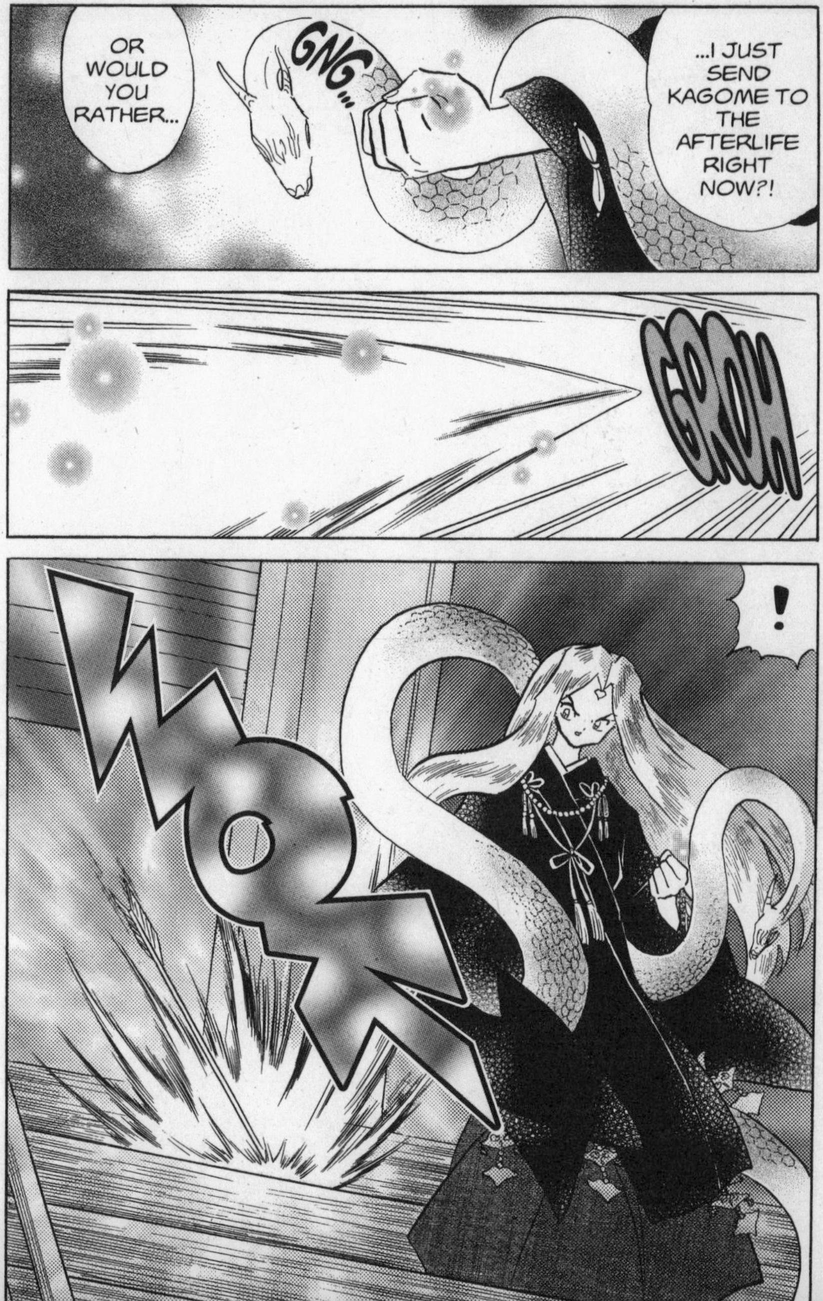
OR WOULD YOU RATHER...
GNG...
...I JUST SEND KAGOME TO THE AFTERLIFE RIGHT NOW?!
GROH
WOK
!

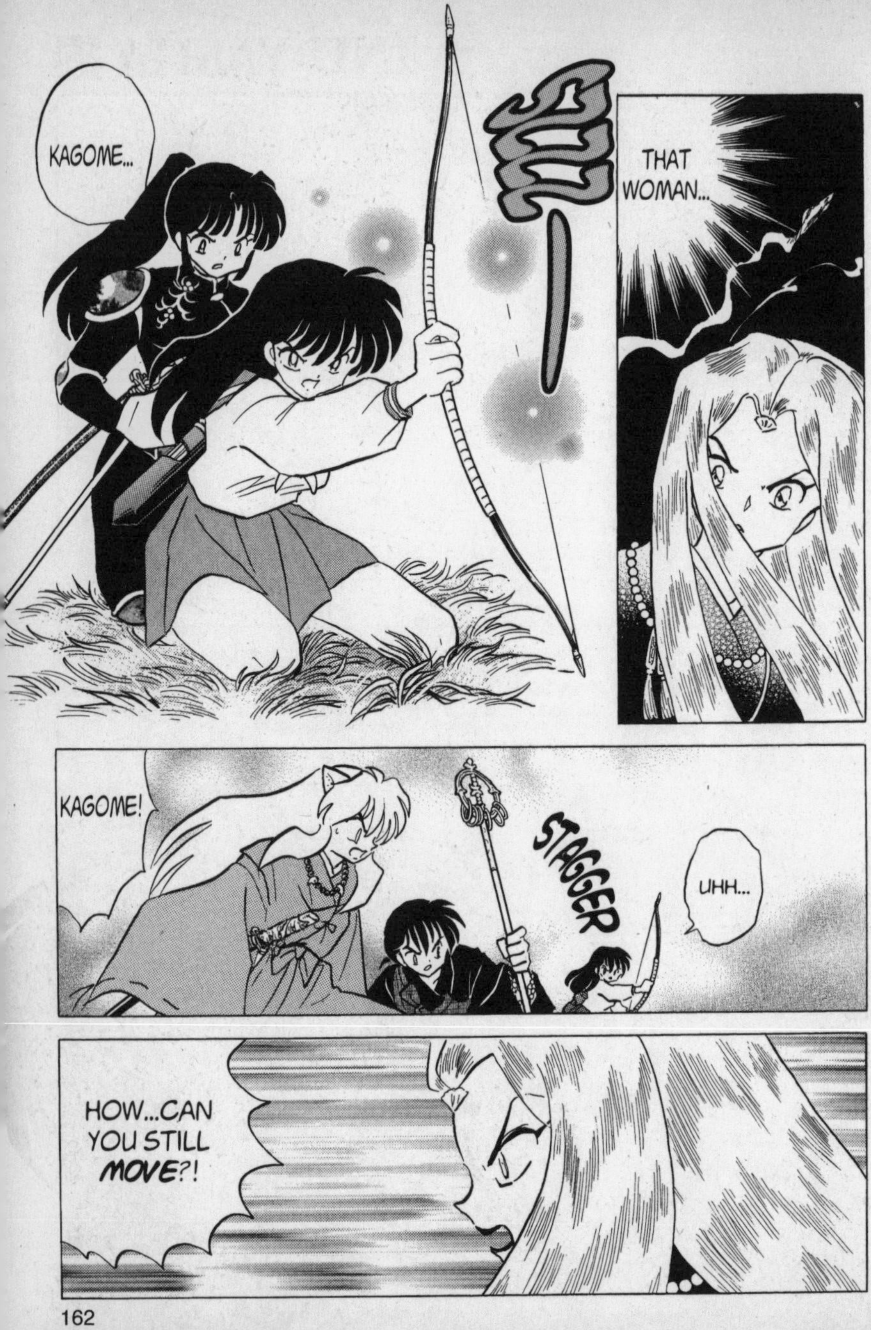

KAGOME...
THAT WOMAN...
KAGOME!
STAGGER
UHH...
HOW...CAN YOU STILL *MOVE*?!

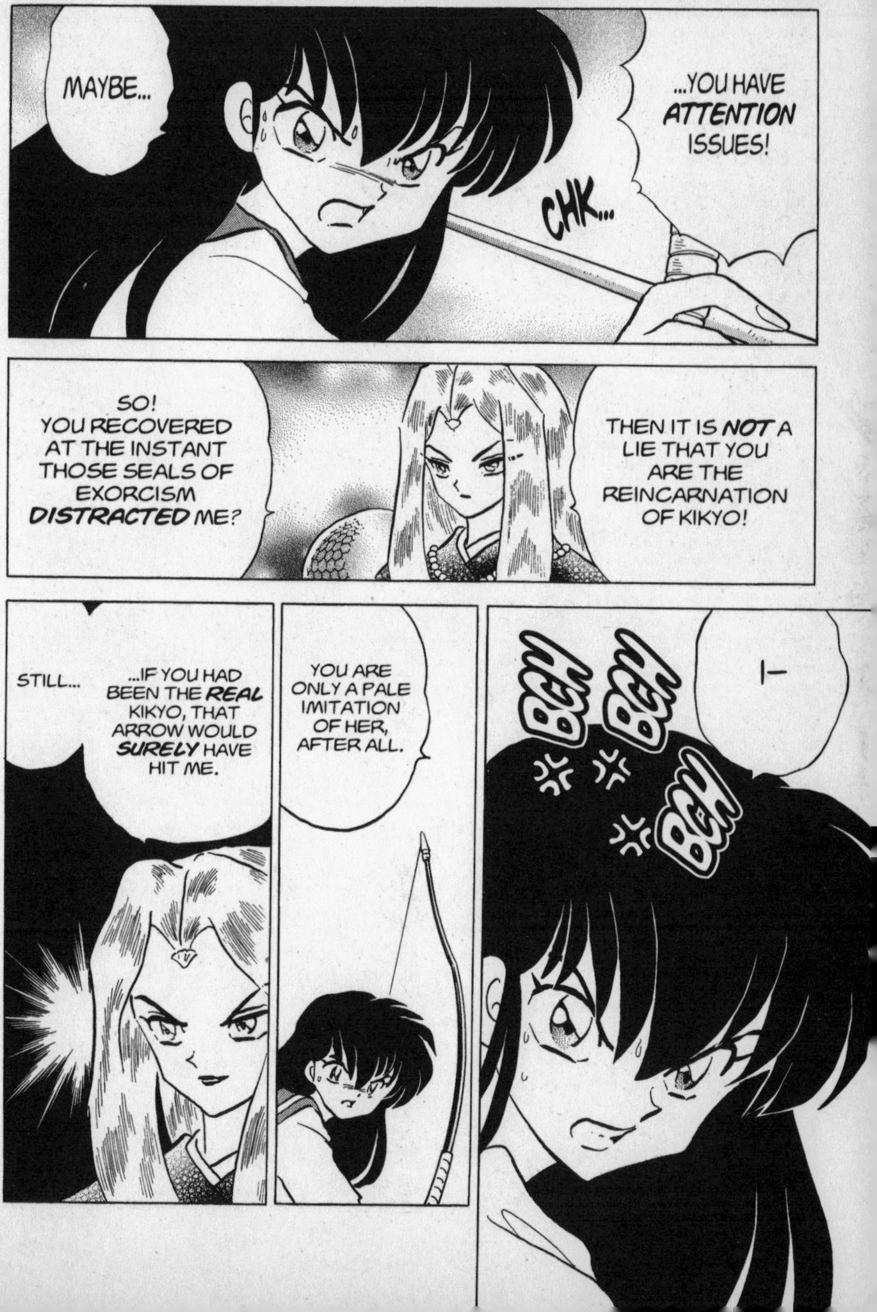
MAYBE...
...YOU HAVE ATTENTION ISSUES!
CHK...
SO! YOU RECOVERED AT THE INSTANT THOSE SEALS OF EXORCISM DISTRACTED ME?
THEN IT IS NOT A LIE THAT YOU ARE THE REINCARNATION OF KIKYO!
STILL...
...IF YOU HAD BEEN THE REAL KIKYO, THAT ARROW WOULD SURELY HAVE HIT ME.
YOU ARE ONLY A PALE IMITATION OF HER, AFTER ALL.
BCH
BCH
BCH
I—

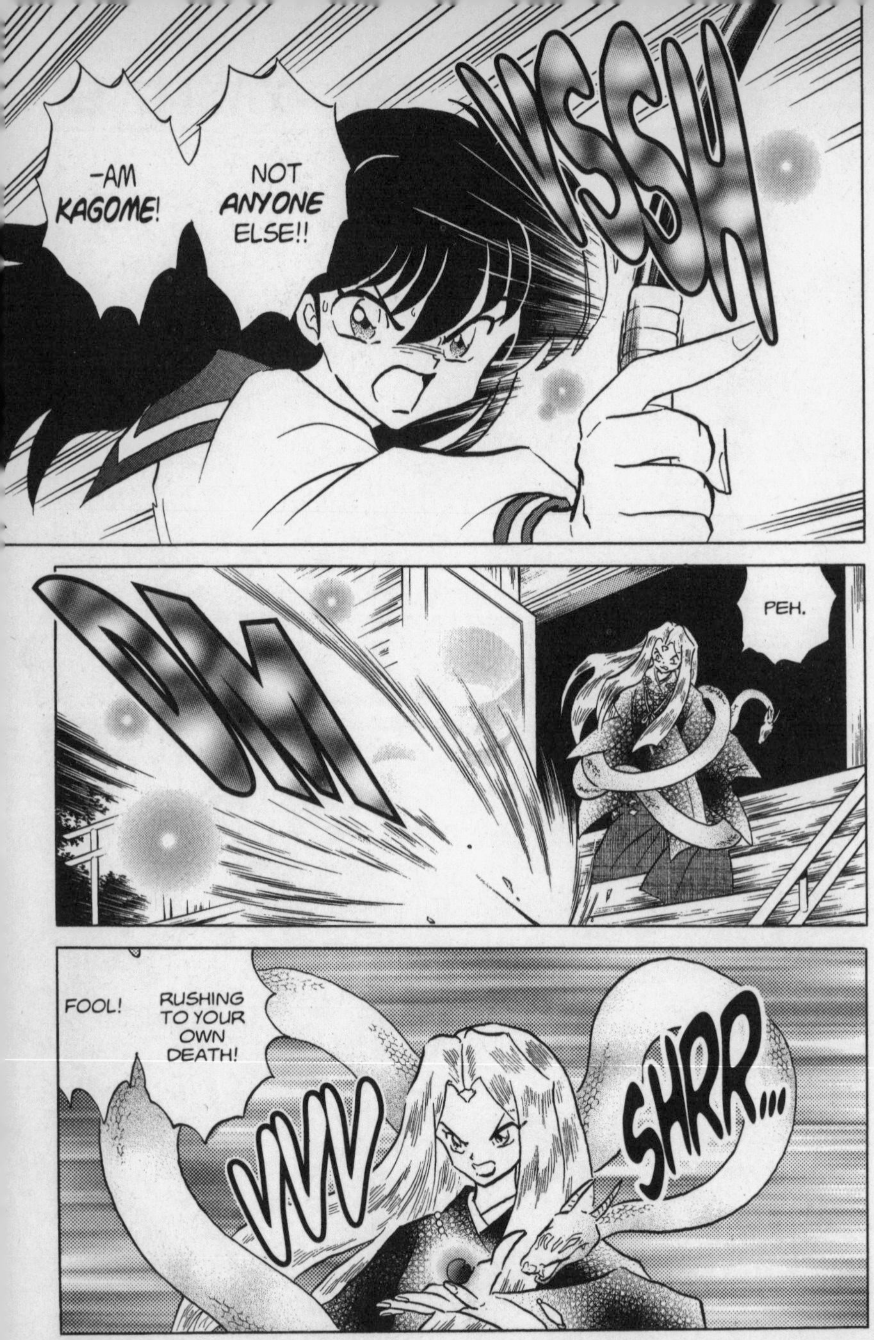
–AM KAGOME!
NOT ANYONE ELSE!!
PEH.
FOOL!
RUSHING TO YOUR OWN DEATH!
SHRR...

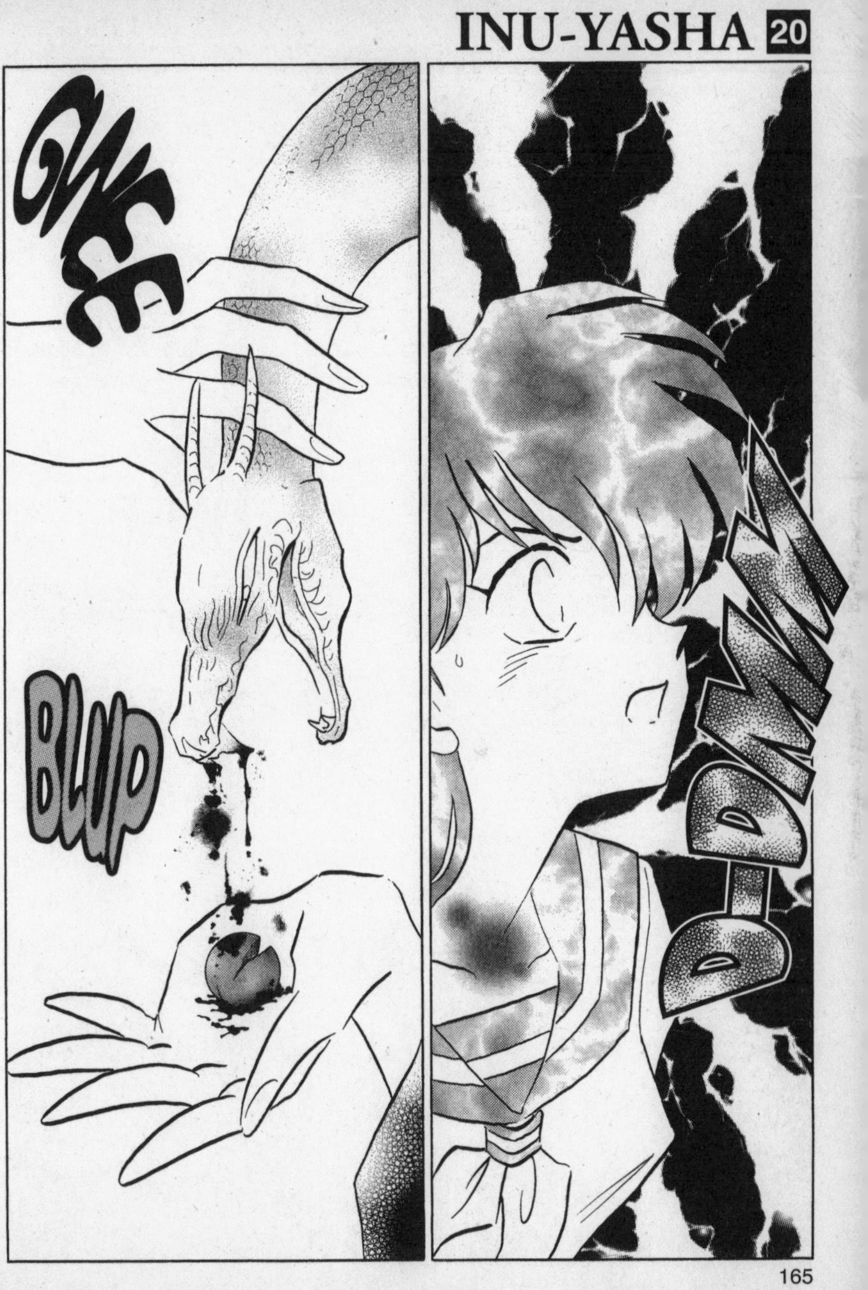
GYEE
BLUP
D-DMMM

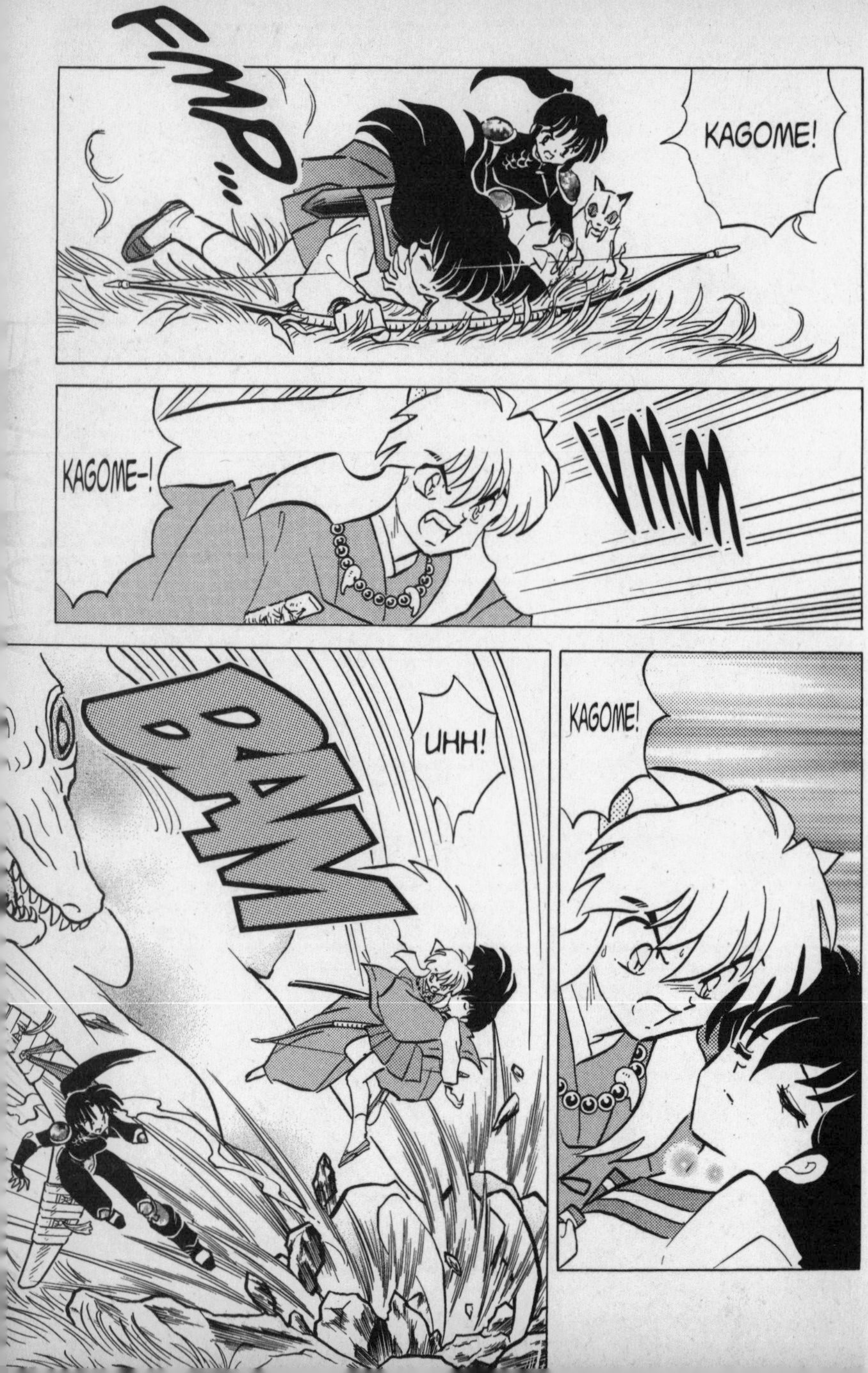
FMP...
KAGOME!
KAGOME-!
VMM
BAM
UHH!
KAGOME!

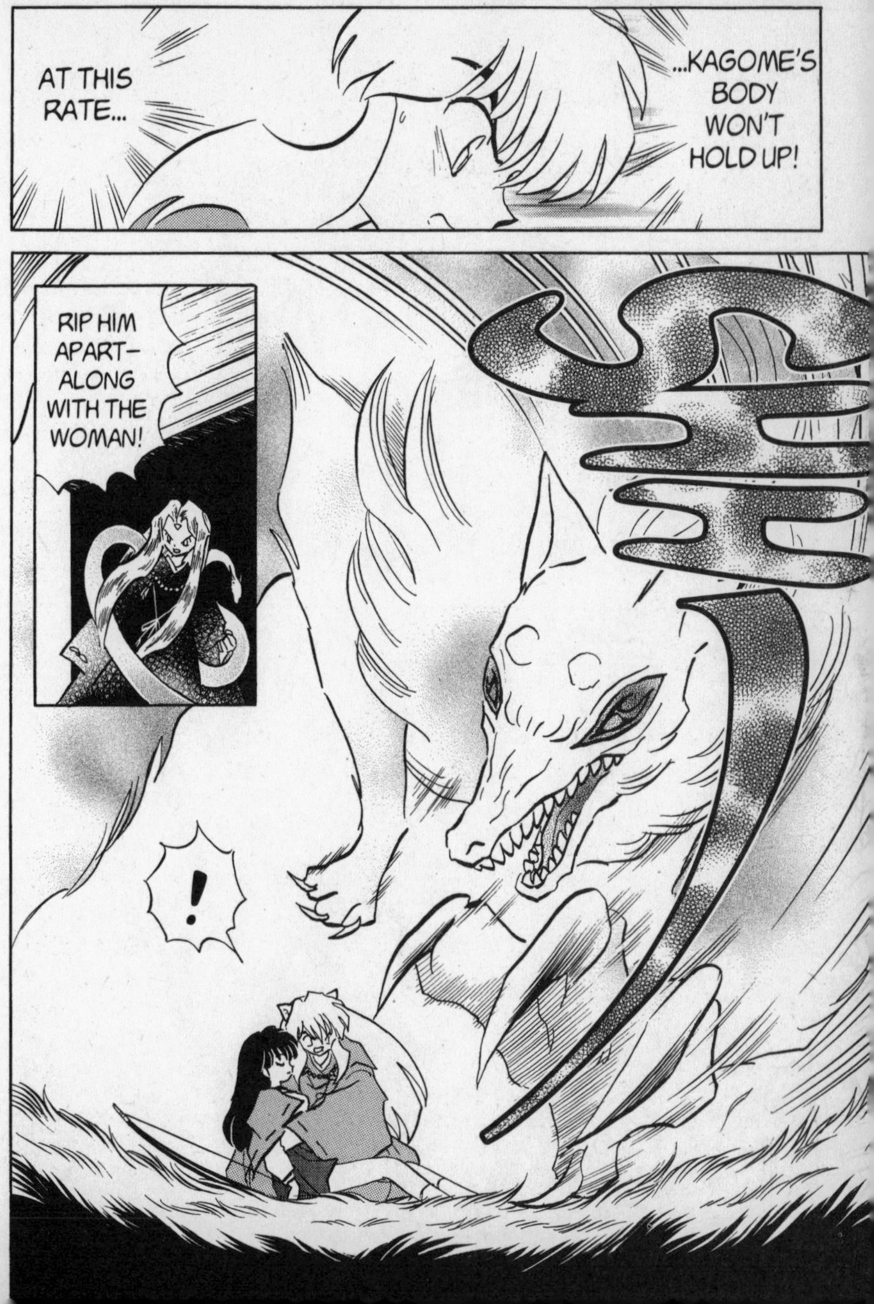
AT THIS RATE...
...KAGOME'S BODY WON'T HOLD UP!
RIP HIM APART-ALONG WITH THE WOMAN!
!

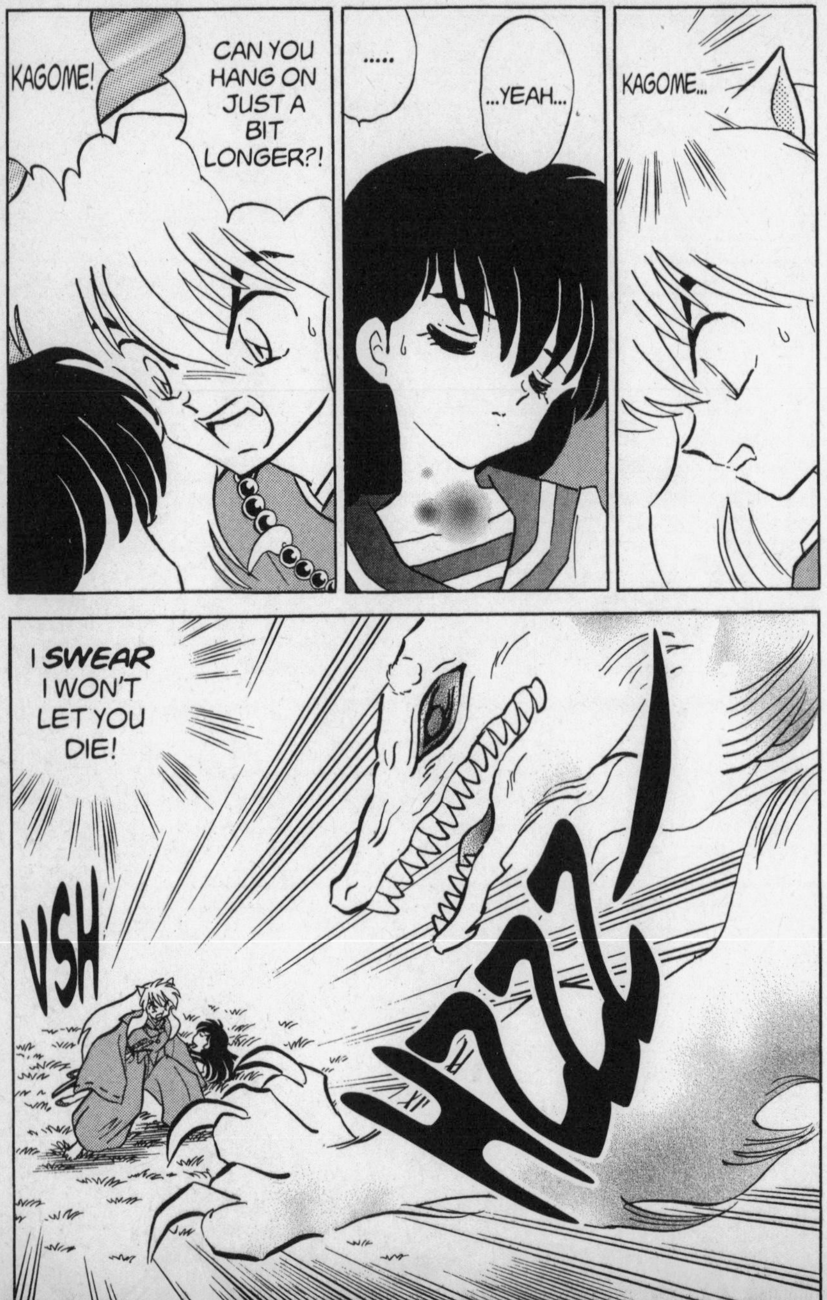
KAGOME!
CAN YOU HANG ON JUST A BIT LONGER?!
.....
...YEAH...
KAGOME...
I SWEAR I WON'T LET YOU DIE!
VSH
HZZZ

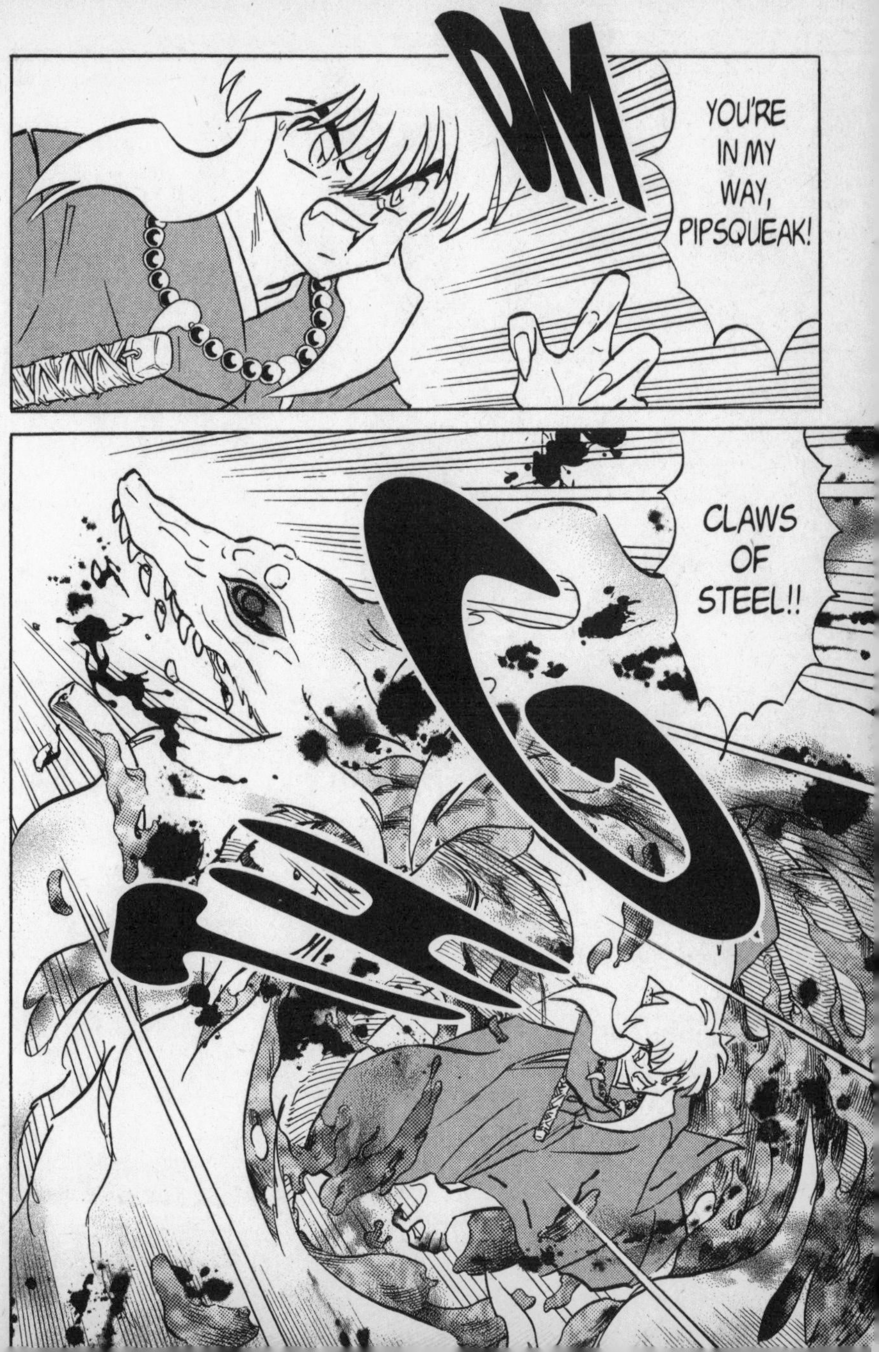
DM
YOU'RE IN MY WAY, PIPSQUEAK!
CLAWS OF STEEL!!

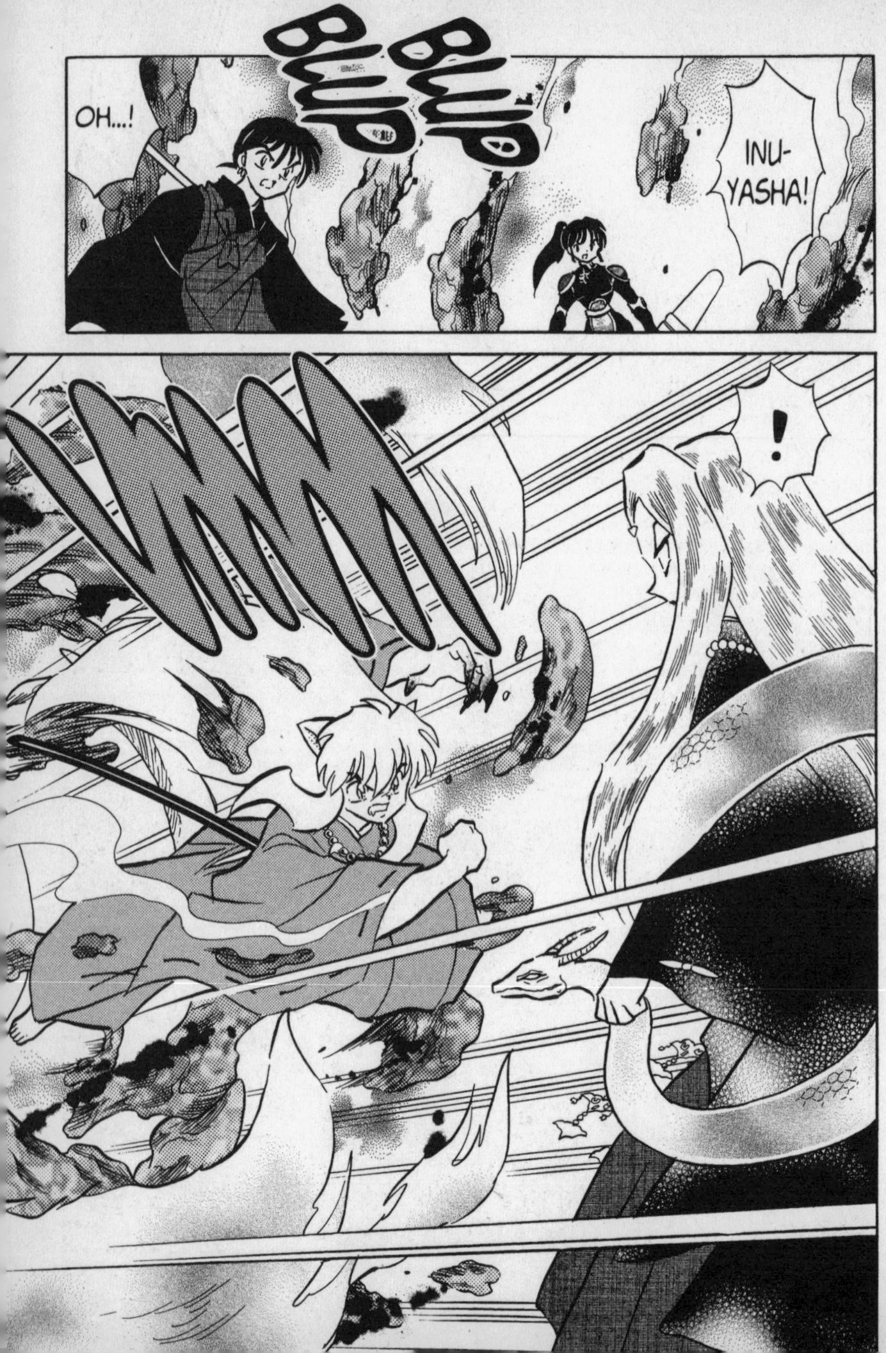

BLUP BLUP
OH...!
INU-YASHA!
!

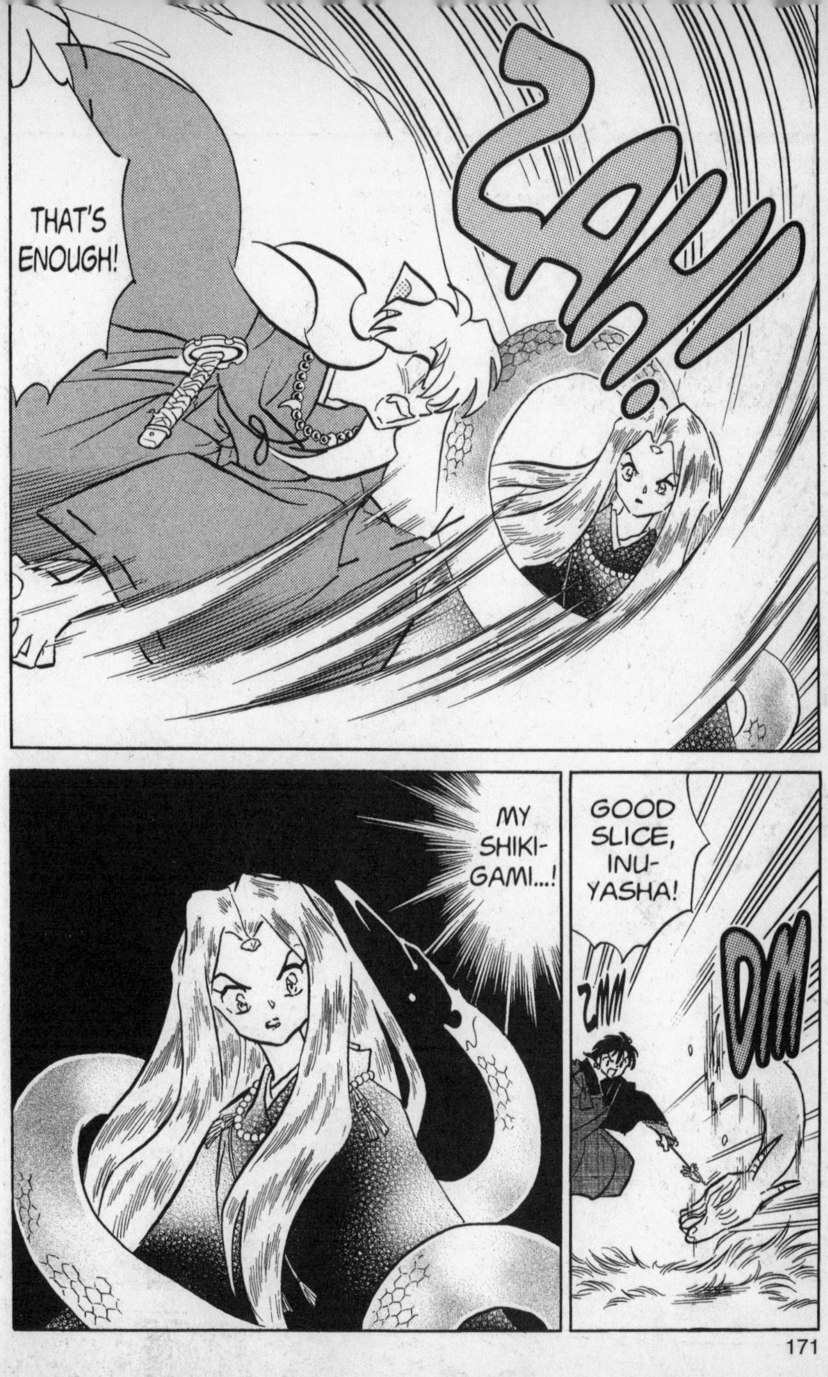
THAT'S ENOUGH!
ZAH!
MY SHIKI-GAMI...!
GOOD SLICE, INU-YASHA!
ZMM
DM

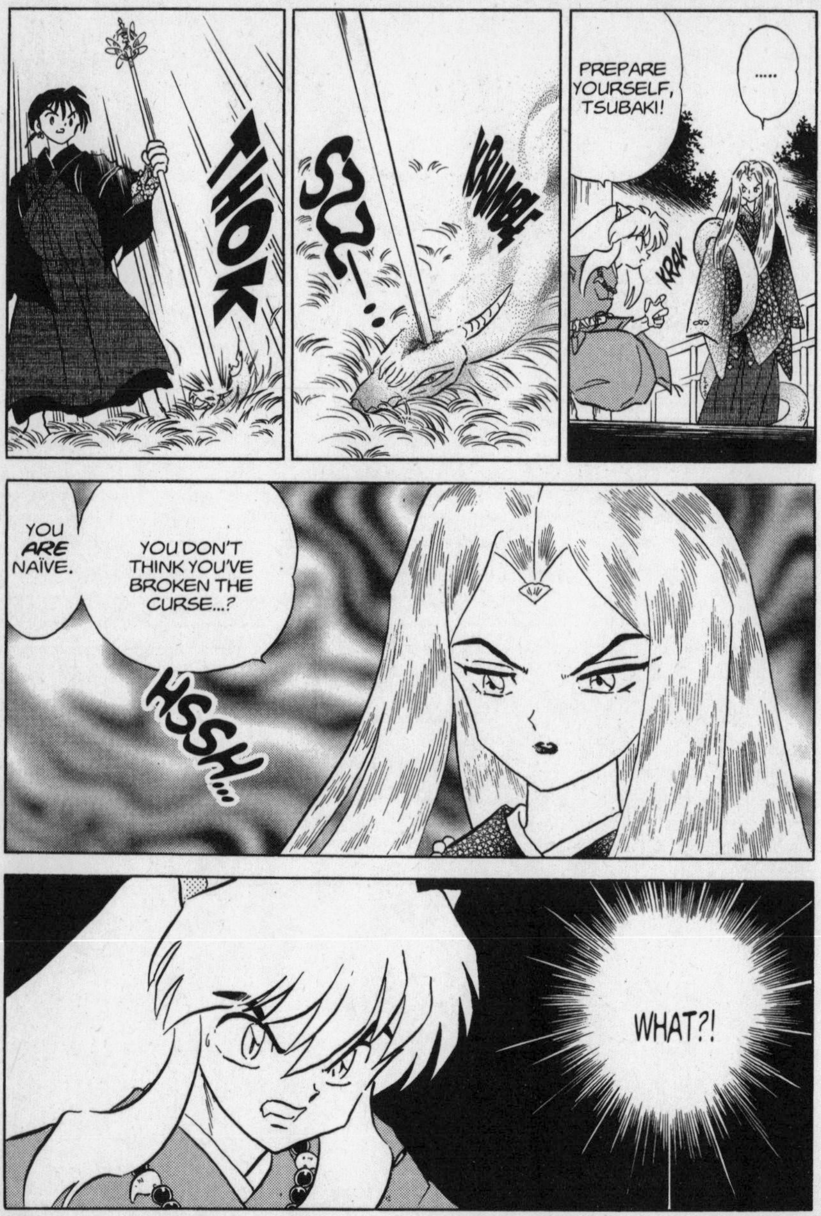
THOK
SZZ—!!
KRUMBLE
PREPARE YOURSELF, TSUBAKI!
......
KRAK
YOU *ARE* NAÏVE.
YOU DON'T THINK YOU'VE BROKEN THE CURSE...?
HSSH...
WHAT?!

SCROLL TEN

THE CURSE REFLECTED

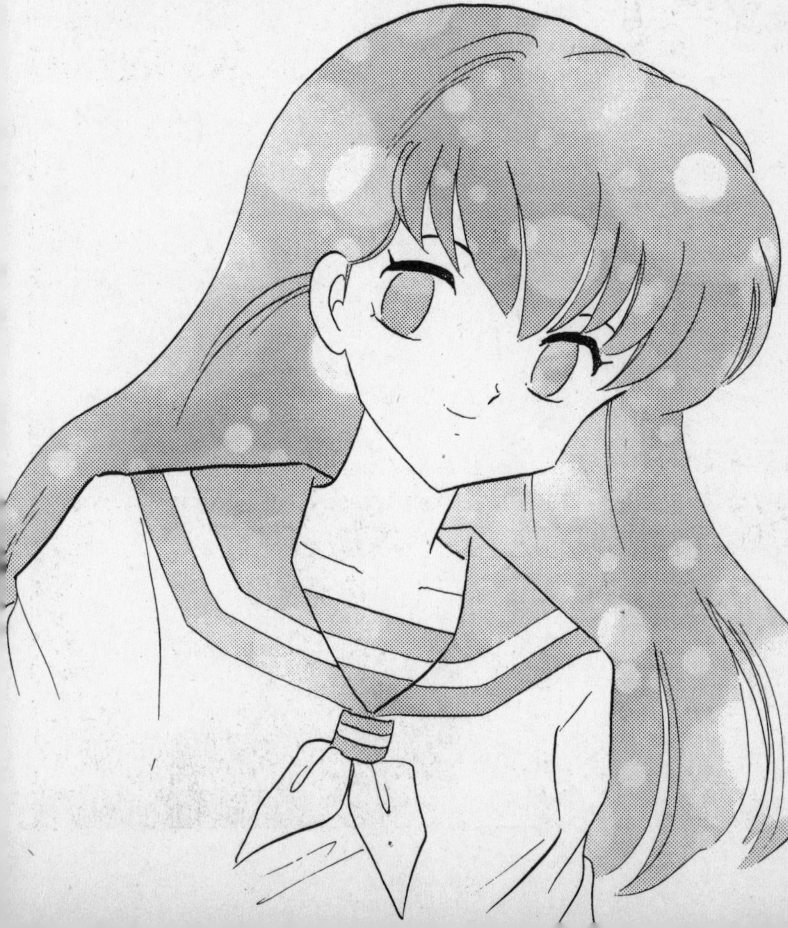

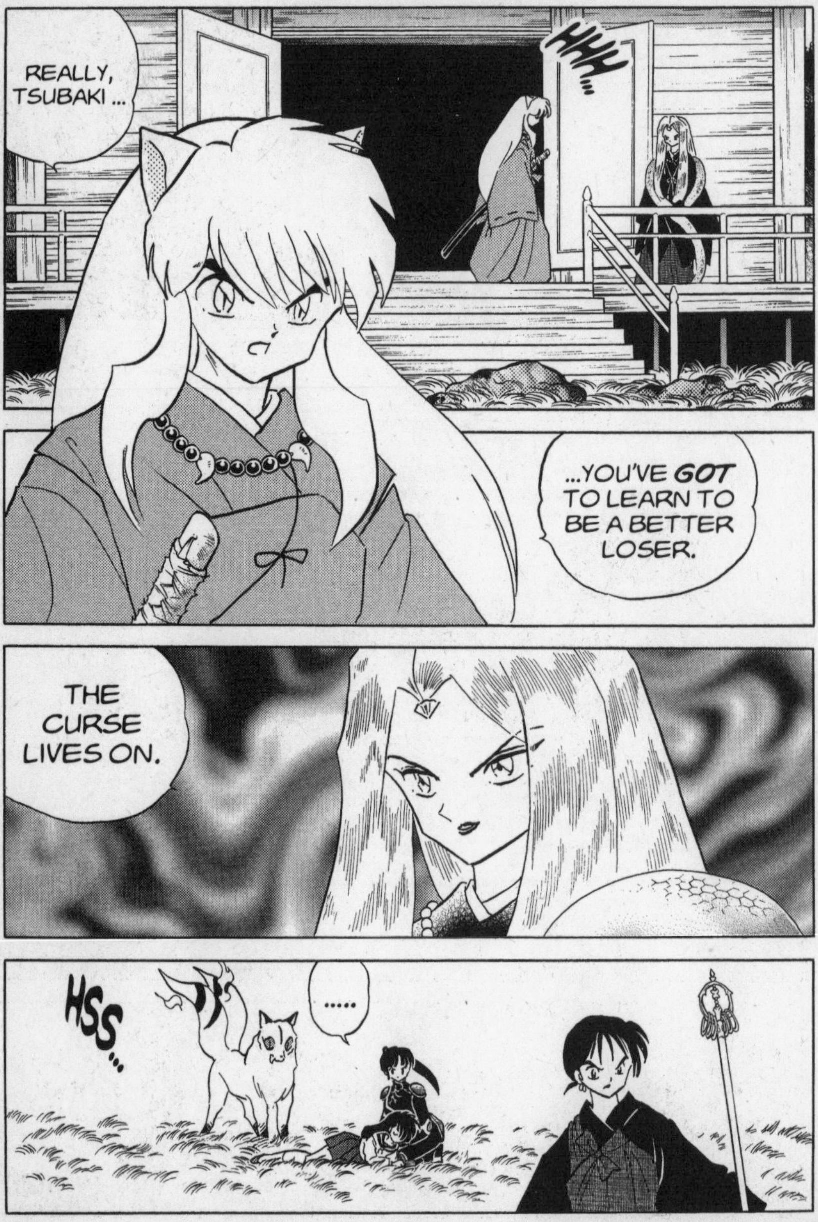
REALLY, TSUBAKI ...
HHH...
...YOU'VE GOT TO LEARN TO BE A BETTER LOSER.
THE CURSE LIVES ON.
HSS...
......

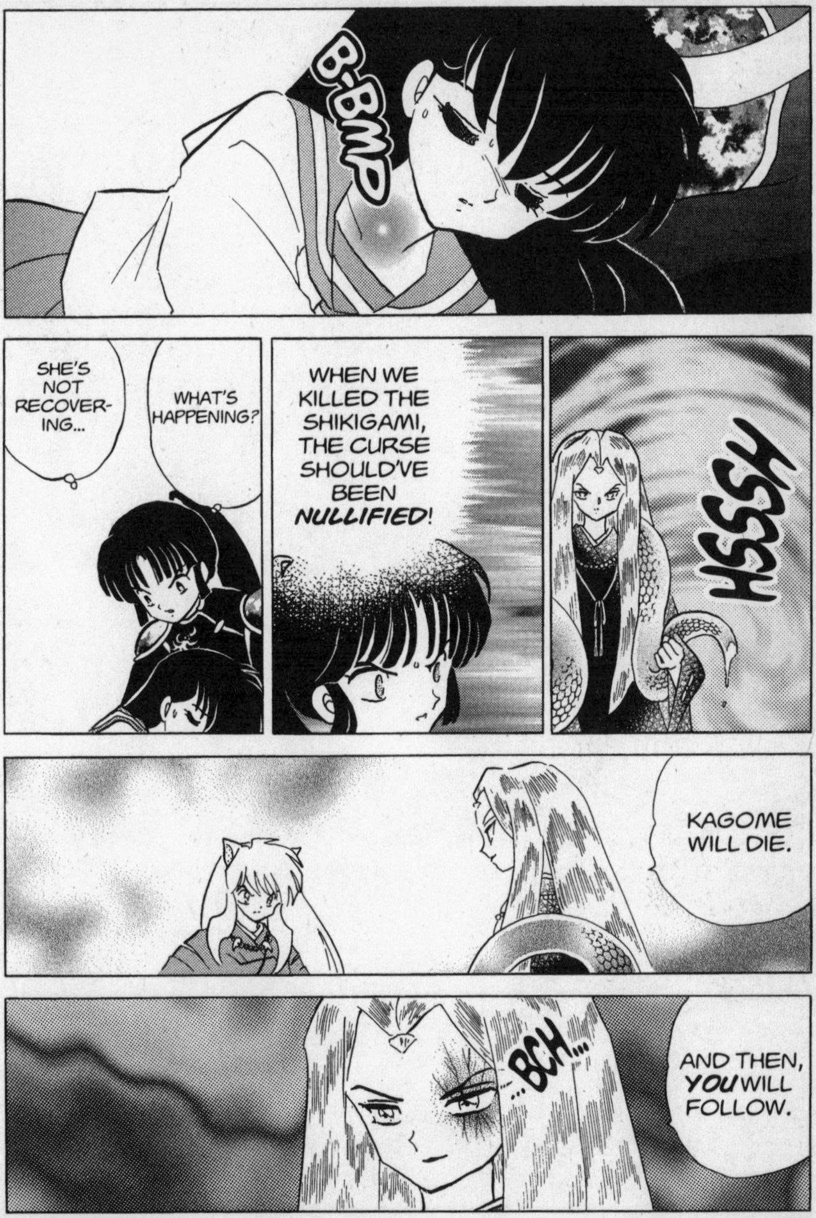
B-BMP
SHE'S NOT RECOVER-ING...
WHAT'S HAPPENING?
WHEN WE KILLED THE SHIKIGAMI, THE CURSE SHOULD'VE BEEN *NULLIFIED*!
HSSSH
KAGOME WILL DIE.
...BCH...
AND THEN, *YOU* WILL FOLLOW.

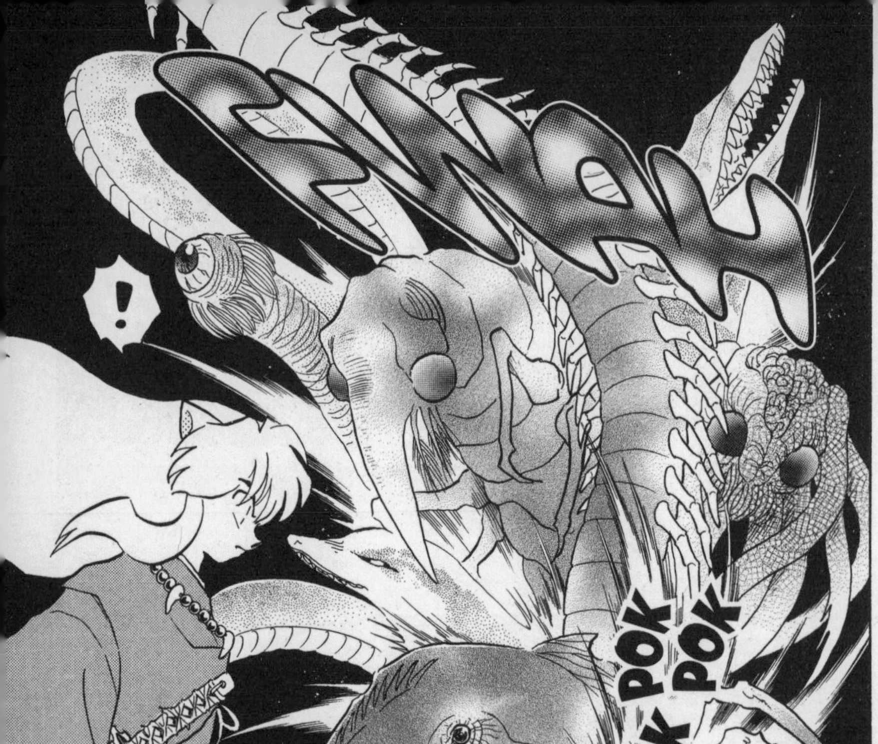
!
POK POK POK POK

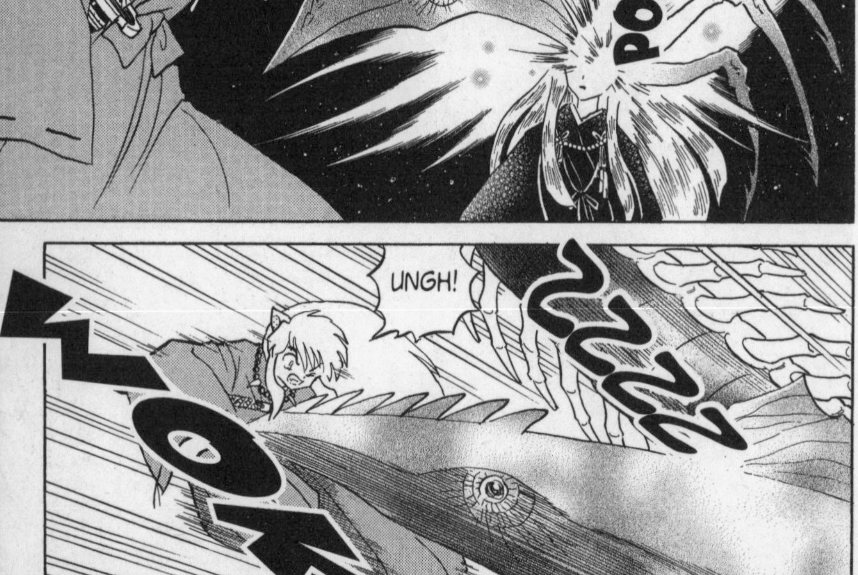
UNGH!

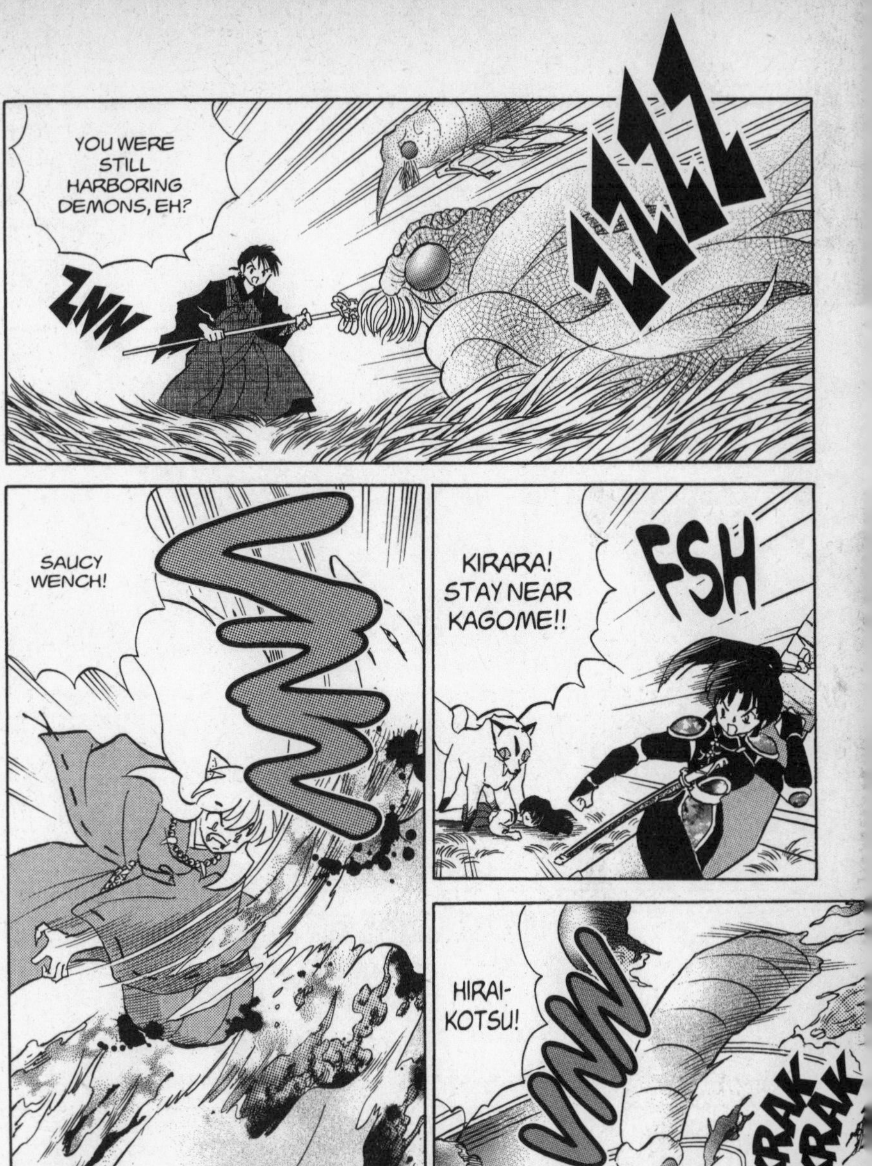
YOU WERE STILL HARBORING DEMONS, EH?
ZNN
SAUCY WENCH!
KIRARA! STAY NEAR KAGOME!!
FSH
HIRAI-KOTSU!
KRAK KRAK

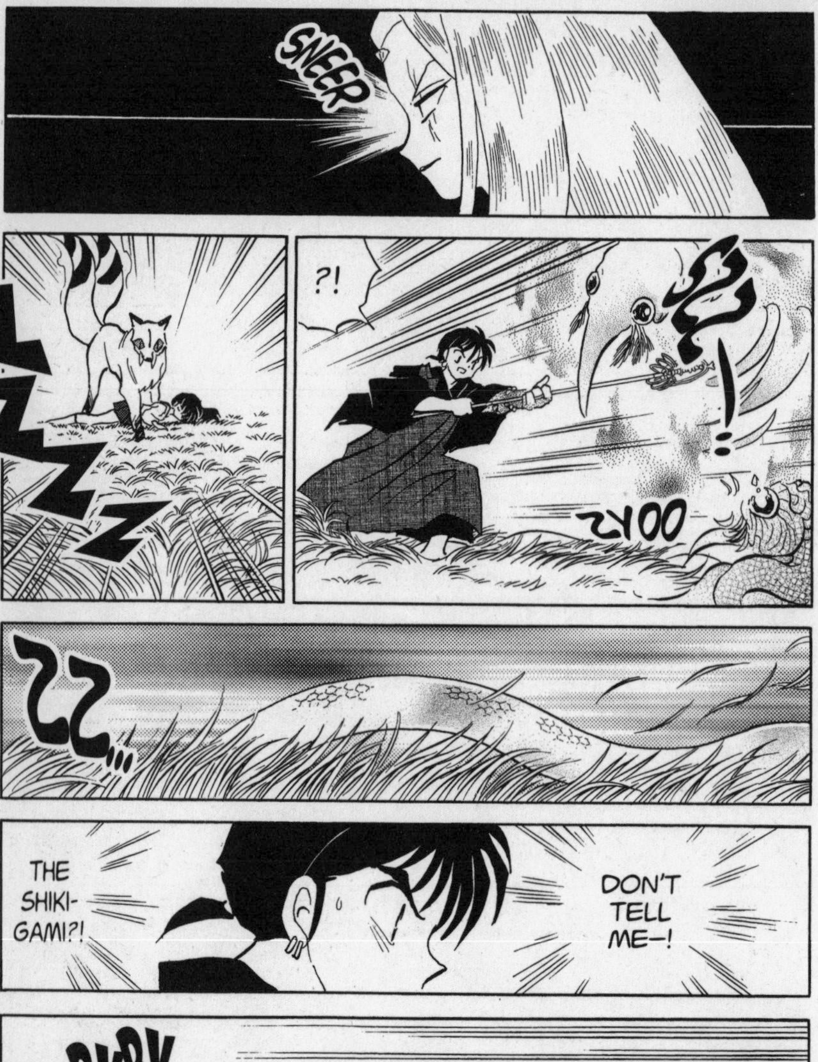
SNEER
?!
ZYOO
ZZ...
THE SHIKI-GAMI?!
DON'T TELL ME–!
BKBK

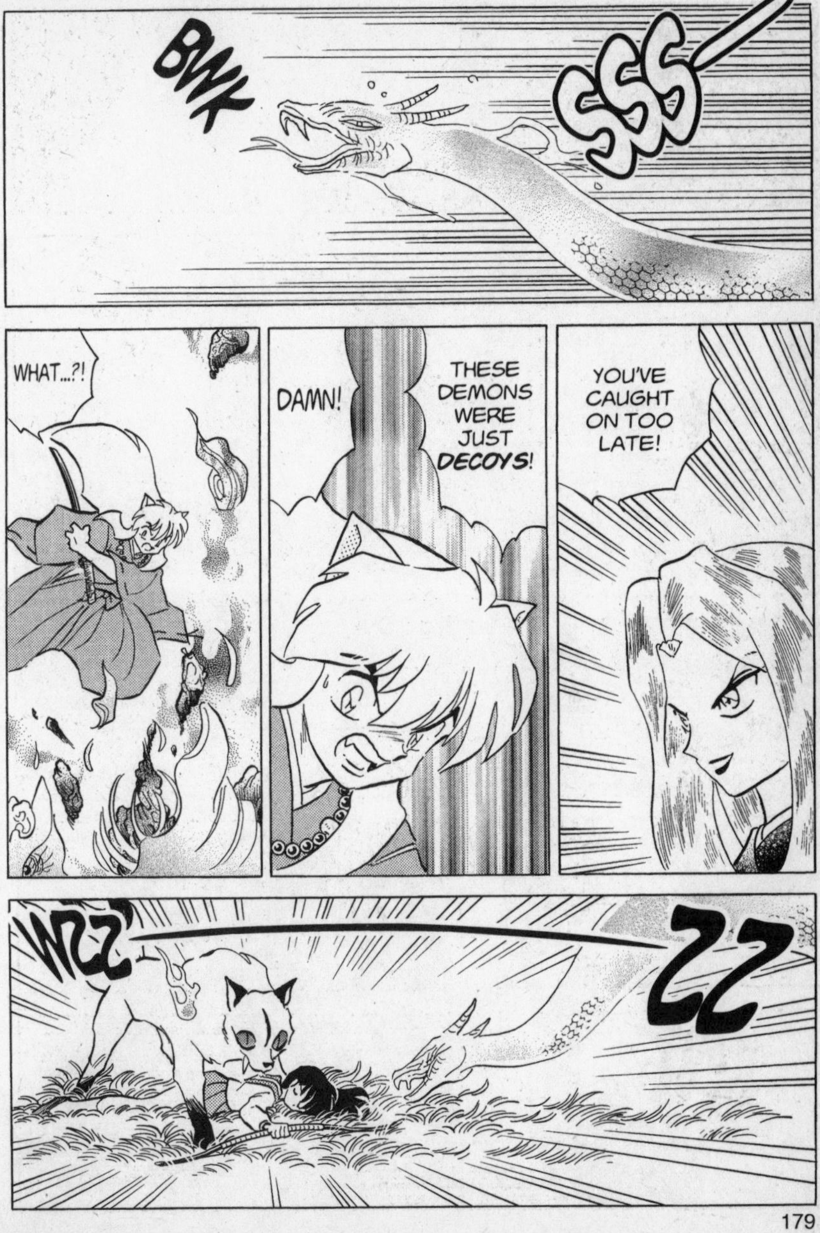

BWK
SSS
WHAT...?!
DAMN!
THESE DEMONS WERE JUST DECOYS!
YOU'VE CAUGHT ON TOO LATE!
WZZ
ZZ

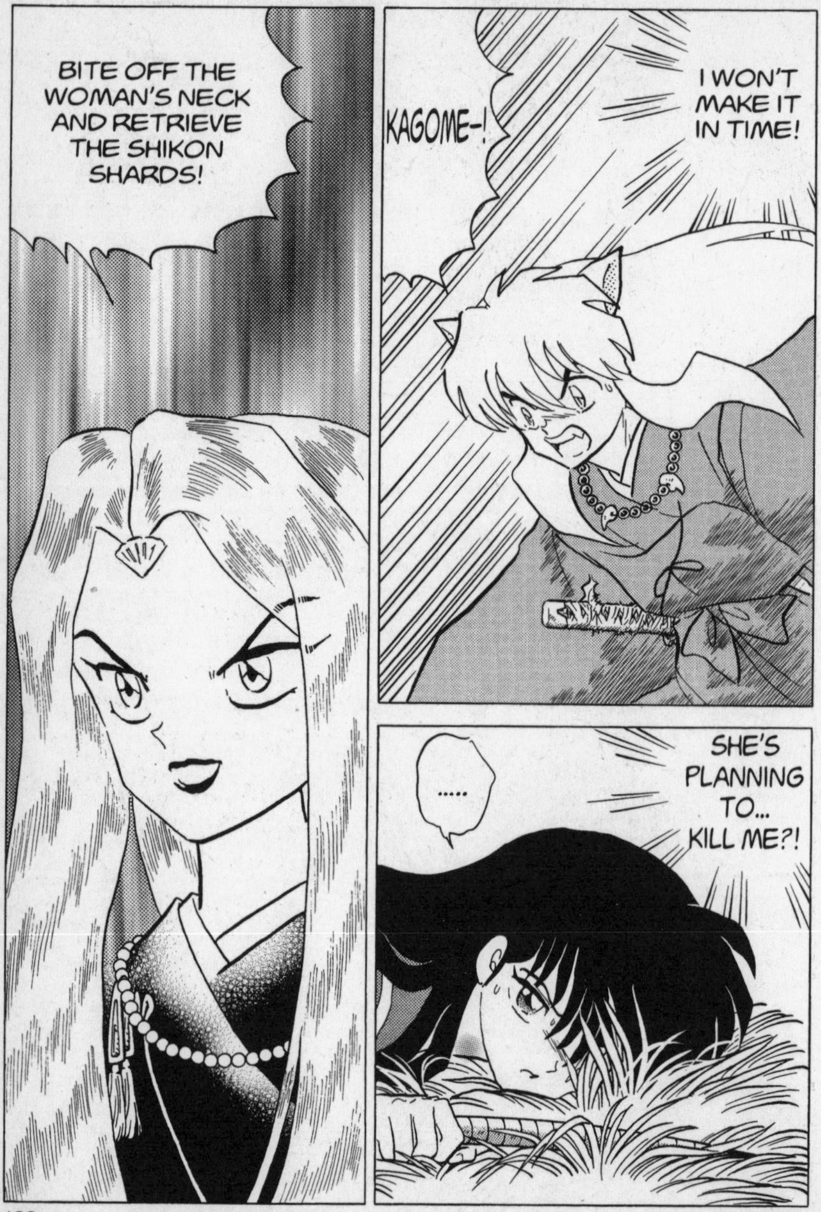
BITE OFF THE WOMAN'S NECK AND RETRIEVE THE SHIKON SHARDS!
KAGOME-!
I WON'T MAKE IT IN TIME!
......
SHE'S PLANNING TO... KILL ME?!

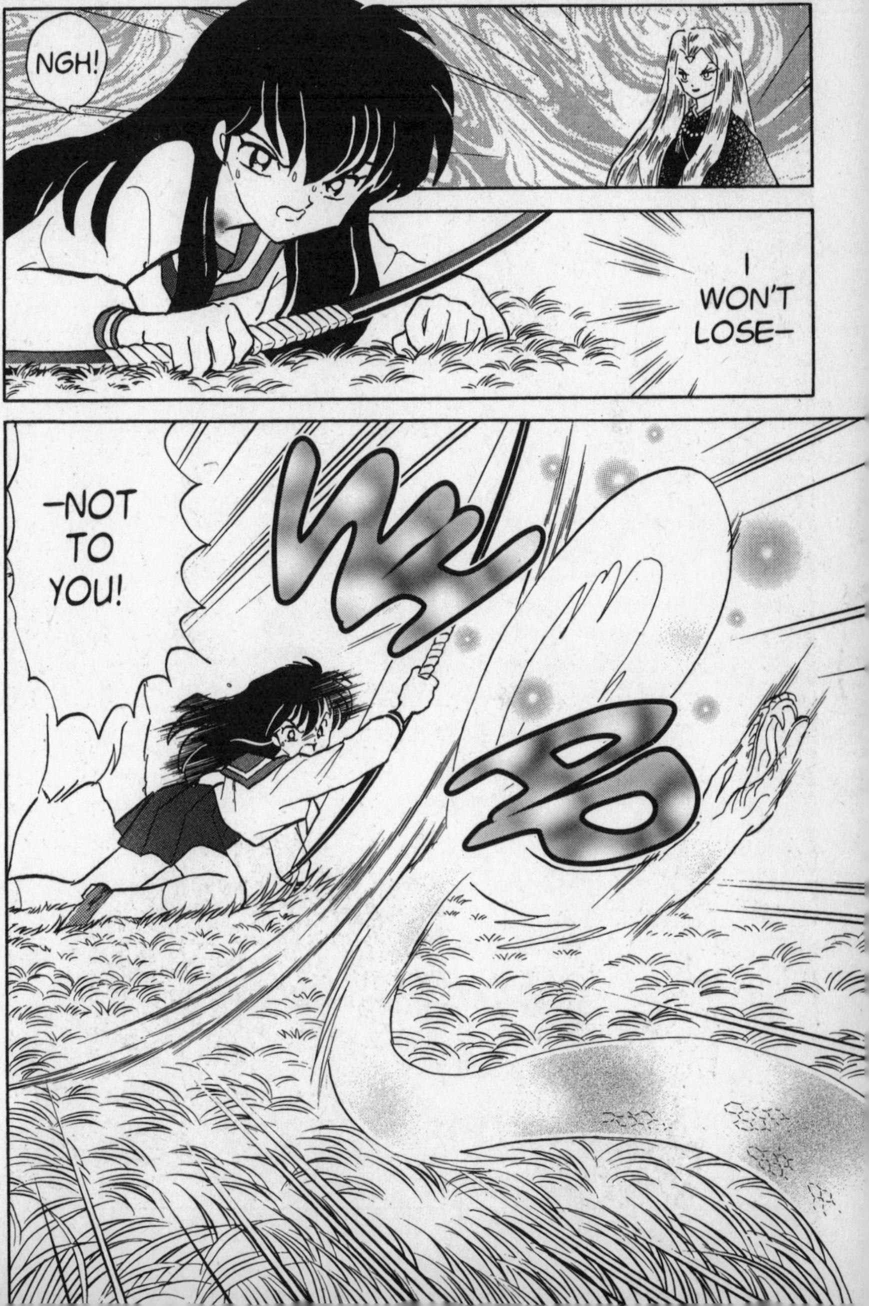
NGH!
I WON'T LOSE–
–NOT TO YOU!

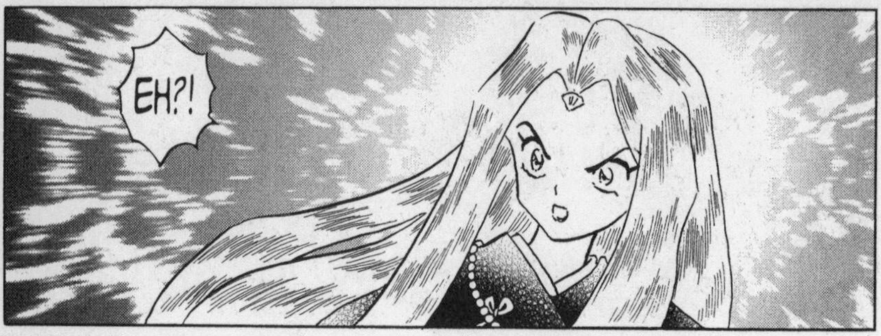
EH?!
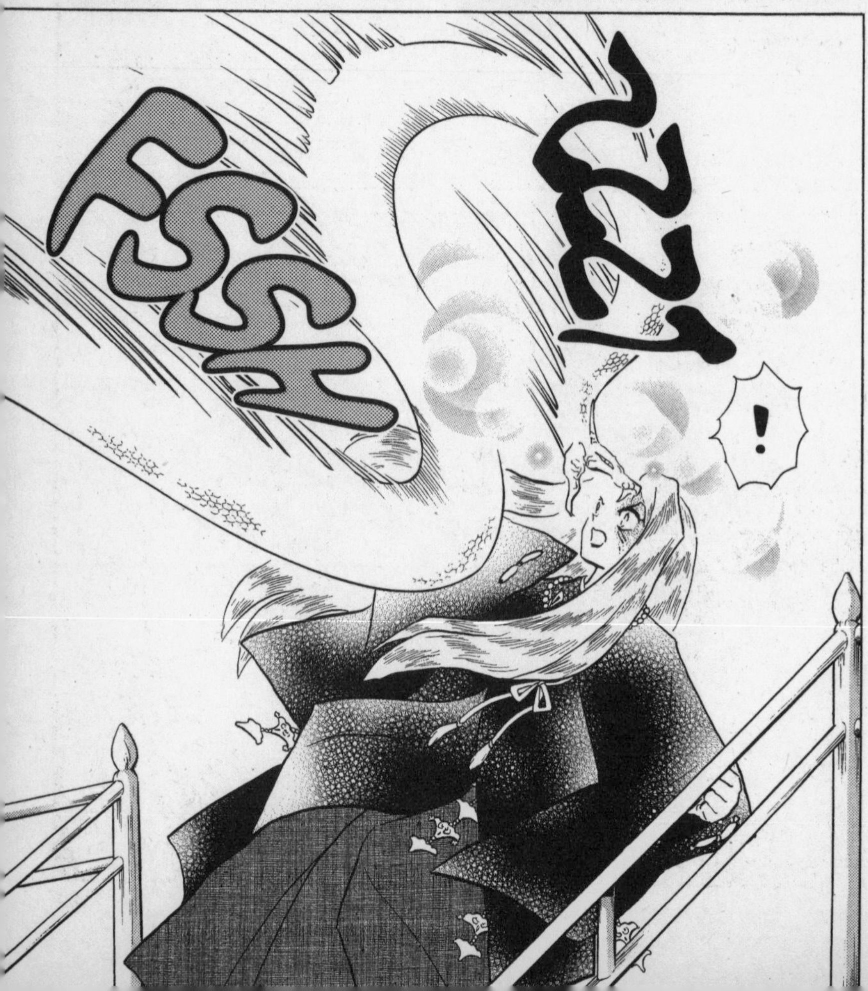
FSSH
ZZZ
!

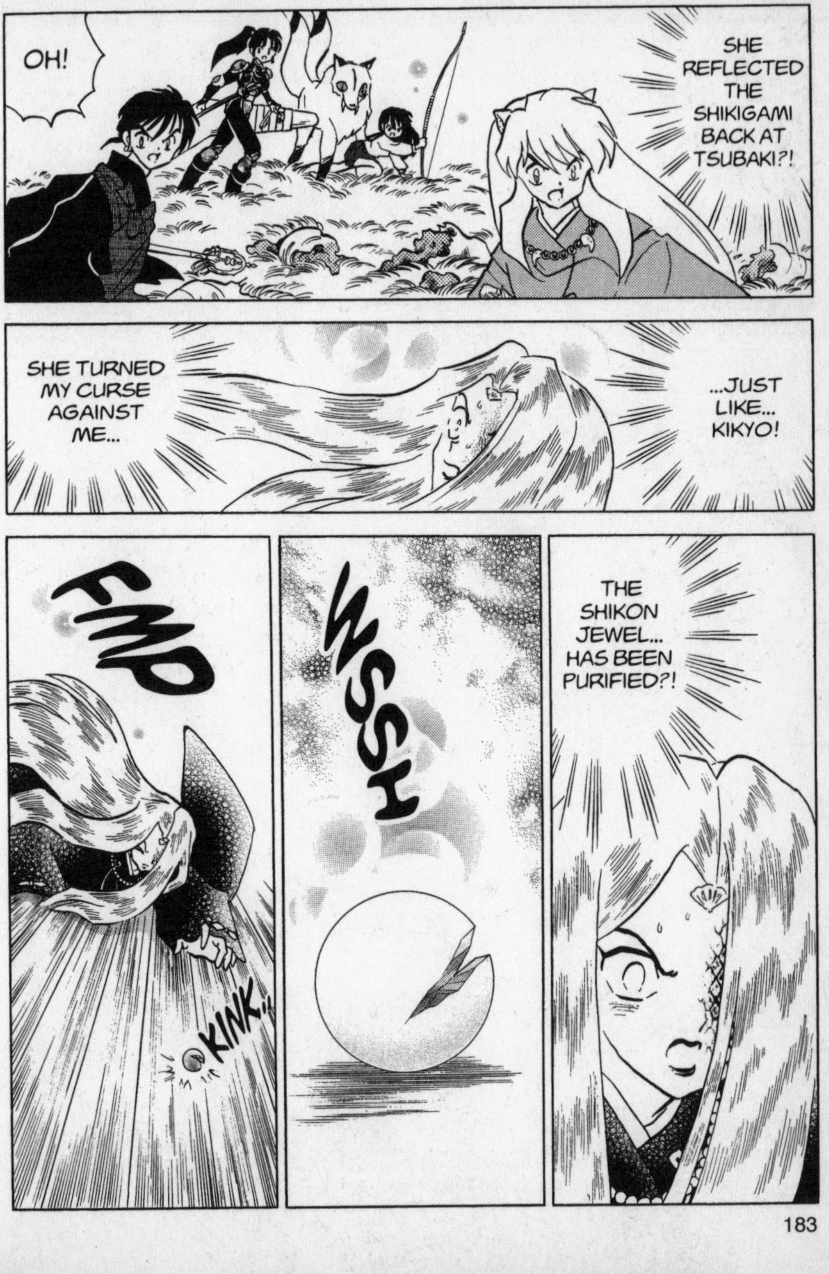
OH!
SHE REFLECTED THE SHIKIGAMI BACK AT TSUBAKI?!
SHE TURNED MY CURSE AGAINST ME...
...JUST LIKE... KIKYO!
FMP
KINK..
WSSH
THE SHIKON JEWEL... HAS BEEN PURIFIED?!

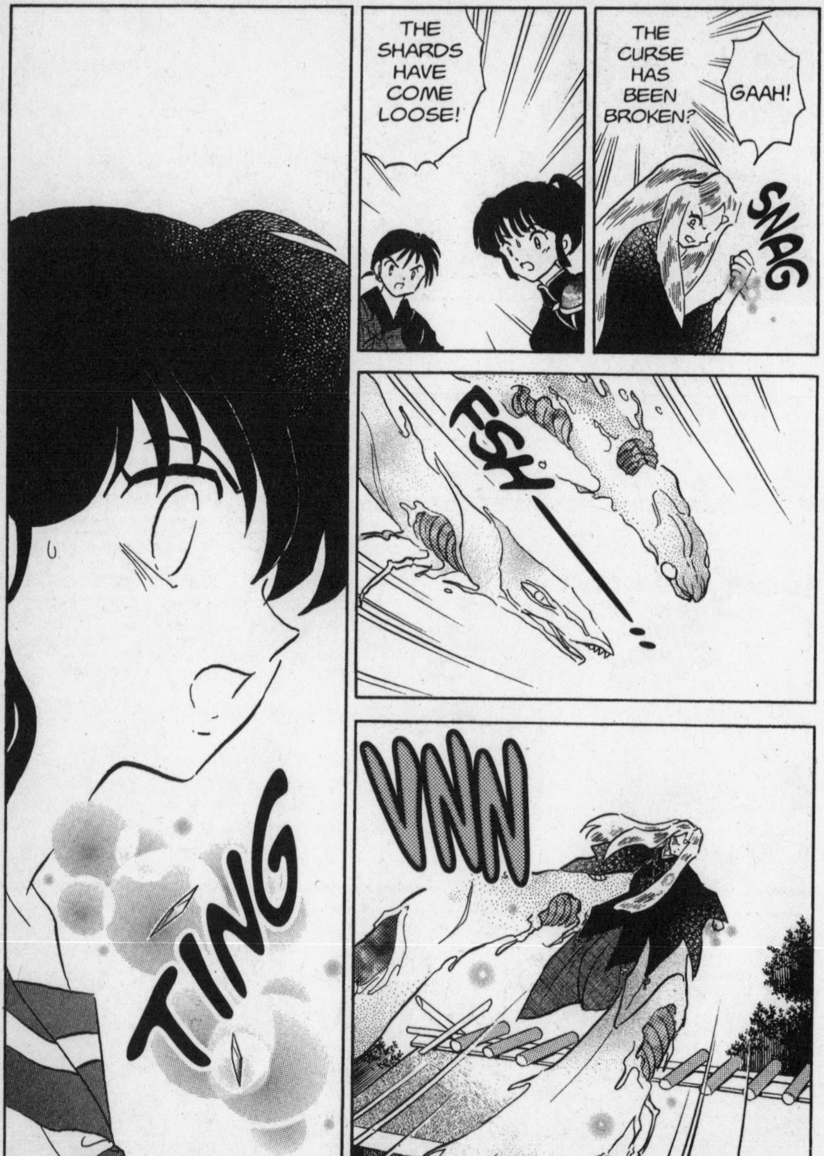
TING
THE SHARDS HAVE COME LOOSE!
THE CURSE HAS BEEN BROKEN?
GAAH!
SNAG
FSH
VNN

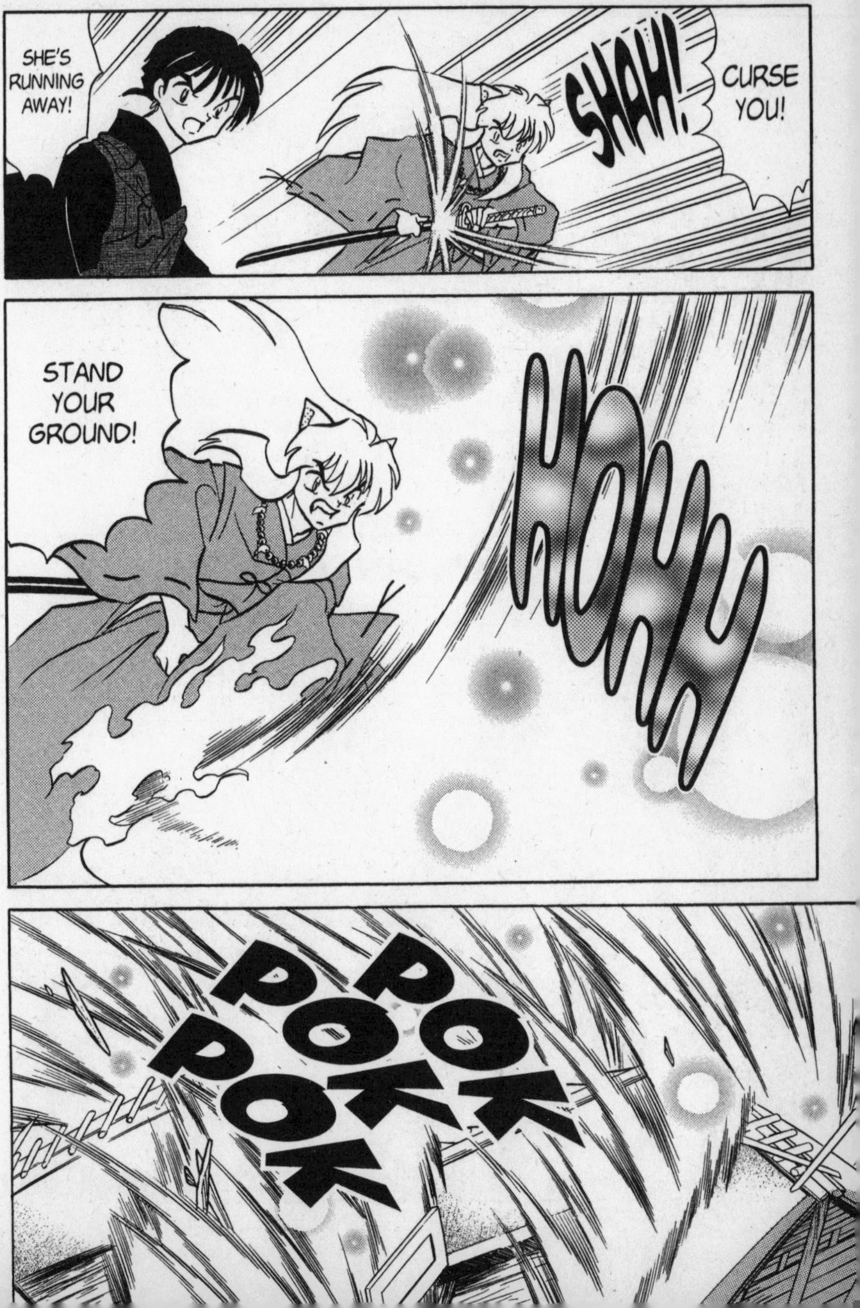
SHE'S RUNNING AWAY!
SHAH!
CURSE YOU!
STAND YOUR GROUND!
POK
POK
POK

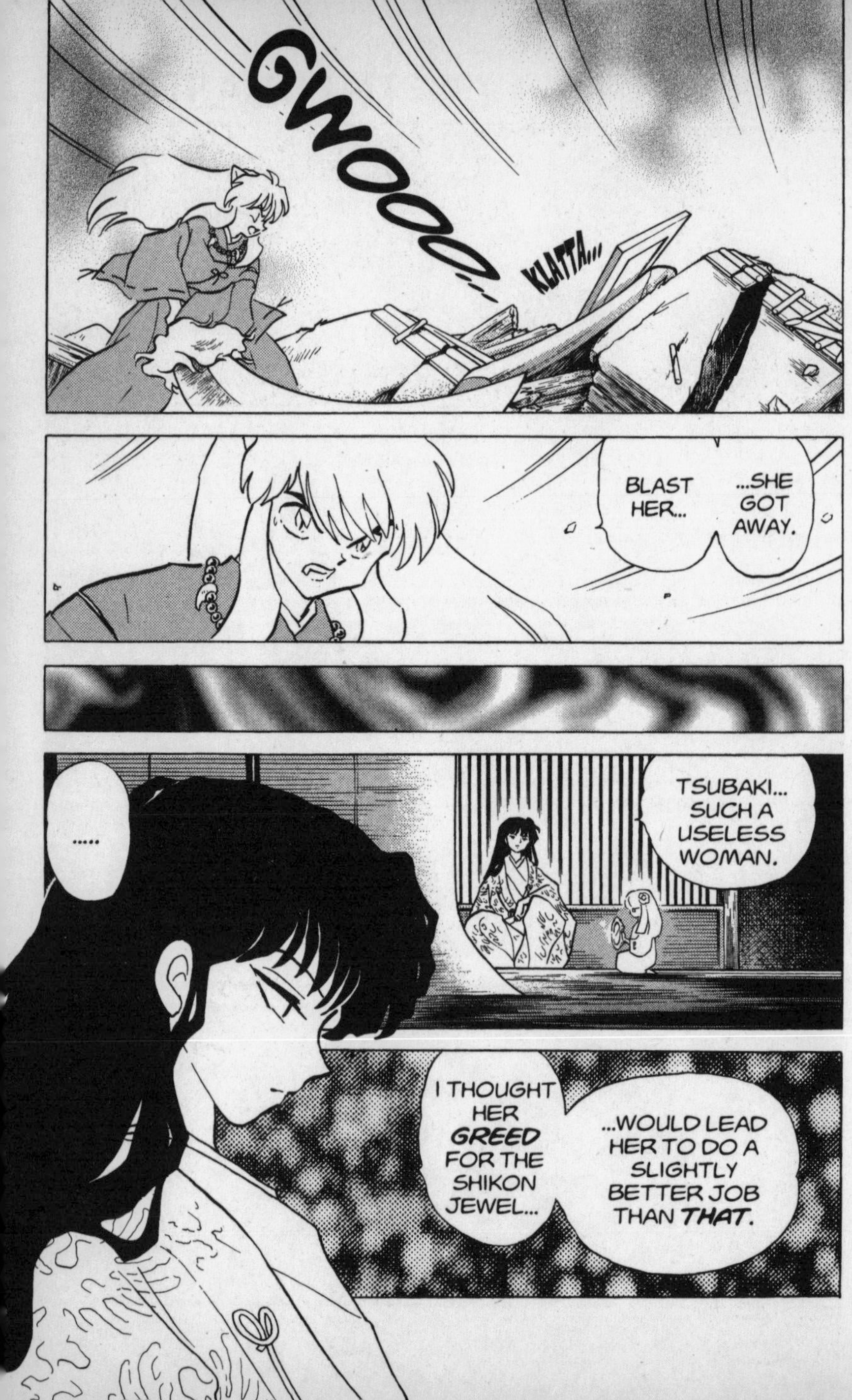
GWOOO...
KLATTA...
BLAST HER...
...SHE GOT AWAY.
.....
TSUBAKI... SUCH A USELESS WOMAN.
I THOUGHT HER GREED FOR THE SHIKON JEWEL...
...WOULD LEAD HER TO DO A SLIGHTLY BETTER JOB THAN THAT.

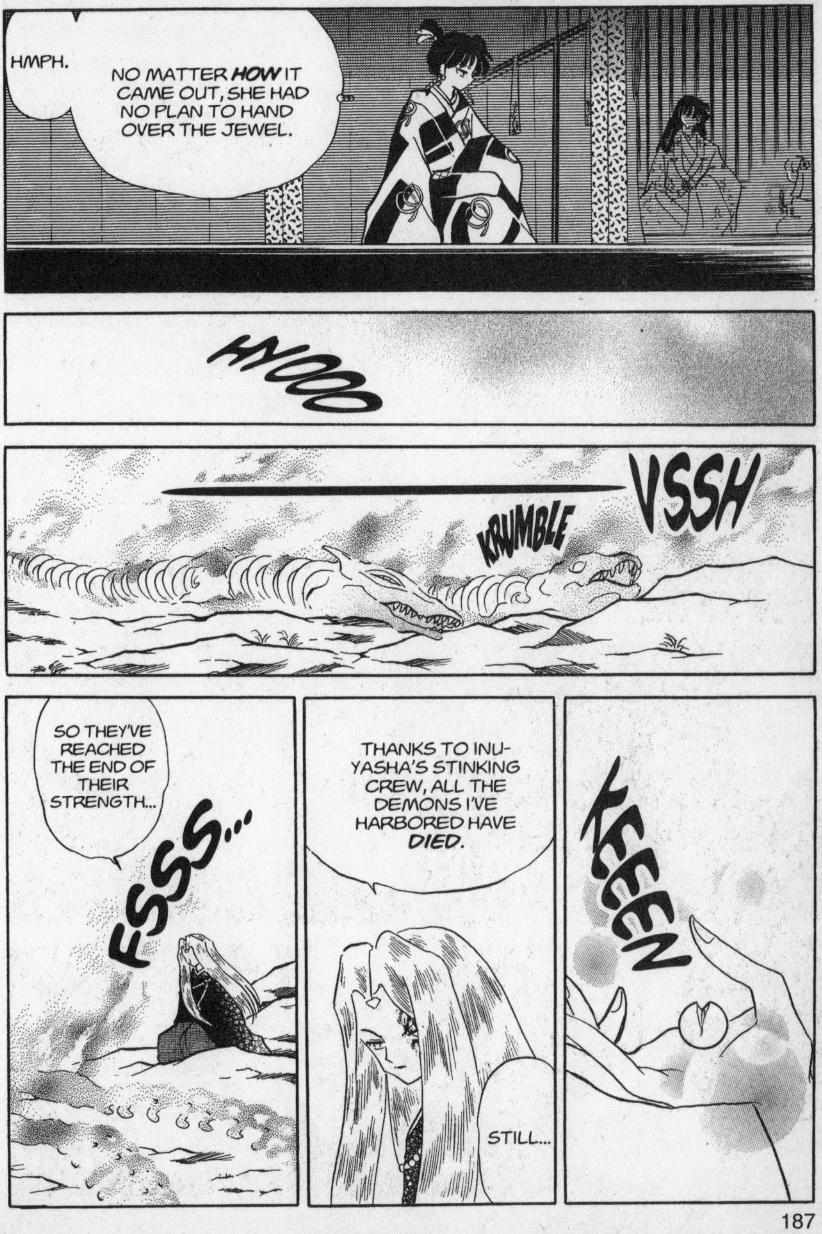
HMPH.
NO MATTER HOW IT CAME OUT, SHE HAD NO PLAN TO HAND OVER THE JEWEL.
HYOOO
VSSH
KRUMBLE
SO THEY'VE REACHED THE END OF THEIR STRENGTH...
FSSS...
THANKS TO INU-YASHA'S STINKING CREW, ALL THE DEMONS I'VE HARBORED HAVE DIED.
STILL...
KEEEN

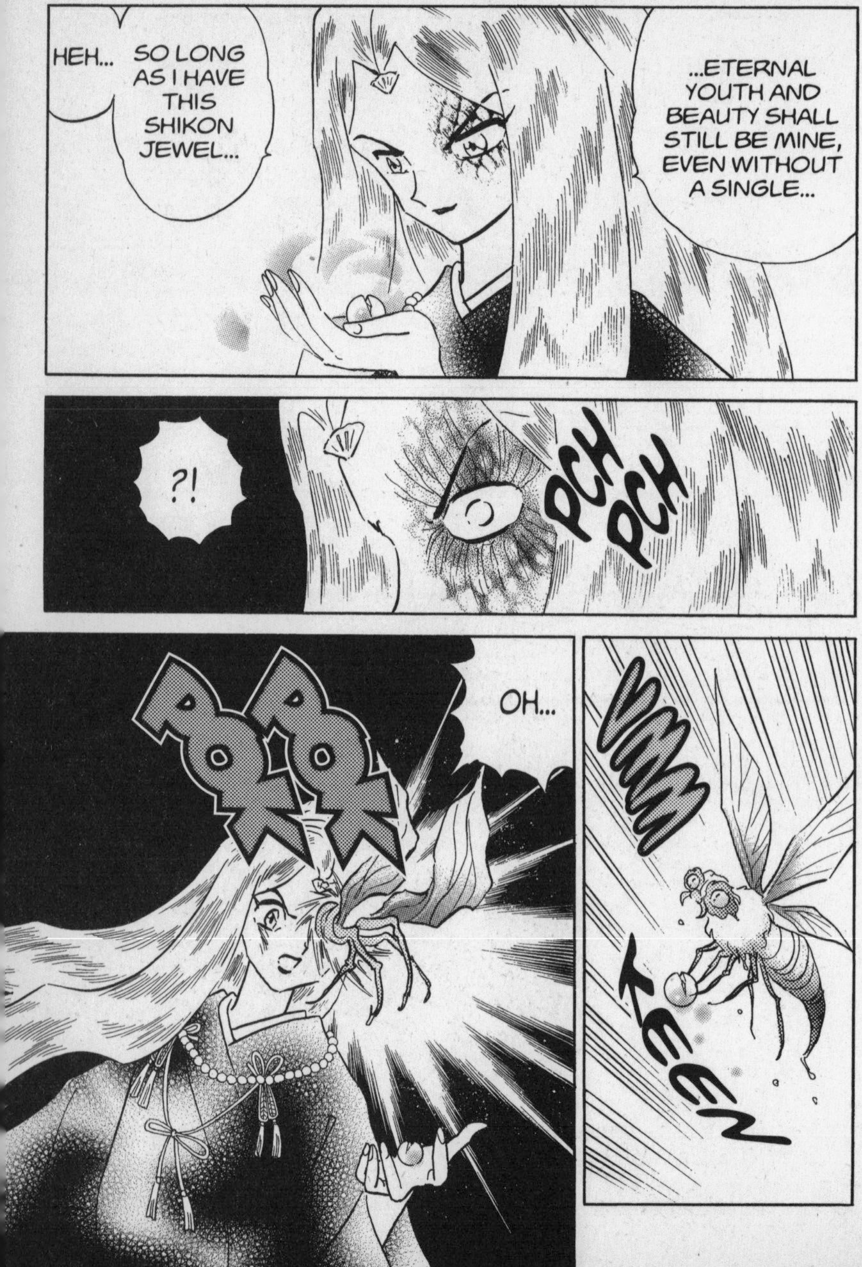
HEH...
SO LONG AS I HAVE THIS SHIKON JEWEL...
...ETERNAL YOUTH AND BEAUTY SHALL STILL BE MINE, EVEN WITHOUT A SINGLE...
?!
PCH PCH
POK POK
OH...
KEEN

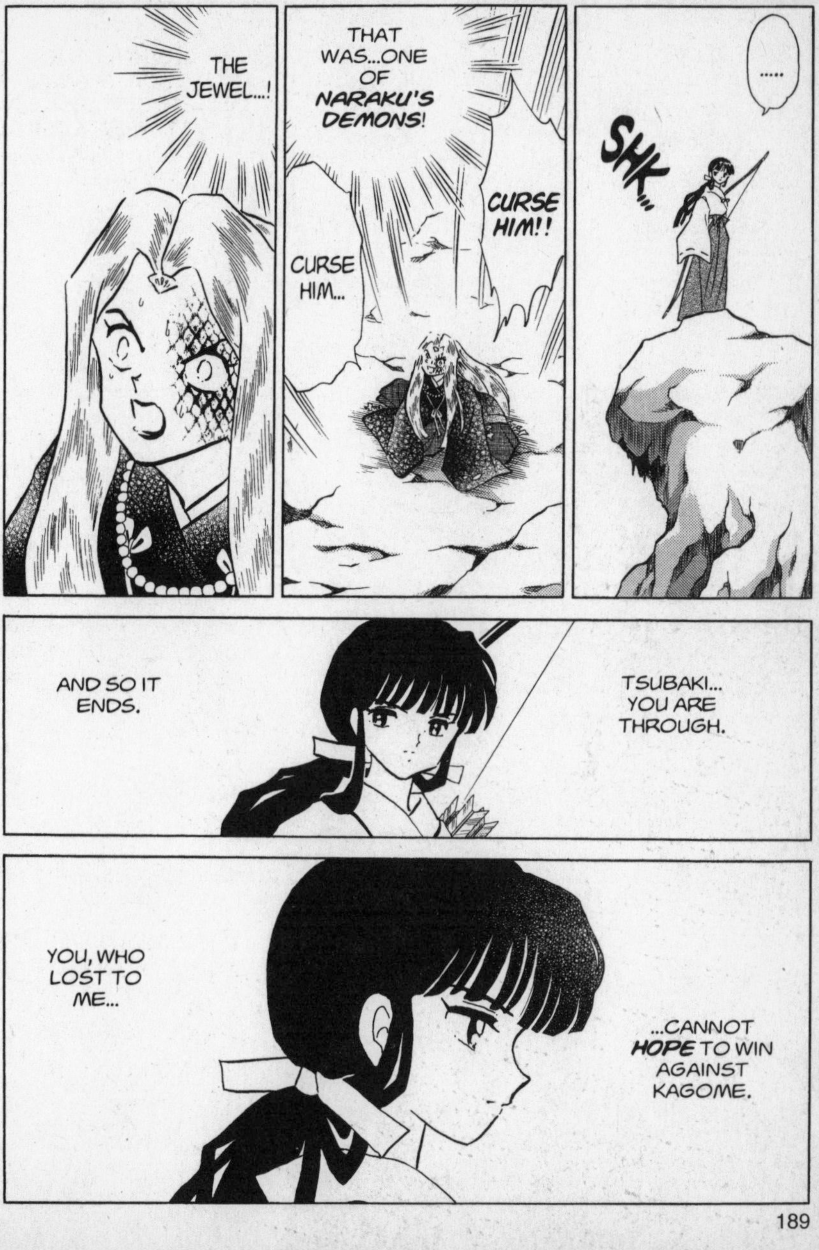
THE JEWEL...!
THAT WAS...ONE OF NARAKU'S DEMONS!
CURSE HIM...
CURSE HIM!!
.....
SHK...
AND SO IT ENDS.
TSUBAKI... YOU ARE THROUGH.
YOU, WHO LOST TO ME...
...CANNOT HOPE TO WIN AGAINST KAGOME.

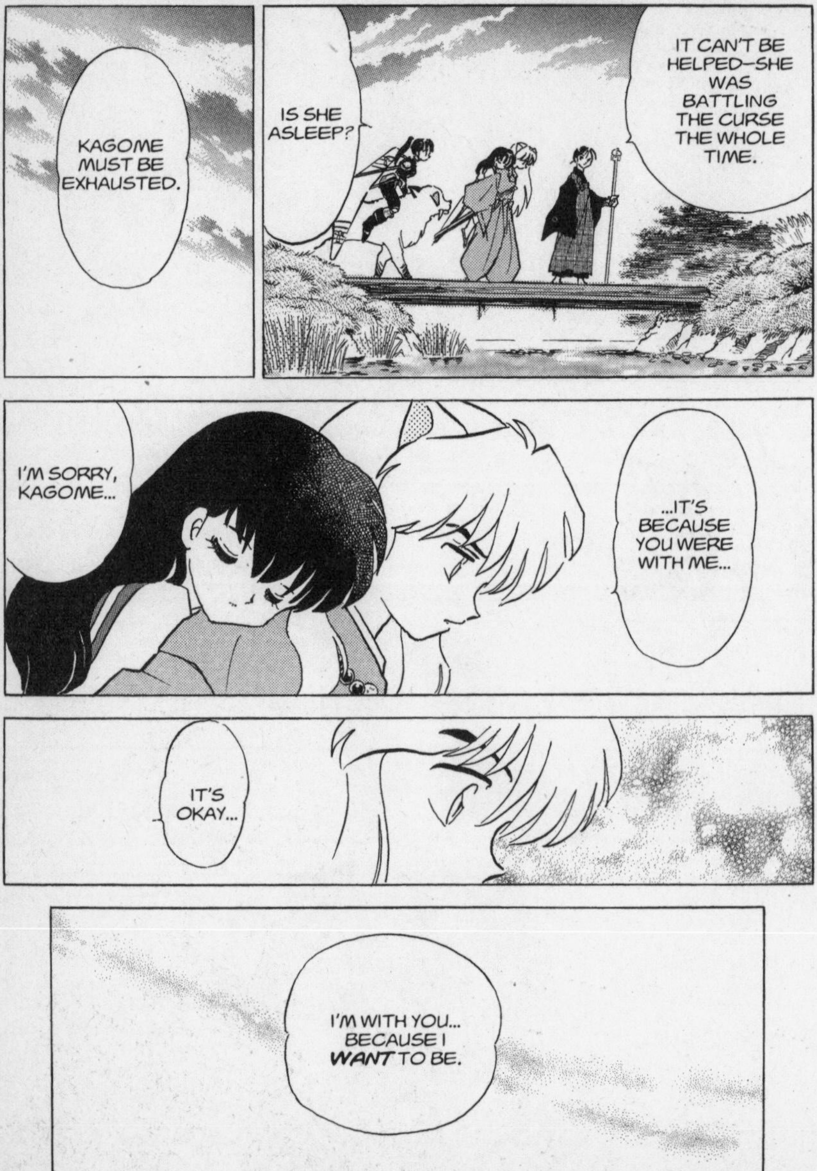
KAGOME MUST BE EXHAUSTED.
IS SHE ASLEEP?
IT CAN'T BE HELPED—SHE WAS BATTLING THE CURSE THE WHOLE TIME.
I'M SORRY, KAGOME...
...IT'S BECAUSE YOU WERE WITH ME...
IT'S OKAY...
I'M WITH YOU... BECAUSE I *WANT* TO BE.

TO BE CONTINUED...

About Rumiko Takahashi

Born in 1957 in Niigata, Japan, Rumiko Takahashi attended women's college in Tokyo, where she began studying comics with Kazuo Koike, author of CRYING FREEMAN. She later became an assistant to horror-manga artist Kazuo Umezu (OROCHI). In 1978, she won a prize in Shogakukan's annual "New Comic Artist Contest," and in that same year her boy-meets-alien comedy series URUSEI YATSURA began appearing in the weekly manga magazine SHÔNEN SUNDAY. This phenomenally successful series ran for nine years and sold over 22 million copies. Takahashi's later RANMA 1/2 series enjoyed even greater popularity.

Takahashi is considered by many to be one of the world's most popular manga artists. With the publication of Volume 34 of her RANMA 1/2 series in Japan, Takahashi's total sales passed *one hundred million* copies of her compiled works.

Takahashi's serial titles include URUSEI YATSURA, RANMA 1/2, ONE-POUND GOSPEL, MAISON IKKOKU and INUYASHA. Additionally, Takahashi has drawn many short stories which have been published in America under the title "Rumic Theater," and several installments of a saga known as her "Mermaid" series. Most of Takahashi's major stories have also been animated, and are widely available in translation worldwide. INUYASHA is her most recent serial story, first published in SHÔNEN SUNDAY in 1996.

EDITOR'S RECOMMENDATIONS

Did you like INUYASHA?
Here's what we recommend you try next:

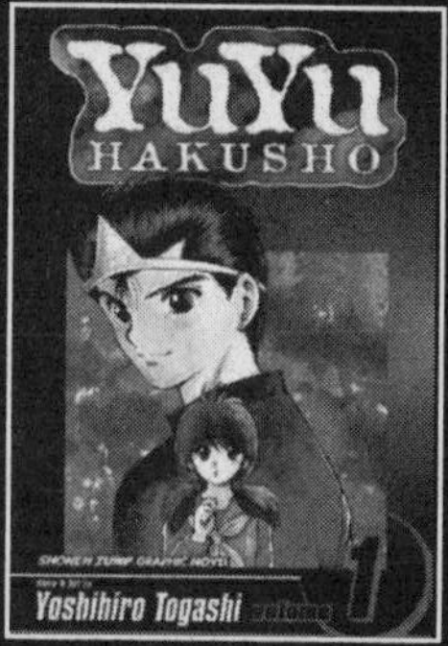

YuYu
HAKUSHO
Yoshihiro Togashi
1

YuYu Hakusho

Yusuke Urameshi was everyone's least favorite thug. An all-around rebel, he often got into fistfights and hardly ever showed up for school. He was cruising along life on the wrong side of the highway when, one day, he decides to do a selfless act. He put himself in front of a boy about to get smashed by a speeding car and lost his life in the process. And that's when he meets Botan, the ferrywoman of the Sanzu River, who offers him a chance to rectify his mistakes and be reborn—at the cost of fighting demons of the Underworld.

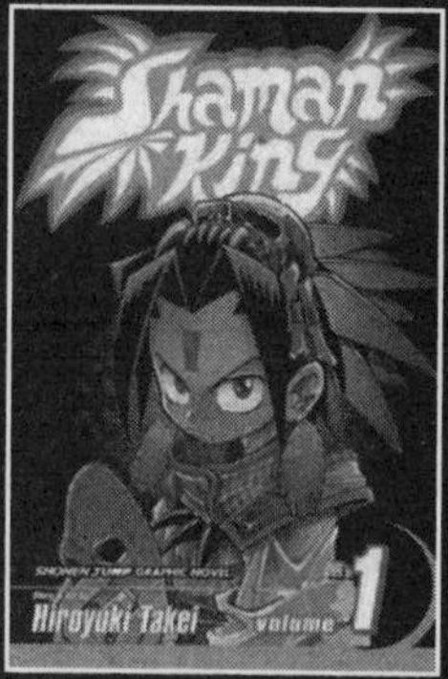

Shaman King
Hiroyuki Takei
volume 1

Shaman King

Yoh Asakura is a junior-high shaman: one of the chosen few who can communicate with ghosts, commune with the spirits of nature, and send a message to the other world. In contrast to home in rural Japan, Tokyo is a metropolis swarming with ghosts: spirits with unfinished business, spooks, revenants, specters—all of which are only visible to Yoh. Along with friends Manta and Amidamaru, he takes on challenges both real and otherwordly—but who or what is the "Shaman King," and what shamans and spirits anticipate his presence beyond the seas of Japan?

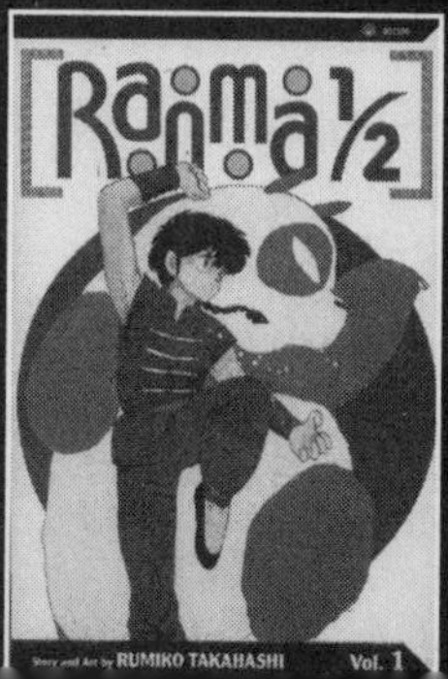

Ranma 1/2
RUMIKO TAKAHASHI
Vol. 1

Ranma 1/2

One day, teenaged martial artist Ranma Saotome went on a training mission with his father and accidentally fell into one of the many cursed springs at Jusenkyo, a legendary training ground in China. Now, every time he's splashed with cold water, he transforms into a busty girl, while his father, Genma, transforms into a panda bear! And only hot water reverses the effect! To make matters worse, Ranma's supposed to be engaged to someone who claims not to like him—but does she...?